Code Listings

D1474497

Linux DNS Server Administration

Craig Hunt

SYBEX

San Francisco Paris Düsseldorf Soest London

Associate Publisher: Neil Edde
Contracts and Licensing Manager: Kristine O'Callaghan
Acquisitions & Developmental Editor: Maureen Adams
Editor: Sarah Lemaire
Production Editor: Molly Glover
Technical Editor: Will Deutsch
Book Designer: Bill Gibson
Graphic Illustrator: Tony Jonick
Electronic Publishing Specialist: Adrian Woolhouse
Proofreaders: Dave Nash, Laurie O'Connell, Nancy Riddiough, Suzanne Stein, Nathan Whiteside
Indexer: Matthew Spence
Cover Designer: Ingalls & Associates
Cover Illustrator: Ingalls & Associates

Library of Congress Card Number: 00-105386

ISBN: 0-7821-2736-3

To Jon Postel, one of the selfless pioneers of the Internet.

Foreword

Linux deserves its own line of system administration books. It is too important to be considered the stepsister of another operating system. Many Linux system administrators rely on books that were written for the Unix operating system because Linux and Unix are almost the same. Since when was "almost" good enough for a professional system administrator? Imagine telling your boss or your users that you almost know what you're doing! Linux is not a hobbyist operating system. It is an enterprise and departmental server operating system used for mission-critical applications. As the administrator of such a system, you cannot settle for information that is almost correct. You require accurate information that is focused on the operating system that you will actually be using—Linux.

Even when a system administrator manages to assemble a bookshelf full of books focused on Linux, there are problems. The books probably come from several different publishers and thus have very different structures and styles. Even within a single publisher, different editors are responsible for different books, so consistency is elusive. Without a consistent approach, it is difficult to locate the information you need in the book. Worse yet, the information may not even be in the book because you cannot count on completeness. Because of these problems, I designed this line of books so that every book has a consistent structure and every book focuses on Linux.

 As the series editor, I read every word of every book in this series and have done my utmost to ensure that the content is complete, accurate, and consistent. If you're familiar with any of my books, such as *TCP/IP Network Administration* or *Linux Network Servers 24seven*, you know that I believe in giving the system administrator complete information in a clear and concise manner. Without interfering with the unique style of each author, I have done that across this entire line of books.

The result is a Linux bookshelf that you can rely on. These books will have the information you need exactly where you expect to find it. Linux is too important for any less than the best!

Craig Hunt

May 2000

Acknowledgments

No book is the work of one person. It is a team effort from the very start. Sharing a platter of oven-roasted mussels with Neil Edde at Zibibbo's in Palo Alto, I tossed out the idea for this series. Neil, who wasn't even assigned to work on this project, encouraged me to present it to the publishers at Sybex so he deserves a big thank-you for getting the ball rolling.

Maureen Adams, the acquisition editor for this series, deserves special thanks. The business side of publishing is driven by deadlines because production people are scheduled based on deadlines and marketing people are promising deliveries based on those deadlines. Maureen ran interference to extend the deadlines so that we had the time to create the technical quality that this series requires.

Keeping me on schedule was Molly Glover's task, and she did it very well. She provided just enough push to keep me moving forward but not so much as to knock me off course. During the intense effort of producing a book, it is good to have someone as level-headed as Molly on hand.

Sarah Lemaire edited the text. Her light touch can be seen everywhere in the improved grammar and structure. I particularly want to thank her for respecting my personal style of writing and blending her edits into it.

This is the second book for which Will Deutsch (UC Davis) has been my technical editor. Will's suggestions are always appreciated. His academic and research background provides a different perspective and often provides insight into topics that will soon be of interest to the administrators of operational systems. Will helps me look a little further down the road than most system administrators have time to do.

I would like to thank all the production people and artists for their hard work in creating the final product: the electronic publishing specialist, Adrian Woolhouse; the illustrator, Tony Jonick; the proofreaders, Dave Nash, Laurie O'Connell, Nancy Riddiough, Suzanne Stein, and Nathan Whiteside; and the indexer, Matthew Spence. The Sybex team produces a superior publication.

I also want to thank the dedicated people who maintain the BIND software, and all the others who contributed to the design of DNS and the development of BIND. Not just because they created an awesome piece of code that is available to everyone, but because that code and the DNS system it created have literally changed the world. Everyone who uses the Internet owes these people a debt of gratitude.

Finally, I want to thank Kathy. With the kids out of the house, she is my only sounding board. Thank goodness she has the patience of Job.

Contents at a Glance

Contents

Introduction

Two technologies are largely responsible for the incredible growth of the Internet. One of these is the World Wide Web—the Internet's killer application. The other is the Domain Name System (DNS). Prior to the widespread introduction of DNS in 1988, the number of hosts on the Internet could be counted in the thousands. Today they can be counted in the tens of millions. This is not just a matter of demand; it is also a result of availability.

The Domain Name System is the tool that makes millions of Internet host names available. Before DNS, all of the registered Internet host names were stored in a flat file that had to be replicated on every computer on the network. The limitations of that file were a barrier to growth. DNS broke that barrier by replacing the flat file with a distributed, hierarchical database system. We are no longer limited by a centrally maintained host file. Now, every organization on the network is responsible for maintaining its own piece of the domain database. As a system administrator, you are the one responsible for maintaining DNS on your system. This book will show you how.

Linux is an excellent platform upon which to build a DNS server. The reliability of Linux itself is already legendary. Everyone has heard of someone who has a Linux server that has been running without interruption for a year or more. (If you hadn't before, you have now because I had such a system.)

As important as the reliability of the operating system is the reliability of the name server software running on that system. Again, Linux is a winner because it uses the Berkeley Internet Name Domain (BIND) software. BIND is the software that first introduced DNS to widespread use back in the 1980s, and it is still the most widely used DNS software today. BIND has been put to the test and proven reliable by millions of users.

This book provides complete coverage of DNS and BIND running under Linux. It focuses exclusively on Linux. Books that attempt to cover every version of Unix are doomed to cover every version of BIND, even those that are long out of date, because some commercial versions of Unix that are still in widespread use were shipped with the older versions of BIND. Linux does a great job of providing the latest software and of making it easy for you to keep that software updated. Every example in this book is based on the latest version of BIND and it is a Linux example that you can use on your own system. There is no need for you to sift through unrelated examples from various flavors of Unix. As a result, the BIND examples are consistent and easy to follow. These factors create a book that is better organized and easier to read.

Who Should Buy This Book

This book is for anyone who wants to run DNS under Linux, or anyone interested in knowing more about how DNS works. If you have read this far into the introduction, that's probably you.

Linux system administrators will find this book invaluable as their primary resource for DNS information. It provides detailed instructions about how to build a DNS server on a Linux platform. Examples of compiling, installing, and configuring BIND to run with Linux are provided. Security features specific to Linux are discussed. Information about Linux that is overlooked by other DNS books is included here.

Even administrators of Unix and Windows NT systems will find this book a useful companion text. This book provides a detailed description of the underlying DNS protocols, and it ties that discussion to the values used to configure DNS. It provides this information in a clear and organized manner. The insights into how DNS works and why certain configuration values are used will be helpful to anyone running DNS—even if they don't use Linux.

This book does not assume that you know a lot about DNS, but it does assume that you have a good understanding of Linux and system administration. If you feel that you need to brush up on these topics, start with *Running Linux*, Welsh and Kaufman, O'Reilly, 1999, and *Linux Network Servers 24seven*, Craig Hunt, Sybex, 1999. Those books will provide you with all the background you need.

This book takes a practical approach that emphasizes what you really need to know to master DNS. The book's structure is task oriented. It provides detailed, step-by-step instructions that tell you what to do and when to do it. But more than that, it explains *why* you do it. The book explains how DNS works so that you can make intelligent decisions about your own server's configuration.

How This Book Is Organized

This book is divided into five parts: "How Things Work," "Essential Configuration," "Advanced Configurations," "Maintaining a Healthy Server," and "Appendixes." The five parts are composed of twelve chapters and four appendixes.

The book is designed as a unit and is meant to be read as a whole. It starts with foundation material that explains DNS, moves through the essential BIND configuration skills that every system administrator needs, discusses specialized configuration options that are needed for special situations, and then concludes with information about maintaining an operational DNS server.

Many chapters reference material covered in other chapters. When such a reference is made, it contains a pointer to the chapter that covers the relevant material. A reader who understands the fundamentals of the DNS protocols and architecture can jump to the Essential Configuration section. An experienced administrator who understands all of the basics of BIND configuration can jump to the Advanced Configurations part of the book. However, most system administrators will benefit from reading the entire text.

While this book is intended to be read as a whole, I understand that many system administrators simply do not have the time to read an entire text. They must go to the topic in question and get a reasonably complete picture of the "why" as well as the "how" of that topic. To facilitate that understanding, necessary background material is summarized where the topic is discussed and accompanied by pointers to the part of the book where the background material is more thoroughly discussed.

Part 1: How Things Work

Part 1 provides the information you need to understand how name service works. This part describes the distributed hierarchical database system and the protocols used by DNS, and the BIND software used to implement DNS on Linux systems.

Chapter 1: The DNS Architecture   Chapter 1 explains the architecture of DNS. The features of DNS that facilitated the growth of today's Internet are described. The structure of domain names, how names are obtained, the top-level domains, and the delegation of domains are explained. Additionally, the role of the root servers, the processing of queries, the dynamic distribution of information, and the relationship among servers are discussed.

Chapter 2: The DNS Protocols   Chapter 2 examines the processing of queries in more detail. It explains the packets that are exchanged to resolve a host name to an IP address. This chapter also describes the protocols used to keep the distributed DNS databases synchronized.

Chapter 3: The BIND Software   DNS is implemented through the BIND software. Chapter 3 explains the components of BIND, the different server configurations that BIND makes possible, and how BIND servers are combined to create an enterprise DNS architecture. The named command and the ndc command are explained. This chapter also provides instructions on downloading and compiling the latest version of BIND for your Linux system.

Part 2: Essential Configuration

Part 2 covers the basic configuration skills needed by every domain name administrator. This part provides you with a step-by-step view of how a Linux DNS system is configured, from a client configuration to a master server configuration.

Chapter 4: Configuring the Resolver   Every networked system has a resolver to create the queries that a client sends to the name server. Configuring the resolver is a task that must be done on every client and server. Chapter 4 describes the default resolver configuration. It also describes every resolver configuration option that you can use to create a custom configuration. It provides examples of realistic resolver configurations. The configuration of the `host.conf` and the `nsswitch.conf` files, which set the order in which the various name services are used, is also covered.

Chapter 5: Caching and Slave Server Configuration   Most Linux name servers are caching-only servers or slave servers. Chapter 5 covers the configuration of both types of servers. The `named.conf` configuration file, the root cache file, and the local host file are all covered.

Chapter 6: Creating a Master Server   Every domain has one master server that holds the domain databases. Chapter 6 describes the configuration of a master server and the construction of basic DNS database files. Both the domain database and the reverse domain database are covered. The DNS database records, called resource records, are also explained.

Part 3: Advanced Configurations

Part 3 describes those configuration options that go beyond the basics. The process of delegating your own subdomains and the configuration features that can be used to handle special situations are covered in this part of the book.

Chapter 7: Creating Subdomains   Once you have been given a domain, you have the authority to create subdomains within that domain. Chapter 7 explains the process of delegating authority for a subdomain within your domain and within your reverse domain. Care and maintenance of subdomains is also discussed.

Chapter 8: Special BIND Configurations   Average configurations are not adequate for every site. Chapter 8 covers features such as forwarders, preferred servers, performance tuning, wildcarding, and private roots that can be used to create a special configuration. The advantages and disadvantages of these features are discussed.

Chapter 9: Dynamic DNS   Sites that use DHCP want some way for the DHCP server to tell the DNS server about host name-to-IP address mappings. Dynamic DNS (DDNS) is a technique for doing this. Chapter 9 explains the benefits and risks of DDNS. It also explains how to configure DDNS and how to use it.

Part 4: Maintaining a Healthy Server

Part 4 focuses on tasks that are essential to maintaining a secure and reliable server. The ongoing maintenance tasks of security, testing, and monitoring are covered in Part 4.

Chapter 10: DNS Security   Every system attached to the Internet is a potential target for intruders. DNS servers are no exception. Chapter 10 discusses general Linux security procedures and describes the specific BIND features that help you secure your system.

Chapter 11: Testing DNS   A variety of test tools available on your Linux system allow you to test your own server and remote servers. Chapter 11 describes the features of the nslookup, dig, and host test tools. Examples of using these tools to test specific problems are provided.

Chapter 12: The BIND Log Files   The BIND software creates extensive log files that allow you to examine the DNS protocol interactions between your server and its clients. Chapter 12 examines the BIND log file (named.run), the dump file (named_dump.db) and the statistics file (named.stat). The configuration options that you have available to build the log files are also described.

Appendixes

The book concludes with four appendixes. Two of the appendixes are detailed references to the BIND configuration commands and the resource records supported by BIND. The other two appendixes cover topics, BIND 9 and NIS, that are not directly related to configuring an operational Linux DNS server, yet are of interest to a domain administrator.

Appendix A: BIND 9   Appendix A describes the features and changes that are coming in the future, as part of BIND version 9. The functionality of the BIND 9 beta release is described.

Appendix B: *named.conf* Command Reference   All Linux BIND servers are configured in the named.conf file. Examples of using the named.conf configuration commands are provided throughout this text. Appendix B provides a detailed syntax reference for all of the named.conf commands.

Appendix C: Resource Record Reference   Appendix C is a reference to all of the standard resource records supported by BIND.

Appendix D: Configuring Network Information Service   NIS is a service that provides access to a centrally maintained host table, as well as access to other system administration databases. Appendix D describes the installation and configuration of this optional service.

Conventions

This book uses the following typographic conventions:

`Inline_Program_Font` is used to identify the Linux commands, filenames, and domain names that occur within the body of the text.

`Program_Font` is used in listings and examples.

Bold is used to indicate something that must be typed as shown. This might be user input in a listing, a recommended command-line, or fixed values within the syntax of a command. For example, a command syntax written as **key** *key_id* means that the command **key** must be typed exactly as shown.

Italic is used in command syntax to indicate a variable for which you must provide the value. For example, a command syntax written as **key** *key_id* means that the variable name *key_id* must not be typed as shown, and that you must provide your own valued for *key_id*.

[ ] in a command's syntax an item enclosed in square brackets is optional. For example, **ls** [−l] means that −l is an optional part of the **ls** command.

| is a vertical bar that means choose one keyword or the other in a command's syntax. For example, **yes|no** means choose yes or no.

Help Us Help You

Things change. In the world of computers, things change rapidly. Facts described in this book will become invalid over time. When they do, we need your help locating and correcting them. Additionally, a 400-page book is bound to have typographical errors. Let us know when you spot one. Send your improvements, fixes, and other corrections to support@sybex.com. To contact the author for information about upcoming books and talks on Linux, go to www.wrotethebook.com.

Part 1

How Things Work

Featuring:

- The role of the host table and its limitations

- What the structure of a domain name reveals

- How zones and domains differ

- How queries are resolved

- The role of the IP protocols that support DNS

- The components of DNS query/response messages

- How the distributed DNS databases stay synchronized

- The role of the BIND software

- What the resolver is and how it works

- What named is and how it is run

- How a name server is managed with ndc

- Downloading, compiling, and installing BIND

The DNS Architecture

A great deal of ink is wasted explaining why you need to translate computer names to numeric addresses. System administrators already know the reason: Users like names and networks like numbers. And as a system administrator, it is your job to keep both the users and the network happy and productive.

In this chapter, you'll learn how names are translated into numbers on networks that use the Internet Protocol (IP). This chapter explains terms used later in this book and lays the groundwork for understanding why certain tasks are required to create a running domain name server.

You will begin by looking at the file that was originally used for this job. You will see how the limitations of that file lead to the distributed hierarchical database system structure of today's Domain Name System (DNS). The structure of domain names and what they show about the domain hierarchy are discussed along with your server's place in the hierarchy and the role of the root servers. For those readers who are completely new to DNS, how you obtain your own domain name is explained. All of this begins with a look into the past.

The */etc/hosts* File

In the beginning, the host table was the only tool used to map host names to Internet addresses. All Linux systems still have a host table, which is stored in the /etc/hosts file.

In fact, all IP network servers have a host table. If you have experience with Unix, you recognize the name /etc/hosts because that is where Unix systems store the host table. If your background is Windows NT, you know the host table as the %SystemRoot%\ System32\Drivers\etc\hosts file. The structure and content of the hosts file is the same on all of these systems. Listing 1.1 contains an example from a Linux system that illustrates the structure of the hosts file:

Listing 1.1   Structure of the /etc/hosts File

```
$ cat /etc/hosts
#
# Table of IP addresses and host names
#
127.0.0.1               localhost
172.16.5.5              crow
172.16.5.1              wren ns1
172.16.5.4              hawk gw5
172.16.5.20             kestrel kestral
172.16.5.2              robin redbreast bob
172.16.5.6              eagle www
172.16.5.7              bluebird blue news
```

Lines that begin with a sharp sign (#) are comments. All other lines define data for the host table and all of these lines have the same format: A data line begins with an IP address that is followed by a list of names that map to that address. The first name in the list is the primary name assigned to the address. All of the other names are aliases or nicknames.

Host name aliases are used to provide shorter names, historic names, generic names, and alternate spellings for a given host name. All of these things are done as a convenience for users. The convenience of a shorter name is obvious and needs no explanation. *Historic names* are used to ease a name transition. When the name of a host is changed, the old historic name may still be used by some users or may still be embedded in some old scripts. *Generic names* are the names that users expect to find for given services. For example, www for the Web server, mail for the mail server, and news for the news server are names the user expects to find. Alternate spellings can help when host names are difficult to spell.

> **TIP** If you must create alternate spelling aliases or you frequently change host names, then you probably chose the wrong host name in the first place. Host names should be easy to spell and should be independent of things that can easily change such as location, user, or task. See RFC 1178, "Naming Your Computer," for advice on choosing a host name.

Using the sample hosts file in Listing 1.1, a user could specify bluebird, blue, or news, and the system would return the IP address 172.16.5.7. From the system's point of view, all of these names are the same because they all point to the same IP address. Given this, you might wonder why the first name in the list is called the *primary name*. The primary name is the name used when the system does a *reverse lookup* to convert a numeric address back into a name. Numeric addresses are converted to names to create more readable displays. For example, the netstat command obtains IP addresses when it determines the network status but, by default, it displays host names for those addresses, as follows:

```
$ netstat --inet
Active Internet connections (w/o servers)
Proto R-Q S-Q Local Address Foreign Address   State
tcp    1   0 robin:1967    eagle:80          CLOSE_WAIT
tcp    1   0 robin:1966    eagle:80          CLOSE_WAIT
tcp    1   0 robin:1964    eagle:80          CLOSE_WAIT
tcp    1   0 robin:1963    eagle:80          CLOSE_WAIT
tcp    0 126 robin:23      hawk:1449         ESTABLISHED
```

As this example shows, the netstat command uses the primary name for each host in its display. The netstat --inet command displays the TCP/IP network connections. Each line lists the hosts and the ports involved in a connection. If the local computer only has access to a host table for address-to-name resolution, the name that shows up for each host is the primary name associated with that host's address in the host table.

Analyzing the Host Table

A line-by-line analysis of the host table in Listing 1.1 explains the various types of host table entries, including those entries you probably have in your own host table. These first two lines represent two lines found in every host table:

```
127.0.0.1    localhost
172.16.5.5   crow
```

The first line defines the loopback address 127.0.0.1 and assigns it to the host name localhost. The *loopback address* is a software construct that allows the systems to send data through the TCP/IP stack to itself without actually sending the data out on the network. The loopback facility simplifies testing, permits the system to use the same code used for network communications when sending data between two local processes, and reduces the amount of traffic on the network.

The second line defines the name and address of the local computer. In this example, the local computer is named crow and is assigned the address 172.16.5.5. Every computer has its own address and name in its host table.

The next two lines in the sample host table represent entries for the local DNS server and the local default router:

```
172.16.5.1    wren ns1
172.16.5.4    hawk gw5
```

These entries are useful when the system is booting. wren, which is the name server for this sample network, has the nickname ns1, which stands for "name server 1." hawk, which is the default gateway for this network, has the nickname gw5, which stands for "gateway 5." These entries illustrate the use of nicknames and represent the types of entries that you might actually have in your own host table.

The next two lines represent the type of entries that might be used to catch spelling errors and to handle historic names:

```
172.16.5.20   kestrel kestral
172.16.5.2    robin redbreast bob
```

In the first line, the system administrator has added a nickname to accept the typo kestral as a valid name because a user has trouble typing kestrel correctly. In the second line, a nickname is included for the historic name bob that was assigned to address 172.16.5.2 before the local network standardized on bird names. These lines were added by the system administrator to handle specific problems experienced by the system's users. Rarely would anything like this be required in your host table.

The last two lines illustrate the use of generic names, such as www and news:

```
172.16.5.6    eagle www
172.16.5.7    bluebird blue news
```

It is unlikely that you will need to put values like this in the local host table because, if you actually have a Web server or a network news server, you almost certainly have DNS running. When DNS is running, all computers can get these values from the DNS server and they don't need to get them from the local host table.

The sample `/etc/hosts` file contains eight lines and yet it is probably twice as long as the `hosts` file you will actually have on your computer. On most computers, the host table has only limited utility and the system relies on a name server for most name-to-address translation. Even small, isolated networks generally rely on a service such as Network Information Service (NIS) to create a centralized host table because it is easier to maintain a single server than it is to maintain a separate copy of the host table on every system. Therefore, even when the host table is the primary means of resolving names, only one server has a large host table and most other computers have very small host tables. (See Appendix D, "Configuring Network Information Service," for a description of deploying an NIS server under Linux.)

Host Table-to-DNS Scripts

There are scripts that convert a host table to a DNS database. The problem with these scripts is that they assume your system has a large host table worth converting. Personally, I haven't had a system with a large host table since 1987! These scripts are easy to use, but creating a large host table on a Linux system that runs DNS just doesn't make sense. Chapter 6, "Creating a Master Server," explains how easy it is to put host information directly into the DNS database. You can safely ignore anything you read about host table-to-DNS scripts.

Uses for the Host Table

Though limited, the role of the host table is important. The host table is used to resolve critical addresses, like the address of the default gateway, at times when DNS is not available, such as during the initial boot. The default gateway is a particularly good example of this. It is very possible that the name server is on the far side of your default gateway. Until your system adds the default gateway to its configuration, it cannot communicate with the remote name server. In this case, placing the address of the default gateway in your local host table allows you to configure the gateway without querying a name server that you might not be able to reach.

Beyond these limited roles, the host table has no real use on most systems. All systems that have access to the Internet rely on DNS for name-to-address resolution. Of course, it is possible that your system is on a small isolated network that does not connect to the Internet and that never needs to communicate with remote systems. In that case, the host table might be adequate for all of your needs, particularly if combined with the central maintenance features provided by NIS. However, that is an extremely rare case. For everyone else, the host table supports the system during the boot and handles a few local aliases. Everything else is done by DNS.

Host Table Limitations

The discussion so far does not provide a good reason for DNS. After all, every system already has and uses a host table that performs the host name-to-address and address-to-host name mappings that are required by a system connected to an IP network. Indeed, the host table was originally the only tool used to provide name service on the fledgling Internet. So why do I say that every system connected to the Internet will have only a small host table and will instead rely on DNS? The problems with the host table all relate to its inability to scale to the size needed for today's Internet.

The host table is a flat file.   The host table is a simple text file, which makes it very easy to edit but not very easy to search. The file is searched sequentially for every host-to-address mapping, and every host name in every line of the file may need to be searched. This is not a problem given the size of the host table shown in Listing 1.1, and the file on your Linux system is probably no larger. However, even a tiny fraction of the names in the current Internet would make a flat file extremely burdensome to search.

The host table requires central maintenance.   As new hosts were added to the Internet, they had to be registered with the Internet Network Information Center (NIC). The NIC then added them to the HOSTS.TXT file, which was the source file used to create the host table. Imagine how impossible it would be for any one organization to enter the name of every individual computer on the Internet into a file! Imagine how much time it would take you to build your network if every computer you wanted to add to your network had to be registered with a government agency! If the host table were still the only way to convert names to addresses, the Internet as you know it today would not exist.

The host table has no scheme for automatic distribution.   Because the Internet host table was centrally maintained, some mechanism was needed to move the host table from the NIC to every computer on the Internet. Unix systems had a couple of commands to download the table and convert it to the correct format. However, there was no way to know if and when the host table was updated and thus no way to know when it needed to be downloaded.

Every system needs its own copy of the host table.   No system can use the host table to resolve a name unless that name is in the system's local host table. Even if a system were developed to automatically distribute the host table, distributing it to every host on the Internet would be an insurmountable task.

Given all of these limitations, it was essential for the growth of the Internet that a new means of mapping host names to IP addresses be developed. In the late 1980s, DNS was deployed to provide name service for the growing Internet.

The DNS Hierarchy

DNS solves all of the problems inherent in the host table system. It is not a flat file; it is a distributed, hierarchical database system. DNS requires only limited centralized maintenance. It has multiple techniques for automatically distributing the database information to the servers that need it. Local systems do not need to maintain complete copies of the database and they can learn what they need when they need it. These benefits come from the distributed nature of the domain database system, the DNS hierarchy that links it together, and the manner in which it is used to locate the correct host and address mappings.

Domain Name Structure

DNS is a rooted, hierarchical structure. For a Linux system administrator, this structure is very familiar because it is the structure of the Linux file system. A domain name shows the rooted hierarchical structure of DNS, just like the full path name of a Linux file shows the directory structure. A full Linux path name starts with the root, moves through a series of directories, and finishes with the filename, e.g., /usr/lib/zsh/zed. The individual parts of the path are separated by slashes. The root is indicated by the null name— a separating slash (/) with no preceding name. A file path name starts with the most general (the root) and moves to the most specific (the file).

A fully qualified domain name (FQDN) has several similarities. Each part of a domain name is separated by a single character, which in a domain name is a dot. The root is assigned the null name—a separating dot (.) with no trailing name. But in this case, the order is reversed. A domain name moves from the most specific (the host) to the most general (the root). For example, in the name royal.terns.foobirds.org.,

- royal is the host name.
- terns is the subdomain.
- foobirds is the second-level domain purchased by this organization.
- org is the lop-level domain under which this organization registered its second-level domain.
- . is the root.

An important feature of this structure is that it enables the creation of enough unique host names for a network the size of the Internet. In the same way that a Linux file system can have two files with the same filename as long as each file has a unique path name, DNS can have many computers with the same host name as long as the fully qualified domain name of each computer is different. Just as `/home/craig/.bashrc` and `/home/sara/` `.bashrc` are two different files, `cow.mammals.org` and `cow.dairies.com` are two different hosts. It is the full path from the root domain to the individual host that defines the host's unique name.

The Top-Level Domains

Immediately below the root domain are the top-level domains. There are two basic types of top-level domain names: organizational domains and geopolitical domains. *Organizational domains* describe an organizational function. For example, the ubiquitous `.com` domain is used for commercial organizations. There are currently seven top-level organizational domains:

`.com` for commercial organizations

`.edu` for colleges, universities, and other institutions of higher learning

`.gov` for U.S. federal government agencies

`.int` for international governmental organizations

`.mil` for U.S. military organizations

`.net` for network-based organizations

`.org` for organizations, such as non-profits, that don't fit in any of the other categories

These seven domains are often called *generic top-level domains* (gTLDs). Several other possible gTLDs have been suggested in the past but none of the other proposed domains has gone into official use. In fact, of the seven possible gTLDs, only three, `.com`, `.net`, and `.org`, still have a heavy load of new registrations. Most U.S. federal agencies, military organizations, and universities registered years ago, and the `.int` domain was never very popular.

The generic top-level domains are by far the most popular in the United States. The `.com` domain has become so popular that providing service for it has become a major burden for the root servers. This concentration led to efforts to create other organizational top-level domains. However, `.com` is so closely tied to the idea of electronic commerce inside the U.S. that it is unlikely that business users would voluntarily move to another top-level domain.

Outside of the U.S., *geopolitical domains* are very popular. The geopolitical domains use a two-character country code largely based on the International Standards Organization (ISO) country codes. These domains are sometimes called *country code top-level domains* (ccTLDs). Examples of ccTLDs are `.uk` for the United Kingdom, `.de` for Germany, and

.bz for Belize. There are more than a hundred of these domains because there are as many possible ccTLDs as there are countries.

Some countries permit second-level registrations directly under the ccTLD. For example, the German branch of amazon.com is registered as amazon.de. For many other ccTLDs, the second-level domains are generic domains for commercial, academic, and governmental organizations. In those countries, an organization registers its domain in the third level. For example, amazon.com is a commercial organization. In the United Kingdom, commercial organizations register in the second-level .co domain, so amazon's domain is amazon.co.uk. The third approach to ccTLDs is to create geo-political second-level domains under the ccTLD.

The United States represents the third way to implement a ccTLD. In the U.S., every state is given a second-level domain under the .us ccTLD. These second-level domains are identified by the two-character U.S. Postal Service state codes. Maryland, where I live, is registered as md.us. The .us ccTLD is used extensively by state and local governments and by K–12 educational institutions.

The names of the various domains under the root are essentially arbitrary. As the description of the ccTLDs shows, there are any number of different approaches that can be used to name the domains under the top-level domains. Additionally, there is nothing magical about the current top-level domains. Others could easily be added or other names could have originally been chosen.

This book uses the imaginary domain foobirds.org for many examples. Imagine that it is the domain of a non-profit organization dedicated to protecting endangered birds. foobirds is the second-level domain that the organization purchased and .org is the top-level domain in which the domain was registered.

Reverse Domains

The foobirds.org domain is used to convert host names to addresses. However, as you saw in the description of the host table, there are times when it is necessary to convert from an IP address back to a host name. For this, DNS uses a special *reverse domain*.

There are two reasons that the domains that map addresses back to names are called reverse domains. First, of course, is that the act of converting a number to a name is the reverse of what is done in a normal DNS query when a name is converted to a number, which makes mapping a number to a name a *reverse lookup*. A second reason that the address-to-name domains are called reverse domains is the fact that the numeric address is written in reverse order. This requires more explanation.

Recall that when describing domain names I said that they move from the most specific (the host) to the most general (the top-level) domain. Thus, in the name `crow.foobirds.org`, the host is named `crow` and the top-level domain is `org`. IP addresses are the reverse of this structure. An IP address starts with the most general (the network) and moves to the most specific (the host). For example, in the address 172.16.5.5, 172.16 is the network number and 5.5 is the host number. (See the sidebar "Address Masks" for more information on how I determined the network and host numbers from this address.)

Because the structure of an IP address is the opposite of the structure of a domain name, the address must be reversed when it is treated as a reverse domain name. To create a reverse domain name, reverse the order of the digits in the IP address and add `.in-addr-arpa` to the end of the string of digits. `in-addr-arpa` is the special top-level domain in which all reverse domains are located. Using these rules, the address 172.16.5.5 yields the reverse domain name `5.5.16.172.in-addr.arpa`. In the reverse domain database, the name `5.5.16.172.in-addr.arpa` points to the host name `crow.foobirds.org`, thus creating the mapping from the IP address back to the host name.

The structure of the reverse domain can be confusing. In Chapter 6 we will create the reverse domain for a DNS server. The examples there will make the structure and purpose of the reverse domain clear.

Address Masks

An IP address is 32 bits long. It is divided between a network address portion and a host address portion. The network address is used to route the IP datagram through the network and the host portion is used to make final delivery. The system determines which part of the address defines the network and which part defines the host by applying an address mask to the IP address.

The address mask is a bit mask. If a bit is on (set to 1) in the address mask, the corresponding bit in the address is a network address bit. If a bit is off (set to 0), the corresponding bit in the address is a host bit. Given the address 172.16.5.5 and the split of 172.16 for the network and 5.5 for the host, the address mask must have the first 16 bits set to ones and the last 16 bits set to zeros.

The address mask can be defined in three ways:

1. You can specify it using dotted decimal notation. Using this notation, the mask described above would be 255.255.0.0.

Address Masks *(continued)*

2. You can specify the mask using an *address-prefix,* which is a decimal number specified with the IP address. For example, to specify a 16-bit network mask for the IP address 172.16.5.5, write the address as 172.16.5.5/16.

3. You can let the address default to its *natural mask,* which is the address mask that is used if you do not define a mask. If the first byte of an address is

- 0 to 127, the natural mask is 255.0.0.0.

- 128 to 191, the natural mask is 255.255.0.0.

- 192 to 223, the natural mask is 255.255.255.0.

- greater than 224, the address is not assigned to a network device.

In the example described earlier in this chapter, the natural mask was applied to the address 172.16.5.5. That is how I determined that 172.16 was the network number and 5.5 was the host number.

Searching for a Domain

From the root of the Linux file system, any file can be found by following the path name of the file through the various directories to the file itself. Likewise, from the root of DNS, any host can be found by following the pointers to the various name servers until the server responsible for that host is located. In both cases, the process begins by locating the root.

The system determines the location of the root of the Linux file system during the boot by reading the location from a configuration file that you, the system administrator, created. You define the location of the root either by specifying it during the initial installation or by manually configuring the `lilo.conf` file with a value such as `root = /dev/hda2`.

Similarly, your system determines the location of the DNS root by reading the location from a configuration file when the name server process starts. In the same way that you are responsible for configuring the location of the file system root, you are responsible for configuring the location of the DNS root. For now, don't worry about the structure and content of that configuration file. It is described in detail in Chapter 5, "Caching and Slave Server Configuration." All you need to know right now is that you tell your server where the DNS root is located. From there on out, the process of finding information about some remote domain is pretty much automatic as your server follows the links through the different levels of the domain hierarchy.

Currently, there are 13 servers that provide root service. They are named `a.root-servers.net` through `m.root-servers.net`. It is possible for the root servers to delegate a top-level domain to any other server, but in the current configuration of the Internet, most root servers are also servers for some of the top-level domains. Two servers, `l.root-servers.net` and `m.root-servers.net`, are pure root servers. They only answer queries about the root and point all queries about top-level domains to other servers. The remaining 11 servers all provide service for some of the top-level domains. The busy `.com`, `.net`, and `.org` domains have additional servers from the `gtld-servers.net` domain, such as `f.gtld-servers.net`, to help the root servers handle queries for these domains.

Some top-level domains are completely delegated to other servers. A query for the servers for the top-level `.uk` domain lists the following servers, none of which are root servers:

- `ns0.ja.net`
- `ns.eu.net`
- `ns.uu.net`
- `ns1.nic.uk`
- `sparky.arl.mil`

All possible domain names create the *domain name space*. Every *authoritative server* is responsible for a piece of the domain name space. A server is said to be authoritative when it can answer a query with complete accuracy. It can answer with authority because the server has the complete database for that part of the domain name space. The part of the domain name space an authoritative server is responsible for is referred to as that server's *zone of authority*.

No server is responsible for all of the domain name space. Even the root servers are only responsible for a small piece. Figure 1.1 illustrates the zones of authority of two of the root servers that have already been discussed.

Figure 1.1 Zones of authority

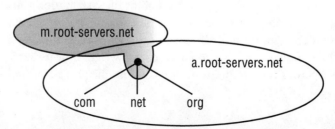

Figure 1.1 shows two of the authoritative servers for the root domain and certain top-level domains. This figure illustrates that the servers can have overlapping zones of authority and shows that zones and domains are different things. The `a.root-servers.net` server has a zone that includes the root, the `.net`, the `.org`, and the `.com` domains, while the zone of `m.root-servers.net` is only the root domain. In the case of the `m.root-servers.net` server, the zone and the domain are equivalent but in the `a.root-servers.net` server case, the zone includes multiple domains.

The root domains and the top-level domains are basically composed of pointers to the servers for lower level domains. Below the top-level domains are the second-level domains that are assigned to organizations around the Internet. For example, the imaginary domain that we will configure in this book is the `foobirds` second-level domain within the `.org` domain. The root server is responsible for the `.org` domain but the server that we create in this book is responsible for running the `foobirds.org` domain. The root server has delegated authority for the second-level domain to your organization. All that the top-level domain has for the `foobirds.org` domain is a pointer to our server.

Limiting the amount of information stored in the top-level domains is one of the keys to limiting the amount of central maintenance required for DNS. The bulk of the DNS database information is distributed among the tens of thousands of servers that are responsible for lower level domains. Building such a server and creating the database information for that server is one of the responsibilities of a domain administrator.

The Role of a Distributed Database

DNS simplifies maintenance and controls the size of individual database files by delegating complete authority over individual domains. You have the ability to add as many or as few host names to that domain as you wish. You can even create new domains within your domain and delegate those domains to whomever you wish.

For example, assume that you own the domain `arts.org`. You could create the domains `graphic.arts.org`, `visual.arts.org`, and `musical.arts.org`, and assign them to anyone. Once you delegate authority for those domains by placing the appropriate pointers in the `arts.org` database, those new domains are valid parts of the Internet namespace, and the organizations to which you delegated them have complete authority over those domains. Delegating these new domains does not require the approval of any "higher authority" because you have already been delegated complete authority over the `arts.org` domain. The `arts.org` domain is the *parent* of the subdomains `graphic.arts.org`, `visual.arts.org`, and `musical.arts.org`. The existence of the subdomains is completely dependent on the placement of the correct pointers in the parent domain.

The benefits of a distributed system go beyond the fact that more people and machines are involved in making sure DNS works effectively. The other advantage of distributed control is that it allows the network to grow more naturally. Whether delegating a subdomain or adding host names, it is much simpler for an administrator close to the needs of an organization to respond to those needs in a timely manner. The distributed structure of DNS places control where it needs to be—close to the action.

Along with all of this authority comes responsibility. Anyone who wants the freedom of running their own domain must accept the responsibility of running it correctly. Problems like lame delegations and poorly synchronized servers can impact Internet users on the other side of the world. A *lame delegation* occurs when the parent domain points to the wrong server for a subdomain. Poorly synchronized servers are caused by incorrect settings in the domain database. As a domain administrator, you are responsible for avoiding these problems. Use the information you gain from this book to make sure that your domain is not a source of these problems.

A look at how your local name server turns the name of a remote host into an IP address illustrates how this highly distributed database system works.

Resolving a Query

The process of finding information about a remote domain starts with the local name server. If the local server knows the answer, it answers the query itself. If it has no information at all about the remote domain, it asks the root servers for help. As noted previously, the local name server always knows how to find a root server.

Generally, the root server does not answer the query itself. Instead, it tells the local server where it can find the answer by sending the local server a pointer to the server that is responsible for the remote domain. Because the root server refers you to another server for the final answer instead of tracking down the answer itself, the root server is called a *non-recursive* server. The enormous number of queries received by the root servers makes it impractical for them to track down the answer to every query. On the other hand, the local server, like most servers, is a *recursive* server because it continues to send out queries until it receives an answer to the original question.

> **NOTE** Like servers, queries can also be recursive or non-recursive. Queries between name servers are generally sent as non-recursive queries because a server can chase down the answers itself. Queries from the resolver to a name server are recursive queries because the stub resolver depends on the server to chase down the answer.

Armed with the information provided by the root server, the local server now sends the query directly to the remote server that the root server indicated is responsible for the domain in question. That server will probably provide the final answer to the question. It is possible that the server the root pointed you to is not the server ultimately responsible for the specific domain about which you're seeking information.

Remember, this is a hierarchy. It is possible that the server you really want to query is subordinate to the server the root pointed to. Regardless of this, you'll frequently get the final answer instead of just a reference because the remote server is often knowledgeable about systems in its subdomains. In fact, you will probably get the final answer as well as pointers to the servers that are actually responsible for the specific domain. Figure 1.2, however, shows the second-level server referring the query to a subdomain server to better illustrate how a server searches the domain hierarchy.

Figure 1.2   A DNS query

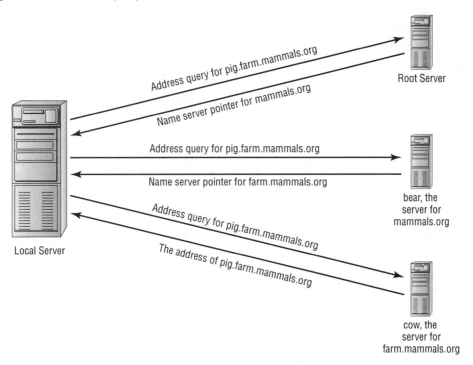

Figure 1.2 illustrates the flow of this query. The local server first sends the query for the address of `pig.farm.mammals.org` to the root server. The root server responds with a

name server pointer to the server for the `mammals.org` domain. The local server then queries that server and gets a pointer to a subdomain server for `farm.mammals.org`. Finally, the local server queries the subdomain server and gets the final answer. The local server saves all of this information for later use.

The Importance of Caching

The first thing the local server did was see if it could directly answer the query. It did this by checking its cache of answers. When a name server learns information about a remote domain, it saves that information and uses it later to directly answer queries for that information without having to re-query the remote domain server.

All of the answers a server receives are cached. Therefore, even if the local server can't directly answer a second query, it may still be able to shorten the search process.

For example, in Figure 1.2, the local server learned the address of `pig.farm.mammals .org` as well as the fact that `cow.farm.mammals.org` is the server for the `farm .mammals.org` domain and that `bear.mammals.org` is the name server for the `mammals.org` domain. If the local server needs to look up the address of `wolf .mammals.org`, it does not need to query the root server even though it does not have that address in its cache, because it has cached the fact that `bear` is the correct remote server for the `mammals.org` domain. Therefore, the local server sends the query directly to `bear`, thereby shortening the query process.

Caching is one of the most powerful features of DNS. It allows the local server to dynamically build up a supply of answers to its most frequently asked questions. The local server has all of the information it needs and no information it doesn't need. This creates a very efficient service.

Of course, the server cannot cache the information forever. Things change and it is possible for cached information to get out of date. For this reason, DNS allows the administrator of a domain to decide how long remote servers are allowed to cache information about the domain. The domain administrator knows best how frequently information in the domain changes and thus is in the best position to decide how long it should be cached. Later in this book, when you create a domain database, you will look at how to define the length of time a database record can be cached.

Obtaining a Domain Name

In all likelihood, your organization already has a domain name and you have been assigned to run the name server. If you do already have a domain name, you can skip this section. But if you are just starting out to build a new domain, read this section to find out how you select and register a new domain name.

Finding a Registrar

Your domain is not part of the official domain name space until it is registered. Only certain organizations are permitted to officially register a domain name. You need to locate an official registrar and obtain their services to register your domain. The place to start is either www.icann.org or www.internic.net. Both of these sites provide listings of official registrars.

ICANN is the Internet Corporation for Assigned Names and Numbers. ICANN is a non-profit organization created to take over management of some functions previously managed through U.S. government contractors. As of this writing, ICANN is new and does not completely manage all of these functions. Instead, ICANN works with existing contractors to ensure that everyone has access to domain names and Internet numbers. ICANN provides pointers to various international registrars.

www.internic.net is a U.S. government Web site designed to point users to official gTLD registrars and to answer any questions that Internet users might have about the domain registration process. The imaginary domain used in this book is registered in .org. For .org, .com, or .net domains, www.internic.net is a good place to start. Figure 1.3 shows part of the alphabetic list of accredited registrars.

Figure 1.3   The registrar listing

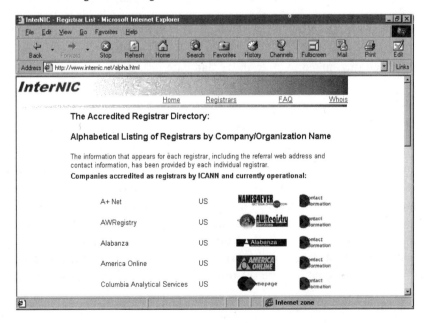

There is not much to choose between registrars. Domain registration is very inexpensive, usually less than $50 a year, so cost is not much of a factor. Service is also difficult to determine because once a domain is registered, it doesn't usually require any maintenance. Some administrators like to choose a registrar that is located close to home, but even this is not really significant in a wired world. Use your own judgment. I frankly can't find anything to recommend any individual registrar. In the following examples, I used Network Solutions as the registrar, in part because they are located a stone's throw away from my home. You, however, should choose your own registrar.

Registering a Domain

Once you select a registrar, go to their Web site for instructions on registering a domain. At www.internic.net, simply clicking the symbol of the registrar should take you to their Web site. Most registrars provide an online Web form for registering your domain name.

For example, if you select Network Solutions from the list at www.internic.net, you go to www.networksolutions.com. There you are asked to select a domain name. This first step searches the existing domain database system to make sure that the name you want is available. If it isn't, you're asked to choose another name. If the name is available, you must provide information about the servers that will be authoritative for the new domain. Some registrars, including Network Solutions, will provide DNS service for your new domain as an optional extra cost service. Because we plan to create our own server for the foobirds.org domain, we will provide our own server information.

First, you're asked to provide the name of the person legally responsible for this domain. This information is used by the registrar for billing purposes and is included in the whois database that provides contact information about the people responsible for domains. If you're already in the whois database, you're asked to provide your NIC handle, which is a unique identifier linked to your whois database record. For example, my NIC handle is cwh3.

If you are a new customer, you're asked to provide the name and address of the people who will be the administrative, technical, and billing contacts. These can be three different people or the same person, depending on how your business is organized.

Next, the system prompts for the names and IP addresses of two servers that will be authoritative for this domain. Enter the names of the master and slave server you have configured for your domain. The servers should already be operational when you fill in this form. If they aren't, you can pay a little extra and have Network Solutions host your domain until your servers are ready. You shouldn't enter the names of servers that aren't yet ready to run because that will cause a lame delegation when the root servers use this information to put pointers into the top-level domain to servers that are not really authoritative. Either preconfigure your servers, even if only with minimal information, or pay the somewhat higher fee to reserve your domain name until your servers are ready.

Check the information. Pay the bill. Now you're ready to run your own domain.

Registering a Reverse Domain

A one-to-one mapping does not exist between names and numbers. Even in the old host table it was possible to have many names assigned to one number. Just because you register a domain name does not necessarily mean that you will register a reverse domain. You are more likely to decide you need a reverse domain because of the IP addresses you own than you are to decide you need one because of the domain names you own.

Where you register your reverse domain depends on where you obtained your addresses. If you obtained a block of addresses from your ISP, you need to talk to them about delegating a reverse domain to you because they have probably already registered the reverse domain for the address space from which that block was taken.

If you obtained your addresses from a national registry, you need to talk to them about registering your reverse domain. An example of a national registry is the American Registry for Internet Numbers (ARIN), www.arin.net. (Other national address registries are listed at www.icann.org.) In all cases, you need to know from whom you bought your addresses and what their policies are regarding reverse domain registration.

> **NOTE**   If you use a private network number, as we do in this book, you do not need to register a reverse domain. The private network numbers listed in RFC 1918, "Address Allocation for Private Internets," are available for anyone to use. The addresses they contain cannot be routed across the Internet and thus are limited to use within a private network. A proxy server or network address translation (NAT) box is required when systems that use private addresses communicate with the outside world.

In Sum

The architecture of DNS permitted the Internet to grow to the size it has reached today. The previous technique for mapping names to addresses used a simple, flat file that could not scale to the size needed to support Internet growth. DNS solved the growth problem by creating a hierarchical database system that provides the centralized control needed for an orderly naming system and still allows the burden of name service to be shared among tens of thousands of name servers.

Each authoritative server is responsible for a small piece of the whole called the server's zone of authority. Non-authoritative servers also share the burden by caching domain information and answering queries from their caches.

Coordinating among all of these servers and moving questions and answers across the network require a range of communications protocols. Chapter 2, "The DNS Protocols," looks at the protocols that underlie DNS and how they are used to keep the system robust and running.

2

The DNS Protocols

A *protocol* is a set of rules that define how two computers should interact to exchange information over a network. Exchanging DNS data requires a set of standardized protocols. Like any distributed database, DNS clients need to retrieve information from the database and servers need to keep the information in the database accurate and up to date. Queries require the exchange of questions and answers in agreed-upon formats. Synchronizing databases among distributed servers requires an agreement on when and how the synchronization is to be done.

The technical details of protocols and packet structure can be complex and intimidating, particularly if your background is system administration and not network design. A protocol designer would probably feel the same way if asked to read one of your shell scripts. If this chapter is not your cup of tea, feel free to jump ahead to more practical chapters. But if you do, I urge you to come back and read this chapter after you have worked with DNS configuration. You will find an elegant linkage between the actions you take in configuring your system and the packets your system puts on the network.

This chapter tells you the rules that DNS uses to exchange information, not so you can master the protocols but so you can master the DNS servers that depend on these protocols. Understanding how data moves through the network helps in understanding why certain configuration parameters are required and what can be done to optimize them. Let's begin by understanding the protocol suite that DNS is part of.

The Internet Protocols Suite

The DNS architecture, described in Chapter 1, is implemented on top of a network architecture. The network upon which DNS runs is the Internet and the software that makes the Internet possible is the Internet Protocol (IP) suite. The DNS protocols are part of that suite.

The Internet Protocol is the foundation of the protocol suite. IP defines the network addressing, thus the term *IP address*, and it defines the basic unit of information that moves though the network. This unit of information is a block of data, called a *datagram*, that contains addressing and administrative information, as well as application-specific data. Because the datagram carries its own addressing information with it, it can move through the network independent of any other datagram. The benefits of this independence are robustness and efficiency. Robustness comes from the fact that each datagram can choose its own path through the network. If part of the network fails, the datagram can move around it on any available path. Efficiency comes from the minimal overhead involved in this scheme. Because each packet is independent, there is no need to keep track of other packets in the flow, which simplifies processing. The weakness of this independence is that sometimes the application data must span multiple datagrams. The IP protocol does not provide a way to sequence the data across datagrams.

Application programs access the IP protocol through two transport protocols: UDP and TCP. The *User Datagram Protocol (UDP)* provides the application with full access to the strengths of IP. With UDP, an application creates a message that becomes the data portion of a datagram. Each UDP message is an independent entity that moves through the network without depending on any other message.

The *Transport Control Protocol (TCP)* offers the application a way to address the weaknesses of IP. When an application needs to send a stream of related data, TCP provides the features necessary for the data to arrive at the remote location reliably and in sequence. TCP maintains the sequence by embedding sequence numbers in the stream of transmitted data and ensures reliability by requiring acknowledgements from the remote end. DNS is a network application that uses both UDP and TCP to send data over IP. Figure 2.1 shows these protocol layers.

Figure 2.1   Protocol layers from DNS to IP

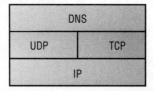

The only time DNS uses TCP is when distributed servers synchronize their databases by transferring entire domain database files. One of the challenges of a distributed database system is ensuring that all of the servers in that system provide accurate answers. The backup servers and the master servers must provide information of the same high quality. DNS keeps each backup server's data accurate by periodically transferring the entire domain database from the master server. During a file transfer, many related records are transmitted and it is important to keep the data in sequence. TCP is perfect for this. It has the reliability mechanisms needed to ensure that the entire database is received by the distributed servers, and it has sequence numbering to guarentee that all of the database records are received in order.

DNS uses UDP for the majority of its network traffic. It sends queries and receives responses as UDP packets. Given the critical nature of DNS, some people question the wisdom of sending DNS data over the unreliable UDP protocol. But the truth is, DNS is a perfect match for UDP. A DNS query fits into a single UDP packet and so does the response to the query—one packet is sent and one packet is received. No overhead is needed to establish a connection and no overhead is needed to sequence records because each DNS message is an independent entity. The response to the query is the acknowledgment of the request so there is no need to use a separate protocol for acknowledgments. Teaming a request/response protocol like DNS with UDP is highly efficient. The queries and responses that DNS sends over UDP have a well-defined message format.

The DNS Message

The format of the DNS message is defined in RFC 1035, "Domain Names—Implementation and Specification." This RFC defines a standard message format composed of up to five parts:

Header   The header section provides administrative information about the message, including information about what is contained in subsequent sections of the message.

Question   The question section defines the question being asked by a query. When the question section is returned in a response, it is used to help determine which question the response is answering.

Answer   The answer section is found in a response and it contains the answer to the specific question sent in the query.

Authority   The authority section is found in a response and it contains pointers to the servers responsible for the domain being queried. Chapter 1, "The DNS Architecture," shows how important these pointers are for locating information within the DNS hierarchy, even when the first server queried cannot provide a real answer to the question.

Additional   The additional section is found in a response. This section contains database records that provide additional, important information that supports the answer. These are not database records directly requested by the query, but they help in interpreting or utilizing the response.

The format of the DNS message is clearly shown by the dig test tool. dig is one of the DNS test tools included with Linux. It is used throughout this text and covered extensively in Chapter 11, "Testing DNS." A nice feature of dig is that it shows the entire DNS message, not just the answer to the query. Listing 2.1 shows the DNS message format, as displayed by dig.

Listing 2.1   The DNS message format shown by dig

```
[craig]$ dig dog.mammals.org

; <<>> DiG 8.2 <<>> dog.mammals.org
;; res options: init recurs defnam dnsrch
;; got answer:
;; ->>HEADER<<- opcode: QUERY, status: NOERROR, id: 4
;; flags: qr aa rd ra; QUERY: 1, ANSWER: 1, AUTHORITY: 2, ADDITIONAL: 2
;; QUERY SECTION:
;;      dog.mammals.org, type = A, class = IN

;; ANSWER SECTION:
dog.mammals.org.        1H IN A         192.168.24.11

;; AUTHORITY SECTION:
mammals.org.            1H IN NS        ns.exodus.net.
mammals.org.            1H IN NS        fox.mammals.org.

;; ADDITIONAL SECTION:
ns.exodus.net.          15M IN A        206.79.230.10
fox.mammals.org.        1H IN A         192.168.24.5

;; Total query time: 249 msec
;; FROM:owl.foobirds.org to SERVER: default -- 10.22.11.61
;; WHEN: Wed Feb 23 09:33:30 2000
;; MSG SIZE  sent: 33  rcvd: 137
```

The first three lines and the last four lines contain information that dig provides in addition to the DNS message. Those lines will be explained when dig is described in more detail. The focus of this chapter is the DNS message. dig prints all five sections of the message that it received in response to its query. Without an understanding of the structure of a DNS message, the dig response can lead to more confusion than enlightenment. Let's look at each section in more detail.

The Header Section

All DNS messages have a header section to describe how the data that follows should be interpreted. The header section, as described in RFC 1035, consists of six 16-bit words. Figure 2.2 shows the header section as it is laid out by the RFC.

Figure 2.2   The DNS message header section

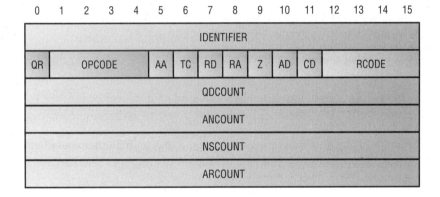

Contents of the Header Section

Many of the values in the header section can be affected by configuration values you define for your server. Examples of the effect you can have on header values are noted and each item in the header section is described in the following sections.

IDENTIFIER   The first word of the header is a 16-bit identifier generated by the server that issued the query. This identifier is used in the response so that the response can easily be matched to the query.

The DNS software that Linux provides has an option called use-id-pool that improves the randomness of the query identifier to avoid duplicates. While not required for basic server operation, the use-id-pool option illustrates the scope of control you have over the DNS configuration and demonstrates that you cannot fully understand the configuration options available to you without understanding the underlying details of DNS. See

Appendix B, "name.conf Command Reference," for a short description of the use-id-pool option.

QR QR stands for query/response. This is a one-bit field that indicates whether the message is a query or a response. 0 means it is a query and 1 means it is a response.

OPCODE The OPCODE is a four-bit field that defines what kind of query is contained in the message. Like the identifier, it is initially set by the server that generates the query and is left unchanged by the server that generates the response. There are five defined OPCODE values:

0   means that this is a standard query. All queries for DNS database information use this OPCODE.

1   means that this is an inverse query. Inverse queries are obsolete and no longer used.

2   means that this is a query for server status, not a query for database information. While defined, this OPCODE is not supported or used.

4   means that this is a DNS NOTIFY message. NOTIFY is a technique used to synchronize the databases on master and slave servers.

5   means that this is an update message. Update messages change the records stored in the DNS database on authoritative servers that support dynamic DNS.

AA AA stands for authoritative answer. This is a one-bit field that is used only when the message is a response. The bit is set to 1 if the response comes from an authoritative server. As explained in Chapter 1, all servers cache answers and can then answer queries from their caches. These answers are not authoritative. Only a server responding to a query for information in its zone of authority can provide an authoritative answer. When an authoritative server provides an authoritative answer, it sets this bit to 1. When a server answers from its cache of answers, it sets this bit to 0, indicating it is a non-authoritative answer. You will create the authoritative servers for your domain.

TC TC stands for truncation. The truncation bit is set to 1 if the response was too large to fit in a message and had to be truncated. If the truncation bit is 0, the entire response fits into one message, which is the normal case.

RD RD stands for recursion desired. This bit is set to 1 to request recursion. Most clients request recursion. RES_RECURSE, an option described in Chapter 4, "Configuring the Resolver," that causes the client to set this bit to 1, is compiled into the DNS software by default. By its very nature, recursion means that the first recursive server to handle the request will send out as many additional queries as are needed to find the answer to the original question. Because the server is already recursively handling the query, it does not need other servers to also recursively pursue an answer. The server normally sets this bit to 0 on subsequent queries so that the other servers don't unnecessarily start their own recursive searches.

RA   RA stands for recursion available. This bit is set to 1 if the name server generating the message supports recursion. It is set to 0 if the name server is a non-recursive server. By default, Linux name servers are recursive servers. However, you control this through the `recursion` configuration option covered in Chapter 8, "Special BIND Configurations."

Unused   This is an unused bit available for future use.

AD   AD stands for authenticated data. This bit is set to 1 when the data in the message has been authenticated using the DNS security (DNSSEC) protocol.

CD   CD stands for checking disabled. Setting this bit to 1 indicates that the server is unable to authenticate the message, not because the data failed authentication, but because the server either does not have or has currently disabled support for the DNSSEC protocols. See Chapter 10, "DNS Security," for more information on DNSSEC.

RCODE   The response code is a four-bit value used for error codes in a response message. Linux software supports ten error codes:

0   No errors occurred. The response is good.

1   There was an error in the format of the query and the name server could not understand the query.

2   Due to a name server failure, the name server was not able to process the query.

3   The domain name referenced in the query does not exist. This is a very useful error code when it comes from an authoritative server. It literally means that the requested domain name does not exist, which is information that is just as important as knowing the address of a domain name. For this reason, this type of information is cached just like an answer containing an address. In fact, this error code is referred to NXDOMAIN (non-existent domain) almost as if it were a real DNS database record. Caching NXDOMAIN information is called *negative caching*. Several times in the discussion of name server configuration, we will examine options relating to negative caching.

5   The request was refused. The server supports the requested function but it won't do it for the client. Security is the primary reason for this response code. You control what DNS services are offered and what hosts they are offered to with configuration options like `allow-query` and `allow-transfer`.

6   The request contained a dynamic DNS update that attempted to add a domain name that already exists. The update was rejected.

7   A dynamic update attempted to add a set of database records that already exist. The update was rejected.

8   The DNS update request attempted to delete or change records that don't exist. The update was rejected.

9   The request asked the server to update a zone for which the server is not authoritative. A non-authoritative server cannot perform a dynamic DNS update. Therefore, the update was rejected.

10   The database records in the DNS update request do not belong to the domain for which the update was requested. The update was rejected.

QDCOUNT   QDCOUNT stands for query data count. This field contains the number of entries in the question section of the message.

ANCOUNT   ANCOUNT stands for answer count. This field contains the number of DNS database records contained in the answer section of the message.

NSCOUNT   NSCOUNT stands for name server count. This field contains the number of DNS name server database records contained in the authority section of the message.

ARCOUNT   ARCOUNT stands for additional record count. This field contains the number of DNS database records contained in the additional section of the message.

Evaluating the *dig* Header Data

Use the information about the header section to interpret the output of the `dig` command in a more meaningful way. Here is the header data from Listing 2.1:

```
;; ->>HEADER<<- opcode: QUERY, status: NOERROR, id: 4
;; flags: qr aa rd ra; QUERY: 1, ANSWER: 1, AUTHORITY: 2, ADDITIONAL: 2
```

`dig` does not display the header data in the order in which it occurs in the header section, but it is still easy to identify:

`opcode: QUERY`   clearly indicates that this is a standard query; in other words, the OPCODE field contains a 0.

`status: NOERROR`   is a little trickier. `status` really refers to the RCODE field and `NOERROR` means that the RCODE field contains a 0.

`id: 4`   indicates that the identifier used for this message was the number 4. This value doesn't seem random. If your server generated this response, you might want to enable the `use-pool-id` option described in Appendix B. It improves the randomness of the identifier at the cost of a small increase in the memory used by the name server.

`flags: qr aa rd ra` really covers four different fields in the header section and gives us information about three others. `dig` uses `flags` to group together all of the one-bit fields. It lists each field that is set to 1. This means that QR is set to 1, indicating this is a response. AA is set to 1 because this answer came from an authoritative server. RD is set to 1 to indicate that recursion was requested by the query. RA is set to 1, indicating that recursion is available on the server. TC is not listed, meaning it is set to 0 and that the response was not truncated. AD and CD are also set to 0 because DNSSEC is not in use.

`QUERY: 1, ANSWER: 1, AUTHORITY: 2,` and `ADDITIONAL: 2` represent the last four fields in the header section, QDCOUNT, ANCOUNT, NSCOUNT, and ARCOUNT. This information tells you that there is one entry in the question section, one database record in the answer section, two records in the authority section, and two records in the additional section.

The Question Section

The question section is the first section after the header. It holds the query sent from the DNS client and is found in both the request and the response message. Each query in the question section is three 16-bit words long. Figure 2.3 shows the format of a query.

Figure 2.3 A DNS query

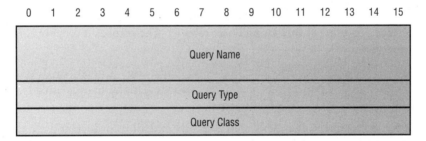

Query Name Field

The Query Name field contains the fully qualified domain name for which information is sought. Recall that a fully qualified domain name ends with the root. For example, `mammals.org.` and `robin.foobirds.org.` are fully qualified domain names. When a domain name is stored in the Query Name field, the separating dots are dropped and each piece of the name is preceded by a byte that defines the length of that piece of the name. `robin.foobirds.org.` is stored as `5robin8foobirds3org0`. Notice the zero length at the end of the name. All query names end in this way because they all end with the root and the root is a null name; a null name is a name with no length.

Query Type Field

The Query Type field defines the type of database records being requested. There are many different types of DNS database records, all of which are defined in Appendix C, "Resource Record Reference." Each record type is assigned a numeric value and it is that value that is used in the Query Type field. For example, a 1 in the Query Type field means that the client wants the IP address of the host identified in the Query Name field. A domain name can have more than one type of database record assigned. The Query Type field permits the client to request an individual record type or groups of records. The values used to request multiple records are listed here:

250   This value, called TSIG, requests the transaction signature record for a domain. These records are used for authentication to improve DNS security. See Chapter 10 for more information.

251   This value requests an incremental zone file transfer (IXFR). The zone file is the database file that contains all of the records for a specific zone of authority. Distributed servers synchronize the database by transferring the zone file. This is one of the techniques used to transfer the file.

252   This value requests a full zone file transfer (AXFR). This is the technique used by a backup name server to synchronize its database with the master server for the specified domain. This is a basic function of DNS. Protocols relating to this function are covered later in this chapter.

253   This is an obsolete value that is no longer used. Called MAILB, it was designed to retrieve various mailbox records. The records it retrieves are no longer used.

254   This is an obsolete value that is no longer used. Called MAILA, it was designed to retrieve various mail agent records. This value was already obsolete in 1987 when RFC 1035 was written.

255   This value, called ANY, retrieves any and all records relating to the query name. This is a powerful and popular query type.

Query Class Field

The third word in the query entry is the Query Class field. There are five possible class values: Internet (1), Hesiod (3), Chaosnet (4), NONE (254), and ANY (255).The ANY and NONE values are used for special purposes, such as dynamic updates. Hesiod is a server developed almost 20 years ago at MIT as part of Project Athena. Cool stuff like X Windows and the Kerberos authentication server came from that project, but Hesiod is no longer widely used. Chaosnet also dates to about 20 years ago. It was the network used by the Lisp machines that were once very popular in the articficial intelligence research community. Your Linux server will always work with Internet database records so the query class used for all of your queries will be Internet, which is abbreviated as IN and has a numeric value of 1.

Evaluating the *dig* Query Data

The `dig` command used in Listing 2.1 displayed this query data:

```
;; QUERY SECTION:
;;        dog.mammals.org, type = A, class = IN
```

Using information from the header, you know that this query section contains only one query. The three fields of this query are clearly shown. You know the query is asking for information about `dog.mammals.org` because that is the query name. Specifically, the query is asking for the Internet address of `dog`. You know that because the query type is A, which is the record type of address records, and the class field is IN, stating that the client is only interested in Internet records. An Internet address query is the most common query and it is the one that `dig` defaults to if no arguments are added to the `dig` command line.

The Answer, Authority, and Additional Sections

The three remaining sections of the response message all have the same format. The answer, authority, and additional sections all contain a list of DNS domain records. The number of records in each section is specified in the header. The records are laid out as shown in Figure 2.4.

Figure 2.4   The format of database records in a response

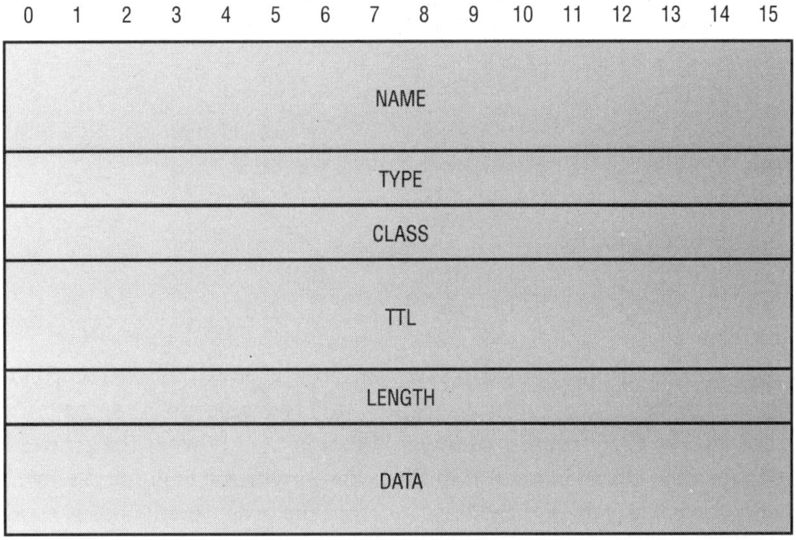

As you'll see in Chapter 6, "Creating a Master Server," most of these fields are entered by you when you create the domain database for the master server. Although not entered in exactly this order, the meaning of the fields will become very familiar to you as you build your own database files. The fields are as follows:

NAME   This is the domain name of the object to which this record relates.

TYPE   This is the database record type. It can be any of the record types listed in Appendix C.

CLASS   This is the class of the database. It can be IN for Internet, HS for Hesiod, or CH for Chaosnet. It is usually IN.

TTL   This is the time-to-live field. It defines how long the database record can be saved in a remote server's cache.

LENGTH   This is the only field that is not created by the domain administrator. It specifies the length of the following data field in bytes.

DATA   This is the data field that relates to this type of resource record. For example, in an address record, this would be an address. On a name server record, this would be the domain name of the name server. The data field varies in content and length depending on the record type.

Evaluating the *dig* Data for the Answer, Authority, and Additional Sections

The dig command in Listing 2.1 displayed the following answer, authority, and additional sections:

```
;; ANSWER SECTION:
dog.mammals.org.        1H IN A        192.168.24.11

;; AUTHORITY SECTION:
mammals.org.            1H IN NS       ns.exodus.net.
mammals.org.            1H IN NS       fox.mammals.org.

;; ADDITIONAL SECTION:
ns.exodus.net.          15M IN A       206.79.230.10
fox.mammals.org.        1H IN A        192.168.24.5
```

The header section displayed by dig says that there is one database record in the answer section, two records in the authority section, and two records in the additional section. The query asked for the address of dog and that is exactly what the answer section provides. dig displays the information in the order in which it is entered when building a database record, which is slightly different from the order in which it is transmitted in a response message. The answer shows the full domain name of dog. It shows that the TTL for this record is 1 hour (`1h`). The class is `IN` for Internet, the type is `A` for address, and the data field of the record is the Internet address of `dog`, 192.168.24.11.

The authority section lists the servers that are authoritative for the `mammals.org` domain to which `dog` belongs. There are two name server records, each providing the name of an authoritative server. From this, we know that `fox.mammals.org.` and `ns.exodus.net.` are authoritative for `mammals.org`.

The additional section completes the message by providing the address of each of the authoritative servers. The addresses are important because if the local server wants to send future queries directly to the authoritative servers for the `mammals.org` domain, it needs to know the address of those servers. In this case, the addresses are 206.79.230.10 and 192.168.24.5.

All of the information from all of these sections is cached by the local server. If it receives a query for the addresses of `dog.mammals.org` or `fox.mammals.org`, it can now answer those queries directly from its own cache—at least for the next hour. The longest TTL on any of these records is one hour.

The DNS message is the building block of all DNS client/server activity. It is the unit sent to a server as a query and the unit with which the server responds to a query. Most DNS information is exchanged in DNS messages sent over UDP. The exception is when servers need to synchronize an entire domain database.

Synchronizing Databases

Synchronizing databases begins with the exchange of request and response packets over UDP just like any other DNS interaction. The request message sent depends on the technique being used to update the backup domain files. There are two techniques:

- A traditional pull technique in which the backup servers pulls the data down from the master server.
- A newer push technique in which the master server pushes database updates out to the backup servers.

Slave-Initiated Zone Pull

When the pull technique is used, the backup server sends a query to the master server asking for administrative information about the zone. This information is held in the Start of Authority (SOA) record for the zone, so the slave server queries the master for an SOA record. The data field of the SOA record contains a lot of information, but one item, the zone's serial number, is particularly important to the slave server. The slave compares that serial number to the serial number of its copy of the zone. If the serial number of the master file is greater than the serial number of the slave's copy of the zone, the slave assumes that it needs to download an updated database from the master.

The slave server can download the entire database with a zone file transfer (AXFR) or it can request just the changes to the zone with an incremental zone file transfer (IXFR). For a full zone file transfer, the question section of the slave's request message contains the name of the domain being transferred in the query name field, IN in the Query Class field, and AXFR in the Query Type field. The question section and a properly formatted header section are all that is required for a zone file transfer request.

The request message for an incremental zone file transfer is slightly more complex. As you might expect, the message contains a properly formatted header and a question section that contains the name of the requested domain, the class IN, and the type IXFR. In addition, an incremental zone transfer request contains the slave's SOA record in the authority section. The slave sends its SOA record to the master so that the master knows how far out of synchronization the database files are. The master then sends the slave those records that have changed between the version of the zone the slave has and the current version of the zone on the master. Unlike the AXFR, which transfers the entire file, only the individual database records that have changed are sent in an IXFR.

The incremental zone transfer has the potential to greatly improve zone transfer efficiency. But like many things that look good, it is not as easy as it sounds. IXFR reduces network load at the cost of increased processing.

First, IXFR forces the master server to maintain a history of database updates in order to know what should be sent to the slave. This history may need to be several changes deep, depending on the frequency with which the zone changes and the slave checks for changes.

Second, the slave needs to understand how to process these changes in a manner that guarantees that the database files are synchronized. These requirements increase the complexity of the DNS software. Some DNS servers avoid the complexity by treating an IXFR as an AFXR. In the long run, however, I expect that all name servers will comply with the RFCs and support incremental zone transfer requests. Linux DNS servers do support IXFR.

Master-Initiated Zone Push

The master server starts the process of pushing an updated zone down to its slave with a standard DNS request message sent over UDP. In the header section of the message, the OPCODE is set to 4, which is the NOTIFY code. The question section of the request message contains a query for the SOA record of the slave server. When the slave receives the request message, it flips the QR bit from query to response and sends the message right back to the master. This is fine because the master server isn't really interested in the slave's SOA record. It wants a positive acknowledgement that the slave server has received the domain NOTIFY message and it gets that when it receives the slave's response message.

After responding to the master, the slave server begins to retrieve the updated zone file. The slave can use either a full zone file transfer or an incremental zone file transfer to get the update. NOTIFY simplifies the processing of an incremental zone transfer because it limits the amount of history that the master server is forced to maintain. The NOTIFY is sent every time the zone changes so only those records changed in the last zone update need to be sent for the IXFR. There is no need to stored changes from earlier updates because the slave has already received them in response to earlier NOTIFY messages. NOTIFY also simplifies the IXFR process for the slave because only one set of changes needs to be processed. By simplifying IXFR, NOTIFY makes it more useful.

Using these various techniques, the servers responsible for a zone ensure that the database information on every authoritative server is accurate.

In Sum

The Domain Name System is a network-based, distributed database service. DNS uses standardized protocols to communicate over the network. The network that DNS is built on is the Internet. The Internet is a logical network created by the IP suite, which is composed of IP, the transport protocols UDP and TCP, and application protocols. The DNS network protocol is one of the application protocols. DNS works by exchanging standardized request and response messages over the network.

The DNS protocols are implemented in the Berkeley Internet Name Domain (BIND) software. Every Linux name server uses BIND to construct the request and response messages and perform all of the tasks associated with DNS. Chapter 3, "The BIND Software," introduces the BIND client/server software and describes how it is installed in your Linux DNS server.

3

The BIND Software

Linux DNS servers use the Berkeley Internet Name Domain (BIND) software. BIND is one of the original implementations of DNS and it is the most widely used implementation in the world today. BIND is found on all Unix systems and has been ported to many operating systems, including Linux. One of the things that makes Linux such an excellent platform for building a DNS server is the fact that it uses the most thoroughly tested and widely used DNS software in existence.

The release of BIND at this writing is BIND 8.2.2pl5. All recent versions of Linux ship with BIND 8. If you're moving to Linux from a commercial Unix operating system, you may have used BIND 4. BIND 8 is very different, particularly in its configuration syntax. This book focuses exclusively on BIND 8 because that is the version of BIND that Linux uses and it is the version you should be using. (The proposed features of BIND 9, which is not yet available, are covered in Appendix A, "BIND 9.")

This chapter describes the BIND software. It covers the components that make up the BIND package, the various types of configurations that you can build with BIND on Linux, and how those configurations can be used to create your DNS architecture. This chapter also describes how you can install BIND on your Linux systems, including how to download and compile the latest BIND release.

BIND is a client/server system and thus is composed of two fundamental parts:

- The resolver, the client side of the system
- named, the name server daemon

This chapter describes both components of BIND, beginning with the resolver, which is found on every DNS client and server.

The Resolver

The resolver creates the query that is sent to the name server. Despite its name, it does not actually resolve the query. It simply sends the query to the server for resolution. Because all it does is build the query and wait for another process to answer the query, the BIND resolver is called a *stub resolver*.

To build a query that is in the correct form for the name server, the resolver uses the information entered by the user and values that you have placed in the configuration. Assume the user enters the following command:

```
[craig] $ telnet crow
```

The resolver routines are called by `telnet` and given the host name `crow` to resolve into an IP address. The resolver cannot simply pass the name `crow` to the name server for resolution because there is no way for the name server to know which domain `crow` is part of. The name server needs a full domain name if it is going to locate the correct address.

Building Fully Qualified Domain Names

The resolver applies the following rules to determine if it should add a domain name to a host name before sending it to the name server and to determine exactly how the host name should be modified:

- If the host name passed to the resolver by the application doesn't contain a dot (`.`), the search list is used first. The search list can contain one or more domain names that are either defined by you or derived from the `hostname` command on the local system. (The details of how the search list is defined are discussed in Chapter 4, "Configuring the Resolver.") Domain names are taken from the search list and appended to the host name to create a fully qualified name. The resolver builds a query with the first domain name in the search list. If the name server tells the resolver that the name it is asking for is a non-existent name, the resolver sends out a query using the second name in the search list. It continues in this manner until all of the domain names in the search list are exhausted or the name server responds to the query. If none of the queries results in a positive answer from the name server, the resolver makes one last attempt using the name exactly as the user typed it in. The query order for a name that does not contain a dot is first to use the search list and then to use the name as typed.

- If the host name passed to the resolver contains any dots, the resolver assumes the name already has a domain name attached so it sends the name to the name server as it is. If the server cannot answer the query, the resolver sends additional queries using the domain names from the search list. When a name contains a dot, the query order is to first send the name as is and then to use the search list.

Resolver Timeouts

The query process is complicated by the fact that the Internet is a best-effort network. Unless it receives an answer from the name server, the resolver cannot assume that the name server received the query. Therefore, the resolver must reissue the query when it determines that the name server did not receive the query. It does this by maintaining a timer and by assuming that when the timer expires, the query should be sent again.

> **NOTE** The timeout values can all be configured in the latest version of BIND. To provide examples that are applicable to the widest range of Linux systems, these examples assume that BIND is configured to use traditional timeout values.

The standard timeout for the first query is set to 5 seconds. You can define up to three name servers for your resolver to use. The resolver sends the first query to the first server in the server list with a timeout of 5 seconds. If the first server fails to respond, the query is sent to the second server in the list with a timeout of 5 seconds. If the second server fails to respond, the query is sent to the third server in the list with a timeout of 5 seconds. Each server in the list is given a chance to respond and each server is given the full 5-second timeout. This first round of queries can take as little as 5 seconds if you have defined only one server or as long as 15 seconds if you have defined three servers.

If no server responds to the first round of queries, the previous timeout is doubled and divided by the number of servers to determine the new timeout value. The query is then sent again. By default, the current version of BIND retries two times, but you can configure more retries if you wish. Traditionally, this process was repeated three times, for a total of four queries, before the resolver abandons its attempt to resolve the query. Assuming that the resolver is configured for three retries, it uses the following timeouts:

Timeouts with one server The first query has a timeout of 5 seconds, the second has 10 seconds, the third has 20 seconds, and the final query has a timeout of 40 seconds. Given this, the resolver waits up to 75 seconds before abandoning the query when one server is defined.

Timeouts with two servers The first round of queries has a timeout of 5 seconds for each server, the second round is also 5 seconds, the third round is 10 seconds, and the fourth round is 20 seconds. This gives a total timeout value of 40 seconds for each server, which means the resolver waits up to 80 seconds before abandoning a query when two servers are defined.

Timeouts with three servers   The first round of queries has a timeout of 5 seconds for each server, the second round is 3 seconds, the third round is 6 seconds, and the fourth round is 13 seconds. This gives a total timeout value of 27 seconds for each server, which means the resolver waits up to 81 seconds before abandoning a query when three servers are defined.

NOTE   Dividing 10, 20, or 40 by 3 does not yield a whole number. The timeout values 3, 6, and 13 are truncated, whole number values.

Without the formula described in this section, which reduces the timeout based on the number of servers, three servers would take up to 225 seconds to time out if the resolver used the same 5-, 10-, 20-, and 40-second timeout values it uses for one server. Even the most patient user would become exasperated! Additionally, when multiple name servers are used, it is not necessary to give each of them as much time to resolve the query. It is highly unlikely that they will all be down at the same time. A query timeout when three servers are configured probably indicates that there is something wrong with your local network, not with all three remote servers. Because of this timeout formula, the added reliability of three servers only costs, at most, 6 seconds.

The BIND resolver does not actually exist as a distinct process. It is really a library of software routines that are linked into any process that needs to query DNS. The programmer who creates a network application makes use of the resolver by placing the appropriate calls within the source code of the application.

The reason that the resolver can be implemented as library routines called by other processes is that it is a reasonably simple procedure. All the resolver really does is turn the query into a full domain name, send it to the name server, and wait for an answer. The bulk of the work takes place in the name server.

The Name Server

named is the BIND name server daemon. As a daemon, named is started during the Linux boot by one of the startup scripts and continues to run as long as the system is running. named implements the server side of the DNS protocols described in Chapter 2. It listens on UDP port 53 for DNS queries, finds the answer to the queries, and returns the answer to the resolver that asked the question.

The *named* Command

The name server daemon is run by the named command. In practice, the syntax of the named command is usually very simple, although there are several command-line options. The command-line options are:

−c   defines the path name of the configuration file. By default, the name of the configuration file is named.conf. Use a different filename only if you're testing an alternative configuration. Don't change the name of the configuration file of an operational server. That makes it difficult for the other administrators of your system to find and debug the configuration when you're not available. An alternate configuration file can also be specified with either the −b option or by placing the name of the configuration file at the end of the named command line. All three of the following commands perform the same function:

```
[root]# named -c test.conf
[root]# named -b test.conf
[root]# named test.conf
```

−u   defines the user id under which named is run. The option is used to select a user id that has less privilege than the root user id under which the name server usually runs. Chapter 10, "DNS Security," describes how this option is used to improve security.

−g   defines the group id under which named is run. This option is used for the same reasons as the −u option and these options are often used together. If the −g option is not specified when the −u option is used, named is run under the group id associated with the user id defined by −u. If neither −u or −g is used, the default group id assigned to root is used.

−t   defines the chroot directory for named. If −t is not defined, named does not use the chroot command to change to a secure directory. Chapter 10 describes how a chroot jail is used to enhance the security of a Linux name server.

−w   defines the working directory used by named. The working directory can also be defined in the named configuration file, as described in Chapter 5, "Caching and Slave Server Configuration."

−d   turns on debugging. A numeric value from 1 to 11 is passed with the −d option. The higher the number associated with the −d option, the greater the level of detail included in the debug information. The debug information is written to the named.run file. Chapter 12, "The BIND Log Files," provides detailed examples of using debug information to troubleshoot a server. On most servers, debugging is not required but when it is, it is enabled with the –d option or with the nde trace command. The –d option is useful when you want to debug what happens to named during startup.

–q logs all incoming queries. This option is still available but is no longer used. Query logging is now defined in the named configuration file, as described in Chapter 12. Don't use the –q option.

–r turns off recursion, making this a non-recursive server. Normally, you want to keep your server set as a recursive server, and even if you don't, don't use the –q option. This option is deprecated, which means that it is still available but is no longer used. Recursion can be enabled and disabled in the named configuration file as described in Chapter 8, "Special BIND Configurations." If you must create a non-recursive server, do it in the configuration file.

–f runs named as a foreground process. By default, named runs in the background as a daemon, which is exactly what you want on a Linux system. This option prevents that default behavior. Don't use the –f option on your Linux system. It is really intended to support certain System V Unix systems that start foreground processes from the inittab file.

–p changes the port number associated with named. By default, the named port is port 53. You specify an alternate port with the –p option. This option is rarely used because all of your clients expect to find the server on port 53. Moving it to another port means that the clients will not be able to communicate with the server unless their configurations are also modified. This should only be used for testing or other similar specialized configurations.

Most of these named command-line options are either implemented in the configuration file or are used only for specialized configurations. Because of this, these options are rarely used. On most systems, running named is as simple as typing:

```
[root]# named
```

Generally, however, named is not started from the command line. A name server is not something started at the administrator's discretion. Once a system becomes a name server for a network, it must be up and running at all times. For this reason, named is started at boot time.

Starting *named*

On Linux distributions like Red Hat and Caldera that use System V-style boot procedures, the script that starts named is found in the /etc/rc.d/init.d directory where it is stored, sensibly enough, under the name named. On distributions like Slackware that use BSD-style boot procedures, the commands that start named are stored in one of the rc scripts used to start the network. For example, on Slackware 4.0, the command to start named is found in the rc.inet2 script located in the /etc/rc.d directory. Regardless of the name of the script used for this purpose, some startup script is used to start the name server at boot time.

TIP   To locate the named startup script on your Linux system, go to the directory that holds startup scripts and run the command grep named * to search every file for references to named. Not sure where the startup scripts are stored? Go to /etc and look for files or directories that begin with the string rc. Those are startup files and directories.

The ps command reveals whether or not named is running on a system:

```
[root]# ps -C named
  PID TTY          TIME CMD
  427 ?        00:00:36 named
```

The low process ID (PID) shows that this process was started during the boot. Running this ps command on a Linux workstation may give you a surprise. Many desktop Linux users have named running and don't even know it. Despite the fact that they plan to use the desktop computer as a BIND client, many users are running named unnecessarily because they answer configuration questions incorrectly during the initial installation.

Generally, the decision to run named is made when you first install Linux. You know that the computer is going to be a name sever so you install and enable the name server software during the initial installation. It is possible, however, to enable or disable named after the system is installed and there are several tools to do this. These tools are discussed in the following sections.

Enabling *named* on a BSD-Style Linux System

Linux systems that use BSD-style boot procedures start named by executing the named command directly from one of the main startup files. Listing 3.1 shows the code, found in /etc/rc.d/rc.inet2 on a Slackware 4.0 system, that starts named:

Listing 3.1   Starting named from a Slackware boot script

```
# # Start the NAMED/BIND name server:
if [ -f ${NET}/named ]; then
  echo -n " named"
  ${NET}/named -u daemon -g daemon
fi
```

Listing 3.1 shows a Slackware system that is ready to run named. The first line is a comment, as indicated by the fact that it starts with a sharp sign (#). The next line is an if statement that checks whether or not the file that contains the named program is available. If the program is found, a message is displayed on the console indicating that named is starting and the named program is run. In Listing 3.1, named is passed the –u and –g command-line arguments.

Be aware that your Slackware system might not look exactly like this. By default, the code to start named is commented out of the rc.inet2 file, so you must remove the sharp signs at the beginning of all four lines of the if statement to enable named.

There are two ways to prevent Slackware from starting named at boot time, but both are essentially brute-force methods. The most straightforward method is to comment the lines shown in Listing 3.1 out of the rc.inet2 script by placing a sharp sign (#) at the beginning of each line.

Alternately, you could move named out of the ${NET} directory. ${NET} is a script variable defined in rc.inet2 as /usr/sbin. Moving named out of the /usr/sbin directory means that [–f ${NET}/named] evaluates to false, making rc.inet2 skip the named startup. These techniques disable named, but they are far from elegant.

Directly editing a startup script is easy, but dangerous. Most system administrators worry that an editing error will have a major negative impact on the next boot. I have never really had a major boot problem caused by an editing error, but I understand the fear.

Enabling *named* on a System V-Style Linux System

One of the advantages of the System V-style boot procedure is that major services have their own startup scripts and those scripts are indirectly invoked, which makes it possible to control whether or not a service is started at boot time by controlling whether or not the script is invoked. For example, Red Hat, which uses a System V-style initialization, stores the script that starts named in the file /etc/rc.d/init.d/named. The script is invoked indirectly from the runlevel directories that support multi-user networking by the S55named script. An examination of that script shows that it is just a symbolic link to the real named script:

```
[root]# cd /etc/rc.d/rc3.d
[root]# ls -l S55named
lrwxrwxrwx 1 root root Oct 31 S55named -> ../init.d/named
```

To enable or disable the named startup script for a specific runlevel, simply add or remove the symbolic link in that runlevel's directory. In and of itself this would be simple enough, but Red Hat and other Linux systems make it even easier by providing tools to manage the runlevel directories.

NOTE A detailed description of the Linux boot process is beyond the scope of this book. To learn more about the boot process, runlevels, and startup scripts, see *Linux Network Servers 24seven*, Craig Hunt, Sybex, 1999.

Enabling *named* with *tksysv*

tksysv is an X Windows tool provided for the purpose of controlling scripts started at each runlevel. Figure 3.1 shows the main tksysv screen.

Figure 3.1   Enabling named with tksysv

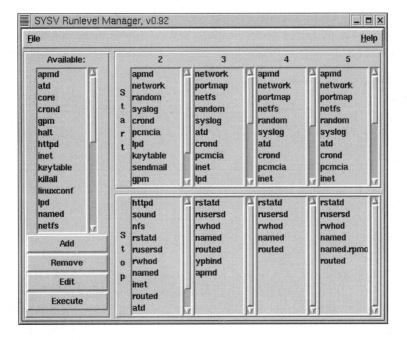

All of the scripts that can be controlled by tksysv are listed on the left-hand side of the screen. On the right are the services that are started and stopped for runlevels 2, 3, 4, and 5. To disable a service for a specific runlevel, simply highlight the service in the Start list for that runlevel and click the Remove button. For example, to remove named from runlevel 5, which is traditionally used as the runlevel for dedicated X Windows workstations, click named in the Start list under runlevel 5 and then click Remove. After that, named will no longer start when the system boots under runlevel 5.

To add named to a runlevel, highlight named in the Available list and click Add. You'll be asked to select a runlevel. An example might be runlevel 3, which is traditionally the default runlevel for multi-user servers. Select the runlevel and click Done. You're then asked to select a script number. Use the default, which is 55 for named. Click Add and the script is added to the startup. The next time the system reboots under runlevel 3, named will be started.

Of course you don't want to reboot your system just to run the named startup script. Use the Execute button to run the named script immediately.

tksysv has a couple of nice features. First, it comes bundled with different versions of Linux. It runs just as well on Caldera as it does on Red Hat, and it runs just as well under Red Hat 5 as it does under Red Hat 6. Second, a clone of tksysv called ntsysv runs in text mode and therefore doesn't require X Windows. A dedicated NFS server might not be running X Windows. In that case, you want a tool like ntsysv that runs in text mode.

Enabling *named* with *ntsysv*

ntsysv is even easier to use because it doesn't bother you with lots of questions about runlevels. It just presents you with a list of services that can be automatically started at boot time. One of these is named. The startup script for every item in the list that has an asterisk next to it will be run during the next boot. Use the arrow keys to scroll down to the named entry in the list and then use the space bar to select or deselect named. When the settings are just what you want, tab over to the OK button and press Enter. That's all there is to it. Figure 3.2 shows the main ntsysv screen.

Figure 3.2   Enabling named with ntsysv

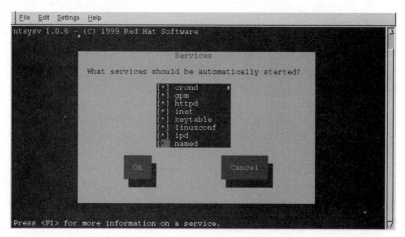

Enabling *named* with *linuxconf*

Another tool that is popular on Red Hat 6 systems is `linuxconf`. `linuxconf` is a general-purpose system administration tool. One of the features it provides is a way to manage the startup scripts. Figure 3.3 shows the `linuxconf` screen that is used to manage startup scripts.

Figure 3.3 Enabling named with `linuxconf`

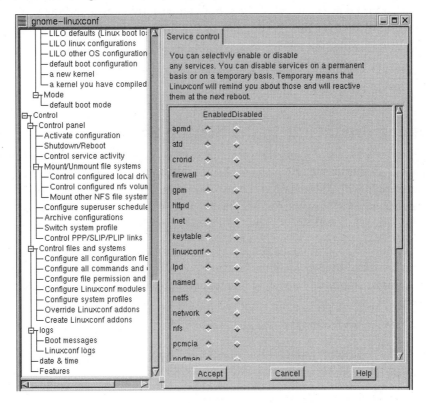

From the menu on the left-hand side of the `linuxconf` window, select Control ➢ Control Panel ➢ Control Service Activity. A list of services appears on the right-hand side of the window; it is the same list of services displayed by `ntsysv`. Again, like `ntsysv`, you don't have to worry about runlevels. Simply enable or disable the `named` script by selecting the appropriate button next to the `named` entry.

Enabling *named* with *chkconfig*

One final tool that can be used to control the scripts that are run at boot time is `chkconfig`. This is a command-line tool based on the `chkconfig` program from the Silicon Graphics

IRIX version of Unix. The Linux version has some enhancements, such as the ability to control which runlevels the scripts run under. The `--list` option of the `chkconfig` command displays the current settings:

```
[root]# chkconfig --list named
named 0:off 1:off 2:off 3:on 4:on 5:on 6:off
```

To enable or disable a script for a specific runlevel, specify the runlevel with the `--level` option, followed by the name of the script you wish to control and the action you wish to take, either on to enable the script or off to disable it. For example, to disable named for runlevel 5, enter the following:

```
[root]# chkconfig --level 5 named off
[root]# chkconfig --list named
named 0:off 1:off 2:off 3:on 4:on 5:off 6:off
```

Passing Arguments to the Startup Script

The previous section discussed several different ways to do essentially the same thing—enable or disable named at boot time. All of these approaches work. Choose the one that is compatible with the version of Linux you're running and that suits your tastes. But remember, most of the time you will install and enable named during the initial system configuration and will never again need to fiddle with the boot files.

It is far more likely that you will need to control a named process that is already running on your system. On some systems this can be done by manually invoking the boot scripts. For example, on a Red Hat system, the following command can be used to stop the name server:

```
[root]# /etc/rc.d/init.d/named stop
```

When you're ready to resume name service, the server can be manually started with the following command:

```
[root]# /etc/rc.d/init.d/named start
```

On most Linux DNS server systems, when you need to manage the named process, you do not do it with the boot files. Instead, you use ndc. In fact, as of release 6.1, even the Red Hat boot scripts use ndc to control the named process.

Managing *named* with *ndc*

The named control (ndc) program is an effective tool for managing the named process. It comes with the BIND software, so it is included with your Linux system and is installed when you install BIND. ndc is used for a variety of functions. Table 3.1 lists the options that are available with the ndc command and the purpose of each of these options.

Table 3.1   ndc Options

Option	Purpose
status	Displays the process status of named.
dumpdb	Dumps the cache to the named_dump.db file.
reload	Reloads the name server.
stats	Dumps statistics to the named.stats file.
trace	Turns on tracing to the named.run file.
notrace	Turns off tracing and closes the named.run file.
querylog	Toggles query logging, which logs each incoming query to syslogd.
start	Starts named.
stop	Stops named.
restart	Stop the current named and starts a new one.

There are a couple of different versions of ndc in use on different Linux distributions. One version is a shell script that implements many of the ndc options by using the signal-handling capabilities of named, which are covered in the next section. The other version is a binary program that provides some additional features but at the cost of increased complexity. Both versions work fine and provide all of the control options listed in Table 3.1, which are sufficient to manage the named process.

Several of the command-line options available with ndc perform the same functions as those provided by the signal-handling capabilities of named. Features such as the reload option, which causes the name server to reload its database, or the dumpdb option, which causes named to dump its cache to an ASCII file called named.db, are easier to use as ndc commands than they are as named signals. The command I use most often is ndc reload, which forces an immediate reload after the database is updated. This isn't necessary because the system automatically reloads the database after an update. But if you're as compulsive as I am, you just can't wait.

Most ndc options are simple and easy to use. The following commands would stop, then restart the named process:

```
[root]# ndc stop
[root]# ndc start
new pid is 795
```

This command sequence assumes that there is some length of time between stopping the old named process and starting a new one. If you really want to quickly kill and restart the named process, use the restart option:

```
[root]# ndc restart
new pid is 798
```

Passing Arguments with *ndc*

The start and restart commands from the previous two examples start named without any options. The newer, binary version of ndc can accept named arguments. If you decide to use any named command-line options, such as the security options described in Chapter 10, they can be passed to named on the ndc command line, as shown here:

```
[root]# ps -1C named
  F S UID PID PPID C PRI NI ADDR SZ WCHAN TTY   TIME    CMD
040 S   0 798   1 0  65  0   - 566 do_sel ? 00:00:00 named
[root]# ndc 'restart -u daemon'
new pid is 806
[root]# ps -1C named
  F S UID PID PPID C PRI NI ADDR SZ WCHAN TTY    TIME CMD
140 S   2 806   1 0  76  0   - 615 do_sel ? 00:00:00 named
```

The first ps command displays the status of the current named process. Notice that it is running under the root UID of 0, which is the default for named. This example restarts the name server and passes named the –u command-line option that tells it to run under another user id. The example uses the user id daemon, which is the numeric UID 2 on this Red Hat 6 system. The second ps command shows that named is, in fact, running with a UID of 2, so the value was successfully passed by ndc to named. Personally, I never do this. If I need to run named with command-line options I just do it, as in the following example:

```
[root]# named -u daemon
[root]# ps -1C named
  F S UID PID PPID C PRI NI ADDR SZ WCHAN TTY    TIME CMD
140 S   2 814   1 0  60  0   - 615 do_sel ? 00:00:00 named
```

I think this is cleaner and easier to understand than passing the arguments through ndc. But it is just a matter of taste. Both approaches work—if you have the latest version of ndc. The older, script version of ndc does not accept named arguments with the start and restart options. To add arguments to the start and restart commands of the older ndc, you need to edit the ndc script file and add them yourself. This variability between different versions of ndc is another reason why I prefer to use the named command directly when I need to pass arguments to named. I know that no matter which distribution I'm using, this approach will always work.

Using *ndc* Interactively

I have described ndc as a simple tool, but the newer version can be confusing. It is more powerful than the older version and with that power comes complexity. The new version can be run from the command line, as illustrated by all of the examples shown thus far in this section.

ndc can also be run as an interactive process by typing **ndc** at the command prompt. In the following example, ndc is run as an interactive process and the help command is used to print out a list of the interactive commands, as shown in Listing 3.2.

Listing 3.2   ndc interactive commands

```
[root]# ndc
Type  help  -or-   /h   if you need help.
ndc> /h
       /h(elp)   this text
       /e(xit)   leave this program
       /t(race)  toggle tracing (protocol and system events)
       /d(ebug)  toggle debugging (internal program events)
       /q(uiet)  toggle quietude (prompts and results)
       /s(ilent) toggle silence (suppresses nonfatal errors)
ndc> /t
tracing now on
ndc> /e
```

I rarely use ndc as an interactive process. Most of the things I do with ndc, such as reloading the database or restarting the name server, can be done just as well, or better, from the command line. But the feature is there if you need it.

ndc Control Modes

The new version of ndc also runs in two different control modes: pidfile-mode and channel-mode. When ndc is running in pidfile-mode, it reads the process id (PID) of the named process from the /var/run/named.pid file and manages that process on the local computer. Use the –p argument to change the name of the file from which ndc reads the PID or to make sure that ndc is running in pidfile-mode. On a Linux system, normally there is no need to use the –p argument because /var/run/named.pid is the file that Linux systems use to store the named PID.

Channel-mode allows ndc to manage named on a remote system. It is enabled by the –c ndc command line argument that allows you to define the control channel. By default, the channel is /var/run/ndc, which is a Unix domain socket. The ls command can be used to check for the existence of this channel control point, and the netstat –a command, which shows all active sockets, can be used to display the status of the control point, as follows:

```
[root]# ls -l /var/run/ndc
srw-------   1 root     root              0 Jan  4 13:31 /var/run/ndc
[root]# netstat -a | grep ndc
unix  0   [ ACC ]   STREAM   LISTENING  1485 /var/run/ndc
```

The Unix socket that ndc uses can be replaced with a network socket by specifying an IP address and a port number with the –c argument. For example, the following command would cause the local system to use TCP port 54 as the ndc control channel:

```
[root]# ndc -c 127.0.0.1/54
```

To bind the client side of the control channel to a specific address, use the –l command-line argument, as in this example:

```
[root]# ndc -c 172.16.12.3/31 -l 172.16.12.1/31
. . .
[root]# netstat -na
Active Internet connections (servers and established)
Proto Recv-Q Send-Q Local Address   Foreign Address State
tcp       0      1 172.16.12.1:31 172.16.12.3:31 SYN_SENT
tcp       0      0 172.16.12.3:53     0.0.0.0:*  LISTEN
tcp       0      0 127.0.0.1:53       0.0.0.0:*  LISTEN
. . .
```

In this example, the control channel is located at TCP port 31 of the server at IP address 172.16.12.3. The ndc client is located on the host at IP address 172.16.12.1. A quick netstat command displays the TCP connection status and shows that a SYN has been sent to start the TCP handshake.

Remotely managing a named process with ndc is potentially a cool feature, but I can't swear to it because I never use it. I worry too much about security, particularly for a service as critical as name service. Generally, I find that the domain administrator works very close to the domain server and therefore remote management is not an issue. But if it is an issue for your organization, you may find this feature of ndc useful.

A downside to the fact that the new version of ndc runs in two different modes is that sometimes ndc options do not work as you expect. A simple test with the help command on a Red Hat 6.1 system shows this in Listing 3.3.

Listing 3.3   Conflicting results from different ndc modes

```
[root@]# ndc -c /var/run/ndc
Type   help  -or-   /h   if you need help.
ndc> help
ndc: [220 8.2]
ndc: [214-]
ndc: [214-getpid]
ndc: [214-status]
ndc: [214-stop]
ndc: [214-exec]
ndc: [214-reload]
ndc: [214-dumpdb]
ndc: [214-stats]
ndc: [214-trace]
ndc: [214-notrace]
ndc: [214-querylog]
ndc: [214-qrylog]
ndc: [214-help]
ndc: [214 quit]
ndc> /e
[root]# ndc -p /var/run/named.pid
Type   help  -or-   /h   if you need help.
ndc> help
        help        this output
        status      check for running server
        stop        stop the server
        start       start the server
        restart     stop server if any, start a new one
        dumpdb      dump cache database to a file
        reload      reload configuration file
        stats       dump statistics to a file
```

```
trace              increment trace level
notrace            turn off tracing
querylog           toggle query logging
qrylog             alias for querylog
ndc> /e
```

At first, these differences are surprising but after a little thought, a simple explanation comes to mind. When ndc runs in pidfile-mode, it has a fixed set of valid commands. But when ndc runs in channel-mode, the set of commands are dynamic to allow them to be defined by the remote server. This is done for security reasons, to allow the remote server to define as many or as few commands as are really needed for remote management. Still, the differences can be disconcerting and sometimes commands just don't run as you think they should.

If a command doesn't work as you expect, try adding the –p option to the ndc command. On most Linux systems, the status option displays a multi-line report similar to the following:

```
[root]# ndc status
named 8.2.2 Thu Nov 11 1999 redhat.com:/usr/src/bind/bin/named
number of zones allocated: 64
debug level: 0
xfers running: 0
xfers deferred: 0
soa queries in progress: 0
query logging is OFF
server is DONE priming
server IS NOT loading its configuration
```

On some other Linux systems, the status option displays a simple line of text similar to the text displayed by ps. But occasionally, the status option displays nothing unless it is teamed with the –p option, as shown in the following example:

```
[root]# ndc status
[root]# ndc -p /var/run/named.pid status
pid 814 is running
```

With these few tips you should not be surprised by the variations in ndc you might encounter on different Linux distribution. Regardless of these problems, I think you'll find ndc an effective tool and easier to work with than using signals to control named. However, understanding the signals that are handled by named is important because all versions of named, even older versions, handle the same signals. If you're called upon to troubleshoot a name server that doesn't have an ndc command, the signals could be invaluable.

named Signal-Handling

named handles several different signals. The most commonly used, at least for me, is SIGHUP.

The SIGHUP Signal

The SIGHUP signal causes named to reread its configuration file and reload the name server database. Using SIGHUP causes the reload to occur immediately. On the master server for a domain, this means that the local database files are reloaded into memory. On a backup domain server, this means that the backup system immediately reloads its local disk copies of the database and then checks with the master server to see if there is an update to the database. SIGHUP performs the same function as the ndc reload command.

The SIGINT Signal

The SIGINT signal causes named to dump its cache to the file named_dump.db, which is exactly what the ndc dumpdb command does. The dump file contains all of the domain information that the local name server knows. Examine this file. You'll see a complete picture of the information the server has learned. Examining the cache is an interesting exercise for anyone who is new to DNS. Chapter 5 uses the dump file as a way to illustrate the role of the cache initialization file. The full dump file is described in Chapter 12.

The SIGUSR1 and SIGUSR2 Signals

Use the SIGUSR1 signal to turn on tracing. Each subsequent SIGUSR1 signal increases the level of tracing. Trace information is written to the file named.run. Tracing can also be enabled with the -d option on the named command line if the problem you are looking for occurs so early in the startup procedure that the SIGUSR1 signal is not useful. The advantage of the SIGUSR1 signal is that it allows tracing to be turned on when a problem is suspected, without stopping and restarting named. SIGUSR1 is equivalent to the ndc trace command.

The opposite of the SIGUSR1 signal is the SIGUSR2 signal. It turns off tracing and closes the trace file. After issuing SIGUSR2, you can examine the file or remove it if it is getting too large. The SIGUSR2 signal performs the same function as the ndc notrace command.

The SIGWINCH Signal

Another signal that can be used to log trace data is SIGWINCH. SIGWINCH toggles query logging. The first SIGWINCH causes named to start logging all of the queries the server receives. The next SIGWINCH turns off query logging. Logging queries can be useful for debugging server problems or just for learning about how name service works. However, a query log can grow very large, very fast, so use this signal with caution. The ndc querylog command is also used to start and stop query logging.

The SIGILL Signal

Use the SIGILL signal to write the name server statistics out to the `named.stats` file. The contents of this file and how to interpret them are discussed in Chapter 12. The `ndc stats` command does the same thing as SIGILL.

The SIGTERM Signal

The SIGTERM signal saves data modified by dynamic updates back to the database files before the system is shut down. It can only be used and is only useful if `named` is compiled with dynamic updating enabled. Dynamic DNS is discussed in Chapter 9, "Dynamic DNS."

Passing signals to `named` is somewhat more complicated than managing it with `ndc`. The system administrator uses a number of commands when passing signals to `named`. Two of these are `kill` and `killall`.

The *kill* and *killall* Commands

The `kill` command is used to send a signal to a running process. As the name implies, by default, it sends the kill signal (SIGTERM). To use it to send a different signal, specify the signal on the command line. For example, specify `-INT` to send the SIGINT signal. The PID is usually provided on the `kill` command line to ensure that the signal is sent to the correct process.

As usual, there is more than one way to do something on a Linux system. You can learn the PID of `named` using the `ps` command:

```
[root]# ps -ax | grep named
  415 ?        S      0:00 named
```

You can learn the PID of `named` by displaying the `named.pid` file:

```
[root]# cat /var/run/named.pid
415
```

You can learn the PID of `named` using the Linux `pidof` command:

```
[root]# pidof named
415
```

You can even learn the PID using the `kill` command:

```
[root]# /bin/kill -p named
415
```

This last example is the most interesting because it shows that kill (at least a certain version of kill) does not require a PID. The example clearly shows that kill can find the PID from the process name. Notice, however, that the full path name /bin/kill was used to execute kill. That is because bash, like most shells, has its own integrated kill command. The kill command integrated into the shell, which is the kill command most administrators use, requires a PID.

> **NOTE** Most Linux systems, including Red Hat and Caldera, have /bin/kill. But it is possible that your system won't. Don't worry; you can always use the bash kill command.

Combining some of these commands, you can send a signal directly to named. For example, to reload the name server, you could enter the following command:

```
[root]# kill -HUP 'cat /var/run/named.pid'
```

The cat /var/run/named.pid command that is enclosed in single quotes is processed by the shell first. On our sample Red Hat system, a cat of named.pid returns the PID 415. That is combined with the shell's kill command and then is processed as kill -HUP 415. This works, but I find it easier to use /bin/kill or killall, there is less to type and less to remember.

As noted earlier, /bin/kill does not require a PID. It can work with a process name, as in the following example:

```
[root]# /bin/kill -HUP named
```

killall is another command that can be used to send a signal to a process. killall is designed to process names instead of PIDs. For example:

```
[root]# killall -HUP named
```

The downside of using a process name with killall or /bin/kill is that there can be more than one process running with the same name. This is highly unlikely in the case of named, but it is possible. If you create an exotic configuration that has more than one copy of named running, use PIDs to make sure that you signal the correct process.

Personally, I use ndc to control named and avoid using signals to the greatest extent possible. I find ndc easier to use, and there have been some rumblings from the developers at the Internet Software Consortium that future versions of named might not support signal-handling. You might as well learn ndc now, while you still have options.

Exploring the ISC Web Site

BIND is one of the most important open source software products in the world. Most of the root servers depend on BIND and the entire Internet depends on the root servers. This important piece of software is maintained by the Internet Software Consortium (ISC). ISC is a non-profit company that develops and maintains open source software. ISC has three main software products:

- Internet Network News (INN) software
- Dynamic Host Configuration Protocol (DHCP) software
- The DNS server software BIND

Additionally, ISC offers consulting, support, and training for its products. If you're interested in the latest BIND release or the latest documentation, the ISC Web site www.isc.org is a great place to start.

Figure 3.4 shows an example of the online documentation available at ISC. Go to the ISC home page, select BIND, select the release of BIND you're interested in, and then select the links to the appropriate documentation. Figure 3.4 is the start of the configuration guide for BIND 8.2.2.

Figure 3.4   BIND online documentation

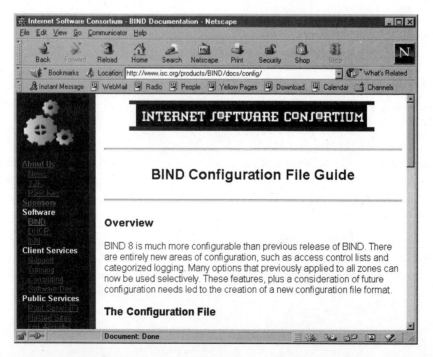

At the ISC home page, you can find the latest BIND software by following essentially the same links you used to get to the online documentation. However, instead of selecting one of the documentation links, you select a download link. Figure 3.5 shows this decision point.

Figure 3.5 Downloading BIND

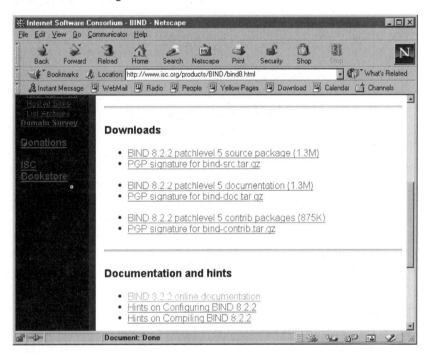

In Figure 3.5, you can see that for BIND 8.2.2, ISC offers three possible downloads:

The BIND source code   This is the package you need in order to install BIND from source on your Linux system.

The documentation download   You'll definitely want this. Not only does it contain essential man pages, it has other useful documentation, such as the BIND Operations Guide, which is a little out of date but still an interesting read.

A collection of DNS tools contributed by developers around the world   These DNS tools can be interesting, but they are not required for a server installation and you don't need to download them. The only user-developed tool used in this book is the update software described in Chapter 9.

Once BIND is downloaded, it must be compiled. An example of compiling BIND 8.2.2pl5 on a Caldera 2.3 Linux system is shown in the next section.

Compiling the Latest BIND Release

BIND is available at ISC as a `gzip` compressed `tar` file. Create a directory for BIND, download the BIND source and documentation tarballs, and unpack them in the new directory. In the following example, the directory is named `/usr/local/src/bind8.2.2`:

```
[home]# mkdir /usr/local/src/bind8.2.2
[home]# cd /usr/local/src/bind8.2.2
[bind8.2.2]# tar -zxf /home/craig/bind-src.tar.gz
[bind8.2.2]# tar -zxf /home/craig/bind-doc.tar.gz
[bind8.2.2]# ls -l
total 5
-rw-rw-r--   1 716    root      2537 Nov  4 23:52 Makefile
drwxrwxr-x  10 716    root      1024 Nov 12 00:39 doc
drwxrwxr-x   9 716    root      1024 Nov 12 00:44 src
```

With the files in place, change to the new `src` directory and run the `make` command to compile the source. The instructions for Linux in the `src/INSTALL` file tell you not to run `make` without the `links` or `stdlinks` options. Take this advice and run `make` with no options.

On my test system, BIND compiled, but it might not compile on yours. The BIND 8.8.2pl5 documentation states that the compile was only tested on Red Hat 5.2 and Debian 2.2.9. Obviously, there are many other Linux distributions and the predefined compile parameters might not be correct for those systems. Before running `make`, check that the parameters are correct for your system.

Linux Compile Parameters

The first thing the BIND installation does is check the type of system you're running and determine if a port of BIND exists for your system. These ports are stored in the `src/ports` directory as subdirectories. A listing of `src/ports/linux` shows that a Linux port does exist.

```
[bind8.2.2]$ ls -l src/port/linux
total 8
-rw-rw-r--   1 716    root      2380 Feb 21  1999 Makefile
-rw-rw-r--   1 716    root       312 Jun 11  1999 Makefile.set
```

```
drwxrwxr-x   2 716   root    1024 Nov 12 00:40 bin
drwxrwxr-x   4 716   root    1024 Nov 12 00:40 include
-rw-rw-r--   1 716   root      35 Nov 19  1996 noop.c
-rwxrwxr-x   1 716   root     108 Dec  4  1996 probe
```

The *Makefile.set* File

From a system administrator's perspective, `Makefile.set` is the most important file in the `src/port/linux` directory. It contains the `Makefile` variables used to compile BIND on a Linux system. Each source directory has a `Makefile` with predefined variables. The variables defined in `Makefile.set` override those predefined variables at runtime. If the values defined in `Makefile.set` are correct for the distribution of Linux you're using, BIND should compile. The contents of the Linux `Makefile.set` file are shown in Listing 3.4.

Listing 3.4   Linux `Makefile.set` file

```
[bind8.2.2]$ cd  src/port/linux
[linux]$ cat Makefile.set
'CC=gcc -D_GNU_SOURCE'
'CDEBUG=-O -g'
'DESTBIN=/usr/bin'
'DESTSBIN=/usr/sbin'
'DESTEXEC=/usr/sbin'
'DESTMAN=/usr/man'
'DESTHELP=/usr/lib'
'DESTETC=/etc'
'DESTRUN=/var/run'
'LEX=flex -8 -I'
'YACC=yacc -d'
'SYSLIBS=-lfl'
'INSTALL=install'
'MANDIR=man'
'MANROFF=cat'
'CATEXT=$$N'
'PS=ps -p'
'AR=ar crus'
'RANLIB=:'
```

The `Makefile.set` file defines the syntax of commands, such as the C compiler (`gcc`) and the lexical analyzer (`flex`), that are needed to compile and install BIND. It describes the location of the directories where the documentation and the executable programs should be installed after compilation. These are called the *destination directories,* hence the prefix DEST on those variables.

In addition, the `Makefile.set` file defines some libraries that the loader will need to link the executable files. Check that all of the commands and libraries are found on your system and that the destination directories are correct for your system. If all of these things are right, you should be able to make and install BIND without problems. See the sidebar, "Problems, Problems," for a description of what happens when things go wrong.

Problems, Problems

Compiles do not always go as you planned, at least not for me. Fresh from compiling BIND on a Caldera 2.3 system, I sat down at a second Caldera 2.3 system belonging to a friend of mine and attempted to do the same. Full of confidence, I didn't bother to check that all of the commands defined in the `Makefile.set` file were available. Of course, things went wrong.

About 80% of the way through the make, the linker (`ld`) displayed an error message saying, "the file or directory –lfl was not found." –lfl is not literally the name of the file. –l is a linker option and fl is the value being passed to that option. The linker constructs the real filename by adding `lib` before the value being passed and adding `.a` after the value. Therefore, fl really means that the linker is looking for the file `libfl.a`. A `find / -name libfl.a -print` command showed that the file was not on my friend's system, even though it was on mine.

Why the difference? After all, these were both Caldera 2.3 systems. The difference comes about by the manner in which the system was initially installed. My system was installed with all of the code-development options because it was intended as a code-development platform. My friend's system was installed as a desktop client. He had installed the C compiler and several other things, but he had not installed everything. In this specific case, he did not install the `flex` package that `libfl.a` is a part of.

There are two simple approaches to resolving this problem. One, of course, is to simply install the missing library and rerun the make. The other is to copy the already compiled binary files from my system to my friend's system. The systems are completely compatible so there is no reason why a program compiled on my system won't run on his system. This technique of compiling on a development system and then moving the binary file to the DNS server is very common. For security reasons, it is not a good idea to have a C compiler and other development tools lying around on a dedicated DNS server. You'll hear more about the security advantages of a dedicated DNS server in Chapter 10.

Other Ways to Install BIND

It is not usually necessary for you to compile your own version of BIND. BIND is delivered with every major Linux distribution. On a DNS server, BIND is normally installed as part of the initial Linux installation. If it is not installed at that time, it can easily be added later using one of the package-management systems available for Linux.

To simplify the task of adding and deleting software on a running server, Linux vendors have developed package-management systems. Debian and Slackware uses their own systems, but Red Hat, SuSE, Mandrake, TurboLinux, and Caldera all use the Red Hat Package manager (rpm). rpm is an excellent example of how all package managers work.

Using *rpm* to Install BIND

Use the rpm command with the –q option or the --query option to check which packages are already installed in the system.

```
[root]# rpm -q bind
bind-8.1.2-1
```

This example queries rpm for the string bind. The response shows that BIND 8.1.2 is installed. If this is not the version you want because you are downloading and compiling your own version of BIND, remove the old one with the --erase option or the –e option, as in this example:

```
[root]# rpm --erase --nodeps bind
```

The --nodeps option is added to this command line to force rpm to erase the BIND software, even though other packages are dependent on BIND. Attempting to erase BIND without using the --nodeps option displays an error message stating that other software depends on BIND; BIND is not removed. Failing to remove the BIND RPM package before installing a non-RPM version of BIND, such as a version that you compile yourself, means that the system will still think the old RPM version of BIND is installed and will assume that something is wrong with BIND when it fails the verification tests. The –V option is used to verify an RPM package. Here is what happens when the components of BIND are upgraded without using rpm and then are versified by rpm:

```
[root]# rpm -V bind
S.5....T    /usr/sbin/named
S.5....T    /usr/sbin/named-bootconf
S.5....T    /usr/sbin/named-xfer
S.5....T    /usr/sbin/ndc
```

The –V option prints out a line for each file in the package that fails verification. Values are printed at the beginning of the line to indicate which tests were failed. Each letter or number indicates a failure and each dot indicates a test that was passed. The possible values are as follows:

5   indicates that the file has an incorrect MD5 checksum.

S   indicates that the file has the wrong file size.

L   indicates that the file is improperly a symbolic link.

T   indicates that the file has the wrong file creation time.

D   indicates that the file is located on the wrong device.

U   indicates that the file has the wrong user id (UID) assigned.

G   indicates that the file has the wrong group id (GID) assigned.

M   indicates that the file is assigned the wrong file permissions or file type.

In the previous example, the files have the wrong checksum, the wrong creation time, and they are the wrong size. These are all things you would expect because these are not the original files; they are files that I compiled and installed over the original files. Everything else about the new files checks out ok. But even these three errors might set off alarm bells with the system's computer security officer.

Generally, it is much better to upgrade an existing RPM package with a new package than it is to delete the package and replace it with software you compile yourself. First, using the rpm command is much easier than compiling software. Second, the features of rpm, such as verifying the integrity of the software, are unavailable if you don't use rpm. To upgrade an existing version of BIND with the rpm command, use the –U option.

```
[root]# rpm -U bind-8.2.2_P3-1.i386.rpm
warning: /etc/rc.d/rc5.d/K45named saved as /etc/rc.d/rc5.d/K45named.rpmorig
[root]# rpm -q bind
bind-8.2.2_P3-1
```

The –U option removes the old version of BIND, which in this case is BIND 8.1.2, when it installs the new version. The warning message states that rpm made a backup copy of the named kill script. The reason it does this is so that you can gracefully kill the copy of named that is running before starting the new version of named that you just installed. named, which is the only daemon in the BIND package, is constantly running on a name server.

rpm does not take it upon itself to interrupt a running process. It leaves that up to you. To ensure that the kill script for the old version of named is exactly what it should be, it saves the old script when it installs a new one. In this case, it is actually unnecessary to save the old script but rpm does it anyway. In reality, you'll start the new version of named with the command ndc restart. The kill script will not be invoked until the next system shutdown.

X Tools for Installing BIND

In all of the previous examples, I used the command-line version of rpm. It is easy to use, easy to explain, and it runs on all Caldera and Red Hat systems, even those systems that don't have X Windows running. If you are using X Windows, there are some graphical tools for running the Red Hat package manager. Older versions of Red Hat and Caldera use a tool named glint. Caldera 2.3 uses a tool named **kpackage** and Red Hat 6 uses a tool called **gnorpm**. Figure 3.6 shows **gnorpm**, which is the graphical version of rpm for Red Hat 6 systems.

Figure 3.6   Installing BIND with gnorpm

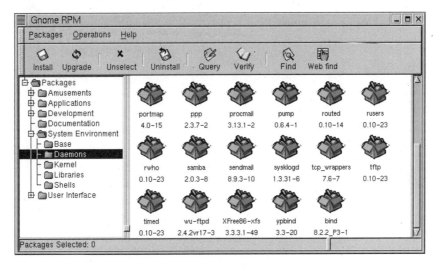

Understanding gnorpm is easy once you understand the rpm command. The icons near the top of the window clearly parallel the –U (upgrade), –q (query), –V (verify) and –e (uninstall) command-line options available with rpm. Simply highlight the package you're interested in and select the action you want to take. Figure 3.6 shows the test system after BIND was upgraded to release 8.2.2.

Of course, to upgrade BIND with rpm you need to locate an updated BIND RPM package. RPM packages are not available from ISC. You need to look for them at your Linux vendor's Web site or at a site like www.rpmfind.net.

Locating Pre-Compiled BIND Software

Because DNS name service is so important, all of the major Linux vendors make an effort to update their version of BIND when a critical bug is fixed or when a major new feature is added. They do this by making updated versions of BIND available online. Figure 3.7 shows the Red Hat Web site, which lists an update to BIND.

Figure 3.7   Red Hat support Web site

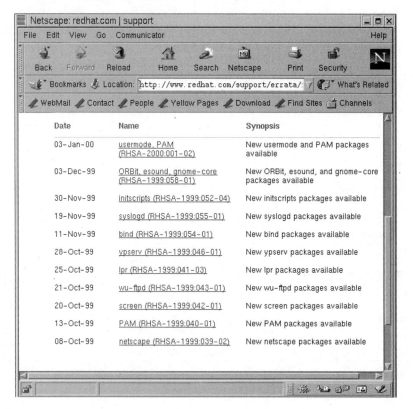

Click the Red Hat Errata icon located on the desktop of a Red Hat 6.1 system to look at the software updates, bug fixes, and security advisories that are available online. Check all of them for the latest BIND updates. The window in Figure 3.7 is the Security Advisories window. This tells you that the fixes to BIND are security-related fixes and thus very important. Clicking the BIND link in the window in Figure 3.7 explains the fix and provides links from which the fix can be downloaded. In this case, the fix is the BIND 8.2.2 RPM package that we installed in the previous section.

RPM packages are also available via anonymous FTP. `ftp.rpmfind.net` provides RPM packages for several Linux distributions. Red Hat provides updates at `updates.redhat.com`. Updates are available for the various Red Hat releases and for the various hardware architectures that Linux runs on. To obtain fixes for release 6.1 running on the Intel *x*86 architecture, log in to `updates.redhat.com` and change to the `6.1/i386` directory. For other releases, choose the appropriate release directory, and for other architectures, choose a different architecture directory, e.g. `5.2/Alpha`.

The following example shows an anonymous login to `updates.redhat.com` and a download of the BIND 8.2.2 update. This particular update to BIND is provided in three RPM packages:

`bind-devel`   provides tools for code developers.

`bind-util`   provides optional utilities for use with BIND.

`bind-8.2.2`   provides the heart of the system, including `named` and the other components you expect to find on a Linux DNS name server.

In the following example, user input is shown in bold. The example has been edited to better fit on a book page, but is essentially what you would see if you performed this download.

```
[root]# ftp updates.redhat.com
Connected to updates.redhat.com.
220 FTP server ready.
Name (updates.redhat.com:craig): anonymous
331 Guest login ok, send your e-mail address as password.
Password: craig@sybex.com
230 Guest login ok, access restrictions apply.
Remote system type is UNIX.
Using binary mode to transfer files.
ftp> cd 6.1/i386
250 CWD command successful.
ftp> ls bind*
200 PORT command successful.
150 Opening ASCII mode data connection for /bin/ls.
-rw-rw-r-- root root 1671783 bind-8.2.2_P3-1.i386.rpm
-rw-rw-r-- root root  402350 bind-devel-8.2.2_P3-1.i386.rpm
-rw-rw-r-- root root  649547 bind-utils-8.2.2_P3-1.i386.rpm
226 Transfer complete.
```

```
ftp> prompt
Interactive mode off.
ftp> mget bind*
local: bind-8.2.2_P3-1.i386.rpm
200 PORT command successful.
150 Opening BINARY mode data connection
226 Transfer complete.
1671783 bytes received in 1.09e+03 secs (1.5 Kbytes/sec)
local: bind-devel-8.2.2_P3-1.i386.rpm
200 PORT command successful.
150 Opening BINARY mode data connection
226 Transfer complete.
402350 bytes received in 263 secs (1.5 Kbytes/sec)
local: bind-utils-8.2.2_P3-1.i386.rpm
200 PORT command successful.
150 Opening BINARY mode data connection
226 Transfer complete.
649547 bytes received in 425 secs (1.5 Kbytes/sec)
ftp> quit
```

Red Hat is not the only vendor that makes pre-compiled BIND upgrades available. It is not even the only vendor that makes RPM packages available. Caldera also uses RPM. The Red Hat examples shown previously are just that, examples. Check your vendor's Web site for information about pre-compiled software, including pre-compiled BIND software.

Once BIND is installed, it needs to be configured. Configuring BIND is the topic of the remainder of this book. However, before you begin to configure BIND, you need to understand the basic BIND configuration types to plan the configuration for each server installation. These topics are covered next.

Possible BIND Configurations

The two components of BIND, the resolver and the name server (named), are combined to create a variety of configurations that provide all of the parts necessary to build your organization's DNS architecture. The details of the files used to create these different configurations are covered later in this book. This section discusses the possible configurations and looks at how the systems they create are used to build an overall architecture.

BIND has four basic configurations:

master server   The master server is an authoritative server for a zone. It is the ultimate source of all information about the zone. It loads the zone database from local disk files that are created by the domain administrator. There should only be one master server for a zone.

slave server   A slave server is an authoritative server for a zone because it has complete, current knowledge about that zone. It periodically downloads the entire zone database from the master server and stores a copy of the zone on its local disk drives. A slave server is a backup server for a zone. Generally, two or three backup servers are enough for most domains.

caching-only server   A caching-only server is not authoritative for any zone. It handles queries for local systems, tracking down the answers and storing those answers in its cache. It only directly answers queries from its cache. All other queries are sent to an authoritative server. Most of the servers on a large network are caching-only servers.

resolver-only client   A Linux system can be a pure DNS client just like a Windows 98 system. Simply configure the resolver and make sure you don't run named on the Linux client. Far too many Linux systems run a copy of named unnecessarily, which creates a potential security problem. Only servers need to run named; clients only need the resolver. The majority of systems on your network are clients.

There are some variations on these basic configurations that, although rarely used, may be of use in creating your DNS architecture. One of these is the *forwarder*. All name servers cache answers and use the cache to answer queries locally. The more queries a system handles, the more answers it has in its cache. A server with lots of cached information is said to have a *rich cache*. A forwarder is a server on your enterprise network that handles all external queries for your network. The intent of having one server handle all of the queries is to build a rich cache within the enterprise network to limit the number of queries sent to external networks.

A second variation on the standard configurations is the *unadvertised slave server*. Normally, the master server lists all of the official slave servers as servers for the zone. When a remote name server queries the zone, it receives this list of servers along with the answer. An unadvertised slave is a slave server that is not included in this list. Because of this, an unadvertised slave is unknown to external clients, which has earned it the nickname *stealth server*. It is essentially a variation of the caching-only server that uses the slave server download mechanism as a way to prime its cache with information about the local zone. Like a normal caching-only server, it is used primarily by local DNS clients.

Architecting Your DNS Hierarchy

Use the various configurations described in the previous section to create your own DNS architecture. The types and numbers of servers you use and their placement on your network depend on the size and layout of your network and on the type of network connection it uses. Use the guidelines described here to help plan your server installations and your overall DNS architecture.

The vast majority of systems on your network should be configured as resolver-only clients. If you consider Windows 98 desktop systems, this goes without saying, because those systems are only capable of being clients. In the Linux world, however, every desktop system is fully capable of being a DNS server. Frequently, the user who installs Linux on their desktop mistakenly installs and runs named. Sometimes the user mistakenly thinks they must run named on the desktop to get DNS service. Sometimes they think they will get better service if they run named on the desktop, and sometimes they don't even know named is running. In reality, named is not needed on a client system and can even be a potential source of problems. Make sure your Linux desktop users know that a client system should not be configured as a server.

Each zone should have exactly one master server. A single computer can be the master for multiple zones but one zone should not have multiple master servers. Your enterprise network should have several master servers only if your enterprise domain has several zones. Remember that a zone does not exactly map to a domain because it is possible for a zone to hold multiple domains and it is possible for a domain to contain multiple zones. (In Chapter 1, "The DNS Architecture," you saw examples of these domain-to-zone mappings.)

Each zone should have only one master server because a master server does not validate the contents of its zone file against the data held on any other server. The reason for this is that the zone file created by the domain administrator, who is the ultimate source of DNS information, is read directly off the local disks by the master server. Creating more than one master server means that multiple servers will rely on local disk files as the ultimate source of domain information. This can lead to serious database synchronization problems and it undermines the built-in database synchronization features of BIND. It is possible to create more than one master server for a zone, but doing so is a mistake.

Planning the number of slave servers is a little more complicated than deciding to use one master. Each master server is backed up by at least one slave server. Therefore, you must have at least one slave server backing up each zone. Beyond that, you're free to decide how many additional backup servers are required by your network's topology and load.

Load is not as significant a factor as topology. Servicing a zone that gets 100 or so queries a second is not a significant load for a modern computer system. Using slave servers for load-sharing is probably not of significant importance until the number of queries per second grows much larger.

The real importance of slave servers is to make sure that the DNS database information is available when the master server is unreachable. This can be caused by two things: the master server is down or its connection to the network is broken. For this reason, organizations often use two backup servers. One slave is located within the enterprise network so that queries within the organization do not have to leave the enterprise network when the master server is down. The other slave is located so that it does not share the same connection to the Internet as the master server for those occasions when that connection goes down.

A large organization may have multiple independent connections to the Internet. In that case, the organization may combine both of these backup functions into a single system that is both located on the enterprise network and independently connected to the Internet. Smaller organizations may use the name service facilities of their ISP as a backup server.

The topology of your network can also affect the number of servers needed. A large, far-flung enterprise that has remote facilities on separate continents should have slave servers located close to those facilities. In fact, any time that the connectivity between a remote office and the master server is inadequate is a time to consider placing a backup server at the remote office.

Placing a caching-only server at a remote office is an alternative to placing a slave server there. A caching-only server can limit the amount of traffic passed through the external network. Use caching-only servers to bring name service close to the clients. Many administrators place a caching-only server on each subnet to reduce the amount of DNS traffic handled by the routers.

A good example of this is a multi-homed Linux system used as the router for a small subnet. (A *multi-homed* system is a computer directly connected to more than one network.) The Linux system is fully capable of being a DNS server as well as a router. Turning it into a caching-only server reduces the number of queries sent from the subnet to the authoritative server. Caching-only servers are frequently multipurpose departmental servers, and DNS is viewed as just one more service provided by the departmental server.

Any average Linux system makes a great name service. Name service is not a demanding application. It requires very little CPU power, very little disk space, and only a modest amount of memory. A mid-range Pentium-class CPU with 128MB of RAM and an 8GB disk will do nicely for most enterprises. If the name server services a large number of large, active domains, a more powerful system may be needed. Of course, if you run name service on a system that performs other functions, those functions may demand a more powerful system. You need to use your judgment. But don't assume that because DNS is a highly important system, it requires a large system. Linux on a PC makes a great DNS server platform.

In Sum

The BIND software is the most widely used DNS software in the world. It is included in all Linux distributions and can be downloaded from the Internet Software Consortium, the organization that develops and maintains BIND.

DNS is a client/server system. BIND provides the client software in the form of the resolver library and the server software in the form of the name server daemon (named). BIND permits you to configure Linux DNS clients and a variety of Linux DNS servers. In the next part of the book, we begin the task of configuring BIND in all of its variety. The next chapter starts this process with a look at resolver configuration.

Part 2

Essential Configuration

Featuring:

- Configuring the `resolv.conf` file

- Resolver environment variables

- Understanding the `host.conf` file

- Configuring the `nsswitch.conf` file

- Configuring the `named.conf` file for caching, slave, and master servers

- The role of the `hints` file

- Creating the `localhost` file

- Creating a domain database file

- The structure and purpose of resource records

- The role of reverse domains and how they are configured

4

Configuring the Resolver

Part 1, "How Things Work," described the architecture of the Domain Name System and the DNS protocols used to move domain information through the network. It also introduced the Berkeley Internet Name Domain (BIND) software that is used to implement DNS on a Linux system. Part 2, "Essential Configuration," describes how BIND is configured on a Linux system to handle most client and server configurations.

This chapter begins Part 2 with an examination of resolver configuration. Every Linux system runs the resolver because every client and every server needs to resolve host names into addresses. The default resolver configuration and the environment variables and configuration files used to modify that configuration are discussed. Let's begin by looking at the default resolver configuration.

The Default Configuration

The resolver is configured in the /etc/resolv.conf file. If no resolv.conf file is found, the resolver uses a default configuration. The default configuration is almost never used on Linux systems because most Linux installation programs create a resolv.conf file automatically. Despite this, a system administrator needs to understand how this default configuration is derived in order to troubleshoot Linux and Unix systems that don't have a resolv.conf file, and to better understand how the resolver works.

The default resolver configuration uses the following values:

- If no name server is defined, the resolver attempts to use the name server on the local host. This means that a system that uses the default resolver configuration must run `named`. Therefore, to create a resolver-only configuration, you must create a `resolv.conf` file to specify a remote host to act as the name server for the resolver.

- If no domain search list is defined, the resolver uses the domain name of the local host as the only domain in the search list.

The resolver determines the domain of the local host using the `gethostname` and `gethostbyname` functions. `gethostname` returns the host name that is then used in the `gethostbyname` call to obtain the fully qualified domain name (FQDN).

For this reason, the FQDN of the local computer must be defined in the `/etc/hosts` file when running the resolver with the default configuration. Everything after the first dot in the value returned for the FQDN is assumed to be the local domain name. You can examine these values with the `hostname` and `dnsdomainname` commands:

```
[root]# hostname
24seven
[root]# hostname --fqdn
24seven.wrotethebook.com
[root]# dnsdomainname
wrotethebook.com
```

The resolver runs without the `resolv.conf` file, but I strongly recommend against running it this way. I prefer to have the configuration clearly documented in the `resolv.conf` file. Doing so makes it easier for the other people who administer your system to understand what is going on. It also provides consistency in case the default behavior of the resolver changes at some time in the future. The next section examines the configuration options that are available in the `resolv.conf` file.

Configuring the *resolv.conf* File

The `resolv.conf` file is a simple text file. It is easy to read and can be created and modified with any text editor. Each line in the configuration file contains exactly one configuration command. Each configuration command starts with a keyword that defines the purpose of the command. The keyword is then followed by one or more configuration values. Most commands accept only one value after the keyword, but there are two exceptions: Two commands, `nameserver` and `domain`, accept only one value after the keyword, and three commands, `search`, `option`, and `sortlist`, all accept a list of values. Before looking at some sample resolver configurations, let's look at the possible configuration commands.

The *nameserver* Command

Each `nameserver` command defines one of the name servers that the resolver should use. If the `resolv.conf` file contains no `nameserver` commands, the resolver assumes that the name server is running on the local host. The `resolv.conf` file can have up to three `nameserver` commands to define a total of three name servers. Actually, the file can contain more than three `nameserver` commands but the excess commands are ignored. Chapter 3, "The BIND Software," in the discussion of resolver timeout values, showed that the resolver uses, at most, three name servers. You must define at least two servers for redundancy's sake, and because three servers only increase the timeout by one second over two servers, most administrators use three servers, as in this example:

```
nameserver 172.16.5.3
nameserver 172.16.5.1
nameserver 10.252.116.61
```

The server in each `nameserver` command must be defined by its IP address. The resolver reads `resolv.conf` each time it starts. Until the resolver starts, there is nothing to resolve host names to IP addresses, but values entered as IP addresses don't need to be resolved.

One server address that causes some debate is the address for the name server running on the local computer. The local system can be defined by its primary IP address, by the `localhost` address, or by an address of all zeros. Each address has its advocates. Some administrators recommend the `localhost` address 127.0.0.1 because it is well documented as the official `localhost` address.

Others recommend the IP address assigned to the local computer, e.g., 172.16.12.3. They feel that the IP address is the easiest address to identify as being the address of the local computer. I generally use the address 0.0.0.0 for the local computer, which is defined as the first address assigned to the local computer. When the resolver runs under the default configuration, it uses the 0.0.0.0 address, and if it is good enough for the resolver, it is good enough for me.

Also, the address 127.0.0.1 does not work right on some old computers. This is not a problem for Linux systems, but if someone copies my configuration on an old operating system I don't want them to have problems. Finally, I think 0.0.0.0 is more distinctive than the regular IP address and thus makes it clearer that the name server is the local computer. However, all of these addresses work, so feel free to use the one you like best.

The *domain* Command

The `resolv.conf` file can contain exactly one `domain` command. The `domain` command defines the default domain. The default domain is used to create a domain search list that contains only one domain. The domain search list is used as described in Chapter 3 to create fully qualified domain names out of host names that do not contain a dot. Assume that the `resolv.conf` file contains the following `domain` command:

```
domain terns.foobirds.org
```

Furthermore, assume that the resolver is asked to resolve the host name `sooty` into an IP address. Because `sooty` does not contain a dot, the resolver extends it with the domain names contained in the domain search list. In this case, the list contains only one value, so first the resolver queries for the address of `sooty.terns.foobird.org`. If that name does not resolve to an address, the resolver makes a final attempt by asking the name server to resolve `sooty` into an IP address.

Notice that only the domain name found in the search list and the host name as originally entered by the user are used in attempts to resolve the name to an address. This is different than the old behavior of the `domain` command. In older versions of BIND, the `domain` command served a special purpose. The resolver would search the domain and the parents of the domain defined by the `domain` command. Thus, for the `domain` command in the previous example, an old version of BIND would have searched `terns.foobirds.org` and `foobirds.org`. In current versions of BIND, the `domain` command is no different than a `search` command with only one domain argument. For this reason, I no longer use the `domain` command. Instead, I stick with the more powerful `search` command.

The *search* Command

The `search` command defines the domain search list. Unlike the `domain` command, which accepts only one domain as an argument, the `search` command accepts a list of up to six domains. For example, here is a search list with two domains:

```
search terns.foobirds.org foobirds.org
```

In this example, the resolver is configured to search the `terns.foobirds.org` domain and its parent domain, `foobirds.org`. This type of configuration, searching the local domain and its parent, is popular because it emulates the old BIND behavior that many users are used to. However, the `search` command is not limited to emulating old BIND behavior. It can also expand the search to sibling domains or unrelated domains. For example:

```
search terns.foobird.org ducks.foobirds.org foobirds.org
```

In this example, the administrator adds the sibling domain `ducks.foobirds.org`. Using this search list, a query for `crow` would cause the resolver to first look for `crow.terns.foobirds.org`, then `crow.ducks.foobirds.org`, then `crow.foobirds.org`, and finally, if none of the queries produced an answer, the resolver would look for `crow` without any domain extension. The ability to define the complete search list makes the `search` command much more flexible than the `domain` command.

Use either a `domain` command or a `search` command in the `resolv.conf` file. Don't use both because you might not get the behavior you expect. It all depends on which command is processed last when the resolver reads the `resolv.conf` configuration file.

If neither a `domain` command nor a `search` command is found in the `resolv.conf` file, the resolver derives the default domain name from the local computer name, as described earlier in the default resolver configuration. Personally, I recommend using the `search` command and explicitly defining the search list you want to use. That way, the configuration is self-documenting and confusion is reduced.

The *sortlist* Command

The `sortlist` command changes the order of addresses returned by the name server in order to prefer certain addresses over others. BIND 8 provides configuration commands that can reorder address records in the server or the resolver.

The addresses specified on the `sortlist` command are the preferred addresses, and the order in which they are specified shows the order of preference, with the first address listed being the most preferred. Addresses are specified in dotted decimal notation and can be optionally accompanied by a network mask. If no network mask is defined, the natural mask is used. (Address masks are covered in Chapter 1, "The DNS Architecture.")

The following example prefers the local subnet address the most, followed by the address of the enterprise network. Notice that no mask is provided for the enterprise address so it defaults to the natural mask of 255.255.0.0.

```
sortlist 172.16.12.0/255.255.255.0 172.16.0.0
```

The value defined by `sortlist` is used only when the name server provides multiple addresses in answer to a query. Additionally, it has an effect only if at least one of the addresses provided by the name server is a preferred address. To use it to greatest effect, you need to have a clear idea of which addresses you want the resolver to sort. Figure 4.1 illustrates a network where `sortlist` might be effective.

Figure 4.1 A host with multiple addresses

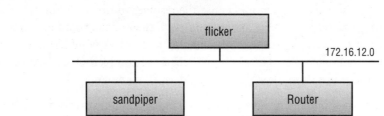

Figure 4.1 shows several computers on an enterprise network. flicker and grackle are both pure DNS clients. The DNS server is a separate system. A multi-homed host named sandpiper is a file server that provides service to both subnet 172.16.12.0 and subnet 172.16.9.0. The two subnets are connected via a router.

The file server is multi-homed so that its traffic does not need to flow through the router. If either flicker or grackle uses the wrong address for sandpiper, in other words, if grackle uses the 172.16.12.0 address or flicker uses the 172.16.9.0 address, the purpose of dual-homing the file server is defeated because the traffic would flow through the router. In this case, the administrators of these systems can use sortlist to ensure that the clients use the right addresses. On flicker, the resolv.conf file would contain the following command:

```
sortlist 172.16.12.0/255.255.255.0
```

On grackle, it would contain the following command:

```
sortlist 172.16.9.0/255.255.255.0
```

A sortlist command that prefers the local subnet address above all others, such as those shown in the previous examples, is a safe bet. Many administrators use such a sortlist command as a matter of course. But trying to use the sortlist command to sort addresses from remote networks can do more harm than good unless you have a very clear understanding of exactly how the networks are configured and how they talk to each other. I almost never use sortlist for sorting any remote addresses.

The *options* Command

The `options` command defines processing options for the resolver. In BIND 8.2.2, there are several possible options:

debug turns on debugging. When the `debug` option is set, the resolver prints debugging messages to standard output. These messages are very informative for debugging resolver or server problems, but in reality, this option is of marginal value. Turning on debugging in the basic resolver configuration produces too much output and produces it at inappropriate times. Use the debugging tools described in Chapter 11, "Testing DNS." All of those tools allow you to turn on resolver debugging when you're ready to run the test in order to get the additional output at a time that you can actually use it.

ndots:*n* defines the number of dots that must appear in a host name for the resolver to decide not to modify it with the search list before sending it to the name server. By default, the resolver will not modify a host name if it contains one dot. As a result, the host name `crow` will be extended with a value from the search list before being sent to the name server, but the host name `sooty.terns` will not. Use the `ndots` option to modify this behavior. Consider the following example:

```
ndots:2
```

This value tells the resolver to use the search list on any host name that contains fewer than two dots. With this setting, both `crow` and `sooty.terns` are extended with a value from the search list before being sent to the name server for the first time.

The `ndots` option changes how the resolver handles queries, but it really only changes the order in which things are done. As Chapter 3 points out, the unmodified host name is either the first or the last query sent to the name server. If `ndots` is set to 1, the default setting, `sooty.terns` is sent to the server without modification. When the server fails to resolve that name, the resolver issues additional queries with the search list values until it gets an answer or the list is exhausted. If `ndots` is set to 2, `sooty.terns` is modified with the first value in the search list before it is sent to the name server. If the server fails to resolve the name, the resolver tries every value in the search list and then sends the unmodified host name to the name server. In either case, exactly the same queries are made. Only the order of the queries is changed.

About the only time that `ndots` is required is if some component of your domain could be confused with a top-level domain and you have users who consistently truncate host names at that domain. In that rare case, the queries would first be sent to the root servers for resolution in the top-level domain before eventually getting back to your local server. It is very bad form to bother the root servers over nothing. Use ndots to force the resolver to extend the troublesome host names with your local domain name so that they will be resolved before ever reaching the root servers.

timeout:*n*   sets the initial query timeout for the resolver. By default, the timeout is 5 seconds for the first query to every server. Subsequent queries time out based on a formula that uses this initial value and the number of servers; see Chapter 3 for a detailed explanation. I have never had occasion to change this value, but if you know for certain that your name server generally takes longer than 5 seconds to respond, you can increase this value to reduce the number of duplicate queries.

attempts:*n*   defines the number of times the resolver will retry a query. The default value is 2, which means the resolver will retry a query two times with every server in its server list before returning an error to the application. The attempts value might need to be increased if you have a poor network connection that frequently loses queries, such as the connection to a remote office in a developing country or at the end of a narrow-band satellite link. In most cases, this value does not need to be changed.

rotate   turns on round-robin selection of name servers. Normally, the resolver sends the query to the first server in the name server list and sends the query to another server only if the first server does not respond. Traditionally, the second and third name servers were defined to provide backup name service. They were not intended to provide load-sharing. The rotate option makes it possible for you to tell the resolver to share the name server workload evenly among all of the servers.

Here's how it works. Assume that the resolv.conf file has the following nameserver entries:

```
nameserver 172.16.5.1
nameserver 172.16.5.3
nameserver 172.16.55.1
```

Furthermore, assume that FTP has asked the resolver for the address of crow, Telnet has asked for the address of kestrel, and Apache has asked for the address of grackle. Without the rotate option set, all three address queries are sent to the name server at 172.16.5.1. With the rotate option set, the query for crow is sent to the server at 172.16.5.1, the query for kestrel is sent to the server at 172.16.5.3, and the query for grackle is sent to 172.16.55.1. The resolver starts at the top of the server list, sends a query to each server in the list, and then starts at the top again.

Implementing load-sharing at the resolver level makes sense only if you have a large number of resolvers involved and you have more than one robust server. For example, assume that you have a large enterprise with 50,000 clients and that the resolvers of all of those clients are configured in exactly the same way. All 50,000 would send all of their queries to the first server in the list of name servers. The `rotate` option would spread the work evenly among all of the central servers.

This, however, is not usually the case. Most resolver configurations list a local name server, such as the name server on the local subnet, first and list other servers only as backup servers. With this model, there are as many different resolver configurations as there are subnets and no server is targeted by more than the number of clients on a single subnet. In this, the average case, setting the `rotate` option is unnecessary and even undesirable because the topology of the network already balances the load.

`no-check-names`   disables the checking of domain names for compliance with RFC 952, "DOD Internet Host Table Specification." By default, domain names that contain an underscore (_), non-ASCII characters, or ASCII control characters are considered to be in error. If you must work with host names that contain an underscore, you should use this option.

Philosophically, I'm not crazy about checking for bad names during the query process. Checking names at this point does not seem to be in the spirit of the old interoperability adage, "Be conservative in what you send and liberal in what you accept." Personally, I prefer to control compliance with the RFCs at the source. The sources of incorrect domain names are the zone files that contain those names. I find it much better to use the name server features that check for incorrect names when the zone file is loaded rather than to check the names one at a time during a resolver query process. Therefore, I use this option to disable checking in the resolver.

`inet6`   causes the resolver to query for IPv6 addresses. The version of the Internet Protocol (IP) used in today's Internet is IPv4. IPv4 uses the 32-bit addresses we are all familiar with. IPv6 expands those to 128-bit addresses. IPv6 is a future protocol toward which networks are evolving. Use this option only if you connect to an experimental IPv6 network. This option would not be used in a normal business environment.

One of the best ways to understand how the `nameserver`, `domain`, `search`, `sortlist`, and `options` commands are combined to make a resolver configuration is to look at some sample `resolv.conf` files. Let's do that now.

Sample *resolv.conf* Files

Despite the fact that the resolver can run with a default configuration, you won't run your Linux system without a `resolv.conf` file. The reason is simple: When you install Linux, the installation program asks you if you use DNS. If you answer yes, the installation program automatically creates the `resolv.conf` file. To run without a `resolv.conf` file, you have to go to the trouble of removing the one that Linux created for you, and since it is better to run with a configuration file, very few administrators go to the trouble of removing it.

A Configuration Created by Lizard

The contents of the configuration file created by the Linux installation file naturally varies depending on what you told the system during installation. Listing 4.1 contains the `resolv.conf` file created by the Lizard installation program when I installed Caldera 2.3 on an old Pentium.

Listing 4.1   A System-Generated `resolv.conf` File

```
# /etc/resolv.conf - DNS setup file
#
# !!! Automatically generated by lizard. Do not edit !!!
#
nameserver 172.16.5.1
nameserver 172.16.5.3
domain foobirds.org
search foobirds.org
```

I removed most of the comments from the `resolv.conf` file shown in Listing 4.1 to save space, but the critical lines are essentially as they appear on the Pentium system. The lines that begin with sharp signs (#) are comments. The first real configuration lines define two name servers. The `domain` line defines the default domain and the `search` line defines the search list. Both of these were created by the installation program from the Pentium's host name. There is really no reason to have both a `domain` command and a `search` command in the same `resolv.conf` file. In this case, only the `search` command has any effect because it comes after the `domain` command. A simple test can prove that the `domain` command is a wasted line.

Testing the Lizard *resolv.conf* File

First, you need to edit the `resolv.conf` file so that the `domain` command and the `search` command are not identical. Otherwise, you won't be able to tell which command is in effect. Listing 4.2 contains the `resolv.conf` file from Listing 4.1 with the `search` command edited for the test.

Listing 4.2   Revising `resolv.conf` to Test the `domain` and `search` Commands

```
# /etc/resolv.conf - DNS setup file
#
# !!! Automatically generated by lizard. Do not edit !!!
#
nameserver 172.16.5.1
nameserver 172.16.5.3
domain foobirds.org
search terns.foobirds.org foobirds.org
```

Now invoke the `nslookup` test program and ask it to show you the current resolver settings with the `set all` command. Listing 4.3 shows that the default domain name and the search list are both set from the `search` command, which occurs after the `domain` command in the `resolv.conf` file that we just created. Also, notice that even though the `search` command can have multiple domains for the search list, it is the first domain listed on the `search` command that `nslookup` assumes is the default domain.

Listing 4.3   `nslookup` Test of `search` Command Settings

```
[craig]$ nslookup
Default Server: wren.foobirds.org
Address:  172.16.5.1

> set all
Default Server: wren.foobirds.org
Address: 172.16.5.1

Set options:
   nodebug         defname        search        recurse
   nod2            novc           noignoretc    port=53
   querytype=A     class=IN       timeout=5     retry=2
   root=a.root-servers.net.
   domain=terns.foobirds.org
   srchlist=terns.foobirds.org/foobirds.org

> exit
```

NOTE To change a resolver setting during an nslookup session, use the set command with the new value. For example, the command set debug turns on debugging, which I find easier and more effective than turning on debugging with the options debug command in the resolv.conf file.

If you then edit the resolv.conf file we created in Listing 4.2 and move the domain command after the search command, rerunning nslookup, as shown in Listing 4.4, shows that the position of the command is all important and that two commands are not needed.

Listing 4.4 nslookup Test of domain Command Settings

```
[craig]$ nslookup
Default Server: wren.foobirds.org
Address: 172.16.5.1

> set all
Default Server: wren.foobirds.org
Address: 172.16.5.1

Set options:
  nodebug         defname        search          recurse
  nod2            novc           noignoretc      port=53
  querytype=A     class=IN       timeout=5       retry=2
  root=a.root-servers.net.
  domain=foobirds.org
  srchlist=foobirds.org

> exit
```

NOTE These examples show you how to examine the operation of the resolver and how to check the configuration using the nslookup program. nslookup is one of the test tools that come with BIND. This powerful and effective tool is used extensively throughout the text and is covered in detail in Chapter 11.

Clearly, the Caldera installation program was mistaken when it put both a domain command and a search command in the same resolv.conf file. Doing so didn't cause any problems because both of the commands were set to the same value. However, it is not a mistake you'll make if you create the configuration file manually, which is what I always prefer to do. In the following sections, we will create `resolv.conf` files manually for a few different configurations.

A Configuration Running *named* on the Local Host

By default, the resolver looks for `named` running on the local host, but the default configuration looks for only that one name server. If you want to have backup name servers for those times when `named` is shut off for maintenance, you must create a `resolv.conf` file. The example in Listing 4.5 shows a local server with two external backup servers.

Listing 4.5   A Local Server `resolv.conf` File

```
# A local server configuration
#
nameserver 0.0.0.0
nameserver 172.16.5.1
nameserver 172.16.5.3
search foobirds.org
```

The local name server is defined by the address 0.0.0.0, which literally means the first address assigned to this host. There are alternative ways to define the local host, as described earlier in this chapter. They all work on Linux systems, but 0.0.0.0 is the most popular.

A Resolver-Only Configuration

A pure DNS client does not run a copy of `named` on the local host. It is a resolver-only client because the resolver is this client's only link to the DNS system. A resolver-only client must have a `resolv.conf` file because the default configuration assumes that the local host is running `named`. The only way to create a resolver-only client is to create a `resolv.conf` file that points all queries to external name servers.

The sample configuration in Listing 4.6 was created on a Linux client that had the BIND 8.2.2 resolver installed. The name of the client is `puffin.foobirds.org` and its IP address is 172.16.5.17.

Listing 4.6   A Resolver-Only `resolv.conf` File

```
# A resolver-only configuration
#
nameserver 172.16.5.1
```

Essential Configuration

PART 2

```
nameserver 172.16.5.3
nameserver 10.252.116.61
search foobirds.org
options nochecknames
```

Notice that the IP address of the local host does not appear in any of the nameserver commands. All of the name servers used by the resolver on this system are external name servers. Furthermore, notice that I have added the options nochecknames line. This option is available under BIND 8.2 but is not available in earlier versions of the resolver. Earlier versions did not do RFC 952 name-checking. Using this option causes the new resolver to emulate the old behavior, which might be necessary if any of the host names queried by your users do not comply with the RFC.

A Load-Sharing Configuration

A load-sharing configuration makes sense only for a resolver-only configuration. If one of the servers is running directly on the local host, that server should always be preferred. Even in a resolver-only configuration, there is usually a single server that should be preferred for all queries. Perhaps it is the server on the local subnet. On occasion, however, there is no reason to prefer a single server and there is some benefit to sharing the query load across all of the servers. In the example in Listing 4.7, the resolver-only configuration shown in Listing 4.6 is modified to use load-sharing.

Listing 4.7   A Load-Sharing resolv.conf Configuration

```
# A load sharing configuration
#
nameserver 172.16.5.1
nameserver 172.16.5.3
nameserver 10.252.116.61
search foobirds.org
options nochecknames rotate
```

The rotate option is used for load-sharing. Notice that it was added to the existing options command. Multiple options can be defined on a single command by separating the options with whitespace. The next section describes how options and other resolver parameters can be modified on a user-by-user basis.

Resolver Environment Variables

Resolver Environment Variables

The `resolv.conf` file defines the resolver configuration for the entire system. Some of the values defined in the configuration file can be overridden by environment variables that are set by individual users. The environment variables do not affect the system-wide configuration and they have no affect on queries issued by other users. They are used to tune the actions of the resolver to the needs of an individual user. There are currently three resolver environment variables:

LOCALDOMAIN defines the domain search list, overriding the search list defined by the `resolv.conf search` command.

RES_OPTIONS defines processing options for the resolver, overriding the options defined by the `resolv.conf options` command.

HOSTALIASES defines the path to a user's personal host alias file. This variable does not have a counterpart in the `resolv.conf` file. It is specifically a user-level feature.

Using the Environment Variables

The syntax of the LOCALDOMAIN and RES_OPTIONS variables is very similar to their counterparts in the `resolv.conf` file. Both variables accept a list of values separated by whitespace. In the case of the LOCALDOMAIN variable, the list is a list of domain names. In the case of the RES_OPTIONS variable, the list is the list of values that are valid for an `options` command. Listing 4.8 shows a user setting the variables.

Listing 4.8 Setting and Testing Environment Variables

```
[craig]$ LOCALDOMAIN='terns.foobirds.org foobirds.org'
[craig]$ echo ${LOCALDOMAIN}
terns.foobirds.org foobirds.org
[craig]$ RES_OPTIONS='attempts:3 timeout:10'
[craig]$ echo ${RES_OPTIONS}
attempts:3 timeout:10
[craig]$ export LOCALDOMAIN RES_OPTIONS
[craig]$ nslookup
Default Server:  wren.foobirds.org
Address:  172.16.5.1

> set all
Default Server: wren.foobirds.org
Address:  172.16.5.1
```

```
Set options:
  nodebug          defname          search         recurse
  nod2             novc             noignoretc     port=53
  querytype=A      class=IN         timeout=10     retry=3
  root=a.root-servers.net.
  domain=terns.foobirds.org
  srchlist=terns.foobirds.org/foobirds.org

> exit
```

In Listing 4.8, the variables are being set at the bash shell prompt. The user then displays the value that was just set using the echo command. (Perhaps this user is a compulsive checker!) Sure that the variables are set correctly, the user exports them to processes outside of the shell. Running nslookup and using the set all command shows that the resolver configuration has been changed for this user.

> **NOTE** Most of the time, the environment variables are not set at the command prompt. Usually, a user with special requirements stores the variable assignments in one of the user's initialization files, such as .bashrc.

The HOSTALIASES variable is a little different. It does not have a parallel in the resolv.conf file and it is not really useful as a system-wide service. It allows the user to define a file containing short aliases for host names that they frequently use. Listing 4.9 is an example:

Listing 4.9   Using the HOSTALIASES Variable

```
[craig]$ cat hostaliases.txt
jack     beanstalk.veggies.org
sprat    www.nist.gov
phat     ftp.sunsite.unc.edu
[craig]$ HOSTALIASES=/home/craig/hostaliases.txt
[craig]$ echo ${HOSTALIASES}
/home/craig/hostaliases.txt
[craig]$ export HOSTALIASES
[craig]$ host sprat
www.nist.gov is a nickname for potomac.nist.gov
potomac.nist.gov has address 129.6.13.23
potomac.nist.gov has address 129.6.13.23
```

In Listing 4.9, the user has created a file containing three host aliases and has named the file `hostaliases.txt`. The `cat` command at the beginning of this listing displays the contents of this file. Each line in the alias file contains an alias/host name pair. Each line starts with an alias that is separated from the host name it maps to by some whitespace.

In Listing 4.9, the user then stores the path name of the alias file in the HOSTALIASES variable. After exporting the variable, a query for the alias `sprat` returns the same value as a query for `www.nist.gov`.

NOTE   The host command used in Listing 4.9 is a test tool that comes with the BIND software. It is used extensively in this text and is described in detail in Chapter 11.

As the system administrator, you're not usually involved in setting environment variables for individual users. Normally, you'll determine the best resolver configuration for the entire system and define that configuration in the `resolv.conf` file. Rarely will you need to change that setting for a user who has special requirements. Frankly, I have never had to do this. But if you have an individual user who seems to be getting strange results from the resolver, you might want to enter the `echo` command just to see if they have been fooling with the configuration.

A Peek Inside the Header File

The process options defined by the RES_OPTIONS variable and the `options` command all have default values. Those defaults can be viewed in the `resolv.h` header file. Some defaults are simple integer values; the others are binary values that can be a little more difficult to understand.

A peek at the integer values in the `resolv.h` file shows some of the default values we have already discussed, among several others. Here are the variables that hold the default integer values for some of the commands we have already discussed:

MAXNS   defines the maximum number of name servers that the resolver will use. This value is set to 3.

RES_TIMEOUT   defines the initial timeout value used by the resolver. This value is set to 5 and can be overridden by the `timeout:n` option.

RES_DFLRETRY   defines the number of times the resolver will retry a query. This value is set to 2 and can be overridden by the `attempts:n` option.

RES_MAXRETRY   defines the absolute maximum number of tries the resolver will retry a query. This value is set to 5. If you set `attempts:n` above this number, it will be ignored.

PART 2

Essential
Configuration

MAXRESOLVSORT   defines the maximum number of addresses that can be specified on a `sortlist` command. This value is set to 10.

Unlike the integer values that tend to set maximums and minimums for the resolver, the binary values in the `resolv.h` file do not set thresholds. These values are basically switches. If one of the binary values is OR'd into RES_DEFAULTS, the feature represented by that binary value is enabled. As shipped in BIND 8.2.2, RES_DEFAULTS enables RES_RECURSE (request recursion), RES_DEFNAMES (use the default domain), and RES_DNSRCH (search up the domain tree).

Several of the binary values are easy to identify as options we have already discussed. RES_DEBUG, RES_USE_INET6, RES_ROTATE, and RES_NOCHECKNAME are easily mapped to the `debug`, `inet6`, `rotate`, and `no-check-names` options by their names alone. Only a few of the other values might arouse your curiosity:

RES_NOALIASES   can be used to turn off the HOSTALIASES feature described in the previous section.

RES_USEVC and RES_STAYOPEN   cause the resolver to run over TCP instead of UDP. Because DNS queries and responses normally fit into a single packet, running DNS over TCP reduces rather than enhances performance. So don't make the mistake of thinking that you should run DNS over TCP.

This discussion is not intended to encourage you to modify the `resolv.h` file. I strongly recommend against changing any of the values in the header file. All of the values worth changing can be configured through the `resolv.conf` file. The point of this discussion is to explain what the header values mean when you look inside the `resolv.h` file, and you will look because this is Linux. It is an open source environment. You have the source code for everything; nothing is hidden. So it is nice to have some idea of what the code is doing.

The real resolver configuration file is `resolv.conf`. It, along with a few other files, defines the entire resolver configuration. The next section describes some of the other files involved in resolver configuration.

The *host.conf* File

Frequently, discussions of configuring the resolver begin and end with a description of the `reslov.conf` file. It is the file that tells the resolver where the name servers are, defines the domain search list, and sets optional parameters for the resolver process. It can easily appear that this is the entire configuration, and it would be if DNS were all there was to Linux name service. Yet the reality is that while DNS is the most important component of name service, it is not the only name service your system will use. This book started with a description of the host table and every Linux system has one. Sometimes the host table is used to resolve a name and sometimes DNS is used. One part of configuring the resolver is telling it what service it should use and when it should use it.

The `host.conf` file is one of the configuration files used to set the order of precedence among the various name services. The `host.conf` file defines several options that control how the `/etc/hosts` file is processed and how it interacts with DNS. To illustrate this, Listing 4.10 displays a sample `host.conf` file that contains every possible option.

Listing 4.10   All Possible `host.conf` Options

```
# Define the order in which services are queried
order bind hosts nis
# Permit multiple addresses per host
multi on
# Verify reverse domain lookups
nospoof on
# Log "spoof" attempts
alert on
# Remove the local domain for host table lookups
trim foobirds.org
```

The `order` option defines the order in which the various name services are queried for a host name or an IP address. The three values shown in the example are the only three values available:

- `bind` stands for DNS.
- `hosts` stands for the `/etc/hosts` file.
- `nis` stands for the Network Information Service (NIS), which is the name service created by Sun Microsystems that is described in Appendix D, "Configuring Network Information Service."

The resolver tries these services in the order they are listed. Given the `order` command shown above, the resolver queries DNS first, then the `/etc/hosts` file, and finally NIS. The search stops as soon as a service answers the query.

The `multi` option determines whether or not multiple addresses can be assigned to the same host name in the `/etc/hosts` file. This option is enabled when `on` is specified and is disabled when `off` is specified. You may be wondering why you would want to do this. Well, assume that you have a single computer directly connected to a few different networks—this is called a *multi-homed* host. Each network requires an interface, and each interface requires a different IP address. Thus, you have one host with multiple addresses. But also assume that this is your Web server and that you want everyone to refer to it by the host name www regardless of the network they connect in from. In this case, you have one host name associated with multiple addresses, which is just what the multi option was designed for. multi affects only host table lookups; it has no effect on DNS. DNS inherently supports multiple addresses.

DNS permits you to look up a host name and get an address, as well as to look up an address and get a host name; names to addresses are in one database and addresses to names are in another database. The nospoof option tells the resolver to reject the host name and return an error unless the values returned from both databases match. For example, if the name wren.foobirds.org returns the address 172.16.5.1, but a lookup for the address 172.16.5.1 returns the host name host0501.foobirds.org, the system rejects the host as invalid. The keyword on enables the feature, and off disables it.

The alert option is related to the nospoof option. When alert is turned on, the system logs any of the host name/address mismatches described previously. When alert is turned off, these events are not logged.

The trim option removes the local domain name before the name is looked up in the /etc/hosts file. This permits the system to match the host name alone, even if the user enters the host name with the domain name. With this, the /etc/hosts file can be created without full domain names and still be useful. Given the trim command in Listing 4.10, a query for hawk.foobirds.org would cause a host table query for hawk. Multiple trim commands can be included in the host.conf file to remove several different domains from host table queries. trim affects only host table lookups; it has no effect on DNS.

Real host.conf files don't actually use all of these commands. The host.conf file that comes with Red Hat 6 and the one that comes with Caldera 2.3 have only two lines, as shown in Listing 4.11.

Listing 4.11   A Realistic host.conf File

```
order hosts,bind
multi on
```

The heart of the host.conf file is the order command, which defines the order in which the name services are searched. The search order shown in Listing 4.11 is the order that is most commonly used. It causes the resolver to check the local host table before querying the name server. Most administrators think this makes sense because the host table contains only a few entries and is therefore very quick to search. On the other hand, it means that the host table is searched every time the resolver has a query.

To me this seems like a waste of time. The host table answers only a very small percentage of the queries generated by the system. After the failed search of the host table, the resolver sends the query to DNS. If the query were sent to DNS first, it would have been answered without a sidetrack into the host table. On my systems, the host table is used only on those occasions when DNS is unavailable because DNS contains everything that is in the host table and much more. Therefore, I use the following `order` command:

```
order bind,hosts
```

With this setup, DNS answers all queries as long as the name server is reachable. The host table is used only when the DNS server cannot answer. Because I configure the host table to have only those values needed to boot the system, this setup works well and runs more efficiently than the other search order. However, I control DNS on my network. If I need a special value, I can put it there. Using the local host table to define special addresses is very useful when you don't control DNS but do control the host table on your local host. If you put special values in the host table that are not found in DNS, you should use the other search order and search the host table first.

The other commands have very little significance. For example, the `multi` command shown in Listing 4.11 is significant only if the host table stores multiple addresses for a single host. As you saw in Chapter 1, "The DNS Architecture," the host table of most Linux systems contains only a few lines and would not normally have multiple addresses for a single host. The other options are useful only if you plan to build and maintain a large host table.

The other possible value for the `order` command is `nis`. Listing 4.11, like most `hosts.conf` files, doesn't mention NIS. NIS handles more than the name service, and another, more complicated configuration file, `nsswitch.conf`, was developed to define the order of precedence when NIS is involved. Most Linux systems have a `hosts.conf` file defined for those old applications that might need it. But the real file for defining the sources of system information, including the order of precedence for the resolver, is the `nsswitch.conf` file.

The *nsswitch.conf* File

The `nsswitch.conf` file handles much more than just the order of precedence between the host table and DNS. It defines the sources for several different system administration databases because it is an outgrowth of the NIS. NIS makes it possible to centrally control and distribute a wide range of system administration files. Table 4.1 lists all of the administrative databases controlled by the `nsswitch.conf` file. Unless you run NIS on your network, the sources of all of these administrative databases, except for the `hosts` database, will be the local files.

Table 4.1   Databases Controlled by nsswitch.conf

database	Holds
aliases	E-mail aliases
ethers	Ethernet addresses for Reverse ARP (RARP)
group	Group IDs
hosts	Host names and IP addresses
netgroup	Network groups for NIS
network	Network names and numbers
passwd	User account information
protocols	IP protocol numbers
publickey	Keys for secure RPC (remote procedure call)
rpc	RPC names and numbers
services	Network service port numbers
shadow	User passwords

The hosts entry is the one that indicates the source for host name and IP address information for the resolver. In the sample nsswitch.conf file in Listing 4.12, DNS is used as the primary source with the local file as the backup source.

Listing 4.12   Using nsswitch.conf without NIS

```
# Sample for system that does not use NIS

passwd:     files
shadow:     files
group:      files

hosts:      dns files
aliases:    files
```

```
services:    files
networks:    files
protocols:   files
rpc:         files
ethers:      files
netgroup:    files
publickey:   files
```

In this sample file, the `hosts` entry tells the resolver to first check DNS (`dns`). If DNS answers the query, the resolver is finished. If DNS can't answer the query, the resolver then tries the local file (`files`), which in this case is `/etc/hosts`. To check the host table before DNS, simply reverse the order:

```
hosts: files dns
```

All of the other entries in the sample `nsswitch.conf` file point to local files, such as `/etc/passwd` and `/etc/services`, as the source of information for those databases. On most Linux systems, local files are used for all of these databases. Unless you run NIS, your `nsswitch.conf` file can look pretty much like the one in Listing 4.12.

Caldera 2.3 *nsswitch.conf* File

The default `nsswitch.conf` file that comes with a Caldera 2.3 system is a little more complex, as shown in Listing 4.13.

Listing 4.13   An `nsswitch.conf` File with NIS

```
# /etc/nsswitch.conf
#
# Name Service Switch configuration file.
#

passwd:         compat
shadow:         compat
group:          compat
hosts:          files nis dns
networks:       nis files dns

ethers:         nis files
protocols:      nis files
rpc:            nis files
services:       nis files
```

The Caldera nsswitch.conf file shown in Listing 4.13 contains two keywords, nis and compat, that were not in Listing 4.12. nis and compat are valid source values if you run NIS on your network. nis simply means that the NIS server is the source of the data. In the Caldera file, nis is the first source for most of the information. If NIS is not running, the system falls back to the other information sources. If you don't plan to run NIS, edit this file to remove the NIS references. If you do plan to run NIS, see Appendix D for additional advice.

Also, compat is a valid source field value if you run NIS. compat means that the source is a local file, but the local files should be read in a way that is compatible with the old SunOS 4 system. Under SunOS 4, NIS data could be appended to a file by using a plus sign (+) as the last entry in a file. For example, if /etc/passwd ended with a +, the system would use the accounts in the password file plus every account in NIS. SunOS 4 has been out of production for more than five years, and the nsswitch.conf file supersedes the old "plus syntax." However, some people still use it, and the compat function is there if you need it. Unless you really plan to run NIS, I suggest using files instead of compat.

Other Database Sources

The examples in this chapter illustrate the most common cases: Data is read from a file or retrieved from DNS or NIS. There are other, rarely used options and they vary depending on the C library used by the application, either Linux libc5 or GNU C Library 2.x. In addition to the files, dns, compat, and nis sources already described, libc5 supports nisplus as a source. nisplus is the Sun Microsystems NIS+ service. It is an enhancement of NIS that is generally limited to networks that have Sun servers. One limitation of libc5 is that it doesn't support compat as a source for the shadow database. A quick look at the Caldera 2.3 nsswitch.conf sample file shows that Caldera must use the GNU C Library because it lists compat as the source for shadow. The GNU C Library supports all of the sources already mentioned, including nisplus. It also supports db and hesiod.

db provides another method of accessing local files. Normally, all of the administrative files listed in the nsswitch.conf file are flat files, ASCII text files that are searched sequentially. If the files are converted to database files, db can be used to search them with database techniques. A database search is much faster than a sequential search. However, the administrative files are rarely large enough to benefit from a database search. hesiod is a rarely used server developed at Massachusetts Institute of Technology (MIT). The keyword hesiod is not even documented for the nsswitch.conf file, but the source code indicates it is there. Personally, I have never had occasion to use db or hesiod, and only rarely nis and nisplus. For more information about NIS, see Appendix D.

Controlling the Selection Process

The `nsswitch.conf` file allows you to control the sources for many more administrative databases and to select many more sources for those databases than the `hosts.conf` file does. It also gives you much finer control over the conditions under which the system selects a source.

The `nsswitch.conf` file provides several keywords that can be used to test the status of a query. These are

> `success`   means that the query returned the expected value. The default action taken for this status is to return the value to the application that started the query and exit the query process.
>
> `notfound`   means that the query worked correctly but that the expected value was not found. In the case of the resolver querying for an address, this might mean that the name server answered that the host or the domain was unknown. The default action taken in this case is to query the next source in line. In the resolver example, that might mean checking the host table if DNS said that the host did not exist, which allows you to define special aliases in the host file that are unknown to DNS while still retaining the advantages of querying DNS first.
>
> `unavail`   means that the source that was queried is not available. For example, the name server is not running. The default action taken for this status is to continue on and query the next source in line.
>
> `tryagain`   means the source is temporarily unavailable. For example, a source file is locked while being used by another process. The default action taken for this status is to continue on and query the next source in line.

The default actions described in this section can be identified by two keywords: `return` and `continue`. `return` tells the resolver to return the value to the application and end the query. `continue` tells the resolver to continue on to the next source and to query that source.

The status and action keywords can be combined and added to the list of sources in the `nsswitch.conf` file to control when the querying process decides to move on to the next source. The syntax for a status check is

```
[ ( ! ? STATUS = ACTION )+ ]
```

This looks worse than it is and requires some explanation. The square brackets are required and they enclose the entire conditional statement. The parentheses are optional and are only needed to enclose each conditional test if multiple conditional tests are linked together by the plus sign within a single conditional statement. Here is an example of using the parentheses and the plus sign:

```
[(NOTFOUND=RETURN)+(TRYAGAIN=RETURN)]
```

Essential Configuration

PART 2

The question mark means any status value. The exclamation mark negates the status value. For example, `!SUCCESS` means unsuccessful.

Putting all of this together allows you to create some pretty fancy status tests, but if you use this feature at all, you will probably create simple tests. For example, you might want to query DNS and only fall back to the host table if DNS is not running. This is a very reasonable thing to do if, like me, you use the host table only to aid the system during startup. Once the name service is running, there is no reason to query the host table, and avoiding doing so saves a little time on every query. Here is the `hosts` line from `nsswitch.conf` with that conditional test set:

```
hosts:        dns [!UNAVAIL=return] files
```

This line says that for all statuses except `UNAVAIL`, the resolver should return the value to the application and exit. Only when the DNS name server is not running should the resolver continue on to the host table. Unless explicitly changed by the conditional statement, the default action is taken, and the default action for `UNAVAIL` is `continue`.

The `nsswitch.conf` file has superseded the `hosts.conf` file because it provides more control over more resources. Linux systems generally have both files configured, but the action really takes place in the `nsswitch.conf` file.

In Sum

This chapter began the process of configuring DNS on a Linux system by configuring the resolver, which is the one DNS component that runs on every Linux system. Three files have been used in this configuration:

`resolv.conf`   defines the resolver configuration.

`nsswitch.conf`   tells the resolver about alternate sources of host information.

`hosts.conf`   is an old configuration file that does some of what `nsswitch.conf` does and is still in use.

Despite the amount of options available for configuring the resolver, the three configuration files tend to be simple. The simple examples found in this chapter are much more likely to be used than the complex examples.

The next chapter continues the discussion of DNS configuration with a look at how the majority of servers are configured.

5

Caching and Slave Server Configuration

Chapter 4, "Configuring the Resolver," describes the resolver configuration files that are found on every Linux DNS client. This chapter looks at the three configuration files that are found on every BIND server:

- `named.conf` is the file that defines the name server configuration.
- The cache initialization file, usually called `named.ca`, `named.root`, or `root.cache`, contains root server information used by the name server during startup.
- `named.local` is a special zone file used to map the standard loopback address to the special host name `localhost`.

Every server uses these files, and for most servers these are the only files you need to create the complete server configuration. Only the master server requires additional configuration files, and there is only one master server in every zone. All of the other servers in a zone are caching-only or slave servers. The information in this chapter provides complete configuration information for both of these types of servers.

> **NOTE** Chapter 3, "The BIND Software," describes three distinct BIND server configurations: caching-only, slave, and master. If you don't remember what these terms mean, review Chapter 3 now before going on.

The *named.conf* File

The named.conf file defines the environment for named and points to the sources of domain database information. Parameters set inside the named.conf file determine whether a server acts as a caching-only server, or as a master or slave server for a specific zone.

The named.conf file is a simple ASCII text file that contains readable, clear-text configuration commands. The structure of the configuration commands is similar to the structure of the C programming language. A statement ends with a semi-colon (;), literals are enclosed in quotes ("), and related items are grouped together inside curly braces ({}). Comments can be enclosed between /* and */ like a C language comment, can begin with // like a C++ comment, or can begin with # like a shell comment. The examples in this book use C++ style comments, but you can use any comment style that you like.

In BIND 8.2.2, there are nine valid configuration statements for the named.conf file. Table 5.1 lists the valid configuration statements alphabetically and provides a short description of each.

Table 5.1   named.conf Configuration Statements

Command	Usage
acl	Defines an access control list of IP addresses.
control	Defines the control channel used by ndc.
include	Includes another file into the configuration file.
key	Defines security keys for authentication.
logging	Defines what will be logged and where it will be stored.
options	Defines global configuration options and defaults.
server	Defines a remote server's characteristics.
trusted-keys	Defines the DNSSEC encryption keys for the server.
zone	Defines a zone.

All of these commands are used somewhere in this text. acl, key, and trusted-keys are covered in Chapter 10, "DNS Security." logging is covered in Chapter 12, "The BIND

Log Files." A syntax reference for every command is provided in Appendix B, "named.conf Command Reference." But most of these configuration commands are not found in the average named.conf configuration file. An average server configuration requires only the options and zone statements, and this chapter focuses on the average configuration that is used on most servers.

The *options* Statement

Most named.conf files open with an options statement. Only one options statement is allowed in a named.conf file. That statement defines the global parameters that affect the way BIND operates. It also sets the defaults used by other statements in the configuration file. Listing 5.1 contains a short example that illustrates both these uses.

Listing 5.1   A Basic options Statement

```
options {
        recursion yes;
        check-names master ignore;
        transfer-format many-answers;
};
```

The statement starts with the options command. The curly braces enclose a list of options and the keywords define which options are being set. Notice that all of the clauses within the options statement end with a semicolon.

The *recursion* Clause

The value provided for recursion, which can be set to yes or no, tells named if it should act as a recursive or a non-recursive server. Chapter 1, "The DNS Architecture," explains that servers can be recursive or non-recursive and that queries can also be recursive or non-recursive. Chapter 4 points out that the resolver can be configured to send recursive or non-recursive queries. Here we see how to configure a recursive or non-recursive server. You will configure most servers to be recursive servers, although recursion is occasionally disabled for security reasons, as described in Chapter 10. The default for recursion is yes, so there is no need to include the option as set in Listing 5.1 in a real configuration.

The *check-names* Clause

The next two commands in Listing 5.1 set global values that are used by subsequent statements in the named.conf file. The check-names keyword tells named what it should do when it checks domain names for compliance with RFC 952, "DOD Internet Host Table Specification," and discovers a name that is not compliant.

Essential Configuration

PART 2

named checks names when it loads a zone file for which the server is the master, when it transfers the zone from the master, and when it gets a response to a query from a remote server. The first argument in a check-names clause is a keyword that specifies one of these situations. Those keywords are:

master   means when the master server loads a zone file.

slave   means when a slave transfers the zone file from the master.

response   means when a response to a query is received.

A different default action is taken in each of these cases. If the server is the master of the zone, it issues an error message and rejects the non-compliant name. This action is called fail because the non-compliant name found in the zone disk file will fail to be loaded into the name server cache.

The default action for a slave server is to issue a warning message about the non-compliant name transferred from the master server but to go ahead and load the non-compliant name anyway. This action is called warn. Finally, the default action for a server when it receives a response from a remote server is not to do any checking at all; this action is called ignore.

These defaults are correct for most servers. However, the check-names clause permits you to change the action for any situation by specifying the situation (master, slave, or response) and the action (fail, warn, or ignore) that you want associated with the situation.

In Listing 5.1, named is told that when it checks names while loading zone files for which this server is the master, it should go ahead and load the offending name and warn the administrator of any errors it finds. This setting might be used if you have a domain that has a few non-compliant names that still exist for legacy reasons. You don't want to have the zone fail to load them, but you do want to know if you accidentally add non-compliant names to the zone file. Having the name server nag you with warnings about non-compliant names is also a reminder for you to wean your users away from those names.

The *transfer-format* Clause

The transfer-format option tells named whether or not it is allowed to put more than one answer in a single message. Two settings are allowed:

one-answer   for compatibility with older servers

many-answers   for better performance

The default transfer-format setting is one-answer. In the example, the global value for transfer-format is set to many-answers to enhance performance.

> **NOTE** There are several other options that can be set to enhance server perfor-
> mance. See the "Performance Tuning" section in Chapter 8, "Special BIND
> Configurations," for a description of all of them.

The value set in the `transfer-format` statement applies to all remote servers. The
`server` command, listed in Table 5.1, can be used to override the global setting on a
server-by-server basis. The `check-names` value set in the previous section affects the
defaults used by the `zone` command. The `zone` statement, also listed in Table 5.1, defines
which zones are loaded by the server and can be used to override the global setting on a
zone-by-zone basis. The `options` statement sets global default values, while other commands in the `named.conf` file set specific values for individual items.

Several options can be set that affect all zones or all servers. The designers of BIND have
set the defaults correctly for the vast majority of configurations. Zones and servers that
need other values are exceptions and should be treated as such by defining the exceptional
characteristics directly on the `zone` or `server` statement. You'll see examples of this in
the `zone` statement later in this chapter. In most cases, I prefer to set exceptional values
specifically for the zone or server that is being affected. Global values should be used for
the general case, which means that in most cases, the default values do not need to be
changed. For this reason, most `named.conf` files contain very few settings in the `options`
statement.

Setting the Correct Path Names

The most commonly used `options` statement defines the working directory for the
server:

```
options {
        directory "/var/name";
};
```

In this `options` statement, the keyword `directory` defines the default directory for
`named`. The literal enclosed in quotes is the path name of the directory. `named` reads files
from and writes files to the default directory. The default directory name is also used to
complete any filename specified in the configuration file. Therefore, if a command somewhere later in the configuration file includes the filename `named.local` with this default
directory defined, the full path name of the file would be interpreted as `/var/name/
named.local`. If the `directory` clause is not specified in the `named.conf` file, the direc-
tory defaults to the directory from which `named` was run. Most system administrators
decide to explicitly define the directory in the `options` statement to ensure that the correct directory is always used and to document which directory is being used for any other
administrator who might read the configuration.

named writes several different output files that are used to check the status of the name server. In addition to setting a default directory, it is possible to define individual path names in the options statement for several of the files that named produces. Don't do this. It gains you nothing and can confuse others who attempt to diagnose a name server problem on your system.

The options statement can also define the path name of the named-xfer program. named-xfer is the program used by slave servers to transfer the zone file from the master server. By default, the path name of this program is /usr/sbin/named-xfer on most Linux systems. If for some reason the program is not located in the directory where your system expects to find it, named will not be able to complete zone transfers. You can tell named where to find the program by using the options command, as in this example:

```
options {
        directory "/var/name";
        named-xfer "/sbin/named-xfer";
};
```

Despite all of the possible options, the options command in the named.conf file on most Linux name servers is only used to define the default domain. The only other statement found in most named.conf files is the zone statement.

The *zone* Statement

The zone statements are the most important statements in the configuration file, and they constitute the bulk of the named.conf file. A zone statement performs the following critical configuration functions:

- It defines a zone that is serviced by this name server.
- It defines the type of name server that this system acts as for the zone. A server can be a master server or a slave server. And because this is defined on a per-zone basis, the same server can be the master for some zones while being a slave for others.
- It defines the source of domain information for a zone. The domain database can be loaded from a local disk file or transferred from the master server.
- It defines special processing options for the zone.

Listing 5.2 contains a sample zone statement that illustrates all of these functions.

Listing 5.2   A Sample zone Statement

```
zone "foobirds.org" in {
        type master;
        file "foobirds.hosts";
        check-names warn;
};
```

Every zone statement begins with the zone command, followed by the name of the zone written as a literal enclosed in quotes. The in keyword means that this zone contains IP addresses and Internet domain names. This is the default, so it is not really required. The curly braces enclose a list of options for this zone.

Required Clauses

The first two clauses defined inside the curly braces of the example are found in every zone statement. The type master clause says that this server is the master server for the foobirds.org domain. Other possible values for the type clause are

slave   identifies this as a slave server for the domain.

hint   identifies this as the hint file that is used to initialize the name server during startup. Every server has one hint zone.

stub   identifies this as a stub server. *Stub servers* are slave servers that only load the name server pointers from the master server's database. You probably won't use this value. It is primarily useful for non-recursive servers that want to refer a query to another server in the same way that root servers refer questions to other servers. The uses for stub servers are discussed in Chapter 8.

The file "foobirds.hosts" clause points to the file that contains the domain database information. For a master server, this is the file that is created by the domain administrator.

Optional Clauses

Many other clauses, beyond the type and file clauses, can be included in the zone statement. Appendix B, which describes the syntax of the zone statement, provides a complete list. The sample zone statement in Listing 5.2 contains one of these additional clauses.

The last clause is in Listing 5.2 primarily to illustrate that options can be defined for a specific zone. The check-names warn option specifies what the server should do if it finds invalid host names in the zone file. The acceptable values for this option are exactly the same as those for the check-names clause in the options statement: fail, warn, and ignore. In this case, though, there is no need to specify master, slave, or response because the type of zone is defined elsewhere in the zone statement. When I need to define optional processing for a zone, I prefer to do it in the zone statement so that only the zone that really requires the optional processing is affected.

In most named.conf files, the zone statements are even simpler than the example shown in Listing 5.2. For one thing, only one of the servers in a zone is the master for the zone. For another, very few servers need to be configured for any type of optional processing. Let's look at some realistic examples of Linux named.conf configuration files.

A Caching-Only Configuration

The caching-only configuration is the foundation of all server configurations because all servers cache answers. The options and zone statements found in the named.conf file of a caching-only server are also found in the configuration of master and slave servers. Because of this, the caching-only configuration is a great place to start talking about server configuration.

The basic caching-only configuration is so ubiquitous that Red Hat 6 creates one during the Linux installation. Listing 5.3 contains the named.conf file created by Red Hat.

Listing 5.3 Red Hat's Default named.conf File

```
options {
        directory "/var/named";
};


//
// a caching only nameserver config
//
zone "." {
        type hint;
        file "named.ca";
};


zone "0.0.127.in-addr.arpa" {
        type master;
        file "named.local";
};
```

The configuration opens with an `options` statement that defines `/var/named` as the default directory for `named`. Red Hat and most other Linux distributions use this directory for `named` files. All subsequent file references in the `named.conf` file are relative to this directory.

Initializing the Root Cache

The two `zone` statements in this caching-only configuration are found in all server configurations. The first `zone` statement defines the hint file that is used to help the name server locate the root servers during startup. The statement starts with the `zone` command. This is followed by the name of the zone. In this case it is `.`, which is the name of the root. The `type` clause identifies this as a hint file, which tells `named` that this is the special file that contains pointers to the root servers. The `file` clause names the file that contains the pointers. In this case, one of the traditional names, `named.ca`, is used. Other systems use the name `named.root` or `root.cache`. You can name the file anything you like. If your Linux system creates the files for you, like Red Hat 6 does, it doesn't make any sense to go in and change the name of the file. In fact, changing the name can make it harder for other administrators to analyze your server configuration. But you could change the name if you wanted to.

Declaring the Loopback Zone

The second `zone` statement makes the server the master for its own loopback address. Okay, I admit it. Technically, this is a master server, which may appear to contradict what I said about this being a caching-only server. But every server is the master server for its own loopback domain, and no other server will ever ask this server to resolve the loopback address or attempt to transfer the loopback zone from this server. This is simply a basic part of the configuration of every server and it doesn't change the fact that this is a caching-only server.

The second `zone` statement identifies the domain as `0.0.127.in-addr.arpa`, which is the special name assigned to the loopback domain. The `file` clause says that the source of domain information for this zone is a local file called `named.local`. Again, this is a traditional name that you can change if you wish. However, there is no good reason to change the name of this file and doing so could make it harder for others to help you support the server.

The `named.conf` file in Listing 5.3, which the Red Hat installation program generates, can be copied and used on any Linux system where it would run without modification. The only parameter in the entire file that might require modification is the default directory. If you decided to place the `named` files in another directory, you should specify that directory as the default directory. Other than that one possible change, nothing else would ever need to be modified to run this caching-only configuration on any Linux system.

Essential Configuration

PART 2

The Slave Server Configuration

Configuring a slave server is almost as simple as configuring a caching-only server. A slave server's named.conf file starts with the same three configuration statements described earlier. The statements that make it a slave server are added to these basic configuration commands. Because of this, you can start with a caching-only configuration to test your system before you configure it as a slave server and then build the slave server by modifying the caching-only configuration. The best way to describe this process is to build a hypothetical slave server.

Assume that wren (172.16.5.1) is the master server for the foobirds.org domain and the 16.172.in-addr.arpa reverse domain. To configure parrot as a slave server for those domains, you add two new zone statements to the named.conf file on parrot to create the configuration shown in Listing 5.4.

Listing 5.4   A Slave Server's named.conf File

```
options {
        directory "/var/named";
};

// a slave server configuration
//
zone "." {
        type hint;
        file "named.ca";
};

zone "0.0.127.in-addr.arpa" {
        type master;
        file "named.local";
};

zone "foobirds.org" {
        type slave;
        file "foobirds.hosts";
        masters { 172.16.5.1; };
};
```

```
zone "16.172.in-addr.arpa" {
        type slave;
        file "172.16.reverse";
        masters { 172.16.5.1; };
};
```

The configuration file in Listing 5.4 contains all of the statements you have already seen, because all servers use a hint file and a loopback domain database file, and most administrators prefer to define the default directory inside the configuration file. Of the five statements in this file, only two are new.

Slave Zone Statements

The two new `zone` statements declare zones for the domains `foobirds.org` and `0.16.172.in-addr.arpa`. The `type` clause in each `zone` statement says that this is a slave server for the specified domain.

The `file` clause has a different purpose than those that you have seen before. In the previous examples, the file identified by the `file` clause was the source of the zone information. In this case, the file is the local storage for the zone information. The ultimate source for the information is the master server.

The `masters` clause identifies the master server. There can be more than one IP address provided in this clause, particularly if the master server is multi-homed and thus has more than one IP address. In most configurations, only one address is used, the address of the master server for the specified domain.

The slave server downloads the entire zone file from the master server in a process called a *zone file transfer*. When the file is downloaded, it is stored in the file identified by the `file` clause. You do not create or edit this file; it is created automatically by `named` using the zone data provided by the master server. After the zone is downloaded, the slave server can load it directly from the local disk. The slave will not transfer the zone again until the master server updates the zone. (Chapter 2, "The DNS Protocols," provides information on how the slave knows when the zone has been updated.)

Unlike the hint file and the local host file, which use traditional names, the files created to store zone information should be given descriptive names. In Listing 5.4, the `file` clauses assign the names `foobirds.hosts` and `172.16.reverse` to the files that respectively hold `foobirds.org` host information and `172.16.0.0` reverse domain information. Descriptive names are important for the files on a slave server because a slave can provide backup to a large number of domains. Descriptive names make it much easier to figure out which file contains what information.

Essential Configuration

PART 2

The sample slave server configuration appears to involve five files: the named.conf file and the four files that it mentions. But two of those files, foobirds.hosts and 172.16 .reverse, are really just empty shells that will be filled by data from the master server. The other three files, the hint file, and the local host file, along with the named.conf file, are required for every server configuration. The next section takes a closer look at the hint file.

When to Create a Slave Server

The similarities in the configurations of a caching-only server and a slave server can raise questions about when it is appropriate to use a slave server instead of a caching-only server. Clearly, the level of effort required to configure a slave server is not the determining factor.

There are two basic reasons to create a slave server: to improve reliability and to improve performance. Improved reliability is the essential reason. Every zone has at least one backup slave server that is advertised by the master as an official backup. In fact, most zones have two such backups. But it is also possible to create slave servers for branch offices or remote parts of the enterprise to improve service or to reduce cost.

A good example of this is when a branch office has a low-performance connection to the rest of the enterprise. For example, consider a small office connecting through a dial-up PPP connection. In that case, queries for the local domain that must go over the dial-up link to reach an authoritative server may be slow or even unreliable.

Another example is a pay-for-use service, such as ISDN in my home state of Maryland. Each query that goes to a remotely located authoritative server incurs a minimum one-minute connection fee. In those cases, placing an unofficial slave server at the branch office can save time and money.

Here's how: The slave server downloads the entire zone, but only when the zone has been updated by the master server. The zone transfer uses TCP instead of UDP, which solves the problem of an unreliable dial-up connection because TCP ensures reliable data transfer. With complete knowledge of the local domain, the server can answer all queries about the local domain without forwarding them to the domain's official authoritative servers. This solves the charge-per-minute problem because the entire zone can easily be transferred in a minute, thus incurring no more cost than a single query does when it is forwarded to a remote server.

When to Create a Slave Server *(continued)*

An unofficial slave server does not interfere in any way with the operation and duties of the official slave servers because the master server does not advertise it. Because the slave server is not advertised, remote servers never query it. The slave server simply loads its cache with all of the information about the zone that it is slaved to and then acts as a caching-only server. In the past, you could configure your system as an unofficial slave server without even coordinating with the administrator of the master server because zone transfers were unrestricted.

Today, zone transfers are often restricted for security reasons, so if you need to create an unadvertised slave, you should coordinate with the administrator of the master server. The few e-mails or telephone calls needed for this coordination are probably the hardest part of creating an unofficial slave server, because, as you have seen, the configuration of a slave server is very simple.

The Root Hint File

The hint file contains information that **named** uses to initialize the cache. As indicated by the root domain (.) name on the **zone** statement, the hint file contains the names and addresses of the root name servers. The hint file helps the local server locate a root server during the startup. DNS is a rooted hierarchical database system. To find its way through the system, a server must be able to locate the root, which is the source of pointers to all external domain information. Chapter 1 describes how this works and why pointers to the root are so necessary.

The hint file is only used during startup. Once a root server is located, an authoritative list of root servers is downloaded from that server. The hint file is not referred to again until the local server restarts.

Caching the Hints

The special role of the hint file can be seen by looking in the cache. The `ndc dumpdb` command described in Chapter 3 dumps the contents of the cache to `/var/named/named_dump.db`. The `named_dump.db` file has three distinct parts: First is a section of comments that describe the zones defined in the server's `named.conf` file. Next comes a very large section labeled Cache & Data. This section contains all of the active cache data used by the server. After the active data, you'll see a section like the one in Listing 5.5.

Listing 5.5 Caching the Root Server Hints

```
; --- Hints ---
$ORIGIN .
.        3600000    IN    NS    A.ROOT-SERVERS.NET.    ;Cl=0
         3600000    IN    NS    B.ROOT-SERVERS.NET.    ;Cl=0
         3600000    IN    NS    C.ROOT-SERVERS.NET.    ;Cl=0
         3600000    IN    NS    D.ROOT-SERVERS.NET.    ;Cl=0
         3600000    IN    NS    E.ROOT-SERVERS.NET.    ;Cl=0
         3600000    IN    NS    F.ROOT-SERVERS.NET.    ;Cl=0
         3600000    IN    NS    G.ROOT-SERVERS.NET.    ;Cl=0
         3600000    IN    NS    H.ROOT-SERVERS.NET.    ;Cl=0
         3600000    IN    NS    I.ROOT-SERVERS.NET.    ;Cl=0
         3600000    IN    NS    J.ROOT-SERVERS.NET.    ;Cl=0
         3600000    IN    NS    K.ROOT-SERVERS.NET.    ;Cl=0
         3600000    IN    NS    L.ROOT-SERVERS.NET.    ;Cl=0
         3600000    IN    NS    M.ROOT-SERVERS.NET.    ;Cl=0

$ORIGIN ROOT-SERVERS.NET.
K        3600000    IN    A     193.0.14.129           ;NT=4 Cl=0
L        3600000    IN    A     198.32.64.12           ;NT=4 Cl=0
A        3600000    IN    A     198.41.0.4             ;NT=11 Cl=0
M        3600000    IN    A     202.12.27.33           ;NT=2 Cl=0
B        3600000    IN    A     128.9.0.107            ;NT=15 Cl=0
C        3600000    IN    A     192.33.4.12            ;NT=24 Cl=0
D        3600000    IN    A     128.8.10.90            ;NT=3 Cl=0
E        3600000    IN    A     192.203.230.10         ;NT=129 Cl=0
F        3600000    IN    A     192.5.5.241            ;NT=5 Cl=0
G        3600000    IN    A     192.112.36.4           ;NT=12 Cl=0
H        3600000    IN    A     128.63.2.53            ;NT=4 Cl=0
I        3600000    IN    A     192.36.148.17          ;NT=21 Cl=0
J        3600000    IN    A     198.41.0.10            ;NT=12 Cl=0
```

NOTE The named_dump.db file is explained in detail in Chapter 12.

This section of the dump file is clearly marked as containing hints. These values are distinct from the active data in the cache. Once operational, the server does not use this information like it does the other information in the cache. Values placed in the hint file are only used during startup. For this reason, the hint file cannot be used to store general information in the cache. The hints are only used to locate a root server. They can have no other purpose.

Contents of the *named.ca* File

Many Linux installation programs create a hint file for you during the initial installation of name server software. If you download BIND from www.isc.org as described in Chapter 3, you'll find a sample hint file in src/conf/workstation/root.cache. Regardless of where you get the BIND you use, the hint files on all Linux systems are essentially identical. The hint file provided by the Red Hat 6 installation contains the server names and addresses shown in Listing 5.6.

Listing 5.6   The Root Server Hint File

```
.                       3600000   IN   NS   A.ROOT-SERVERS.NET.
A.ROOT-SERVERS.NET.     3600000        A    198.41.0.4
.                       3600000        NS   B.ROOT-SERVERS.NET.
B.ROOT-SERVERS.NET.     3600000        A    128.9.0.107
.                       3600000        NS   C.ROOT-SERVERS.NET.
C.ROOT-SERVERS.NET.     3600000        A    192.33.4.12
.                       3600000        NS   D.ROOT-SERVERS.NET.
D.ROOT-SERVERS.NET.     3600000        A    128.8.10.90
.                       3600000        NS   E.ROOT-SERVERS.NET.
E.ROOT-SERVERS.NET.     3600000        A    192.203.230.10
.                       3600000        NS   F.ROOT-SERVERS.NET.
F.ROOT-SERVERS.NET.     3600000        A    192.5.5.241
.                       3600000        NS   G.ROOT-SERVERS.NET.
G.ROOT-SERVERS.NET.     3600000        A    192.112.36.4
.                       3600000        NS   H.ROOT-SERVERS.NET.
H.ROOT-SERVERS.NET.     3600000        A    128.63.2.53
.                       3600000        NS   I.ROOT-SERVERS.NET.
I.ROOT-SERVERS.NET.     3600000        A    192.36.148.17
.                       3600000        NS   J.ROOT-SERVERS.NET.
J.ROOT-SERVERS.NET.     3600000        A    198.41.0.10
.                       3600000        NS   K.ROOT-SERVERS.NET.
K.ROOT-SERVERS.NET.     3600000        A    193.0.14.129
.                       3600000        NS   L.ROOT-SERVERS.NET.
L.ROOT-SERVERS.NET.     3600000        A    198.32.64.12
.                       3600000        NS   M.ROOT-SERVERS.NET.
M.ROOT-SERVERS.NET.     3600000        A    202.12.27.33
```

The hint file contains only name server (NS) and address (A) records. Each NS record identifies a name server for the root domain (.). The associated A record gives the IP address for each server. These name-and-address pairs are the pointers to the root servers.

Using this list, the local name server can send out queries until one of the root servers responds with the current root server list.

NOTE The structure of these domain database entries is covered in Chapter 6, "Creating a Master Server."

Obtaining a Hint File

It is important to realize that you do not directly create or edit this file. The sample file in Listing 5.6 is provided by the Linux installation. But even if your system doesn't provide a hint file, it is easy to get one. A list of root servers is kept at the InterNIC. Download the file /domain/named.root from ftp.rs.internic.net via anonymous FTP. The file that is stored there is in the correct format for a Linux system, is ready to run, and can be downloaded directly to your hint file, as shown in Listing 5.7.

Listing 5.7 Downloading the Root Cache Hint File

```
[craig]$ ftp ftp.rs.internic.net
Connected to rs.internic.net.
220-*****Welcome to the InterNIC Registration Host  *****
     *****Login with username "anonymous"
     *****You may change directories to the following:
       policy            - Registration Policies
       templates         - Registration Templates
       netinfo           - NIC Information Files
       domain            - Root Domain Zone Files
220 And more!
Name (ftp.rs.internic.net:craig): anonymous
331 Guest login ok, send your complete e-mail address as password.
Password: craig@sybex.com
230 Guest login ok, access restrictions apply.
Remote system type is UNIX.
Using binary mode to transfer files.
ftp> get /domain/named.root /var/named/named.ca
local: /var/named/named.ca remote: /domain/named.root
200 PORT command successful.
150 Opening BINARY mode data connection for /domain/named.root (2769 bytes).
226 Transfer complete.
2769 bytes received in 0.998 secs (2.7 Kbytes/sec)
ftp> quit
221 Goodbye.
```

TIP   Download the named.root file every few months to keep accurate root server information in your hint file.

The final file used to configure all name servers is the local host file. Like the hint file, the local host file is a zone file that contains domain database records. The records it contains define the loopback domain.

The Local Host File

Every name server is the master of its own loopback domain, which only makes sense. The whole point of creating the loopback interface (1o0) is to reduce network traffic. Sending domain queries about the loopback address across the network would defeat that purpose.

The loopback domain is a reverse domain. It is used to map the loopback address 127.0.0.1 to the host name localhost. On our sample Red Hat system, the zone file for this domain is called named.local, which is the most common name for the local host file. Listing 5.8 contains the named.local file that the Red Hat installation provides.

Listing 5.8   Red Hat's localhost file

```
$ cat /var/named/named.local
@       IN      SOA     localhost. root.localhost.  (
                        1997022700 ; Serial
                        28800      ; Refresh
                        14400      ; Retry
                        3600000    ; Expire
                        86400 )    ; Minimum
        IN      NS      localhost.

1       IN      PTR     localhost.
```

Every Linux system that runs named has an essentially identical local host file. The one in Listing 5.8 was created automatically by the Red Hat installation; if your system doesn't create one, you can copy this one. There is really no need to edit or change this file to run it on your system.

The local host file contains three database records:

- The Start of Authority (SOA) record defines the default setting for the entire zone and provides information to slave servers that helps them determine when the zone should be transferred.
- The Name Server (NS) record advertises the authoritative server for this zone to remote servers.
- The Pointer (PTR) record provides the essential data in this file. It maps the loop-back address to the host name `localhost`.

Only the PTR record is needed. No slave servers will query this server for the SOA record of the loopback domain. No remote servers will ask this host what server is authoritative for the loopback domain. After all, every server in existence is configured to be master of the loopback domain. None of them need to ask any remote system about that domain. The SOA record and the NS record are not needed; it is merely traditional to include them. This file could be reduced from three records to one record and it would work just as well. But why would you bother? You don't even create this file. It comes with the Linux system and it works fine even with the extra records.

At this point, the content of the file is not really important, because they are always the same on every system. When something is invariable it does not really require much thought. You will, however, need to master all of these database records to create the configurations in the next chapter.

In Sum

Most name servers are caching-only servers or slave servers. For those servers, you do the following:

- Configure the resolver as described in Chapter 4.
- Create the `named.conf` file. On most Linux systems, the installation program will create a caching-only `named.conf` file for you.
- Download the `named.root` file from `ftp.rs.internic.net` and use it as the hint file. On most Linux systems, the installation program will create a hint file for you. Download one to get the latest list of root servers.
- Create the `named.local` file. On most Linux systems, the installation program will create a local host file for you. If yours doesn't, you can copy the one in Listing 5.8.

Configuring caching servers and slave servers doesn't seem very difficult, so what's the big deal about DNS configuration? The big deal is the master server, and that's what you're going to tackle next.

6

Creating a Master Server

In Chapter 5, "Caching and Slave Server Configuration," you configured all of the servers in your domain zone, all but one. The one remaining server is the zone's master server. It is the most important server in the zone and the most difficult to configure. The master server is the server that loads the zone from local domain database files. You, as the domain administrator, are the person who must create those database files. To do so, you must understand which database records are valid, the structure of those records, and the structure of the files that hold those records. This chapter provides that understanding. Let's start by examining the differences between the `named.conf` file on a master server and those that we used on caching-only and slave servers.

The *named.conf* File

A master server's `named.conf` file looks very much like the configuration files for caching-only servers and slave servers that were described in Chapter 5. In fact, the first sample `zone` command used in Chapter 5 was a `zone` command for a master server configuration. Differences in the `zone` command determine whether a system is being configured as a caching, slave, or master server for a specific zone. If the `named.conf` file does not contain a `zone` statement for a specific zone, the server will only cache answers for that zone and will not be authoritative for the zone. If the `zone` statement contains the `type master` clause, the server is the master server for that zone. If the `zone` statement contains the clause `type slave`, the server is one of the slave servers for the zone.

> **NOTE** While setting the `type` clause to `master` or `slave` tells the local system that it is a master or slave server, it does not make the local system an *official authoritative server*. Only the domain delegation in the parent domain provides the pointers to the official authoritative servers. This chapter assumes that you are creating an official master server.

In Chapter 5, `parrot` was configured as a slave server for `foobirds.org` and `16.172.in-addr.arpa`. That configuration pointed to `wren` (172.16.5.1) as the master server for those domains. Listing 6.1 contains the `named.conf` file for `wren`.

Listing 6.1   `named.conf` File for a Master Server

```
options {
        directory "/var/named";
};


// a master nameserver configuration
//
zone "." {
        type hint;
        file "named.ca";
};


zone "0.0.127.in-addr.arpa" {
        type master;
        file "named.local";
};


zone "foobirds.org" {
        type master;
        file "foobirds.hosts";
};


zone "16.172.in-addr.arpa" {
        type master;
        file "172.16.reverse";
};
```

The `zone` statements for the `foobirds.org` and `16.172.in-addr.arpa` domains declare the zones and say that this is the master server for those zones. The `file` clauses in the `zone` statements identify the files that contain the database records for those zones. The other statements in the file, which are the same statements we used in Chapter 5, specify the processing options, the location of the `hints` file, and the location of the local host file.

The configuration of the master server is much the same as any other server—you create a `named.conf` file, a `hints` file, and a local host domain file. The difference comes from the fact that you must also create the real domain database files used in the example. The `foobirds.hosts` file and the `172.16.reverse` file used in the example can't be downloaded from a repository. You must create them, and in order to do so, you must understand the syntax and purpose of the database records.

Domain Database Records

A domain database is built with standard resource records—also known as *RRs*. The standard resource records are defined in various RFCs and there are lots of them. BIND supports over 40 diffcrent RRs. All of these records are listed in Appendix C, "Resource Record Reference." Many are experimental records that were never widely implemented. Many are older records that have been superceded by newer, more efficient RRs. The remainder are the useful records used to build real configurations, and all of these are used somewhere in this book. Those that are useful in special circumstances are discussed in Chapter 8, "Special BIND Configurations." Those that relate to Dynamic DNS are covered in Chapter 9, "Dynamic DNS." And those that relate to DNS security are covered in Chapter 10, "DNS Security."

This chapter focuses on the half-dozen records that are used to build most DNS database files. Table 6.1 lists these basic database records.

Table 6.1   Essential BIND Domain Database Records

Record Name	Record Type	Function
Start of Authority	SOA	Marks the beginning of a zone's data and defines parameters that affect the entire zone.
Name Server	NS	Identifies a domain's name server.
Address	A	Maps a host name to an address.

Table 6.1   Essential BIND Domain Database Records *(continued)*

Record Name	Record Type	Function
Pointer	PTR	Maps an address to a host name.
Mail Exchanger	MX	Identifies the mail server for a domain.
Canonical Name	CNAME	Defines an alias for a host name.

These records are so ubiquitous that several of them have appeared already in this text and we haven't yet built a database file. The hint file contains NS and A records, and the local host file contains an SOA and a PTR record.

The basic functions of name service that we saw in the host table, mapping names and addresses and providing alternate names for hosts, are handled by the A, PTR, and CNAME records. The NS records provide the essential pointers that are needed to link together the hierarchical DNS databases. The SOA record provides data that is essential for keeping the distributed servers synchronized. Every zone file you build will contain at least some of these records.

The Structure of Resource Records

To read or write a zone file, you need to understand the resource records from which it is built. To understand the resource records, you need to understand the components from which they are built. Thankfully, all standard resource records contain the same basic components. The format of a standard resource record is as follows:

```
[name] [ttl] [class] type data
```

The *name* Field

name is the name of the domain object affected by this record. It could be an individual host or an entire domain. Unless the name is a fully qualified domain name, it is relative to the current domain. Two different A records illustrate this:

```
bear.mammals.org.  IN  A  198.12.83.4

hawk               IN  A  172.16.5.4
```

The name in the first line is easy to understand. It's clear that this record affects bear.mammals.org. With a fully qualified domain name there is no ambiguity. Despite the clarity it brings, a fully qualified domain name is rarely used in the *name* field of a resource record. The second sample line shows a much more common form, although the exact meaning of that line is less clear than the first. The name hawk is interpreted relative to the current domain. Assume the second line is in the zone file for the foobirds.org domain. In that case, hawk would be interpreted as hawk.foobird.org. To really understand what object is affected by the record, you must know the current domain. See the sidebar, "Understanding the Current Origin," for more information.

The at-sign (@) is the special value used in the *name* field to refer to the current origin. It is most commonly used to refer to the origin that the system derives from the zone command in the named.conf file. The domain name on the zone command is used as the initial origin value for the zone file. The very first *name* field in the zone file generally contains an @ to reference this origin value. The named.local file in Chapter 5 contains an example of this. The SOA record that opens that file contains an @ in the name field. Several more examples of this format are presented and explained in this chapter.

It is also very common to have a blank *name* field. When the *name* field is blank, the resource record affects the last named object. The last value of the *name* field stays in force until a new value is specified. Consider the following example:

```
puffin          A       172.16.5.17
                MX      5 wren.foobirds.org.
```

Assume that the current origin is foobirds.org. The first record applies to the domain object with the name puffin.foobirds.org. The second record, because it has a blank *name* field, also applies to puffin.foobirds.org.

Understanding the Current Origin

The term *current domain* used in the preceding section is not completely accurate; correct terminology is *current origin*. It is easy to think of the current origin as the current domain because the origin is a domain name. The reason that "current origin" is used is that the meaning is more precise than the meaning of "current domain." Domain is a fuzzy term. bear.mammals.org is a domain name, but so is mammals.org and org. What you mean when you say "domain" is not clearly defined. Origin, however, is an actual data value stored in the domain database. Recall the hints section of the named_dump.db file in Chapter 5. A short excerpt from the Cache & Data section of that file shows the following:

```
$ORIGIN cerf.NET.
noc 172621      IN A 192.153.156.22         ;NT=149 Cr=addtnl
$ORIGIN GTLD-SERVERS.NET.
J       518221  IN  A       198.41.0.21     ;NT=99  Cr=addtnl
F       518221  IN  A       198.17.208.67   ;NT=2   Cr=addtnl
K       518221  IN  A       195.8.99.11     ;NT=11 Cr=addtnl
```

Understanding the Current Origin *(continued)*

```
$ORIGIN internic.NET.
rs0 86221      IN    A     198.41.0.5     ;NT=17 Cr=addtnl
rs   86221     IN    NS    rs0.internic.net.    ;Cr=addtnl
     86221     IN    NS    ns2.netsol.com.      ;Cr=addtnl
     86221     IN    NS    noc.cerf.net.        ;Cr=addtnl
     86221     IN    NS    ns.isi.edu.          ;Cr=addtnl
     722       IN    A     198.41.0.6           ;Cr=answer
$ORIGIN rs.internic.NET.
ftp 86222 IN CNAME rs.internic.net.      ;Cr=auth
$ORIGIN com.
netsol 172625  IN    NS    NS.NETSOL.com.       ;Cr=addtnl
       172625  IN    NS    ns2.netsol.com.      ;Cr=addtnl
       172625  IN    NS    RS0.INTERNIC.NET.    ;Cr=addtnl
$ORIGIN netsol.com.
ns2    172625    IN   A    198.17.208.83        ;Cr=answer
NS     172625    IN   A    198.41.0.196         ;Cr=addtnl
$ORIGIN edu.
isi    172625    IN   NS   ns.isi.edu.          ;Cr=addtnl
       172625    IN   NS   EAST.ISI.edu.        ;Cr=addtnl
       172625    IN   NS   VENERA.ISI.edu.      ;Cr=addtnl
$ORIGIN isi.edu.
EAST   172625    IN   A    38.245.76.2          ;Cr=addtnl
VENERA 172625    IN   A    128.9.176.32         ;Cr=addtnl
ns     172625    IN   A    128.9.128.127        ;Cr=answer
$ORIGIN 0.127.in-addr.arpa.
0      86400    IN    NS   localhost.     ;Cl=5
       86400    IN    SOA  localhost. root.localhost. (
                  1997022700 28800 14400 3600000 86400 )  ;Cl=5
$ORIGIN 0.0.127.in-addr.arpa.
1      86400    IN    PTR  localhost.     ;Cl=5
```

This excerpt clearly shows the value assigned as the origin for various components of the database. The origin is literally a value in the database that is used by the system to complete relative domain names. The origin can be defined by the $ORIGIN directive, which is explained later in this chapter.

The Time-to-Live Field

The time-to-live (*ttl*) field defines the length of time in seconds that the resource record should be cached. All name servers cache responses and use those cached responses to directly answer queries. Caching vastly improves the efficiency of the DNS system. The problem with caching is that it has the potential for distributing out-of-date material.

Unlike authoritative servers that have built-in mechanisms for keeping zone information up to date, a caching server has no knowledge of when the master server for a zone changes the information it has cached. It will continue to answer queries from its cache until the information in its cache times out, even if the information in its cache is wrong. As the administrator of the domain, it's your responsibility to make sure that the remote servers don't cache stale information about your zone.

The *ttl* field permits you to decide how long remote servers can store information from your domain. You can use a short TTL for volatile information and a long TTL for stable information. If no TTL value is specified, the default TTL value defined for the entire domain is used. To set the TTL for the entire zone, use the $TTL zone file directive, which is discussed in detail in an upcoming section.

The *Class* Field

In practice, the *class* field is always the literal value IN. While IN is the only class value you are likely to use, there are three possible *class* field values for a resource record:

- HS for Hesiod servers
- CH for Chaosnet servers
- IN for Internet servers

Hesiod servers are network servers developed at MIT. Their use is largely limited to MIT. You won't use HS class records on your Linux server. The Lisp machines that used Chaosnet are no longer manufactured. The CH value is never used on a Linux DNS name server. All of the domain information you deal with is for TCP/IP networks and Internet servers, so you will use the IN value on all of your resource records.

If the class value is not defined on an individual record, the value is taken from the zone statement in the named.conf file. The same HS, CH, and IN values are valid for the zone statement. If no value is defined for the zone statement, it defaults to IN. Therefore, if you don't bother to set the class value at all, you'll get the correct setting. The resource record will default to the value of the zone statement and the zone statement will default to IN, which is just what you want.

The *Type* Field

The *type* field defines the type of resource record. The record type is a short acronym, such as NS or SOA, assigned to a resource record by the RFC that defines it. The types used in this chapter, which are the most commonly used record types, are listed in the Record Type column of Table 6.1. All of the record types supported by BIND 8 are listed in Appendix C.

The *Data* Field

The last field in the resource record is the *data* field, which holds the data that is specific to the resource record type. For example, in an A record, the *data* field contains an address. The format and function of the *data* field is different for every record type. When resource records are used in the text, the content and structure of the *data* field is described.

The bulk of a domain database file is composed of standard resource records. Yet they are not the only things you'll encounter in a zone file. BIND also provides some zone file directives that are used when building a DNS database.

Zone File Directives

BIND 8.2 provides four zone file directives that are used to simplify the construction of the zone file or to define a value used by the resource records in the file. The four directives are evenly divided into two commands that simplify the construction of a zone file, $INCLUDE and $GENERATE, and two that define values used by the resource records, $ORIGIN and $TTL.

The $TTL Directive

The $TTL directive defines the default TTL for resource records that do not specify an explicit time to live. The time value can be specified as a number of seconds or as a combination of numbers and letters. Defining one week as the default TTL using the traditional format is as follows:

```
$TTL 604800
```

One week is equal to 604800 seconds.

BIND 8 also supports a new format where one week can be defined as follows:

```
$TTL 1w
```

The possible values that can be used with the new format are as follows:

- w for week
- d for day
- h for hour
- m for minute
- s for second

Using this new format a TTL of 1 week, 4 days, 12 hours, and 10 minutes would be the following directive:

```
$TTL 1w4d12h10m
```

I know the traditional format so that is the one I use. If you like the new format, go for it. It works just as well as the traditional form.

How you define the default TTL is pretty simple. What you define as the default TTL is more complex. As described in the previous section, the TTL value controls how long remote servers cache answers from your zone. The advantage of caching is improved performance and the disadvantage is potentially that out-of-date information about your domain will be distributed. You need to set the TTL to a value that gives you the maximum performance improvement for the least amount of risk of bad data.

Select the correct value based on the volatility of the data in your zone. If your domain data changes constantly, use a short TTL such as an hour. If it changes infrequently, use a long TTL such as a week. Change in this context is not synonymous with growth. A domain that grows rapidly does not need a short TTL because, while more data is being added to the zone, the existing data is not changing. The old data, which may have been cached, is still valid. Change in this context means that the information about a specific network object changes.

For example, one day the address 172.16.12.1 is assigned to `crow.foobirds.org` and another day it is assigned to `wren.foobirds.org`. That type of change demands a short TTL. The rapid address changes that require a short TTL are associated with using the Dynamic Host Configuration Protocol (DHCP) to assign addresses to network clients and Dynamic DNS to update DNS with those address assignments. DHCP and Dynamic DNS are covered in Chapter 9.

In this chapter, we create a static domain. The domain administrator manually creates all of the database entries in the zone file for this domain. The zone has very little change. New records are constantly being added but few records are deleted and very few are changed. For a static zone, the $TTL directive sets a long default TTL for the domain that is then overridden for individual records that are targeted for change.

For example, assume that the nickname www points to the host `wren.foobirds.org` and that you're planning to move the Web service to `crow.foobirds.org`. A few weeks before the planned cutover, you make the following change to the zone file:

```
www 600 CNAME wren.foobirds.org
```

Assume that the $TTL directive in the file sets the default TTL to one week. The CNAME record that defines the www generic host name is given a specific TTL of 600 seconds to override the default TTL. Now, remote servers will only cache this record for ten minutes. When you're ready for the cutover to the new server, a new CNAME record is inserted in the zone that points to the new server. The two servers are left running in tandem for 15 minutes or so to let all of the caches in the Internet clear out the obsolete resource record. Then the old server is shut down and the transition is made without a hitch.

The $TTL directive is not the only zone file directive that sets a default value used by the resource records. The $ORIGIN directive also sets such a value.

The $ORIGIN Directive

The $ORIGIN directive sets the current origin, which is the domain name used to complete any relative domain names. By default, the value assigned to $ORIGIN starts out as the domain name defined on the zone statement. Use the $ORIGIN directive to change the setting. For example, the following directive changes the origin to ducks.foobirds.org:

```
$ORIGIN ducks.foobirds.org.
```

Like all names in a zone file, the domain name on the $ORIGIN directive is relative to the current origin unless it is fully qualified. In previous example, the name ends with a dot and thus is a fully qualified domain name. Assume instead that the zone statement defined the domain foobirds.org and the zone file contained the following $ORIGIN directive:

```
$ORIGIN ducks
```

The effect of this statement would be the same as the previous $ORIGIN directive. The name ducks is relative to the current origin foobirds.org. Therefore, the new origin is ducks.foobirds.org. Relative names in any resource records following this $ORIGIN directive in the zone file are relative to this new origin.

Again, assume that the following statements are excerpted from a single zone file and the zone statement for the file defines the domain name as foobirds.org:

```
crow A 172.16.12.5
$ORIGIN ducks
mallard A 172.16.22.3
$ORIGIN terns.foobird.org.
sooty A 172.16.55.1
```

The first A record applies to a domain object named crow.foobirds.org. The second applies to an object named mallard.ducks.foobirds.org. The last A record affects the object named sooty.terns.foobirds.org. There are three different domains within this one zone file.

> **NOTE**   Notice that a fully qualified domain name is used on the second $ORIGIN directive. If a relative name had been used, it would have been relative to the current origin, which at that point was ducks.foobirds.org.

The $ORIGIN directive allows multiple domains to be placed in a single zone file. The $INCLUDE directive permits multiple files to be placed into a single zone.

The $INCLUDE Directive

The $INCLUDE directive reads in an external file and includes it as part of the zone file. The external file is included in the zone file at the point where the $INCLUDE directive occurs.

The $INCLUDE directive makes it possible to divide a large domain into several different files. This might be done so that several different administrators can work on various parts of a zone without having all of them try to work on one file at the same time. An example might be a large domain with three administrators and 12 subnets, where each administrator is assigned responsibility for four subnets. The resulting zone file might contain the following $INCLUDE statements:

```
$INCLUDE foobirds.nets1to4
$INCLUDE foobirds.nets5to8
$INCLUDE foobirds.nets9to12
```

Each directive begins with the $INCLUDE keyword, which is followed by the name of the file. In this example, there are three separate files: foobirds.nets1to4, foobirds .nets5to8, and foobirds.nets9to12. All of the files are located in the directory pointed to by the directory clause in the named.conf file. In the case of the named.conf file shown earlier in this chapter, that would be /var/named, which is the directory used on most Linux systems. This is one way to use the $INCLUDE directive, but unless the zone is very large and simultaneously supported by multiple administrators, it does not really make sense to divide the zone up this way.

Supporting Multiple Domains in One Zone

It's more useful to use the $INCLUDE directive to support multiple domains within a single zone. Assume that the subdomain terns.foobirds.org and ducks.foobirds.org are not delegated domains. Assume that the same server that handles foobirds.org handles them all. All three domains are in one zone. In this case, it makes real sense to divide the different domains into separate files. It eliminates confusion when maintaining the files and makes it much easier to transition to fully delegated domains at some future date. Two $INCLUDE directives in the foobirds.org zone file would include the subdomains in that zone, as follows:

```
$INCLUDE terns.foobirds.hosts terns
$INCLUDE ducks.foobirds.hosts ducks
```

Again, the directive starts with the keyword $INCLUDE, which is followed by a filename, but this time a third field is added. The third field is the origin. If the origin is included, the file defined by the $INCLUDE directive is processed with that value as its current origin. After the file is processed, the origin is set back to what it was before the $INCLUDE directive.

In this example, the origin of the `foobirds.org` zone file is `foobirds.org`. The new origin on the first $INCLUDE statement is `terns`. Because it is a relative name as opposed to an absolute name, the new origin is interpreted as `terns.foobirds.org`. All of the resource records in the `terns.foobirds.hosts` file are processed as relative to this new origin. After they are processed, the origin returns to `foobirds.org`, only to be changed to `ducks.foobirds.org` by the next $INCLUDE directive. Using the $INCLUDE directive in this way is an excellent technique for maintaining multiple domains in a single zone.

The $INCLUDE directive is not the only directive that inserts zone data directly into the zone file. The $GENERATE directive, discussed next, is also used to insert resource records into the database.

The $GENERATE Directive

The $GENERATE directive is used to create a series of NS, CNAME, or PTR records. The resource records generated by the $GENERATE directive are almost identical, varying only by a numeric iterator. The $GENERATE directive is by far the most complex zone file directive. The following example shows the structure of the $GENERATE directive:

```
$ORIGIN 20.16.172.in-addr.arpa.
$GENERATE 1-4 $ CNAME $.1to4
```

The $GENERATE keyword is followed by the range of records to be created. In this example, the range is 1 through 4. The range is followed by the template of the resource records to be generated. In this case, the template is `$ CNAME $.1to4`. A $ sign in the template is replaced by the current iterator value. In this example, the value iterates from 1 to 4. This $GENERATE directive produces the following resource records:

```
1 CNAME 1.1to4
2 CNAME 2.1to4
3 CNAME 3.1to4
4 CNAME 4.1to4
```

Given that `20.16.172.in-addr.arpa.` is the value defined for the current origin, these resource records are the same as

```
1.20.16.172.in-addr.arpa. CNAME 1.1to4.20.16.172.in-addr.arpa.
2.20.16.172.in-addr.arpa. CNAME 2.1to4.20.16.172.in-addr.arpa.
```

```
3.20.16.172.in-addr.arpa. CNAME 3.1to4.20.16.172.in-addr.arpa.
4.20.16.172.in-addr.arpa. CNAME 4.1to4.20.16.172.in-addr.arpa.
```

These odd-looking records have a very specific purpose for delegating reverse subdomains. Delegating domains is the topic of Chapter 7, "Creating Subdomains." The purpose of these resource records, and the syntax and use of the $GENERATE directive are described there.

Now that you know what records and directives are available and what they look like, you're ready to put them together to create a database file.

The Zone File

There are two basic types of database files associated with most master servers: one I call the *zone file* and the other I call the *reverse zone file*. The zone file contains most of the domain information. Its primary function is to convert host names to IP addresses, so A records predominate, but this file contains all of the commonly used database records. Creating the zone file is both the most challenging and rewarding part of building a name server.

The best way to understand the structure and content of a zone file is to look at one and examine each record it contains. Let's look at the zone file for the foobirds.org domain.

In the foobirds.org domain, wren is the master server. Based on the named.conf file created at the beginning of the chapter, the name of the zone file for the foobirds.org domain is foobirds.hosts. That file contains the records as shown in Listing 6.2.

Listing 6.2   A Sample Zone File

```
$TTL 86400
;
;      The foobirds.org domain database
;
@       SOA    wren.foobirds.org. admin.wren.foobirds.org. (
               2000020501 ; Serial
               21600      ; Refresh
               1800       ; Retry
               604800     ; Expire
               900 )      ; Negative Cache TTL
;Define the nameservers
               NS      wren.foobirds.org.
```

```
                    NS      parrot.foobirds.org.
                    NS      bear.mammals.org.
;  Define the mail servers
                    MX      10 wren.foobirds.org.
                    MX      20 parrot.foobirds.org.
;
;       Define localhost
;
localhost       A       127.0.0.1
;
;       Define the hosts in this zone
;
wren            A       172.16.5.1
parrot          A       172.16.5.3
crow            A       172.16.5.5
hawk            A       172.16.5.4
kestrel         A       172.16.5.20
puffin          A       172.16.5.17
                MX      5 wren.foobirds.org.
robin           A       172.16.5.2
                MX      5 wren.foobirds.org.
redbreast       CNAME   robin.foobirds.org.
bob             CNAME   robin.foobirds.org.
kestral         CNAME   kestrel.foobirds.org.
www             CNAME   wren.foobirds.org.
news            CNAME   parrot.foobirds.org.
```

This zone file opens with a $TTL directive that sets the default TTL for all resource
records to one day. Comments, whether full-line comments or comments appended to the
end of a line, begin with a semicolon. All of the other entries in the file are standard
resource records. These records are a good example of an average domain configuration.

The SOA record

The first resource record in all zone files is an SOA record. There is one and only one SOA
record in a zone file. The SOA record declares that the resource records that follow it are
the authoritative information for the zone. It provides important administrative information about the zone to external servers, including the name of the master server, the name
of the domain administrator, and the information needed by slave servers to keep their
databases synchronized with the master. The name field of the SOA record names the
domain and the data field provides the administrative information.

The SOA Data Field

With all of this information, the data field of the SOA record is so long it normally spans several lines. In the `foobirds.hosts` file, the SOA record is six lines long. The parentheses are continuation characters. After an opening parenthesis, all data on subsequent lines are considered part of the current record until a closing parenthesis. Thus, all six of these lines comprise one resource record, as shown in Listing 6.3.

Listing 6.3   A Sample SOA Record

```
@   IN  SOA     wren.foobirds.org. admin.wren.foobirds.org. (
                2000020501 ; Serial
                21600      ; Refresh
                1800       ; Retry
                604800     ; Expire
                900 )      ; Negative Cache TTL
```

> **NOTE**   The @ in the name field of the SOA record refers to the current origin, which in this case is foobirds.org, because that is the value defined in the zone statement of the named.conf file. Because it ties the domain name back to the named configuration file, the name field of the SOA record is usually an @.

The data field of the SOA record contains seven different components. The components of the data field in the sample SOA record contain the following values.

wren.foobirds.org   This is the host name of the master server for this zone. Because you will only create the zone file on the master server, the value in this field will be one of the valid host names for the local computer. A list of authoritative servers occurs later in the zone file. That list includes all authoritative servers—the master and its slaves. The host name placed here indicates which of the authoritative servers is the master.

admin.wren.foobirds.org   This is the e-mail address of the domain administrator. Notice that the at-sign (@) normally used between the username (`admin`) and the host name (`wren.foobirds.org`) in an e-mail address is replaced with a dot (`.`). This special form of the e-mail address is always used in SOA records.

It is very important to provide a valid e-mail address for this value. Remote administrators may need to contact you about your domain. They can examine the SOA record, look at this field, and discover your e-mail address. Frequently, the username in this address is a generic name, such as `root`, `postmaster`, or `hostmaster`. If you use a generic name, make sure the mail is forwarded to a mailbox that someone actually reads. If you have a large domain maintained by multiple system administrators, use a mailing list that includes all of the domain server's administrators as the e-mail address.

2000020501   This is the serial number, a numeric value that tells the slave server that the zone file has been updated. To make this determination, the slave server periodically queries the master server for the SOA record. If the serial number in the master server's SOA record is greater than the serial number of the slave server's copy of the zone, the slave transfers the entire zone file from the master. Otherwise, the slave assumes it has a current copy of the zone and skips the zone file transfer. The serial number must be increased every time the domain is updated in order to keep the slave servers synchronized with the master. See Chapter 2, "The DNS Protocols," for a full description of the protocols used to keep the databases on the authoritative servers synchronized.

In Listing 6.3, the serial number is formatted to show the date that the zone file was last updated. The format is *yyyymmddrr*, where *yyyy* is the year, *mm* is the month, *dd* is the day, and *rr* is the revision number. The two-digit revision number allows for up to 100 updates a day. In the example in Listing 6.3, this is the first revision (01) created on the fifth day (05) of the second month (02) of year 2000. It is not necessary to format the serial number as a date. A simple sequential number will work, but the date format is the most popular because it provide additional, human-readable information about when the zone was updated.

21600   This number defines the amount of time in the refresh cycle. Every refresh cycle, the slave server checks the serial number of the SOA record from the master server to determine if the zone needs to be transferred. Every time the slave server downloads the zone file, it reads this value from the SOA record. The slave server uses this value as a timer to determine how long it should wait before again asking the master for the SOA record.

The example in Listing 6.3 defines the length of the refresh cycle in seconds. A refresh cycle of 21600 seconds tells the slave server to check four times a day. The refresh cycle can also be defined in weeks (w), days (d), hours (h), minutes (m), and seconds(s) using an alphanumeric format. For example, 6h would specify six hours, which is the same as 21600 seconds.

A low refresh cycle keeps the servers tightly synchronized, but a very low value is not usually required because the DNS NOTIFY message sent from the master server causes the slave to immediately check the serial number of the SOA record when an update occurs. (The DNS NOTIFY protocol is described in Chapter 2.)

Additionally, it is often the case that the DNS database does not change very rapidly. Computers are added to the network periodically, but not usually on an hourly basis.

When a new computer arrives, the host name and address are assigned hours, or even days, before the system is added to the network because the name and address are required to install and configure the system. Thus, the domain information is often disseminated to the slave servers before users begin to query for the address of the new system.

Dynamic DNS is the exception. Dynamic zones change rapidly, but DNS NOTIFY handles the dynamic environment. For Linux DNS servers, all of which understand DNS NOTIFY, the refresh cycle is essentially a redundant backup system to ensure that no update fails to be disseminated.

1800   This number defines the length of time in the retry cycle. The retry cycle tells the slave server how long it should wait before asking again when the master server fails to respond to a request for the SOA record. The time can be defined in seconds, as it is in the example, or it can be defined using the new w, d, h, m, and s alphanumeric syntax. The 1800-second value shown in Listing 6.3 can also be defined as 30m.

Don't set the value too low—half an hour (1800) or 15 minutes (900) are good retry values. If the server doesn't respond, it or the network it connects to may be down. Quickly retrying a down server gains nothing. Use a value that gives the server and the network a chance to recover and stabilize after an outage.

604800   This value is the expiration time, which is the length of time that the slave server should continue to respond to queries even if it cannot update the zone file. The idea is that, at some point in time, out-of-date data is worse than no data. This should be a substantial amount of time. After all, the main purpose of a slave server is to provide backup for the master server. If the master server is down and the slave stops answering queries, the entire network is down instead of having just one server down. A disaster, such as a fire in the central computer facility, can take the master server down for a very long time. The sample SOA record in Listing 6.3 uses a value of one week (604800); a value of one month (259200) would not be excessive. The alphanumeric format is also available for the expiration time. One week could be specified as 1w, and one month could be written as 4w.

900   The last value in the data field of the SOA record is the default time-to-live for negative caching servers. You know that all servers cache answers and the servers use those answers to respond to subsequent queries. Most of the answers cached by a server are standard resource records, as the cache dump found earlier in this chapter clearly shows. The server keeps cached records as long as they are valid and the TTL defines how long that is. Each resource record has a TTL, either a TTL defined specifically for that record or the default TTL defined by the $TTL directive. Yet there is a type of information that can be learned from an authoritative server for which there is no resource record and thus no explicit TTL. That information is *negative information*.

A name server can learn from the authoritative server for a domain that a specific piece of information does not exist. For example, the response to a query for `bittern .foobirds.org` would be that the domain name does not exist. This is valuable information that should be cached. But with no associated resource record, and thus no explicit TTL, how long should it be cached?

The negative cache TTL from the zone's SOA record tells remote servers how long to cache negative information. You decide how long remote systems should cache positive information about your zone using either the $TTL directive or the TTL field in the resource record. You determine how long servers cache negative information about your zone by setting a value on the SOA record.

The SOA record in Listing 6.3 sets the negative cache value to 15 minutes (900 seconds). I generally use a negative cache of no more than 15 minutes and often less—5 minutes isn't bad. My reasoning is this: If repeated queries for non-existent information are caused by a misconfigured system banging on a non-existent addresses, one hit every 15 minutes is not going to cause my system any trouble. But if the repeated queries are caused by a remote user who knows that a system with a certain name will soon come online, I'd hate to make that user wait more than 15 minutes once the system is available. You can, of course, set the negative cache TTL to any value that you find reasonable using either the numeric or alphanumeric syntax.

All of the components of the data field of the SOA record set values that affect the entire domain. All of these items provide information useful to remote servers. You decide how often slave servers check for updates and how long caching servers keep your data in their caches. The domain administrator is responsible for the design of the entire domain.

Defining the Name Servers

NS records are used to specify the name servers for a domain. The name field of the NS record contains the name of the domain being serviced and the data field contains the host name of a server for that domain. The NS records that follow the SOA record in the zone file in Listing 6.2 define the official name servers for the `foobirds.org` domain. The sample file lists three official name servers:

```
NS      wren.foobirds.org.
NS      parrot.foobirds.org.
NS      bear.mammals.org.
```

The NS records that define the official servers often follow directly after the SOA record. When they do, the name field of each NS record is usually blank to use the name value from the SOA record. In the zone file in Listing 6.2, the @ on the SOA record refers to `foobirds.org`. Therefore, these NS records all define name servers for the `foobirds.org` domain.

Although it usually appears near the start, the list of official servers can appear anywhere in the zone file. If you decide to place it later in the file, use an explicit value in the name field of the NS records to ensure that they refer to the correct domain object, as in the following example:

```
foobirds.org.   NS      wren.foobirds.org.
foobirds.org.   NS      parrot.foobirds.org.
foobirds.org.   NS      bear.mammals.org.
```

The zone file in Listing 6.2 contains three official name servers: one master and two slaves. This is a very common configuration. The first two NS records point to the master server `wren` that we configure in this chapter and the slave server `parrot` that we configured in Chapter 5. The third server is external to our network.

Name servers should have good network connections, and at least one of the slave name servers should have a path to the Internet that is independent from the path used by the master server. This enables the slave server to fulfill its purpose as a backup server, even when the network that the master server is connected to is down. Large organizations may have independent connections for both servers; small organizations usually do not. If possible, find a server that is external to your network to act as a slave server. Check with your Internet Service Provider (ISP). They may offer this as a service to their customers.

> **NOTE**   These NS records define the official name servers. These are the only name servers that are advertised as authoritative for this domain. Unless the `also-notify` option is used in the zone statement of the `named.conf` file, these are the only servers that receive a DNS NOTIFY message when the zone is updated. If you use unofficial slave servers as described in Chapter 3, do not add them to the official server list. You don't want them advertised. Instead, use the `also-notify` command as described in Chapter 8.

The SOA record and the NS records perform administrative functions for DNS. The SOA defines values needed by remote name servers and the NS records point to the official name servers for the domain. The first resource records in the sample file that provides information to applications outside of the domain name system are the Mail Exchange (MX) records.

Defining the Mail Servers

MX records tell e-mail applications where to deliver mail. The name field of an MX record contains the host name that appears in the e-mail address and the data field contains the host name of the server to which the mail should be delivered. In Listing 6.2, the first two MX records define the mail servers for the `foobirds.org` domain:

```
MX      10 wren.foobirds.org.
MX      20 parrot.foobirds.org.
```

The name field is still blank, meaning that these records pertain to the entire domain because the @ from the SOA record is still the last named object. If mail is addressed to *user*@`foobirds.org`, the mail is directed to the mail exchangers defined by these records.

The first MX record says that `wren` is the mail server for the `foobirds.org` domain with a preference of 10. The second MX record identifies `parrot` as a mail server for `foobirds.org` with a preference of 20. The lower the preference number, the more preferred the server. Therefore, `wren` is the preferred mail server for the `foobirds.org` domain and `parrot` is the backup server.

NOTE The MX record is only the first step in creating a mail server. The MX record is necessary to tell the remote computer where it should send the mail, but for the mail server to successfully deliver the mail to the intended user, it must be properly configured. How `parrot` handles the mail as `wren`'s backup is a function of how `sendmail` is configured on `parrot`. `sendmail` configuration is beyond the scope of this book; it's covered in *Linux Network Servers 24seven*, Craig Hunt, Sybex, 1999.

These MX records redirect mail addressed to the domain `foobirds.org`, but they do not redirect mail addressed to an individual host. Therefore, if mail is addressed to `jay@hawk.foobirds.org`, it is delivered directly to `hawk`; it is not sent to a mail server. This is a very flexible configuration that permits people to use e-mail addresses of the form *user*@*domain* when they like, or to use direct delivery to an individual host when they want that.

Some systems, however, may not be capable of handling direct delivery e-mail. An example is a Microsoft Windows system that doesn't run an SMTP mailer daemon. Mail addressed to such a system would not be successfully delivered, and worse, would probably be reported to you as a network error! To prevent this, assign an MX record to the individual host to redirect its mail to a valid mail server. There are two examples of this in the Listing 6.2 sample zone file:

```
puffin      A       172.16.5.17
            MX      5 wren.foobirds.org.
robin       A       172.16.5.2
            MX      5 wren.foobirds.org.
```

Look at the resource records for `puffin` and `robin`. The address record of each system is followed by an MX record that directs mail to `wren`. The MX records have a blank name field, but this time they don't refer to the domain. In both cases, the last value in the name field is the name from the preceding address record. It is this name that the MX record applies to. In one case, it is `puffin`, and in the other case, it is `robin`. With these records, mail addressed to `daniel@puffin.foobirds.org` is delivered to `daniel@wren.foobirds.org`.

MX records for individual hosts are not just used for systems that can't accept mail. Sometimes you'll see an MX record that refers back to the host itself. Consider the following example:

```
eagle        MX        5 eagle.foobirds.org.
             MX       10 wren.foobirds.org.
```

In this case, the first MX record says that `eagle` is the most preferred mail exchange server for `eagle`! This type of MX record is not required for mail delivery. It is done to speed mail delivery by reducing the number of DNS queries. The next section examines how mail programs use DNS and explains why this entry could reduce queries.

Processing MX Records

When a remote e-mail program has mail to deliver, it queries DNS for the MX records for the host name in the e-mail address. It then sorts those MX records by preference number. Thus, the lower the preference number, the earlier in the list a server appears, which makes servers with low preference numbers preferable to servers with high preference numbers. The e-mail program then tries to deliver the mail to each mail server in order. It stops processing the list if it finds a server that will accept the mail, or if it finds its own host name in the mail exchange server list. (See the sidebar "Avoiding Mailing Loops" for an explanation of why the remote mailer stops processing the MX list when it encounters its own host name.) If it cannot deliver the mail to any of the servers, it will query for the address of the host and attempt to deliver directly to that host.

It is the second query for the address of the host that can be avoided if the host is included in its own server list. Applying the MX list processing rules to the MX list for `eagle` shows that the remote mailer would first try `eagle` and would only fall back to `wren` if `eagle` did not answer. If both of these attempts failed, the system would not query for the address of `eagle` because it already has that information. Thus, one query is avoided. Sounds good, but the reality is a little different.

Notice that the sample zone file doesn't contain MX records that point back to the host that they service. There are two reasons for this. First, implementations usually vary from the ideal. The process of first querying for MX records, then querying for address records is an idealized process described in RFC 974, "Mail Routing and the Domain System."

In reality, many mail programs use the ANY query to get any and all records about a host. That one query retrieves the MX records and the A records. Therefore, a second query for the address is not needed and creating MX records that point back to the host they serve saves nothing. Second, the MX records in our zone file define domain-level mail servers. We are encouraging users to advertise *user@domain* style e-mail addresses; we don't expect to get much mail addressed to individual hosts.

Avoiding Mailing Loops

A backup mail exchange server determines how to deliver mail by querying DNS for a list of MX records just like any other server. However, it cannot just send the mail to each server in turn in the MX list because, in the hands of an MX server, MX records have the potential to create mail-routing loops.

Assume that we have three MX servers in this order of preference: wren, parrot, and jay. wren is down so the mail is delivered to parrot. parrot fetches the MX records and attempts to deliver the mail to wren. wren is still down. parrot queues the mail and does not attempt to deliver it to any other server on the MX list. This is to avoid loops. If parrot tries to deliver the mail to itself, a tight loop ensues. If parrot tries delivering the mail to jay, a bigger loop ensues because jay then starts sending the mail back to parrot, who sends it back to jay, and so on. To avoid these loops, a mail server stops attempting to deliver the mail when it finds itself in the MX list and queues the mail for later delivery. In effect, a backup server only attempts to deliver mail to MX servers that are more preferred than it is. Thus, in this list of three servers, parrot only tries to deliver mail to wren.

Using the same three servers, wren, parrot, and jay, assume that both wren and parrot are down:

The mail comes to jay.

1. jay discovers that the more preferred servers are down.

2. jay queues the mail for later delivery.

3. Later, jay processes its queue. wren is still down but parrot is back in operation.

4. This time, jay delivers the mail to parrot and it becomes parrot's responsibility to deliver the mail.

5. parrot keeps the mail in its queue until wren finally comes back online.

By only sending mail to more preferred servers, mailers avoid mail-routing loops and gradually move mail closer to its final destination.

Defining the Host Information

The MX record illustrates that the information in the DNS system goes beyond the information that is available in the host table. DNS provides more than name-to-address mapping. It also provides the essential name-to-address mappings and the facilities for defining host nicknames that are provided by the host table. This section describes the two resource records used to define host addresses and nicknames.

Assigning IP Addresses

The primary purpose of DNS is to map host names to IP addresses, so it is not surprising that the bulk of the zone file contains A records that do this mapping. The A record has a simple format. The name field contains the name of the host, and the data field contains the address to which the host name is mapped. The sample zone file contains the eight address records, shown in Listing 6.4.

Listing 6.4   Sample Address Records

```
localhost      A      127.0.0.1
wren           A      172.16.5.1
parrot         A      172.16.5.3
crow           A      172.16.5.5
hawk           A      172.16.5.4
kestrel        A      172.16.5.20
puffin         A      172.16.5.17
robin          A      172.16.5.2
```

The first A record in Listing 6.4 maps the name localhost.foobirds.org to the loopback address 127.0.0.1. This entry is included in the domain database because of the way that the resolver constructs queries. Remember that if a host name contains no dots, the resolver extends it with the local domain. So when a user enters **telnet localhost**, the resolver sends the name server a query for localhost.foobirds.org. Without this entry in the database, the resolver might make multiple queries before finally finding localhost in the /etc/hosts file, depending on how you have your nsswitch.conf file set. If you configure your system to check DNS first and then the host table, it is a good idea to have an entry for localhost.

The remaining seven entries in Listing 6.4 map specific host names to addresses. The host wren is assigned the address 172.16.5.1, parrot is assigned 172.16.5.3, crow is assigned 172.16.5.5, and so on. Use the A record to assign an address to a host manually.

In Listing 6.4, every host name has a unique address and every address has a unique host name. This does not have to be the case, as illustrated in Listing 6.5.

Listing 6.5   Address Records for Multi-Homed Hosts

```
owl          A       172.16.5.15
owl          A       172.16.7.32
owl5         A       172.16.5.15
owl7         A       172.16.7.32
```

In Listing 6.5, owl is a multi-homed host. The name owl is assigned both of the host's addresses, so a query for owl returns both 172.16.5.15 and 172.16.7.32. The remote system's resolver can sort out which address it wants to use. (As you learned in Chapter 4, "Configuring the Resolver," the resolver sortlist option can be used to control which address is used.)

The address of each interface of the multi-homed host is also assigned a unique name—owl5 and owl7 in Listing 6.5. These unique names permit those interfaces to be addressed directly for testing or other purposes. Even simple name-to-address mapping is more flexible in DNS than it is in the host table.

Defining Nicknames

Host name aliases, or nicknames, provide shorter names, "historic" names, generic names, and alternate spellings. (All of these nickname functions are described in Chapter 1, "The DNS Architecture.") The CNAME record is used to define a host alias. The name field of the CNAME record contains the host alias and the data field contains the official (canonical) name of the host. That's why CNAME is short for canonical name record. The last five records in the sample zone file are CNAME records, as shown in Listing 6.6.

Listing 6.6   Sample CNAME Records

```
redbreast      CNAME    robin.foobirds.org.
bob            CNAME    robin.foobirds.org.
kestral        CNAME    kestrel.foobirds.org.
www            CNAME    wren.foobirds.org.
news           CNAME    parrot.foobirds.org.
```

Moving down the list of CNAME records provides the following information: redbreast is a host name alias for robin. bob is also a nickname for robin. In this case, bob is a historic name from a time before we standardized on bird names. It still occasionally pops up out of an old mailing list or newsgroup so we keep the alias around. The kestral alias is used as an alternate spelling of kestrel because we have a user who just can't get the name right. The last two aliases provide the generic names www and news that users expect to find.

Properly Placing CNAME Records

Aliases cannot be used in other resource records. For example, don't use news .foobirds.org in the MX record. Use only the canonical name, which in this case is parrot.foobirds.org.

Because aliases cannot be used on other records, take care when placing CNAME records in the domain database. You have seen several examples of the fact that a blank name field refers to the previously named object. If the CNAME record is placed improperly, a record with a blank name field can illegally reference a nickname. For example, the zone file in Listing 6.2 contains these records for robin:

```
robin          A       172.16.5.2
               MX      5 wren.foobirds.org.
redbreast      CNAME   robin.foobirds.org.
```

A mistake in placing these records could produce the following:

```
robin          A       172.16.5.2
redbreast      CNAME   robin.foobirds.org.
               MX      5 wren.foobirds.org.
```

This would cause named to display the error "redbreast.foobirds.com has CNAME and other data (illegal)" because the MX record now refers to redbreast. Due to the potential for errors, many domain administrators put the CNAME records together in one section of the file instead of intermingling them with other resource records.

The zone does many things that the host file cannot do and almost everything that the host file does. The one thing that the host file does that the zone file doesn't do is map IP addresses back to host names. The reverse zone file handles that function.

The Reverse Zone File

The reverse zone file maps IP addresses to host names. This is the reverse of what the domain database does when it maps host names to addresses. The IP address numbers are the "names" in a reverse domain. The numbers in the address are reversed to make them compatible with the structure of a domain name. The network portion of the IP address becomes the domain name and the host portion of the address becomes a host name within the domain. For example, in the reverse domain, the address 172.16.5.2 is written as `2.5.16.172.in-addr.arpa`. All reverse domains are part of the special `in-addr.arpa` domain. The structure of reverse domain names is covered in Chapter 1.

In our example, the network address 172.16.0.0 becomes the reverse domain `16.172.in-addr.arpa`. Listing 6.7 contains the reverse zone file for this domain.

Listing 6.7   Reverse Zone File for `16.172.in-addr.arpa`

```
;           Address to host name mappings.
;
$ TTL  1d
@    SOA     wren.foobirds.org. admin.wren.foobirds.org. (
             2000021602   ;   Serial
             21600        ;   Refresh
             1800         ;   Retry
             604800       ;   Expire
             900 )        ;   Negative cache TTL
             NS      wren.foobirds.org.
             NS      parrot.foobirds.org.
             NS      bear.mammals.org.
1.5          PTR     wren.foobirds.org.
2.5          PTR     robin.foobirds.org.
3.5          PTR     parrot.foobirds.org.
4.5          PTR     hawk.foobirds.org.
5.5          PTR     crow.foobirds.org.
17.5         PTR     puffin.foobirds.org.
20.5         PTR     kestrel.foobirds.org.
1.12         PTR     trumpeter.swans.foobirds.org.
1.6          PTR     arctic.terns.foobirds.org.
```

Like other zone files, the reverse zone begins with a $TTL directive, an SOA record, and a few NS records. They serve the same purpose and have the same fields as their counterparts in the domain database, which were explained earlier in this chapter. The new record in this file is the PTR record.

Pointing Addresses to Names

PTR records make up the bulk of the reverse domain because they can be used to translate addresses to host names. When used in the reverse zone, the name field of the PTR record contains the IP address reversed and converted to a reverse domain name. The data field contains the host name to which the reverse domain name maps.

Look at the first PTR record in Listing 6.7. The name field contains `1.5`. This is not a fully qualified name, so it is interpreted as relative to the current domain, giving `1.5.16.172.in-addr.arpa` as the value of the name field. The data field is `wren.foobirds.org.`. The host name in the data field is always fully qualified to prevent it from being interpreted as relative to the current domain. A PTR query for `1.5.16.172.in-addr.arpa` (172.16.5.1) returns the value `wren.foobirds.org`. The next eight PTR records provide similar mappings.

NOTE Notice the last two PTR records in Listing 6.7. They point to hosts that are in different domains than the other hosts. There does not have to be a one-to-one mapping between one zone file and one reverse zone file. It is possible for the addresses covered by a reverse zone file to fall in multiple domains. Likewise, it is possible for a zone file to map names to addresses that come from multiple reverse domains.

Maintaining both a zone file and a reverse zone file may seem like a lot of trouble for a little gain; after all, most of the action happens in the zone file. But keeping the reverse zone up to date is important. Several programs use the reverse domain to map IP addresses to names for status displays. `netstat` is a good example. Additionally, some remote systems use reverse lookups to check on who is using a service and in extreme cases, the remote systems won't allow you to use the service if they can't find your system in the reverse domain.

Using Directives in the Reverse Zone File

Despite its special purpose, all of the zone file directives are valid for the reverse zone file. In fact, the $GENERATE directive is specifically designed for use in this file. In Chapter 7, you'll use $GENERATE to delegate reverse subdomains. Reverse domains can also be subdivided without formal delegations just like regular domains by using the $INCLUDE directive.

Assume you have a network, 192.168.30.0, with 256 addresses and two administrators independently assigning those addresses. You decide to give each of those administrators control over half of the addresses. Each administrator maps addresses in their own file and you then include those files in the reverse zone file. You might have the following reverse zone file:

```
$ TTL 1d
@    SOA     wren.foobirds.org. admin.wren.foobirds.org. (
             2000021602   ;   Serial
             21600        ;   Refresh
```

```
             1800          ;   Retry
             604800        ;   Expire
             900 )         ;   Negative cache TTL
             NS     wren.foobirds.org.
             NS     parrot.foobirds.org.
             NS     bear.mammals.org.
    $INCLUDE 192.168.30.0-127.rev
    $INCLUDE 192.168.30.128-255.rev
```

The files 192.168.30.0-127.rev and 192.168.30.128-255.rev contain the PTR records that are maintained by the two different administrators. You maintain the SOA record and NS records in the central reverse zone file. To do this, you need to update the serial number in the SOA record and issue an ndc reload command whenever the other administrators update their files.

An alternative to using a single reverse domain is to use the origin argument on the $INCLUDE directive to create undelegated reverse domains within the zone. Assume that your network address is 172.20/16 and that you have assigned responsibility to the addresses in 172.20.5/24 to one group and those in 172.20.6/24 to another group. The first group puts its PTR records in 172.20.5.rev and the other puts its PTR records in 172.20.6.rev. You might create the reverse zone file contained in Listing 6.8.

Listing 6.8   Using $INCLUDE in a Reverse Zone

```
    $ TTL 1d
    $ ORIGIN 20.172.in-addr.arpa.
    @    SOA    wren.foobirds.org. admin.wren.foobirds.org. (
             2000021602    ;   Serial
             21600         ;   Refresh
             1800          ;   Retry
             604800        ;   Expire
             900 )         ;   Negative cache TTL
             NS     wren.foobirds.org.
             NS     parrot.foobirds.org.
             NS     bear.mammals.org.
    $INCLUDE 172.20.5.rev 5
    $INCLUDE 172.20.6.rev 6
```

In a reverse domain, numbers are the domain names. The 5 at the end of the first $INCLUDE directive is a name that is interpreted relative to the current origin, which is 20.172.in-addr.arpa. This creates a subdomain name of 5.20.172.in-addr.arpa.

The 6 in the second $INCLUDE directive creates `6.20.172.in-addr.arpa`. These two subdomains are populated by the resource records from the files identified on the $INCLUDE directives.

Again, you'll need to manually update the serial number in the SOA record and reload the zone files when the administrators of the subdomains tell you that they have made a change. For large networks, it is this manual intervention that makes techniques such as using the $INCLUDE directive to create subdomains less desirable than fully delegated subdomains. Delegating subdomains is the topic of the next chapter.

In Sum

Only one name server in every zone is a master name server. It is the name server that has the original source files for that zone's domain database.

This chapter concludes Part 2, "Essential Configuration," with a basic master server configuration that includes the six basic domain resource records used to build most master server configurations. Part 2 began in Chapter 4 with a description of how to configure the resolver, which is required by every DNS client and server. It progressed in Chapter 5 with a description of how to configure the caching-only and slave servers for your network, which covers all servers except the master server. This chapter put the last piece in the basic configuration puzzle by covering the master server. With the information from Part 2, you can configure more than 90% of all of the name servers you will ever use. But it is that last 10% that causes most of the headaches!

Part 3, "Advanced Configurations," describes advanced configurations that will help you deal with that troublesome 10% of server configurations. The next chapter begins that discussion by looking at how to delegate subdomains, which is something you will need to do if your domain grows large.

Part 3

Advanced Configurations

Featuring:

- How to create non-delegated subdomains within a zone
- When, why, and how to create delegated child domains
- The role of glue records
- Using the $GENERATE directive to delegate reverse domains
- How and why forwarders and other specialized servers are used
- Using options to tune performance, notify unadvertised servers of updates, organize responses, and operate compatibly with older servers
- Using SRV records to advertise network services
- Understanding the Dynamic DNS (DDNS) protocol
- The benefits and dangers of DDNS
- Pre-populating zones to avoid DDNS
- Installing and using DDNS on a Linux system

7

Creating Subdomains

The reason that most organizations obtain a domain name is to assign names and addresses to individual hosts, but that is only part of the story. Your domain gives you the authority to create domains just as easily as you can create hosts. Purchasing a domain from an official registrar is a *delegation of authority*. You have both the responsibilities and the privileges that come with that delegation. You can, in turn, delegate authority to others to run domains that are subordinate to your domain. In the same way that subdirectories are used to better organize the information in a directory, subdomains rationalize a large domain.

Top-level domains, domains, and subdomains can all be called *domains*, which creates confusion. It is possible to differentiate domains as top-level, second-level, third-level, and so on, but this too can be clumsy. This chapter refers to domains as *parents* and *children*. A parent domain is the domain that creates the subordinate domain through delegation. The top-level domain `.org` is the parent of `foobirds.org` that, in turn, is the parent of `terns.foobirds.org`. A subordinate domain is the child of the domain that created it. Thus, `terns.foobirds.org` is the child of `foobirds.org`. Terminology based on the relationship between domains is essential for explaining subdomains and how they are created. To understand how subdomains are created, we must first understand delegation and when it is used.

Why Delegate Subdomains?

Some choose delegation and some have delegation thrust upon them! Okay, so I'm getting a little carried away by this election year. But this statement is not far from the truth. There are two basic reasons that organizations break a domain into subdomains: rational need and political necessity.

The rational reasons for creating subdomains are exactly the same as those reasons that motivated the creation of the domain name system:

size   A large domain, in either the number of hosts or the geographic dispersal, can benefit from the use of distributed servers.

growth   The demand for names can be handled better by distributing the service closer to the source of the demand.

management   A large volume of domain maintenance is more effectively handled by distributing the load to more servers and administrators.

reliability   Distributed servers provide redundancy for critical parts of the domain.

automation   Subdomains can take advantage of the BIND tools that automatically synchronize distributed servers.

These benefits are available to any subdomain. The rational need for these benefits is usually driven by a number of hosts that is so large it cannot be effectively served as a single zone. Perhaps the current servers are overwhelmed. More likely, the current administrative staff is overwhelmed. Delegating subdomains brings more equipment and more people to bear on the problem. The net result is improved responsiveness and performance.

Rational need, however, is not the only reason things get done. Anyone who has worked in an organization knows that office politics is a powerful force that is influenced very little by reality. Even a small domain may be subdivided into even smaller subdomains that reflect the structure of the organization more than any technical need.

Non-Delegated Subdomains

Frequently, organizational domains that do not have an underlying technical need are created without delegating a zone. Recall that zones and domains are not the same things, and that it is possible to have more than one domain in a zone file. Child domains contained within the parent's zone are subdomains, just like any other subdomains, except that the authority for these domains is not delegated to other servers or administrators.

Domains are really just names. Adding a subdomain to a parent zone can be as simple as adding names for that subdomain to the parent's zone file. For example, assume you administer the domain `small.org` and the influential sales department has demanded their own subdomain, despite the fact that they only have three computers. You could create the zone file shown in Listing 7.1.

Listing 7.1   Multiple Domains in One Zone

```
$ORIGIN small.org
$TTL 86400
;
@       SOA     tiny.small.org. logan.tiny.small.org. (
                2000020501 ; Serial
                21600      ; Refresh
                1800       ; Retry
                604800     ; Expire
                900 )      ; Negative Cache TTL
; Define the nameservers
                NS      tiny.small.org.
                NS      bear.mammals.org.
; Define the mail servers
                MX      10 tiny.small.org.
                MX      20 bitty.small.org.
; Define the hosts in small.org
teenie          A       192.168.30.4
tiny            A       192.168.30.1
itty            A       192.168.30.5
bitty           A       192.168.30.3
; Define the hosts in sales.small.org
sales           NS      tiny.small.org.
                NS      bear.mammals.org.
inside.sales    A       192.168.30.20
outside.sales   A       192.168.30.17
upside.sales    A       192.168.30.21
```

Domain names within the zone file are interpreted relative to the current origin. The default origin is taken from the `zone` statement in the `named.conf` file. To simplify the example, Listing 7.1 starts with a $ORIGIN directive to show clearly the domain name being used as the origin. Given this origin, the first four A records in the zone file assign addresses to `teenie.small.org`, `tiny.small.org`, `itty.small.org`, and `bitty .small.org`. The last three A records assign addresses to `inside.sales.small.org`,

outside.sales.small.org, and upside.sales.small.org. A remote user looking for
the address of upside.sales.small.org could easily believe that sales.small.org
was an independent zone with its own name servers.

The NS records are added to complete the charade. A query for the name servers of
sales.small.org returns a list that is identical to the server list for small.org. Since
these servers have a complete copy of the small.org zone, they also have a complete copy
of the information about sales.small.org. So in a way, they really are the authoritative
servers for sales.small.org.

Using Zone Directives for Non-Delegated Subdomains

Chapter 6, "Creating a Master Server," introduces some techniques for using zone file
directives to include more than one domain in a single zone file. Two of these directives,
$ORIGIN and $INCLUDE, can help create a subdomain within the parent zone file.

The $ORIGIN directive sets the current origin. Using it to change the origin makes it
easier to enter the database records for sales.small.org. Listing 7.2 contains the same
zone file as Listing 7.1 with the addition of a $ORIGIN directive.

Listing 7.2   Using $ORIGIN to Simplify a Zone File

```
$ORIGIN small.org
$TTL 86400
;
@       SOA   tiny.small.org. logan.tiny.small.org. (
                2000020501 ; Serial
                21600      ; Refresh
                1800       ; Retry
                604800     ; Expire
                900 )      ; Negative Cache TTL
;  Define the nameservers
              NS      tiny.small.org.
              NS      bear.mammals.org.
;  Define the mail servers
              MX      10 tiny.small.org.
              MX      20 bitty.small.org.
;  Define the hosts in small.org
teenie        A       192.168.30.4
tiny          A       192.168.30.1
itty          A       192.168.30.5
bitty         A       192.168.30.3
```

```
;  Define the hosts in sales.small.org
$ORIGIN sales.small.org.
@              NS      tiny.small.org.
               NS      bear.mammals.org.
inside         A       172.19.20.20
outside        A       172.19.20.17
upside         A       172.19.20.21
```

Listing 7.2 is essentially the same zone file as Listing 7.1—it is just slightly easier to maintain. But even with the $ORIGIN directive, I would not want to maintain a subdomain that was more than a few records long in this manner. Mistakenly adding the A record of a new host at the end of this file could put the host in the sales.small.org subdomain, even if you really wanted it in small.org.

Having everything in one file when multiple domains are involved is confusing. The $INCLUDE directive reduces the chance of this type of error by allowing you to put parts of a single zone into different files. In Listing 7.3, the zone is divided into two different files.

Listing 7.3   Using Separate Files for Non-Delegated Subdomains

```
[craig]$ cat /var/named/sales.hosts
;        Define the hosts in sales.small.org
@              NS      tiny.small.org.
               NS      bear.mammals.org.
inside         A       172.19.20.20
outside        A       172.19.20.17
upside         A       172.19.20.21
[craig]$ cat /var/named/small.org.hosts
$ORIGIN small.org
$TTL 86400
;
@      SOA   tiny.small.org. logan.tiny.small.org. (
             2000020501 ; Serial
             21600      ; Refresh
             1800       ; Retry
             604800     ; Expire
             900 )      ; Negative Cache TTL
;  Define the nameservers
               NS      tiny.small.org.
               NS      bear.mammals.org.
```

```
;  Define the mail servers
                MX        10 tiny.small.org.
                MX        20 bitty.small.org.
;  Define the hosts in small.org
teenie          A         192.168.30.4
tiny            A         192.168.30.1
itty            A         192.168.30.5
bitty           A         192.168.30.3
$ORIGIN sales.hosts sales
```

Listing 7.3 shows two different files, each displayed by a `cat` command. The first file, which I arbitrarily named `sales.hosts`, contains the name server and address records that I created for the `sales.small.org` subdomain. The second file is the zone file for `small.org`. The $INCLUDE directive incorporates everything from the `sales.hosts` into the `small.org` zone file. The first field on the $INCLUDE directive is the name of the file being loaded and the second field is the origin for that file, in this case, `sales` `.small.org`. (Don't remember the $INCLUDE syntax? It's covered in Chapter 6.)

The $INCLUDE directive makes it easier to maintain non-delegated subdomains, but non-delegated subdomains are only useful when there is no good technical reason for creating the subdomain. If you need to distribute the load to other servers and other administrators, creating a non-delegated subdomain won't help you. Even when the reasons for creating the subdomain are political instead of technical, a non-delegated subdomain may not be the answer. Sometimes the organization that demands its own subdomain also demands that you delegate authority for the subdomain to that organization. And frankly, I recommend that you always delegate your subdomains if you can. Don't take on responsibility for a subdomain if administrators closer to the action are willing to take the responsibility themselves.

Delegating a Domain

A domain does not really exist until its parent domain delegates it. The reason for this is clear from the DNS architecture described in Chapter 1.

The domain hierarchy is held together by a series of forward pointers. Starting from the root domain at the base of the DNS tree, any leaf on the tree can be found by following the pointers from the root through the parent domains to the domain that is responsible for the leaf. A Linux name server uses the hint file described in Chapter 5, "Caching and Slave Server Configuration," to locate the DNS root. Once the root is located, the pointers in the parent domains, which are the subject of this section, are used to traverse the DNS tree. A domain is delegated by creating a pointer in the parent domain. It is this pointer that brings the child domain into existence.

The pointer that creates a child domain is a list of servers for that domain and any additional records needed to help clients reach those servers, which are usually address records. Placing these records in the parent domain means that when the parent receives a query for information about the child domain, the parent points the client to the servers for the child domain. The client then sends subsequent queries directly to the servers for the child domain. If the pointers do not exist in the parent domain, the parent responds to the client that the child domain does not exist by sending a NXDOMAIN response code and the query stops at that point. Without a parent domain that contains the proper delegation, a child domain cannot exist. The series of dig queries in Listing 7.4 show this.

Listing 7.4   Viewing Subdomain Delegations with dig

```
# dig @a.root-servers.net royal.terns.foobirds.org
; <<>> DiG 8.2 <<>> @a.root-servers.net royal.terns.foobirds.org
; (1 server found)
;; res options: init defnam dnsrch

;; got answer:
;; ->>HEADER<<- opcode: QUERY, status: NOERROR, id: 38592
;; flags: qr; QUERY: 1, ANSWER: 0, AUTHORITY: 2, ADDITIONAL: 2
;; QUERY SECTION:
;;      royal.terns.foobirds.org, type = A, class = IN

;; AUTHORITY SECTION:
foobirds.org.        1D IN NS      wren.foobirds.org.
foobirds.org.        1D IN NS      bear.mammals.org.

;; ADDITIONAL SECTION:
wren.foobirds.org.   1D IN A       172.16.5.1
bear.mammals.org.    1D IN A       198.32.16.12

;; Total query time: 183 msec
;; FROM: almond.nuts.com to SERVER: a.root-servers.net   198.41.0.4
;; WHEN: Mon Mar 20 23:16:47 2000
;; MSG SIZE  sent: 35  rcvd: 121
```

PART 3

Advanced
Configurations

```
# dig @wren.foobirds.org royal.terns.foobirds.org +norecurse
; <<>> DiG 8.2 <<>> @ wren.foobirds.org royal.terns.foobirds.org +norecurse
; (1 server found)
;; res options: init defnam dnsrch

;; got answer:
;; ->>HEADER<<- opcode: QUERY, status: NOERROR, id: 38592
;; flags: qr; QUERY: 1, ANSWER: 0, AUTHORITY: 2, ADDITIONAL: 2
;; QUERY SECTION:
;;      royal.terns.foobirds.org, type = A, class = IN

;; AUTHORITY SECTION:
terns.foobirds.org.  1D IN NS    sooty.terns.foobirds.org.
terns.foobirds.org.  1D IN NS    arctic.terns.foobirds.org.

;; ADDITIONAL SECTION:
sooty.terns.foobirds.org.   1D IN A   172.16.30.250
arctic.terns.foobirds.org.  1D IN A   172.16.30.251

;; Total query time: 183 msec
;; FROM: almond.nuts.com to SERVER: wren.foobirds.org  172.16.5.1
;; WHEN: Mon Mar 20 23:16:47 2000
;; MSG SIZE  sent: 35  rcvd: 121
```

To illustrate that every parent in the path from the root is the child of some other domain, the queries start by showing that the root has delegated the foobirds.org domain. The root responds to the query for the address of royal.terns.foobirds.org with a DNS message that contains the list of servers for foobirds.org in the authority section and the addresses of those servers in the additional section.

The second query goes to the foobirds.org server. That server responds with the names and addresses of the servers responsible for terns.foobirds.org. The answer sections of both responses are empty, but the pointers provided by the authority and additional sections allow the client to query sooty.terns.foobirds.org directly for the address of royal.terns.foobirds.org.

Every domain must have a complete path all the way back to the root. A query to the root for dodo.extinct.foobirds.org points the client to the server for foobirds.org. But a query to the foobirds.org server for the domain extinct.foobirds.org returns an

NXDOMAIN error. The dig commands in Listing 7.5 show that the NXDOMAIN response code is returned when a domain is not delegated.

Listing 7.5   Results of dig Command When a Domain Isn't Delegated

```
# dig @a.root-servers.net dodo.extinct.foobirds.org
; <<>> DiG 8.2 <<>> @a.root-servers.net dodo.extinct.foobirds.org
; (1 server found)
;; res options: init defnam dnsrch

;; got answer:
;; ->>HEADER<<- opcode: QUERY, status: NOERROR, id: 38592
;; flags: qr; QUERY: 1, ANSWER: 0, AUTHORITY: 2, ADDITIONAL: 2
;; QUERY SECTION:
;;      dodo.extinct.foobirds.org, type = A, class = IN

;; AUTHORITY SECTION:
foobirds.org.        1D IN NS      wren.foobirds.org.
foobirds.org.        1D IN NS      bear.mammals.org.

;; ADDITIONAL SECTION:
wren.foobirds.org.   1D IN A       172.16.5.1
bear.mammals.org.    1D IN A       198.32.16.12

;; Total query time: 183 msec
;; FROM: almond.nuts.com to SERVER: a.root-servers.net   198.41.0.4
;; WHEN: Mon Mar 20 23:20:12 2000
;; MSG SIZE   sent: 35   rcvd: 121


# dig @wren.foobirds.org dodo.extinct.foobirds.org +norecurse

; <<>> DiG 8.2 <<>> @wren.foobirds.org dodo.extinct.foobirds.org +norecurse
; (1 server found)
;; res options: init defnam dnsrch
;; got answer:
;; ->>HEADER<<- opcode: QUERY, status: NXDOMAIN, id: 2552
;; flags: qr aa ra; QUERY: 1, ANSWER: 0, AUTHORITY: 1, ADDITIONAL: 0
```

```
;; QUERY SECTION:
;;       dodo.extinct.foobirds.org, type = A, class = IN

;; AUTHORITY SECTION:
foobirds.org.   900 IN SOA   wren.foobirds.org. admin.foobirds.org. (
                             2000020501      ; serial
                             21600           ; refresh
                             1800            ; retry
                             604800          ; expiry
                             900 )           ; negative ttl


;; Total query time: 160 msec
;; FROM: almond.nuts.com to SERVER: wren.foobirds.org  129.6.13.2
;; WHEN: Mon Mar 20 23:20:39 2000
;; MSG SIZE  sent: 39  rcvd: 91
```

The root believes that the domain extinct.foobirds.org could exist, and that if it does exist, the servers for foobirds.org will know about it. The NXDOMAIN response from the foobirds.org server clearly states that extinct.foobirds.org does not exist. The answer and additional sections of the response are empty, but the authority section provides the SOA record so that the remote server will know how long to cache this negative answer. Perhaps someone has created a domain they called extinct.foobirds.org and has told their friends all about it. They may have already created a zone file with all of the necessary records, but until the administrator of the parent domain creates the pointers for the new domain, it does not really exist. Unless the delegation is properly defined in the parent, the child cannot be reached.

Creating a Child Domain

Bringing a child domain into this world is fairly simple. In the parent domain, the following steps are taken:

- Define the name of the child domain.
- Name the servers responsible for the child domain.
- Define the addresses of the servers.

Listing 7.6 shows the foobirds.org domain with two subdomain delegations: one for terns.foobirds.org and one for ducks.foobirds.org.

Listing 7.6   A Zone File with Subdomain Delegations

```
$TTL 86400
;
;       The foobirds.org domain database
;
@       SOA   wren.foobirds.org. admin.wren.foobirds.org. (
                2000020501 ; Serial
                21600      ; Refresh
                1800       ; Retry
                604800     ; Expire
                900 )      ; Negative Cache TTL
;  Define the nameservers
                NS      wren.foobirds.org.
                NS      falcon.foobirds.org.
                NS      bear.mammals.org.
;  Define the mail servers
                MX      10 wren.foobirds.org.
                MX      20 parrot.foobirds.org.
;
;  Define localhost
;
localhost       A       127.0.0.1
;
;  Define the hosts in foobirds.org
;
wren            A       172.16.5.1
parrot          A       172.16.5.3
crow            A       172.16.5.5
hawk            A       172.16.5.4
kestrel         A       172.16.5.20
puffin          A       172.16.5.17
                MX      5 wren.foobirds.org.
robin           A       172.16.5.2
                MX      5 wren.foobirds.org.
redbreast       CNAME   robin.foobirds.org.
bob             CNAME   robin.foobirds.org.
kestral         CNAME   kestrel.foobirds.org.
```

Advanced
Configurations

PART 3

```
www             CNAME    wren.foobirds.org.
news            CNAME    parrot.foobirds.org.
; Delegate the terns.foobirds.org domain
terns           NS       sooty.terns.foobirds.org.
                NS       arctic.terns.foobirds.org.
; Delegate the ducks.foobirds.org domain
ducks           NS       ruddy.ducks.foobirds.org.
                NS       wren.foobirds.org.
                NS       bear.mammals.org.
; Glue records
sooty.terns     A        172.16.30.250
arctic.terns    A        172.16.30.251
```

The zone file shown in Listing 7.6 builds on the zone file we created for the foobirds .org domain in Chapter 6. All of the records in this file are identical to those shown in Listing 6.2, except for the last seven resource records. The first two new records define the name servers for the terns.foobirds.org domain:

```
; Delegate the terns.foobirds.org domain
terns           NS       sooty.terns.foobirds.org.
                NS       arctic.terns.foobirds.org.
```

The name field of the first NS record contains terns. It is not a fully qualified name so it is interpreted as relative to the current zone, which gives the name terns.foobirds.org. The second NS record has a blank name field so it also applies to terns.foobirds.org. These records define sooty.terns.foobirds.org and arctic.terns.foobirds.org as the servers for the new domain.

The next three NS records define the servers for the ducks.foobirds.org domain. Notice that wren.foobirds.org is one of the servers. wren is also a server for the parent domain foobirds.org.

It is very common for a server of the parent domain to be a slave server for its children. (Come to think of it, most of us wind up slaving for our children!) Using a server from the parent domain slightly reduces the number of queries that a client must send because the parent server answers the first query, as well as providing pointers to the other servers for the child domain. Even more important, the parent server often has better network connectivity than its children, and thus provides a more reliable backup service.

Glue Records

The last two records added to the zone file are special address records called *glue records*. Most address records assign addresses to hosts within the zone. Glue records are special because they define addresses for hosts that are not in the zone. In Listing 7.6, the glue records define the addresses of `sooty.terns.foobirds.org` and `arctic.terns.foobirds.org` as follows:

```
; Glue records
sooty.terns          A      172.16.30.250
arctic.terns.ducks   A      172.16.30.251
```

Listing 7.6 lists the `foobirds.org` zone. The hosts `sooty.terns.foobirds.org` and `arctic.terns.foobirds.org` are not in the `foobirds.org` zone. A separate zone has been delegated for `terns`. The administrator of that domain has the right to assign addresses to these hosts. So why are these addresses declared in the `foobirds.org` zone file?

The reason is simple. If the addresses weren't declared here, the addresses wouldn't be available to clients searching for information about the `terns.foobirds.org` domain. No client would be able to reach these servers because network connections depend on IP addresses, not names.

Imagine what happens when the parent zone doesn't contain the address for `sooty` or `arctic` and a remote client asks for information about a host in the `terns.foobirds.org` domain. `wren` provides the names of the servers but no addresses. The client is stumped. Without an address, it is unable to connect to `sooty` or `arctic` directly and it doesn't know who else to ask for the addresses. It can't ask `wren` because `wren` has already said it doesn't have the addresses. The query can't be resolved.

Glue records, however, are not required for all of the child domain servers defined in Listing 7.6. No glue record is needed for `wren` because its address is already defined in the zone file. No glue record is needed for `ruddy` because `wren` is a server for the `ducks.foobirds.org` domain and thus has access to the address of `ruddy` in its copy of the `ducks` zone file. Finally, no glue record is necessary for `bear.mammals.org` because its address can be obtained directly from the `mammals.org` zone, independent of the `foobirds.org` zone.

The basic rule for glue records is this: You must assign a glue address record when the server is located in a zone that is subordinate to the parent zone. When in doubt, it doesn't hurt to include the glue record.

Avoiding Lame Delegations

I opened this section on creating child domains by stating that a domain does not really exist until it is delegated by its parent domain. The great advantage of this is that you can develop and test a domain before activating it. In fact, you should always have the child domain running on all of its servers before putting the pointers to the domain in the parent domain. Doing so avoids lame delegations.

A *lame delegation* is a domain that has been delegated to servers that are not ready to handle the domain. As the administrator of the parent domain, it is your responsibility to ensure that you don't create lame delegations. Test each name server in the server list before delegating the domain. Listing 7.7 shows a test using the host command, which is described in detail in Chapter 11, "Testing DNS."

Listing 7.7   Checking the Servers Before Delegating

```
[craig]$ host -r -t soa ducks.foobirds.org wren.foobirds.org
Using domain server:
Name: wren.foobirds.org
Address: 172.16.5.1
Aliases:

ducks.foobirds.org SOA ruddy.ducks.foobirds.org dan.ruddy.ducks.foobirds.org(
                 2000032201    ;serial (version)
                      10800    ;refresh period
                       1800    ;retry refresh this often
                     604800    ;expiration period
                        900    ;negative TTL
                          )

[craig]$ host -r -t soa ducks.foobirds.org ruddy.ducks.foobirds.org
Using domain server:
Name: ruddy.ducks.foobirds.org
Address: 172.16.50.1
Aliases:

ducks.foobirds.org SOA ruddy.ducks.foobirds.org dan.ruddy.ducks.foobirds.org(
                 2000032201    ;serial (version)
                      10800    ;refresh period
                       1800    ;retry refresh this often
```

```
                     604800      ;expiration period
                        900      ;negative TTL
                          )
[craig]$ host -r -t soa ducks.foobirds.org bear.mammals.org
Using domain server:
Name: ns1.foobirds.org
Address: 172.22.13.2
Aliases:

Host not found.
```

Every zone must have an SOA record. Testing for the SOA record of the new zone lets you know if the zone exists and if the servers are ready to run. All three of the servers in this test are supposed to be authoritative for ducks.foobirds.org, but bear.mammals.org says it has never heard of that domain. Based on this result, I would not add the delegation for the ducks.foobirds.org domain to the foobirds.org zone. Instead, I would send a letter to the administrators of ducks saying that the zone isn't ready and telling them that they should check with the administrator of bear.mammals.org to see what's wrong.

So far, delegating subdomains looks pretty easy. First, check that all of the servers are running and if they are, add a few NS and A records to the zone file. Simple! Well, not always. Delegating subdomains for reverse domains can be much more complex.

Delegating Reverse Domains

An IP address is not the same thing as a host name. This is clear from the way that the structure of an IP address is reversed to create a host name for the reverse domain. Yet the difference is even more fundamental than this simple conversion implies. IP addresses are often written in dotted decimal notation as four distinct byte values. It is this four-byte value that is reversed to created the reverse domain name.

But an IP address is not made up of four distinct bytes; it is really a contiguous 32-bit value. Interpreting an address as four separate bytes severely limits its flexibility. The problem with reverse domain names is that they do interpret an IP address as four separate bytes.

Delegating on a Byte Boundary

All of the reverse domains discussed so far in this book treat the IP address as four separate bytes. Doing so simplifies the concept of reverse domains because it is easy to see how reverse domains map to addresses written in the classic dotted decimal style. It also simplifies the creation of reverse subdomain delegations.

The network address of foobirds.org is 172.16.0.0. The reverse domain 16.172.in-addr.arpa that we created for this network address is shown in Listing 6.7 in Chapter 6. Delegating subdomains within the reverse domain is as easy as delegating subdomains in a normal domain—if the reverse subdomains are delegated on byte boundaries. Listing 7.8 adds subdomain delegations to the 16.172.in-addr.arpa zone file.

Listing 7.8   Delegating Reverse Subdomains

```
$ORIGIN 16.172.in-addr.arpa.
$ TTL 1d
@    SOA      wren.foobirds.org. admin.wren.foobirds.org. (
                2000021602   ;   Serial
                21600        ;   Refresh
                1800         ;   Retry
                604800       ;   Expire
                900 )        ;   Negative cache TTL
;  Define the name servers
              NS      wren.foobirds.org.
              NS      falcon.foobirds.org.
              NS      bear.mammals.org.
;  Point addresses back to host names
1.5           PTR     wren.foobirds.org.
2.5           PTR     robin.foobirds.org.
3.5           PTR     parrot.foobirds.org.
4.5           PTR     hawk.foobirds.org.
5.5           PTR     crow.foobirds.org.
17.5          PTR     puffin.foobirds.org.
20.5          PTR     kestrel.foobirds.org.
1.12          PTR     trumpeter.swans.foobirds.org.
;  Delegate the addresses in 172.16.50.0
50            NS      ruddy.ducks.foobirds.org.
              NS      wren.foobirds.org.
;  Delegate the addresses in 172.16.6.0 and 172.16.30.0
6             NS      arctic.terns.foobirds.org.
              NS      sooty.terns.foobirds.org.
30            NS      arctic.terns.foobirds.org.
              NS      sooty.terns.foobirds.org.
```

The last six resource records in Listing 7.8 are the records that delegate the subdomains. Each is an NS record that defines a name server for the new domains. The first two of these NS records define the servers for 50.16.172.in-addr.arpa. These two servers will manage the address-to-name mappings for the 256 addresses from 172.16.50.0 to 172.16.50.255. The last four NS records give control over the addresses 172.16.6.0 to 172.16.6.255 and 172.16.30.0 to 172.16.30.255 (a total of 512 addresses) to the name servers arctic and sooty.

Delegating these domains was easier than delegating a normal domain; it didn't even require glue records. The cost of this simplicity is reduced flexibility. Delegating on a byte boundary means that addresses can only be delegated in blocks of 256. This is cumbersome if you don't want to delegate in multiples of 256, and it can be a big problem if you don't have 256 addresses to delegate.

Dividing Reverse Subdomains Without Delegation

Assume you have a network, 192.168.30.0, with 256 addresses and two administrators independently assigning those addresses. Clearly you cannot give them each a byte-boundary reverse subdomain—you only have 256 addresses. One approach to this problem is to keep everything in one zone while dividing the responsibilities for that zone between the administrators. Zone file directives help you do this.

Let's say you decide to give each of those administrators control over half of the addresses. Each administrator maps addresses in their own file and you then include those files in the reverse zone file using the $INCLUDE directive. You might have the reverse zone file shown in Listing 7.9.

Listing 7.9 $INCLUDE Directives in a Reverse Domain

```
$ TTL 1d
@    SOA      tiny.small.org. admin.tiny.small.org. (
             2000020501    ;    Serial
             21600         ;    Refresh
             1800          ;    Retry
             604800        ;    Expire
             900 )         ;    Negative cache TTL
             NS     tiny.small.org.
             NS     bear.mammals.org.
$INCLUDE 192.168.30.0-127.rev
$INCLUDE 192.168.30.128-255.rev
```

The files `192.168.30.0-127.rev` and `192.168.30.128-255.rev` contain the PTR records that are maintained by the two different administrators. You maintain the SOA record and NS records in the central reverse zone file. For this to work, you need to update the SOA serial number and issue an `ndc reload` command whenever the other administrators update their files.

Because you'll need to manually update the serial number and reload the zone files based on changes made by other administrators, I don't recommend using a non-delegated subdomain when you can use a real subdomain. The only time I use a non-delegated subdomain is when there is no technical reason for creating a real subdomain, and thus no other administrators to coordinate with. Therefore, using the $INCLUDE directive to create subdomains for the zone file in Listing 7.9 is less desirable than creating fully delegated subdomains. Luckily, BIND provides another zone file directive to deal with tough reverse subdomain delegations like this one.

Generating a Reverse Domain Delegation

Delegating a subdomain avoids the problem of manually reloading the zone that is associated with non-delegated domains. For that reason, you might want to turn the $INCLUDE directives shown in Listing 7.9 into delegated domains. The problem is that the simple byte-aligned delegation used for the `16.172.in-addr.arpa` domain in Listing 7.8 cannot be used for the `30.168.192.in-addr.arpa` domain. The two subdomains defined in Listing 7.9 share the values of a single byte. Dividing that byte is the challenge.

Because DNS treats the IP address as four distinct bytes, it can appear that the solution is to use all four bytes and delegate every address. This requires hundreds of NS records, but the $GENERATE zone file directive described in Chapter 6 makes it easy to generate hundreds of nearly identical records. Here's how the $GENERATE directive can be used:

```
$ORIGIN 30.168.192.in-addr.arpa.
$GENERATE 0-127 $ NS mini.small.org.
$GENERATE 0-127 $ NS micro.small.org.
$GENERATE 128-255 $ NS nano.small.org.
$GENERATE 128-255 $ NS little.small.org.
```

The four $GENERATE lines create 512 separate NS records—two for every address in this reverse domain because there are two servers defined for each delegated zone. This is easy to do but the problem with it leaps out at you as soon as you read the word *zone*. These NS records are delegating zones! A separate zone file will need to be created for every address on this network. That's 256 zone files! Clearly this is *not* the way to go for this small domain.

Surprisingly, delegating small reverse domains is sometimes more difficult than dealing with large domains. For large domains, delegating addresses in blocks of 256 is not usually a problem. Assume that you want to divide the addresses in the 16.172.in-addr.arpa zone into blocks of 10,000. Simply accepting a delegation of 10,240 addresses, which is a multiple of 256, makes it possible to delegate the addresses with two $GENERATE statements:

```
$GENERATE 10-49 $ NS buzzard.foobirds.org.
$GENERATE 10-49 $ NS condor.foobirds.org.
```

These directives delegate the 40 subdomains from 10.16.172.in-addr.arpa to 49.16.172.in-addr.arpa, creating 40 zones encompassing 10,240 addresses. Of course, this requires the remote servers to maintain 40 zone files, but that is probably no more difficult than maintaining one file with 10,000 entries. In fact, most system administrators find it easier to maintain the smaller files.

Using Indirection in Reverse Domains

While maintaining 40 files that each contain a few hundred entries is acceptable, maintaining hundreds of files that each contain only one line is not. Delegating a separate zone for each address in a small reverse domain is not the answer. The solution to this problem comes from realizing that domain names are just that—names. The names can be divorced from the numbers, which eliminates the four-byte barrier that we are struggling with. Simply create descriptive domain names for the two zones you want to create, delegate those two zones, and make the limiting four-byte names to be nicknames for names in the new domains you just created.

Here's how: In the 30.168.192.in-addr.arpa zone file, delegate two new subdomains and add CNAME records for every address assigning them canonical names in the new domains, as shown in Listing 7.10.

Listing 7.10 Using Indirection to Simplify Reverse Domains

```
$ORIGIN 30.168.192.in-addr.arpa.
$ TTL 1d
@    SOA    tiny.small.org. admin.tiny.small.org. (
            2000020501    ;   Serial
            21600         ;   Refresh
            1800          ;   Retry
            604800        ;   Expire
            900 )         ;   Negative cache TTL
     NS     tiny.small.org.
     NS     bear.mammals.org.
```

```
;  Delegate subdomain 0-127.30.168.192.in-addr.arpa.
0-127           NS mini.small.org.
0-127           NS micro.small.org.
; Create a CNAME record for every address from 0 to 127
$GENERATE 0-127 $ CNAME $.0-127
$GENERATE 0-127 $ CNAME $.0-127
;  Delegate subdomain 128-255.30.168.192.in-addr.arpa.
128-255         NS nano.small.org.
128-255         NS little.small.org.
; Create a CNAME record for every address from 128 to 255
$GENERATE 128-255 $ CNAME $.128-255
$GENERATE 128-255 $ CNAME $.128-255
```

The first interesting records in this file are the two NS records that define the name servers for 0-127.30.168.192.in-addr.arpa, thus delegating that new domain. 0-127 is not valid in an IP address, but it doesn't have to be. Even in a reverse domain, the value in the name field of a resource record is a name; names are not constrained by the rules of IP addresses.

The two $GENERATE directives that follow the subdomain delegation create CNAME records that map names in the 30.168.192.in-addr.arpa zone to names in the new 0-127.30.168.192.in-addr.arpa zone. The CNAME records define the names in the 30.168.192.in-addr.arpa zone as the aliases and the names in 0-127.30.168.192 .in-addr.arpa as the canonical names. Even though you have created a new domain to hold the address to name pointers, you must create these CNAME records. Remote servers don't know about the new domain. They will create reverse map queries using the standard rules for converting an IP address to a reverse domain name. They will look for address-to-name mappings in the 30.168.192.in-addr.arpa zone. The CNAME records will then link the query to the new domain.

The next four records do the same things for the 128-255.30.168.192.in-addr.arpa domain. The NS records delegate the zone and the $GENERATE directives create the CNAME records that link to that zone.

To complete the creation of the new zones, the subdomain administrators must create the named.conf files and the zone files for the new zones. A server for 0-127.30.168.192 .in-addr.arpa would have the following zone statement in its named.conf file:

```
zone "0-127.30.168.192.in-addr.arpa" {
        type master;
        file "192.168.30.0-127.rev";
};
```

This **zone** statement says that this server is the master server for the 0-127.30.168.192 .in-addr.arpa zone. Furthermore, it says that the zone file for this domain is named 192.168.30.0-127.rev. As shown in Listing 7.11, that zone file looks like any normal reverse zone file and is mostly composed of PTR records.

Listing 7.11 The 0-127.30.168.192.in-addr.arpa Zone

```
$ORIGIN 0-127.30.168.192.in-addr.arpa.
$ TTL 1d
@     SOA     mini.small.org. admin.mini.small.org. (
              2000020501   ;   Serial
              21600        ;   Refresh
              1800         ;   Retry
              604800       ;   Expire
              900 )        ;   Negative cache TTL
              NS  mini.small.org.
              NS  micro.small.org.
1             PTR tiny.small.org.
3             PTR bitty.small.org.
4             PTR teenie.small.org.
5             PTR itty.small.org.
17            PTR outside.sales.small.org.
20            PTR inside.sales.small.org.
21            PTR upside.sales.small.org.
```

Listing 7.11 contains the normal PTR records that you expect to find in a reverse zone. But remote servers will not directly query this zone. They will first go to the zone shown in Listing 7.10. Figure 7.1 shows how a query for the PTR record of 3.30.168.192.in-addr.arpa is processed.

Figure 7.1 A sample query with CNAME records

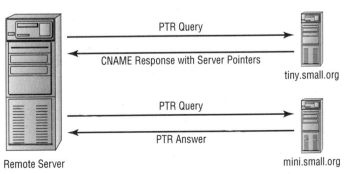

Remote Server

The remote server first sends a query for the PTR record of 3.30.168.192.in-addr.arpa to the server for the 30.168.192.in-addr.arpa zone. The SOA record in Listing 7.10 says that tiny is the master server for that zone. Yet tiny does not respond to the query with the requested PTR record. Instead, it tells the remote server that 3.30.168.192.in-addr.arpa is only an alias and that the real name it should be looking for is 3.0-127.30.168.192.in-addr.arpa.

Furthermore, it tells the remote server that the authoritative servers for the 0-127.30.168.192.in-addr.arpa domain are mini and micro. In Figure 7.1, the remote server then sends the PTR query to mini. mini finds the PTR record in the file shown in Listing 7.11 and responds with the information that 192.168.30.3 is the address of bitty.small.org. This level of indirection adds a step in resolving a reverse domain query, but it makes it possible to delegate subdomains that would otherwise be impossible to create.

This technique for eliminating the byte boundary as a barrier to delegating reverse domains is described in RFC 2317, "Classless IN-ADDR.ARPA Delegation." To me, the most important thing about this technique is that it removes the fog of confusion that surrounds names and addresses, and subnets and subdomains. Domain names and network addresses are not the same thing, and subnets and subdomains are unrelated. A single domain can have names that map to addresses from many different networks, and a network can have addresses assigned names in many different domains.

In Sum

When domains grow, the burden of maintaining those domains can become too great for the administrative staff of one master server. With DNS, the burden can be distributed to other servers by delegating authority over subdomains within the parent domain. Domains are delegated by placing pointers in the parent domain that refer queries for the child domain to the servers for that new domain. Delegation makes DNS flexible enough to grow as your domain grows and it is an essential component of the distributed nature of DNS.

Domain delegation is the most important advanced feature of DNS, and it is one that you will certainly use if your domain grows. There are many other advanced features, although they are not as widely used. These advanced features are the topic of Chapter 8, "Special BIND Configurations."

8

Special BIND Configurations

Not every domain can be described as average. Some domains have special needs that cannot be satisfied by the basic configurations covered in Chapter 5, "Caching and Slave Server Configuration," and Chapter 6, "Creating a Master Server." BIND provides a plethora of configuration options to satisfy almost any reasonable need. Appendix B, "`named.conf` Command Reference," lists them all. This chapter helps you make sense of these options by organizing them into topics.

This chapter is something of a laundry list because it contains several largely unrelated topics. The only real relationship among all of these topics is that they are configuration options that are only needed in special circumstances. Some of these topics generate more curiosity than they deserve. You'll probably discover that you don't need to use most of them, but you'll want to know something about all of them. In this chapter, you'll learn the advantages and the disadvantages of these options to better decide which ones are right for you.

Notifying Unadvertised Servers

DNS NOTIFY, which is described in Chapter 2, "The DNS Protocols," is a powerful feature that keeps the domain database of the slave servers tightly synchronized with the master server. The master sends a DNS NOTIFY message to its slaves telling them to update the database whenever the database on the master is changed. By default, a Linux server enables DNS NOTIFY and sends the NOTIFY messages to every slave server identified as an official domain server by an NS record in the zone file.

Listing 8.1 contains the first few lines in the `foobirds.org` zone file. The three NS records after the SOA record identify the official servers. `wren` is the master, and `parrot` and `bear` are the slaves. With a default configuration, `parrot` and `bear` are sent NOTIFY messages every time `wren` updates the zone.

Listing 8.1   The Official Slave Servers

```
$TTL 86400
;
;      The foobirds.org domain database
;
@      SOA   wren.foobirds.org. admin.wren.foobirds.org. (
             2000020501 ; Serial
             21600      ; Refresh
             1800       ; Retry
             604800     ; Expire
             900 )      ; Negative Cache TTL
;Define the nameservers
             NS    wren.foobirds.org.
             NS    parrot.foobirds.org.
             NS    bear.mammals.org.
```

BIND provides two options in the `named.conf` file that control whether or not the DNS NOTIFY protocol is used and what other servers are sent NOTIFY messages. Use the `notify` option to manually enable or disable the DNS NOTIFY protocol, as in the following example:

```
options {
  notify yes;
};
```

In this example, the DNS NOTIFY protocol is enabled. Because that is the default, enabling the protocol with the `notify` option is unnecessary. Conversely, the `notify no` option is necessary to disable the protocol.

> ***TIP*** Some administrators disable the protocol because they have old slave servers that don't support DNS NOTIFY. I think that approach is wrong. A better approach is to replace the old server with a low-cost Linux server that can do the job right.

Use the `also-notify` option to add computers to the list of servers that receive DNS NOTIFY messages. Adding 172.16.5.3 and 172.16.5.20 to the list of servers could be accomplished with this option:

```
options {
    also-notify { 172.16.5.3; 172.16.5.20; };
};
```

The `also-notify` option is very useful if you have unadvertised slave servers. Unadvertised slave servers, also called *unofficial slave servers* or *stealth servers,* are described in Chapter 5. They are used to overcome certain types of network connection problems. They are only intended for internal use and should not be advertised to the outside world. Nonetheless, they should be configured to provide accurate information to the internal clients that depend on them. Keeping information accurate requires tightly synchronized databases, which DNS NOTIFY gives you. If you have unadvertised slave servers, you should use the `also-notify` option.

The previous examples show `notify` and `also-notify` as global options. Used in the `options` statement, they affect all of the domains for which the server is the master, which could be several.

A better way to use these options is within a `zone` statement. Listing 8.2 shows a `named.conf` file with `notify` and `also-notify` options defined for individual zones.

Listing 8.2   Defining `notify` and `also-notify` for a Zone

```
options {
        directory "/var/named";
};


// the hint and localhost files
//
```

```
zone "." {
        type hint;
        file "named.ca";
};

zone "0.0.127.in-addr.arpa" {
        type master;
        file "named.local";
};

// a master nameserver configuration
//
zone "foobirds.org" {
        type master;
        file "foobirds.hosts";
        also-notify 172.16.5.3 172.16.5.20;
};

zone "16.172.in-addr.arpa" {
        type master;
        file "172.16.reverse";
        also-notify 172.16.5.3 172.16.5.20;
};

zone "swans.foobirds.org" {
        type master;
        file "swans.foobirds.hosts";
        notify no;
};
```

The last three zone statements in Listing 8.2 show that this server is the master of three zones. In the first two zone statements, an also-notify option is added to notify unadvertised slaves of zone updates. The last statement illustrates that the notify option can also be used in the zone statement. The notify no option disables the DNS NOTIFY protocol for the swans.foobirds.org zone, presumably because at least one of the slave servers for that zone cannot handle the protocol. Again, I don't recommend doing this. This example is presented to illustrate the availability of the option—nothing more.

Controlling Recursion

Your server, if left to its own devices, acts as a recursive server. When it receives a query, it does all of the work necessary to find the answer to that query and it does that work for any client that asks it. BIND makes it possible for you to change this behavior. You can disable recursion altogether, and you can control from which clients your server accepts recursive queries.

Use the `recursion` option to enable or disable recursion. By default, this option is set to `yes`, enabling recursion. To disable recursion, simply set this option to `no`.

You rarely want to disable recursion. Most servers receive queries from resolvers. The BIND resolver is a stub resolver that depends on recursion. Recursive searches are an essential part of the design of BIND. Non-recursive servers can only be used in limited circumstances, such as when a server serves only other servers. Unlike resolvers, servers send out non-recursive queries, so a server dedicated to serving other servers can be a non-recursive server.

An ISP might create a non-recursive server that has no direct clients but provides slave services for its customer's domains. You might advertise non-recursive servers to the outside world while providing separate recursive servers for your internal network. But if you create a non-recursive server, it cannot be listed as a name server in any client's `resolv.conf` file or as a forwarder in any server's `named.conf` configuration.

Recursions can also be controlled for individual clients. Use the `allow-recursion` option to identify the hosts from which your server will accept recursive queries. By default, a BIND server accepts recursive queries from any client. The following example limits recursive queries to those clients on the local network (172.16.5.0):

```
options {
    allow-recursion { 172.16.5/24; };
};
```

Most servers are recursive and you want to keep them that way. There are security reasons for limiting recursion to trusted clients, which are covered in Chapter 10, "DNS Security." The `allow-recursion` option lets you keep a recursive server while limiting recursion to the appropriate clients. This is more flexible than creating a completely non-recursive server, and is useful for more situations.

Performance Tuning

The named.conf file provides many options that can be used to tune the performance of your name server. The majority of these options can be ignored when you run DNS on a Linux system. Most options default to give you the best possible performance, but not all of them. Some options favor backward compatibility over performance. This section organizes the performance-tuning options into related topics to help you decide which tuning options may benefit your system.

Tuning Zone Transfers

Zone transfers can be one of the most demanding tasks for your server, particularly if your system is the master or slave for large zones or for a large number of zones. BIND provides several options to increase the efficiency of zone transfers and to reduce the burden they place on the system.

Zone Transfer Formats

The best way to increase the efficiency of the zone transfer is to put more than one resource record in the answer section of each DNS message sent during the transfer. The transfer-format option controls whether or not your server puts more than one resource record in the answer section of each message. This option can be set to one-answer, which is the default, or to many-answers, which increases efficiency.

The default is one-answer because many servers cannot understand the many-answers format. Set the transfer-format option to many-answers only if you're sure that the remote server can understand that format. All systems running BIND 8.2 support the many-answers format and, according to Microsoft's documentation, so does the Microsoft DNS server. Because each remote server might be different, I suggest setting this option inside a server statement, as in the following example:

```
server 172.27.31.6 {
   transfer-format many-answers;
};
```

Setting Inbound Transfer Limits

The transfer-format option affects both outbound and inbound transfers. For outbound transfers, the local server is the master server. All other zone transfer options affect only inbound transfers, those transfers in which the local server is a slave. These options are as follows:

transfers-in   defines the maximum number of inbound zone transfers that can be running at any one time. It defaults to 10, which is a substantial number.

In most business environments, a server is not even authoritative for 10 separate domains. Of course, exceptions exist. A classic example of an exception is an ISP server that provides backup DNS service for hundreds of the ISP's customers. Increasing the number of concurrent transfers should speed things up if the server has sufficient system and network resources to adequately handle the additional simultaneous file transfers.

`transfers-per-ns` defines the maximum number of simultaneous transfers allowed from any one remote server. The default is 2. With this setting, the local server can request only two concurrent zone transfers from any individual master server. In general, this is plenty. The default is a good value because most slave servers back up only a few zones from any one master server. Requesting too many zones from one server at one time can overwhelm that server and wind up reducing performance. Only increase this value in close coordination with the administrator of the master server, and after determining that the remote master and the local slave servers both have sufficient resources to support more concurrent transfers. Remember that the remote master is probably supporting several other slave servers.

`serial-queries` defines the maximum number of concurrent SOA requests the slave server will allow. The default is 4. Each time the slave needs to check the master zone's serial number, it requests the SOA record from the master. The default setting of `serial-queries` permits the slave to simultaneously have unanswered requests for SOA records to four different master servers. Except for ISP servers that back up hundreds of zones, the default should be sufficient.

`max-transfer-time-in` defines the maximum amount of time the local slave server waits for a remote master server to complete an inbound zone transfer. The default is 120 minutes, which is more than enough time. A zone file containing millions of resource records could be transferred in much less than two hours. This value should not need to be increased and there is no benefit in decreasing it.

`transfer-source` identifies the address of the network interface that should be used for zone transfers. By default, the server uses the network interface it considers closest to the remote server. This means that if the local server shares a network with the remote server, the interface to that network is used. Otherwise, the first address assigned to the local server is used. This option is only useful if your server has more than one network interface. If it does, and one of those interfaces provides superior performance when communicating with the remote server, specify that interface with this option. The `transfer-source` option can be specified in the `zone` statement so that the best interface can be selected for each remote server.

Special systems, like root servers handling the enormous .com domains or servers at an ISP providing service to hundreds of zones, can benefit from these tuning parameters. Most businesses do not have these kinds of requirements.

If the domain for your business is overwhelming your domain server, you need to look more at your domain design than at the tuning parameters of your server. DNS is a distributed system. The load of that system should be distributed among many servers and control of that system should be placed close to the users. If your domain is so large that it is overwhelming your server, your design is too centralized. You are ignoring the benefits of DNS and reliving the errors of a centralized host table. Divide and conquer!

Tuning for a Dial-Up Connection

At the opposite end of the spectrum from large systems that provide backup services for hundreds of domains are the very small servers connected to the network through dial-up connections. BIND also offers some configuration options for these small servers.

Use the dialup option to optimize the server for a dial-on-demand connection, such as an ISDN connection. By default, the dialup option is set to no. To tell the server that it is using a dial-up connection, use the following command:

```
options {
    dialup yes;
};
```

Setting dialup to yes reduces the amount of zone maintenance traffic sent by the server and attempts to concentrate the maintenance into a single call. This can be a significant benefit if you have a network that bills for each dial-up connection. When dialup is yes, the server only conducts zone maintenance when the heartbeat interval has expired. This means that a master server with dialup set holds any DNS NOTIFY messages until the timer expires and then sends them to all of its slaves. Likewise, a slave with dialup set holds any serial number checks until the heartbeat interval has expired.

By default, the heartbeat interval is 60 minutes. You can set the interval to the number of minutes you wish with the heartbeat-interval option, as in the following example:

```
options {
    dialup yes;
    heartbeat-interval  240;
};
```

In this example, the heartbeat-interval option is set to four hours (240 minutes). Any time up to a day is probably reasonable. The previous example shows heartbeat-interval being set as a global parameter. It is also possible to apply heartbeat-interval to an individual zone by setting it within a zone statement.

WARNING Setting heartbeat-interval to 0 means that zone maintenance will never occur.

The disadvantage of setting dialup to yes is that it slows the synchronization of domain databases. The advantage is that it husbands a limited and potentially costly resource, the bandwidth of a dial-on-demand connection. In general, critical servers are not located at the end of dial-on-demand connections. Often, these connections attach small offices to the main network. The servers at the end of these links are frequently unadvertised slave servers, as described in Chapter 5. The reason these servers exist is to save bandwidth and money. The dialup option can help.

Other Maintenance Timers

Before leaving the topic of timers, it is worth mentioning that there are other maintenance timers in addition to the heartbeat timer. BIND allows you to set these timers using the options described in the following sections.

The *cleaning-interval* Option

Each time a BIND 8 server retrieves a record from its cache to answer a query, it checks the record's TTL and discards the record if it is out of date. In addition, the server periodically scans the cache and deletes any records with expired TTLs. By default, it does this periodic task every 60 minutes. Use the cleaning-interval option to change this time, if you wish. However, 60 minutes is a good setting. It is often enough to take out the trash and not so often that it puts a load on the system.

Setting cleaning-interval to 0 means the system will never actively clean up the cache. Instead, it will check the TTL of a record and discard it if it is out of date, only when it receives a query for the record. Linux systems never crash and rarely reboot. Don't set cleaning-interval to 0. A lot of garbage can build up in the cache in the months between Linux reboots.

The *interface-interval* Option

Periodically, by default, every 60 minutes, BIND checks the network interface list to see if it has changed. If a new interface has been added, named starts a listener on that interface. If an interface has been removed, named deletes the listener for that interface.

This timer is not used to discover newly installed hardware. Every Linux administrator that I know turns the computer off before installing hardware and uses that time to do lots of other hardware and software maintenance. When the system reboots, named learns of the new interface at boot time. What the interface-interval option is really used for

Advanced Configurations

PART 3

is when a server has multiple network interfaces and runs software, such as the routing package `gated`, that dynamically adds and deletes interfaces from the interface list.

TIP I do not recommend running a single system as both a router and a DNS server, and this is one of the reasons why: If gated decides an interface is down because of a routing protocol problem, named may stop listening to a perfectly good network interface. Generally, I disable this feature by setting interface-interval to 0 when I must run BIND and gated together.

The *statistics-interval* Option

Periodically, the name server writes statistics to the statistics file. This option sets how often that happens. By default, statistics are written every 60 minutes, which I find to be a good value. Again, setting this to 0 prevents the server from automatically writing statistics, although the server will still dump statistics when the `ndc status` command is used.

Handling Clueless Clients and Servers

The reality of the network is that not every server is running BIND 8.2 on a Linux system. You cannot count on remote clients and servers that can handle the latest DNS features. BIND provides several options for backward compatibility with older clients and servers.

The option that is most obviously directed to supporting outdated systems is `has-old-clients`. The sole purpose of this option is to set values in other options. I don't use `has-old-clients` because I think the default values of the options it sets are already correct. Setting `has-old-clients` to yes sets:

- `auth-nxdomain` to yes. Setting `auth-nxdomain` to yes causes the server to set the authoritative bit (AA) in the DNS message header every time it returns a non-existent domain (NXDOMAIN) response. In effect, the local server pretends it is authoritative when it sends out negative information, even if it isn't. `yes` is the default for compatibility with older versions of BIND that expect negative information only from authoritative servers. These older systems will loop until the retry limit is exceeded and then fail if the AA bit is not set on negative information. Don't change this setting to no because it breaks these outdated servers, and there are still plenty of them.

- `rfc2308-type1` to no. The default is no. RFC 2308, "Negative Caching of DNS Queries (DNS NCACHE)," defines four response types for negative information. A Type 1 response includes the zone's SOA record and the NS records in the answer section. Some old resolvers and `sendmail` programs are confused by the NS records and interpret them as a referral to the other servers listed in the records. These older systems require a Type 2 response that contains only an SOA record in the answer section. Setting `rfc2308-type1` to `no` tells the server to send Type 2 responses instead of Type 1 responses. Set this option to `yes` only when you're sure that all of the resolvers and `sendmail` programs in your domain have been updated.

- `maintain-ixfr-base` to `yes`. The default is `no`. Systems running some of the first implementations of incremental file transfer do not maintain an update history file. Setting `maintain-ixfr-base` to `yes` causes the master server to maintain an update history file for its slaves. By default, this file is not maintained, which makes sense because each zone has only a few slaves, and the software on the slaves is usually very well maintained. Generally, a slave that has been updated to support incremental zone file transfers has been updated to do them right.

The discussion of the OPCODE field in Chapter 2 mentions the obsolete inverse query. An *inverse query* was used to learn the value in the name field of a resource record by providing the server with the value from the record's data field. Inverse queries were never recursive. The server would search for the information in its cache of answers and respond on that basis.

In practice, inverse queries were almost never used and then were only used to map addresses back to names—a task that can be handled much more efficiently by the reverse domain. Inverse queries were abandoned a long time ago. (The last program that I'm familiar with that used them was `nslookup` in BIND 4.6.) Despite this, BIND provides the `fake-iquery` option in case someone still has software that uses inverse queries. The `fake-iquery` option defaults to `no`, meaning that inverse queries are refused. Setting `fake-iquery` to `yes` causes the server to send a fake answer when it receives an inverse query.

A common incompatibility between PCs running Microsoft software and Unix systems is the way that each system ends a line of text. A conflict exists between the Unix newline character and the carriage return/linefeed characters used on Microsoft systems. BIND provides the `treat-cr-as-space` option in the unlikely circumstance that the zone file for your DNS server was edited on a PC and contains extraneous carriage returns. The default is `no` because it is assumed that the zone file was created on the DNS server. If you dabble in the Dark Side, you can use `treat-cr-as-space yes` to hide your sins.

Chapter 7, "Creating Subdomains," suggests testing to avoid lame delegations before you delegate a subdomain. Unfortunately, many parent domains don't test first, so lame delegations are common. When your server learns of a lame server delegation, it has learned valuable negative information that should be cached. Use the `lame-ttl` option to define how long a lame server indication should be cached. The default is 10 minutes, which is generally adequate. This can be increased to a maximum of 30 minutes.

Advanced Configurations

PART 3

Organizing Responses

Often, more than one record is returned as the answer to a query. A query for the NS records for the foobirds.org domain returns three NS records. A query for the address record of a multi-homed host might return multiple address records. A group of such records is called an *RRset* for *resource record set*. The order in which the records in an RRset are sent in a response is configurable.

Shuffling Resource Records

By default, BIND shuffles the records in an RRset in a round-robin manner. Using a round-robin shuffle, the NS records for foobirds.org in the first response are sent in the order wren, parrot, and bear. In the second response, the order is parrot, bear, and wren, and in the third response, the order is bear, wren, and parrot. A fourth response returns to the original order. The round-robin shuffle provides a simple form of load-sharing.

The round-robin shuffle has several advantages, but BIND lets you choose alternatives. BIND offers three ways to organize RRsets:

- cyclic is the formal name for the round-robin shuffle described previously. This setting provides basic load-sharing.

- random shuffles the records in a random order. This method emulates earlier versions of BIND that returned records in an unpredictable order.

- fixed returns the records in the order in which they are listed in the zone file. Preserving the order found in the zone file has minimal utility unless you want to direct all traffic to the first record in the set.

Use the rrset-order option to select the ordering method you prefer. Here is an example:

```
options {
    rrset-order {
        class IN type NS name "foobirds.org" order random;
        order cyclic;
    };
};
```

Each line inside the curly braces of the rrset-order statement defines the class, record type, and name field value of each record in the set, and defines the order in which the set should be returned. The first line inside the curly braces of the rrset-order statement in this example says that Internet (IN) name server (NS) records for the foobirds.org domain should be returned in random order.

The second line is `order cyclic`. It does not specify a class, type, or name, so it defaults to all classes, all types, and all domains. In effect, it says that, with the exception of the records defined in the previous line, all RRsets should be shuffled in a round-robin manner.

I don't fiddle with `rrset-order`. I like the load-sharing I get from the round-robin shuffle, which is the default I get if no `rrset-order` option is defined. You, however, might have a reason to change the order of the records your server puts in a response. The `sortlist` command is another way to change the order of records sent by your server.

The *sortlist* Command Revisited

The `sortlist` command organizes the records in an RRset based on the addresses of those records. The `sortlist` command used in the `resolv.conf` file is explained in Chapter 4, "Configuring the Resolver," along with a figure describing when and why it would be used.

Another `sortlist` option is available in the server configuration. It has the same affect on addresses as the resolver's `sortlist` command and it is used for the same reasons as those described in Chapter 4. The benefit of the server `sortlist` option is that it centralizes on the server a complex configuration task that would otherwise need to be done at each client.

Of course, this can only be done for clients that send their queries to the server; these are usually the clients that list the server in the name server list of their `resolv.conf` files. Use the `sortlist` option in the server's `named.conf` file to identify the clients that require address sorting and to define the `sortlist` for those clients. Listing 8.3 shows an example.

Listing 8.3   Using the Server sortlist Option

```
options {
    sortlist {
        { 172.16.9/24; 172.16.9/24; };
        { 172.16.12/24; 172.16.12/24; };
    };
};
```

The `sortlist` option in Listing 8.3 accomplishes exactly the same task as the `sortlist` example in Chapter 4. Each line in a `sortlist` option contains at least two addresses. The first address is the address of the client, which is followed by a list of addresses that are preferred in responses to that client. Look at the first line in the `sortlist` in Listing 8.3:

```
{ 172.16.9/24; 172.16.9/24; };
```

The first address in this line defines which clients are affected. The address is 172.16.9/24, which matches every address that starts with 172.16.9. If the server gets a query from any host on subnet 172.16.9.0, it applies this sort list to the answers it sends back to that client. The second address on this line tells the server to reorder any address records it sends to the client so that records containing an address that start with 172.16.9 are placed before any other address records.

The second line inside the `sortlist` option shown in Listing 8.3 creates a similar sort list for subnet 172.16.12.0. It checks for clients on subnet 172.16.12.0, and prefers addresses that start with 172.16.12 in responses to those clients.

> **NOTE** Recall that in the example in Chapter 4, the hosts on subnet 172.16.9.0 and on 172.16.12.0 depend on the services of a multi-homed host that has addresses on both networks. A query for the address of that host returns both addresses. Naturally, the host on subnet 9 prefers to use the subnet 9 address and the host on subnet 12 prefers to use the subnet 12 address.

Notice that in Listing 8.3, the address used to identify the client is the same as the address used to sort the addresses in the response. When the values in both fields are identical, you don't need to include both. The `sortlist` option shown in Listing 8.3 could be rewritten as follows:

```
options {
    sortlist {
        { 172.16.9/24; };
        { 172.16.12/24; };
    };
};
```

A sort list is not limited to one preferred address. Let's assume that a small company has three separate addresses for its in-house network: 192.168.24/24, 192.168.83/24, and 192.168.91/24. Further assume that you want to prefer in-house addresses in responses to every client. You could use the following `sortlist` option:

```
options {
    sortlist {
      { 192.168.24/24;
          192.168.24/24;
          { 192.168.83/24; 192.168.91/24 }; };
      { 192.168.83/24;
          192.168.83/24;
```

```
            { 192.168.24/24; 192.168.91/24 }; };
        { 192.168.91/24;
              192.168.91/24;
              { 192.168.24/24; 192.168.83/24 }; };
        };
    };
```

This example identifies three possible ways to sort addresses for three possible client addresses. Each definition is three lines long, and each prefers the client's local network, with the other in-house networks given the next highest preference. Here is one of the definitions broken out and explained:

```
{ 192.168.24/24;
      192.168.24/24;
      { 192.168.83/24; 192.168.91/24 }; };
```

The first line contains the address 192.168.24/24. This matches any query from a client whose address starts with 192.168.24. If the response to that client includes addresses, the next two lines are used to determine how those addresses are sorted. Addresses that start with 192.168.24 are the most preferred, and after that, addresses that start with either 192.168.83 or 192.168.91 are equally preferred. And all of these addresses are preferred above any other address.

In addition to addresses, keywords can be used in the sortlist option. localhost matches any address assigned to the server. localnets matches the network address of any network to which the server is directly attached. The sortlist option, which emulates the address-sorting behavior of BIND 4, is probably the most popular sort list configuration:

```
options {
    sortlist {
        { localhost; localnets; };
        {localnets; };
    };
};
```

If the source of a query is the local host, local network addresses are preferred. If the source is a local network, the local network address is preferred. In responses for all local queries, the server places addresses from the local networks before any external addresses. Given the potential complexity of determining the best way to sort addresses, this may be the only sort list you will ever use.

Advanced Configurations

PART 3

Special External Servers

BIND includes several configuration options to define the interaction between your server and other servers. You can decide to prefer some servers and to reject others. This section describes these various options and the reasons they are used.

Using Forwarders

When a server receives a query from a client, it checks its cache to answer the client. The server either answers the client directly with information from the cache, or uses information from the cache to locate a server that can help find the answer for the client, even if the only server it can find is a root server. The `forwarders` option changes this behavior.

When forwarders are defined, the local server uses the list of forwarders instead of the name server pointers in the cache to locate a server that can help it answer a client's query. A server configured to use forwarders sends all of the queries it can't answer directly from its own cache to the servers defined in the forwarders list. The forwarders list is defined with the `forwarders` option, as in the following example:

```
options {
forwarders { 172.16.5.1; 172.16.5.3; };
};
```

The forwarders list is similar to the list of name servers in the `resolv.conf` file. Each server is queried in turn. Subsequent servers are only queried if the preceding server fails to answer. Given the configuration in the previous example of the `forwarders` option, the local server first checks its local cache for the answer to a query. If it doesn't have the answer, it sends the query to the server at 172.16.5.1. If 172.16.5.1 fails to respond to the query, the local server sends the query to 172.16.5.3. If 172.16.5.3 also fails to respond to the query, the local server takes matters into its own hands and pursues an answer to the query, just as it would if the forwarders list didn't exist. This behavior of first asking the forwarders and then pursuing the answer directly can be changed with the `forward` option.

The `forward` option can be set to `first` or `only`. `first` is the default and it is the behavior described in the preceding paragraph. When `first` is set, the server first checks the forwarders and then pursues the answer directly. When `only` is set, the server will only ask the forwarders. If the forwarders do not answer, the query will fail—the local server will not attempt to answer the question on its own.

The purpose of creating a forwarders list is twofold. First, because the forwarders handle so many queries, they develop a rich cache of answers. Many queries are rapidly answered from the forwarders' cache once this rich cache develops.

Second, using forwarders can reduce traffic over the wide area network. The forwarders are normally located within the organization's private network or local area network. In some parts of the world, network connections are billed based on the amount of traffic or the number of connections. Using forwarders in these circumstances can save money.

Other times, it's not cost; it's connectivity. Access to the Internet may be limited. Most often, access is limited by a firewall for security reasons. In that case, the forwarders may be the only DNS servers allowed to connect to the outside world.

There are some good reasons to use forwarders, but don't get carried away. Most networks are not billed based on usage, so nothing is saved by using forwarders. Many firewalls allow DNS traffic or provide a DNS proxy server. Before implementing forwarders, make sure you actually need them.

I for one never use the `forward only` option. Many servers sitting behind firewalls use this setting to prevent the server from sending queries directly to the outside world. But I don't think it is the job of DNS to control outbound traffic—that is the firewall's job. The correct way to handle this is to filter all DNS traffic at the firewall and to decide there if you actually want to control outbound DNS traffic.

Not using `forward only` has the benefit of setting off an alarm at the firewall when servers attempt to query outside servers, which lets you know that either the servers are misconfigured or the forwarders are not doing their job. It also has the benefit of allowing internal queries to resolve even when the forwarders are unavailable. Let me explain.

Assume that you have a slave server in the `foobirds.org` domain seeking information about a host in the `terns.foobirds.org` domain. That server checks its cache. It doesn't have the information to directly answer the query, but it does have the NS records that point to the servers for the `terns.foobirds.org` domain because those records are part of the `foobirds.org` domain for which it is authoritative.

If `forward only` is set, the server cannot directly follow those NS records to the servers for the `terns.foobirds.org` domain, even if the servers in the forwarders list fail to answer the query. But if `forward first` is set, the server can resolve the internal query itself when the forwarders are unavailable. Most queries are internal queries. It is important to be able to resolve them directly, and internal queries are not an issue for the network firewall.

Selecting Preferred Servers

BIND queries the closest name server when multiple name servers are authoritative for the same domain. It determines which name server is closest based on the round trip time (RTT) of packets sent to the remote server. The servers are sorted by RTT and grouped

Advanced
Configurations

PART 3

together into *bands*. The closest band is 32 milliseconds wide and each successive band is 64 milliseconds wide. These bands are designed to separate servers on different continents into different bands.

Within a band, a server is selected if it is topologically closer to the local server. By default, a server is topologically closer if it shares a network with the local server. Use the topology option to change this behavior, as in the following example:

```
option {
    topology {
        192.168.83/24;
        192.168.91/24;
        !172.27/16;
    };
};
```

Name servers are considered "topologically closer" the higher they are in the topology list. Given this topology option, name servers from network 192.168.83.0 are the most preferred and 192.168.91.0 are the next most preferred. The last entry in this list begins with a !, which means that any other server in the same band is preferred over the servers on network 172.27.0.0.

I have never needed to use the topology option in a real configuration. Generally, named does a good job of picking the right server. This option is probably only useful if you have a unique network configuration.

Rejecting Bad Servers

In addition to selecting the best servers for the job, either through the forwarders option or the topology statement, BIND lets you identify servers that it should avoid. Use the blackhole option to define addresses that should be ignored as follows:

```
options {
blackhole { 172.27/16; };
};
```

With the blackhole option set, the local server would not query any server with an address from the network 172.27.0.0, even if the root servers said that a server on that network was authoritative for some domain. Not only that, the local server would not respond to any query, or any other message, coming from an address on that network. blackhole is an extreme measure that is primarily used to block traffic when an administrator believes a security attack or other critical problem is originating from the remote network.

A more common problem is a misconfigured server that gives out bad information. To address that problem, use the bogus option in a server statement. For example, if the server at 172.27.8.1 is badly configured and providing incorrect answers, you can tell your server to stop sending it queries and ignore any response it sends with the following server statement:

```
server 172.27.8.1 {
bogus yes;
};
```

Setting bogus to yes specifies that information coming from this server should be ignored. bogus can only be set within a server statement. Thus it affects only one server. By default, servers are assumed to know what they are talking about.

Defining a Private Root

Creating your own root sounds very sexy. Many domain administrators view the root servers as the ultimate DNS servers. The truth is that, while they are absolutely essential for DNS and are critical for the survival of the Internet, what they actually do is pretty boring. DNS is a distributed system. The really interesting information is on the distributed servers. Root servers point the way to the party, but they don't dance.

However, it is the mystique of the real root servers that generates more interest in private root servers than they deserve. Private root servers are non-recursive servers used in place of the real root servers on networks that are completely isolated from the Internet. When private root servers are used, DNS access is completely cut off from the outside world. In this day and age it is rare to find a network that has absolutely no access to the Internet, but it is possible. If you do not have any access to the Internet, you need to create a private root in order to run DNS.

> **NOTE** People often think of firewalled networks as networks that don't have access to the Internet. When they do, they think of a private root as a possible solution for a firewalled network. Don't believe it. Even in a firewalled network, users need to resolve the names of services located on the Internet. I suggest forwarders for that task. See the discussion in Chapter 10.

The Steps to Create a Private Root

Only a few steps are needed to create a private root. The first two steps take place on the systems that you designate as root servers. The final step takes place on every server in your domain. First, on the private root server, create a `named.conf` file that declares your private root server as a master of the root domain, as in the following example:

```
options {
        directory "/var/named";
};
// Declare the root zone
//
zone "." {
        type master;
        file "root.data";
};
zone "0.0.127.in-addr.arpa" {
        type master;
        file "named.local";
};
```

> **NOTE**   Notice this `named.conf` file does not have a hint file. It is the root so it doesn't need a hint file for the root.

Next, create a root zone file on the private root server that delegates your real domain to the authoritative servers for your domain. For example, assume you created a private root for `foobirds.org` on a system named `lark`. Your root zone file would look something like this:

```
$TTL 86400
;       A private root domain database
.       SOA    lark.foobirds.org. admin.lark.foobirds.org. (
               2000003291 ; Serial
               21600      ; Refresh
               1800       ; Retry
               604800     ; Expire
               900 )      ; Negative Cache TTL
;Define the root servers
               NS      lark.foobirds.org.
               NS      blackbird.foobirds.org.
;Delegate the foobirds.org domain
foobirds.org.  NS      wren.foobirds.org.
               NS      parrot.foobirds.org.
```

```
;  Delegate the 12.172.in-addr.arapa. domain
12.172.in-addr.arapa. NS      wren.foobirds.org.
12.172.in-addr.arapa. NS      parrot.foobirds.org.
;  Define the glue records
wren.foobirds.org.    A       172.16.5.1
parrot.foobirds.org.  A       172.16.5.3
```

Finally, every server on the private network needs to change its hint file from the standard file to one that points to the private root servers, as follows:

```
;  A hint file for the private root
.                        NS      lark.foobirds.org.
.                        NS      blackbird.foobirds.org.
lark.foobirds.org.       A       172.16.34.1
blackbird.foobirds.org.  A       172.16.23.1
```

Following these steps creates a private root. I don't use them and I don't recommend them. But these are the steps if you decide you need to create a private root of your own.

Defining Additional Information

Configuration options in the named.conf file are not the only way of customizing DNS. Special resource records can be used to add optional information to the DNS database. This section looks at how network names are defined in DNS, at how system administrator contact information is made available in DNS, and at a new way to identify network servers.

Defining a Network Name

In the prehistoric days of the Internet, name service depended on the /etc/hosts file and the hosts file was built from the HOSTS.TXT file that came from the Internet Network Information Center. In addition to /etc/hosts, the HOSTS.TXT file built /etc/networks. The /etc/networks file was used to map a network address back to a network name. That file still exists on some Linux systems but it is often empty.

A network address is the address assigned to an entire network. For example, the network address 172.16.0.0 is the network address for our imaginary organization. Assigning a network name to that address allows commands that convert addresses to names for informational displays to display a name for the network in addition to names for hosts. You already know that mapping from numbers to names takes place in the reverse

domain. Adding the following PTR record to the 16.172.in-addr.arpa zone maps the
network address to a name:

```
0.0      IN  PTR   foobirds-net.foobirds.org.
```

So far, this is nothing new. What's different about this mapping is what happens in the
foobirds.org zone file. The network address 172.16.0.0 is a *network* address; it is not
a host address. You can't put an address record in the foobirds.org zone assigning the
address 172.16.0.0 to the name foobirds-net because 172.16.0.0 is not a valid host
address. Instead, put a PTR record in the foobirds.org zone that points the name
foobirds-net.foobirds.org to the name 0.0.16.172.in-addr.arpa. Listing 8.4
shows the first part of the foobirds.org zone file to illustrate this.

Listing 8.4   Using a PTR Record in a Forward Zone

```
$TTL 86400
;
;       The foobirds.org domain database
;
@       SOA   wren.foobirds.org. admin.wren.foobirds.org. (
                2000020501 ; Serial
                21600      ; Refresh
                1800       ; Retry
                604800     ; Expire
                900 )      ; Negative Cache TTL
; Define the nameservers
                NS      wren.foobirds.org.
                NS      parrot.foobirds.org.
                NS      bear.mammals.org.
; Define the mail servers
                MX      10 wren.foobirds.org.
                MX      20 parrot.foobirds.org.
;
; Define the network name
;
foobirds-net    PTR     0.0.16.172.in-addr.arpa.
```

Sometimes people assume that PTR records specifically map numbers to names. PTR
records are frequently used for that purpose, but they do it by mapping one name to
another name. Remember, an IP address must be reversed and converted into a reverse

domain name before it can be used in the name field of a PTR record. PTR records maps names to names and that is just what is happening in this example. The name `foobirds-net` is mapped to the name `0.0.16.172.in-addr.arpa`.

The importance of defining a network name for your network address is marginal. It is done primarily as a courtesy to remote systems. By allowing systems to use DNS to map the network address to a network name, you speed the processing of certain tools on those systems, make the displays of those tools more readable, and provide additional information to remote system administrators that might help them in troubleshooting problems.

A more important piece of troubleshooting information is the name of a person to contact on your site when trouble occurs. Providing that information is the next section's topic.

Defining the Responsible Person

Only person-to-person contact can resolve many network problems. You frequently need to talk to someone, preferably someone technical, at the remote end who can cooperate in troubleshooting the problem. As the domain administrator, the remote system administrators can always find you. Your e-mail address is the second data field in the SOA record. A query for the SOA record points them right to you.

Often you're not the best contact for the problem. The problem might not have anything to do with DNS. It could be a problem with a specific computer. Regardless, the contact will come to you first if the remote administrator cannot find a better contact. Use the responsible person (RP) resource record to give the remote administrator a better contact.

The name field of the RP record defines the domain object for which the person is responsible. The data field contains two components:

- The e-mail address of the responsible person
- A pointer to a TXT record that contains additional information about the responsible person

Listing 8.5 will make this clear. It shows the `foobirds.org` zone with responsible people added for every domain object.

Listing 8.5   Using RP Records to Define Technical Contacts

```
$TTL 86400
;
;  The foobirds.org domain database
;
@       SOA     wren.foobirds.org. admin.wren.foobirds.org. (
```

```
                    2000020501 ; Serial
                    21600      ; Refresh
                    1800       ; Retry
                    604800     ; Expire
                    900 )      ; Negative Cache TTL
;   Define the nameservers
                    NS      wren.foobirds.org.
                    NS      parrot.foobirds.org.
                    NS      bear.mammals.org.
;   Define the mail servers
                    MX      10 wren.foobirds.org.
                    MX      20 parrot.foobirds.org.
;   Define the responsible people for the entire domain
foobirds.org.   RP      admin.foobirds.org. hotline
hotline         TXT     "Support hotline (301)555-2000"
;   Define the network name
foobirds-net    PTR     0.0.16.172.in-addr.arpa.
;   Define localhost
localhost       A       127.0.0.1
;
;   Define the hosts in foobirds.org
;
wren            A       172.16.5.1
                RP      admin.foobirds.org. hotline
parrot          A       172.16.5.3
                RP      logan.parrot.foobirds.org. logan
logan           TXT     "Logan Little (301)555-2021"
crow            A       172.16.5.5
                RP      doris.crow.foobirds.org crowRP
crowRP          TXT     "Doris Nathan (301)555-2078"
hawk            A       172.16.5.4
                RP      clark.foobirds.org hawkRP
kestrel         A       172.16.5.20
                RP      clark.foobirds.org hawkRP
hawkRP          TXT     "Clark Smart (301)555-2099"
puffin          A       172.16.5.17
                MX      5 wren.foobirds.org.
                RP      admin.foobirds.org. hotline
```

```
robin           A       172.16.5.2
                MX      5 wren.foobirds.org.
                RP      admin.foobirds.org. hotline
redbreast       CNAME   robin.foobirds.org.
bob             CNAME   robin.foobirds.org.
kestral         CNAME   kestrel.foobirds.org.
www             CNAME   wren.foobirds.org.
news            CNAME   parrot.foobirds.org.
;  Delegate the terns.foobirds.org domain
terns           NS      sooty.terns.foobirds.org.
                NS      arctic.terns.foobirds.org.
;  Delegate the ducks.foobirds.org domain
ducks           NS      ruddy.ducks.foobirds.org.
                NS      wren.foobirds.org.
                NS      bear.mammals.org.
;  Glue records
sooty.terns     A       172.16.30.250
arctic.terns    A       172.16.30.251
```

In Listing 8.5, several records have been added to the foobirds.org zone. Every object in the zone now has an RP record and an associated TXT record. The first RP and TXT records, shown here, are assigned to the foobirds.org domain itself:

```
;  Define the responsible people for the entire domain
foobirds.org.   RP      admin.foobirds.org. hotline
hotline         TXT     "Support hotline 301-555-2000"
```

The responsible person for the foobirds.org domain can be reached at the e-mail address admin@foobirds.org. As in the SOA record, the @ of the email address is replaced by a dot (.) when it is written on the RP record. You may question adding an RP record for a domain because the e-mail address of the people responsible for the foobirds.org zone is already available in the SOA record. The advantage is that the RP record adds a pointer to a TXT record that provides additional contact information. The pointer is the second item in the data field of the RP record.

The pointer to the TXT record is the name field value from that TXT record. In the example, the value is hotline, which is interpreted as hotline.foobirds.org. A query for a TXT record with that name returns a text string saying that the support hotline phone number is 301-555-2000. The TXT record can contain any arbitrary text information you want. Phone numbers, postal mail addresses, and building locations are commonly provided.

In addition to the zone itself, the people that can be reached at the `admin@foobirds.org` e-mail address and at the hotline phone number also support the hosts `wren`, `puffin`, and `robin`, as indicated by the RP records associated with each of these hosts.

Note that while each host has its own RP record, the text record is not repeated. The `hotline` pointer on each of these RP records ties them back to the TXT record that has already been defined. This illustrates that the central support group is often responsible for the domain and many of the individual hosts within the domain. In addition to supporting those systems that belong to the central computer operation, the central support staff is often responsible for those systems that lack their own adequate technical support.

Of course, the real benefit of the RP record is not found by pointing remote administrators to the same domain administrator advertised by the SOA record. The real benefit comes when you can put the remote administrator directly in touch with the system administrator who is responsible for a specific host. Four hosts in Listing 8.5, `parrot`, `crow`, `hawk`, and `kestrel`, have there own professional support. Logan supports `parrot`, Doris supports `crow`, and Clark supports both `hawk` and `kestrel`.

While advertising the names, e-mail addresses, and phone numbers of system administrators sounds like a great idea to the domain administrator, it may not sound like such a great idea to the system administrators. They may like the fact that you have to filter all trouble calls from external sources before the calls reach them. For this reason, they may be reluctant to provide the information necessary to create the RP and TXT requires shown in Listing 8.5.

The best way to handle this is to require this information for a computer before you register its host name in your domain. It is best to get administrators used to handling their own trouble calls before they start depending on you.

Defining Network Servers

The server selection record (SRV) is defined in RFC 2052, "A DNS RR for Specifying the Location of Services (DNS SRV)." This record is still defined as experimental, but its importance is bound to grow because Microsoft intends to use it as a server discovery mechanism for Windows 2000.

Traditionally, generic names such as `www.foobirds.org` and `news.foobirds.org` are used to identify the hosts that provide specific services so that a remote user has at least a chance of guessing which system provides the service they want. However, this practice was never documented or standardized in any way. RFC 2052 defines a standard method for identifying the server that provides a service. The SRV record eliminates the need to guess.

In addition to providing a standard naming convention, the SRV record offer features for defining backup servers and for implementing load-balancing. The syntax of the SRV resource record shows these features:

> _service._protocol.name **SRV** preference weight port server

The name field contains two arguments that occur before the object name. These are *service* and *protocol*.

service is any valid service name from the /etc/services file. This is the name that identifies the service required by the remote user. For example, in the /etc/services file, the service name for FTP is ftp and the service name for the World Wide Web is http.

protocol is any valid protocol name from the /etc/protocols file, although it must be the protocol that is associated with the selected service in the /etc/services file. This is usually either tcp or udp.

Given these rules, the *service* and *protocol* arguments for a Web server would be _http._tcp, while for a DNS server the arguments would be _domain._udp.

NOTE The underscore characters that precede the service name and the protocol name are used to prevent those names from conflicting with existing domain names.

Figure 8.1 shows how the *service* and *protocol* values can be derived from the /etc/services file. In addition to these values, the value for *port* can also be determined from the /etc/services file. *port* is the numeric port number to which the server listens for network traffic. Normally, the standard port defined in the /etc/services file is used, although it is possible to define a non-standard port in the SRV record if your server is configured to listen to a non-standard port.

Figure 8.1 Finding SRV values in /etc/services

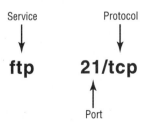

Figure 8.1 contains the /etc/services entry for FTP, which is just one line from the services file. The arrows indicate where the *service*, *protocol*, and *port* values are found. Every record in the /etc/services file has the same format. Looking at the three fields indicated in Figure 8.1 always provides you with the values you need to build an SRV record.

Choosing Between Multiple Servers

Like the MX record, the SRV record has a preference number so that multiple servers can be defined for a single service. The lower the preference number, the more preferred the server. Servers with higher preference numbers are only tried when the servers with the lowest preference numbers are unavailable. In effect, the preference number allows you to define a primary server and its backup servers. Thus, if two FTP servers are defined, one with a preference of 10 and one with a preference of 20, the server with a preference of 20 is only be used when the server with a preference of 10 is unavailable. Otherwise, all FTP traffic goes to the server with the lower preference number.

In addition to a preference number, the SRV record has numeric value, called *weight*, that is used to determine which portion of the total traffic load of a given service should be sent to each server. If multiple servers have the same preference number, the weight factor is used to determine how much of the traffic goes to each server. *weight* is an integer with 1 as the base. If one server has a weight of 1 and another has a weight of 2, the second server should get twice as much traffic as the first. Listing 8.6 contains some sample SRV records.

Listing 8.6   Sample SRV Records

```
_ftp._tcp    IN   SRV   10 2 21 wren.foobords.org.
             IN   SRV   10 3 21 hawk.foobirds.org.
             IN   SRV   20 1 21 crow.foobirds.org.
```

Listing 8.6 contains three SRV records that advertise three FTP servers for the foobirds .org domain. Look at the first record. It has a name field that evaluates to _ftp._tcp .foobirds.org. It has a preference of 10, a weight of 2, and a port number of 21. The FTP server the first record points to is wren. The second record defines hawk as an FTP server that also listens to port 21 and also has a preference of 10. wren and hawk are equally preferred; hawk is not wren's backup. In fact, based on the weight assigned to each server, hawk should get more of the FTP traffic than wren. For every two units of traffic sent to wren, hawk should get three units of traffic.

> ***NOTE*** In this context, a unit of traffic is undefined. Its meaning depends on the application using the SRV record.

The last record in Listing 8.6 says that `crow` is an FTP server with a preference of 20. It will only handle FTP traffic if both `wren` and `hawk` are unavailable. Because no other server is defined with a preference of 20, `crow` will handle all traffic on those occasions that the other two servers are unreachable.

The Reality of SRV Records

The SRV records in Listing 8.6 should make it possible for the remote user to enter the command **`ftp foobirds.org`** and connect to the correct server without actually knowing the server's name. Unfortunately, it doesn't really work that way. DNS provides the records, but the applications are not yet ready to use them. FTP client software, current Web browsers, and anything else you can think of, don't understand preference or weight. They don't even look for SRV records and even if they did, they wouldn't find them because very few domains contain SRV records. For now, if you want the command `ftp foobirds.org` to work, you need to create an address for `foobirds.org`; for example:

```
foobirds.org. IN A 172.16.5.1
```

In this case, the address assigned to `foobirds.org` is `wren`'s address. An attempt to connect to `foobirds.org` actually connects to `wren.foobirds.org`.

Old applications like FTP might not use SRV records, but new applications are using them to locate servers. Kerberos 5, Windows 2000, and the Lucent networked voice messaging system are a few examples.

Of course, the SRV record does a lot more than make it possible to connect to a service with a standardized name. It provides for automatic backup and load-balancing. Add to that the fact that Microsoft is pushing the acceptance of the SRV record, and it is likely that pretty soon more domains will contain these records and more software will use them.

Using Wildcards

Wildcards are one of those things that sound better in theory than they are in practice. A Linux system administrator who knows the incredible power of regular expressions from using `sed` and `grep` may be expecting much more than DNS wildcards offer. DNS has only one wildcard character. It is the asterisk and it is used in the name field to match any name. For example, the line

```
*.foobirds.org. IN MX wren.foobirds.org.
```

matches any `foobirds.org` host name. Therefore, an MX query for the name `sparrow.foobirds.org` gets the response that `wren` is the mail exchanger for `sparrow`.

Sounds great! But there is a big catch. Look back at Listing 8.5. You'll notice that there are no entries in the zone for `sparrow.foobirds.org`. The MX mapping in the preceding paragraph would work just as described.

However, an MX query for `hawk.foobirds.org` would not return the expected mapping. `hawk.foobirds.org` clearly matches the `*.foobirds.org` wildcard, yet the MX record is not returned. That's because `hawk.foobirds.org` has its own records in the zone file.

Look again at Listing 8.5. `hawk` does not have an MX record but it does have an A record. If a name has any kind of resource record in the zone file, it will not match a wildcard even if the wildcard is for a different type of record. Because most zones are heavily populated with resource records, the wildcard has limited applicability.

In Chapter 10, you'll see a type of zone that does not have many resource records and that makes excellent use of the wildcard character. It is the limited zone file that sits outside of a firewall as part of a split domain, which uses a wildcard MX to deliver mail. Beyond that limited case, I rarely use the wildcard character. I prefer to assign resource records to individual hosts.

In Sum

BIND is designed to handle the full range of DNS servers. The BIND default configuration values are correct for most servers, but the system can be optimized for the large servers needed by an ISP or even for the specialized needs of a root server. This chapter provides a wide-ranging discussion of the configuration options that you can use to customize your server.

Despite the advanced nature of many of these options and the fact that they are used for specialized configurations, most of the options covered in this chapter are not highly technical or complex. The next chapter concludes Part 3 with a highly complex advanced configuration option. Chapter 9 covers Dynamic DNS, a feature that not only provides dynamic zone file updates, but also extends the underlying DNS protocol with a new DNS message structure.

9

Dynamic DNS

Dynamic DNS (DDNS) naturally arouses lots of interest. First off, it has a cool name—*dynamic*—the word just sounds good! Second, it promises a lot. In Chapter 6, "Creating a Master Server," you manually built a zone file for the foobirds.org domain. That's how zone files have always been built—manually.

All of the resource records in all of the distributed databases that make up the domain system were created by hand by some person, somewhere. DDNS promises to eliminate this drudge work by having the computer dynamically create the resource records from information that is available on the network.

The Dynamic Host Configuration Protocol (DHCP) has relieved the administrator of the task of manually assigning IP addresses. Perhaps the address assignment information available to DHCP could be used by DDNS to unburden the administrator from the task of manually building the resource records. So far, the only practical application suggested for DDNS requires data from DHCP. The hope is that linking DHCP and DDNS will increase user mobility while lessening system administration.

> **NOTE** DHCP is a complex subject that is outside the scope of this book. To learn more about it, see *The DHCP Handbook*, Droms and Lemon, Macmillan Technical Press, 1999.

This chapter covers the promises and the limitations of DDNS. It examines the interaction between DHCP and DDNS, as well as the configuration options necessary to run DDNS on your Linux server with the current version of BIND 8. Let's begin by taking a closer look at DDNS and exactly what it does.

DDNS Protocol

The DDNS protocol is defined in RFC 2136, "Dynamic Updates in the Domain Name System (DNS Update)." DDNS is built on the basic protocols described in Chapter 2, "The DNS Protocols."

One of the OPCODE values and several of the RCODE values listed in that chapter apply specifically to DDNS. OPCODE value 5 is used in the DNS message header to indicate that the message is a dynamic update. The basic format of the DNS message changes when it is used for a dynamic update. Figure 9.1 shows the format of a dynamic update message.

Figure 9.1   The format of a dynamic update message

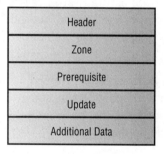

As Figure 9.1 shows, the message is made up of five sections, just like the standard message described in Chapter 2. However, the sections are different from those found in a standard DNS message.

Dynamic Update Message Header

The first section of the dynamic update message is the header. Its form and function is largely unchanged from the basic header covered in Chapter 2. It is still six 16-bit words long. The first word is still a message identifier and the last four words still specify the number of resource records contained in each of the four remaining sections of the message. Figure 9.2 shows the format of the header.

Figure 9.2   The dynamic update message header

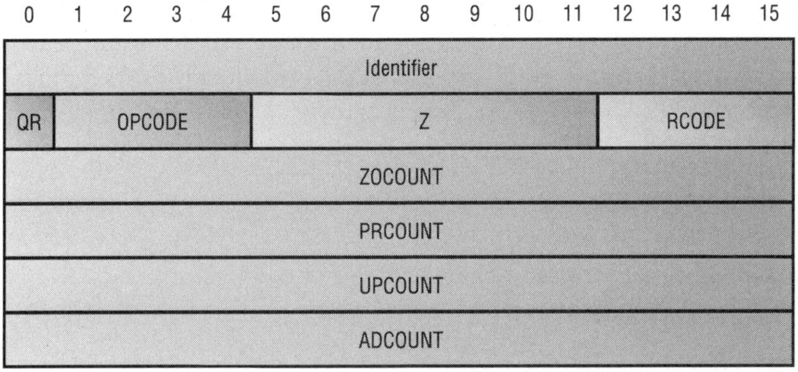

The second word of the header contains fewer fields than the same word in the header of a standard DNS message. The field marked with a Z is unused and must be set to zeros. Only three of the header fields actually contain data. The QR field contains either a 0 for a query or a 1 for a response. The OPCODE field can only contain a 5, although the RCODE field can contain the full range of response codes. In fact, the response codes from 6 to 10 are valid only for dynamic updates. (All of the fields, OPCODE values, and response codes are covered in Chapter 2.)

Zone Section

The zone section of the dynamic update replaces the question section of the standard DNS message. Their formats are the same. Each section contains a name field, a type field, and a class field but their functions are different. While the question section defines a query the client has for the server, the zone section tells the server which zone the client intends to modify.

The name field of the zone section contains a zone name, which is the domain name that appears in the name field of an SOA record. For the sample zone file we created in Chapter 6, the zone name is `foobirds.org.`.

The type field in the zone section is always SOA. This does not mean the SOA record is being changed. In fact, the DDNS protocol specifically prohibits dynamic changes to the SOA record. What this means is that the name defined in the name field is the name found on the SOA record.

Finally, the class field is always IN. Any valid class value is allowed, but for all practical purposes, every zone you deal with will contain Internet class records.

Advanced Configurations

PART 3

Prerequisite Section

Defining the name of the zone to be modified is only the first step. The client also defines the conditions that must be met before the zone is modified. For example, you might not want to add an MX record for a host if an MX record already exists for that host. These conditions are called *prerequisites*. Prerequisites are an extremely important part of dynamic updates. The DDNS protocol defines five types of prerequisites:

- name exists
- name does not exist
- RRset exists with the same name and type
- RRset exists with the same name, type, and data
- RRset does not exist

Prerequisites are defined in the prerequisite section as resource records, using the same format as resource records are defined in the answer, authority, or additional sections of a standard DNS message. The values provided for the various fields of the resource record control the type of prerequisite that is being defined. The following material describes each prerequisite format.

Checking that a Name Exists

This condition tells the server not to do the update unless at least one record exists within the zone with the specified name. This prerequisite does not care which type of record exists with the name; any type of record will do. The prerequisite is defined by placing a single resource record in the prerequisite section with class and type set to ANY, TTL and length set to 0, an empty data field, and the required name in the name field.

Checking that a Name Does Not Exist

This condition tells the server to perform the update only if a specific name does not exist. Again, only the name is significant for this condition; the type of record the name is assigned to does not matter. In this case, the RR in the prerequisite section contains a class of NONE, a type of ANY, TTL and length values of 0, an empty data field, and a name field with the specified name.

Checking for a Specific Name and Type

This prerequisite asks the server to check for a record of a specific type with a certain name before updating the zone. The prerequisite section contains a resource record with the name and type set to the desired values. The class of the record is set to ANY. The TTL and length are set to 0, and the data field is empty.

Checking for a Specific Name, Type, and Data

This condition tells the server that a record of a certain type, with a specific name, containing particular data, must exist before the zone is updated. The prerequisite section contains a complete resource record with the name, type, class, length, and data fields set to the desired values. The only field that is not checked for this prerequisite is the TTL field, which is set to 0.

Checking that Records Do Not Exist

The server is directed by this condition to skip the update if any records of a certain type with a specific name exist. The resource record in the prerequisite section contains the desired name and type. The class is set to NONE, the TTL and length fields are set to 0, and the data field is empty.

Update Section

The update section defines the changes that the client wants to make to the zone. A client can add records to the zone or delete records from a zone. Changes are made to a record by deleting the old record and then adding a new one.

Adding records is simple. Any completely defined resource records found in the update section are added to the zone. A completely defined record needs a name, type, class, TTL, length, and data field. The class must match the class of the zone, which usually means it must be IN.

Deleting records is a little more complicated because there are three ways to delete records. The client can do one of the following:

- Delete all records for a specific name by placing a resource record in the update section with the name field set to the desired name, type and class set to ANY, TTL and length set to 0, and an empty data field.

- Delete all records of a given type for a specific name by placing a resource record in the update section with the name and type set to the desired values, class set to ANY, TTL and length set to 0, and an empty data field.

- Delete a specific record by placing the resource record to be deleted in the update section. Every field must be set to a desired value except TTL. The TTL is set to 0 and is ignored.

Additional Section

The additional section contains other resource records that might be helpful in processing the update. These are not update records. All update records go in the update section.

These are simply records that the client believes might be helpful to the server for completing the update.

For example, a client might define NS records in the update section to create a delegation within the server's zone. The glue records needed to complete the delegation may be outside of the server's zone. (Refer to Chapter 7, "Creating Subdomains," for a discussion of glue records.) Because the glue records are outside of the zone that is being updated, they cannot be placed in the update section. The client could place the glue records in the additional section, where they would be available if the server needs them.

Planning, Policies, and Problems

The discussion of the DDNS protocol in the previous section may alarm you. Repeatedly, the text talks about a client modifying the zone. For most domain administrators, the zone file is sacrosanct. You define one and only one master server to keep the zone accurate and intact. Now along comes a protocol that lets clients fiddle with the zone! Before you deploy this protocol, you need to seriously consider whether or not it is suitable for your organization. You need to compare the benefits of DDNS to the risks, and you need to develop a clear implementation plan for your domain. This section will help you do that.

The Benefits of Dynamic DNS

This chapter opened by mentioning some of the benefits of DDNS:

- simplified maintenance
- dynamic address assignment for servers
- improved mobility
- improve cooperation between configuration servers

Examining each of these benefits helps to separate the hype from the reality, and helps to distinguish the baseless fears from the reasonable domain management concerns.

Simplified Maintenance and Cooperation between Servers

Dynamic updates promise to eliminate the need for manual zone file maintenance. More than that, DDNS should improve the accuracy of zone updates. The addresses assigned by DHCP don't contain typos and DHCP doesn't accidentally assign duplicate addresses. The DDNS server doesn't forget to update the zone serial number. Designing systems in which the DHCP server cooperates with the DNS server to share information should improve performance and accuracy.

But how much will you benefit from these potential improvements? It depends on how much zone maintenance you actually do and which tools you use to do it. Before assuming that DDNS can help you, you should consider a few things.

First, DDNS is only useful if you use DHCP to configure the systems on your network. It is easy to envision other applications designed to take advantage of DDNS, but the reality is that DHCP is currently the only server with plans to dynamically update DNS, and they are just that—plans. The current Linux DHCP server doesn't provide full support for DDNS.

Second, if you use DHCP, how much manual zone maintenance do you currently have? Deploying DDNS can't save you any more work than you're doing. Think of how much time you spend each day adding, deleting, or changing resource records in a zone file. These are the only things that DDNS does. It can't help you answer user questions; it can only do the "typing" for you.

Dynamic Server Addresses and Improved Mobility

Of course, simplified maintenance is only one of the reasons to use DDNS. A more important reason is to exploit features that aren't available without it. Ask yourself if your organization is really happy with the current static technique you use to link DHCP and DNS. If not, DDNS might be of interest to you.

Networks that use DHCP are particularly interested in DDNS, and for good reason. Currently, DHCP can only assign dynamic addresses to hosts that do not offer services to external users. DHCP cannot dynamically assign addresses to servers. A server's name and address must be statically assigned through DNS.

Here's why: A server is only useful if a client can find it. The client must connect to the server using either the server's name or the server's IP address. If the server's address is dynamically assigned, the client cannot know what that address is, so the client is forced to use the server's name for the connection. DNS does the name-to-address mapping, but it can only do this if DNS knows the address. Since the address is dynamically assigned, DNS must get that address from the DHCP server or from the DHCP client. DDNS allows the DHCP server to write the necessary address and PTR records into the zone files on the DNS server to keep DNS informed of dynamic address assignments. Without DDNS, servers cannot be assigned dynamic addresses.

But do you really want dynamic addresses for servers? How many servers does your network have that dynamically come and go from the network? Aren't your servers always running? Why should a server that is always up temporarily lease an address? For official servers, dynamic address assignment does not make sense.

Advanced Configurations

PART 3

Unofficial servers are a different matter. Linux can turn a laptop into a powerful server. It is possible that a system assigned a dynamic address is running a private server that, for instance, directly collects its own e-mail or offers a private Web site. If this private server stayed on one network, it could be given a permanent address just like any other server. But this system might move from network to network within the organization.

Admittedly, mobile users that run their own servers are a small group. Yet providing service to this group is one reason for DDNS. Running private servers and DDNS are not the only alternatives for supporting mobile, high-demand users. With X Windows for remote access, NIS for network-wide logins, and NFS for cross-mounting files with an official server, many of the private services that a user runs directly on a laptop can be handled by a central server. You need a policy to decide which type of private servers you want to allow, and to identify the alternatives you will provide to support those private servers.

The bulk of the systems for which dynamic address assignment is used are desktop PCs running a Microsoft operating system such as Windows 98. These systems are not IP servers. Therefore, you might assume that means they don't need DDNS. You could be wrong. Clearly, no one will `telnet` to one of these desktops or attach to a Web server running on a Windows 98 system. Yet many PCs are peer-to-peer servers in a NetBIOS network. A surprising amount of the push for DDNS comes from those who want to run NetBIOS over TCP/IP to support Microsoft peer-to-peer networking.

Naming Issues

DNS maps names to addresses and addresses to names. In a dynamic update from a DHCP server, the address comes from the DHCP server. But the name has to come from the DHCP client. If it comes from the DHCP server, it is just as dynamic, and therefore just as unpredictable to remote users, as the address. Let's examine the impact of this statement by looking at a PC that gets a different address when it renews its address lease.

If the DHCP server gives names with the addresses, a PC might first get a lease for the address 172.16.27.7 and the name `host7net27.foobirds.org`. Two days later it gets a lease for a different address, 172.16.27.36, and a different name, `host36net27.foobirds .org`. A remote user would not be able to keep track of the names and numbers.

NOTE The names a DHCP server assigns are up to the administrator of the server. Often they are names based on the addresses, which is why I used `host7net27` and `host36net27` as examples. But these are just examples. This is not some special name format generated by DHCP.

On the other hand, the client can select its own host name by filling in the host name field of the DHCP request packet before sending it to the server. Let's assume that the PC sends in the request and includes the name `housefinch.foobirds.org`. With the first lease, the DHCP server assigns the address 172.16.27.7 to `housefinch.foobirds.org`. Two days later, the PC gets a new lease and is assigned 172.16.27.36 for `housefinch.foobirds.org`. In both cases, the clients have the same host name. Remote users can map the name to the correct address through DNS, if DHCP gives the correct address to DNS. If the DHCP server sends dynamic updates to the DNS server, a remote user could connect to `housefinch` without a problem and without knowing that the address of the system had changed. If DHCP does not send a dynamic update to DNS, knowing the host name `housefinch` is useless.

Beyond the difficulties of deploying DDNS, the biggest problem with having the client provide the name is *name conflict*, which happens when more than one client decides to use the same name. Microsoft has several techniques to register names and resolve name conflicts because their NetBIOS network is name based instead of address based. For some time, they have offered Windows Internet Name Service (WINS) as a solution to this problem and they have linked their DHCP and DNS servers to WINS to create a proprietary dynamic update scheme.

A Linux system using Samba software acts as a WINS server. So it is possible to use a Linux box running Samba to resolve name conflicts, a Linux system running DHCP to assign addresses, and finally, a Linux system running DNS to handle the name-address mapping. However, linking these systems can be a great deal of trouble for very little reward and I don't recommend trying it.

On a Linux system, Samba, DHCP, and BIND are not really designed to interact, and the production version of DHCP does not include DDNS support. Additionally, I always avoid making Linux emulate Windows NT. If you really want to make things operate like Windows NT, you probably should use Windows NT. Usually, I find there are simpler ways to do things.

Often it is easier to handle the task of avoiding name conflicts manually. Each domain administrator has a list of available names and assigns a name to each new computer. This works as long as there is not a lot of mobility in the network. If mobile units from remote networks are frequently attached to your network, name conflict may arise even if care is taken to prevent duplicate name assignments. If a system attempts to attach to the network and the name it wants is already used, it will not receive an IP address and will be forced to select another name, which is not a major problem.

Advanced Configurations

PART 3

Security Concerns

The biggest concern any domain administrator has with dynamic DNS is security. Clients are able to change the zone file. The administrator of the DHCP server might not think of his system as a client, but to your DNS server it is a client. Careless security on the part of the DHCP administrator could have a profound impact on your domain. Listing 9.1 shows the process of manually changing the IP address of parrot, the slave DNS server, using the nsupdate tool. If this action was malicious, the results could be devastating.

Listing 9.1   Changing an Address with nsupdate

```
[root]# host parrot.foobirds.org.
parrot.foobirds.org has address 172.16.5.3
[root]# nsupdate
> update delete parrot.foobirds.org. A
> update add parrot.foobirds.org. 86400 A 172.16.5.83
>
> ^D
[root]# host parrot.foobirds.org.
parrot.foobirds.org has address 172.16.5.83
```

Listing 9.1 shows the output of three programs:

- a host lookup to show the original address of parrot
- an interactive nsupdate run to show the commands entered to change the address of parrot
- a second host lookup to show that nsupdate can indeed change the address of the slave server

nsupdate is covered later in this chapter, but the meaning of the update delete and update add commands is pretty clear. The old address record is deleted and a new one is added in its place. The result is that the slave server no longer has the address you might expect.

Listing 9.1 illustrates that when DDNS is running, other computers can change your domain. Think carefully before you use dynamic updates, and make sure to limit the clients that have access to DDNS, as described later in this chapter.

Pre-Populating DNS

After reviewing the benefits and costs of running DDNS on your network, you will decide if DDNS is right for you. If it is, you can skip ahead to the section about enabling DDNS.

On the other hand, if you want to provide DNS support to your DHCP server without DDNS, consider the static techniques for pre-populating the zone that are described in this section.

A Linux DHCP server dynamically assigns addresses from a range of addresses. The scope of possible addresses is fixed and is defined by the DHCP administrator in the DHCP configuration. Listing 9.2 shows the subnet statement and range clause from a Linux DHCP server configuration.

Listing 9.2   Defining a Range of Dynamic Addresses

```
subnet 172.16.70.0 netmask 255.255.255.0 {
    range 172.16.70.100 172.16.70.250 ; }
```

The subnet statement tells the DHCP server to provide service to network 172.16.70.0. Within the subnet statement, the range clause defines the scope of addresses available for dynamic assignment. In Listing 9.2, the server is providing dynamic addressing for the range of addresses from 172.16.70.100 to 172.16.70.250. This information is unknown by the domain administrator until it is communicated to him by the DHCP administrator. But once the range of possible addresses is known, it is possible to pre-populate the DNS server with static name and address mappings for the full range of dynamic addresses. The domain administrator needs to do a couple of things to statically support these dynamic addresses.

Pre-Populating the Reverse Domain

First and most importantly, you need to populate the reverse domain so that the IP numbers assigned by DHCP map back to domain names. Even if no remote user will ever attempt to connect to one of the computers that use dynamic addresses, a fully populated reverse domain is required to support *outbound* connections because some remote servers reject connections unless they can map the client's IP address back to a name.

The DHCP configuration in Listing 9.2 defines the dynamic addresses as 172.16.70.100 to 172.16.70.250, which are the host numbers 100 to 250 on subnet 70 of network 172.16. The approach taken in this section is to create an undelegated subdomain for subnet 70 within the 16.172.in-addr.arpa zone, and then to populate that subdomain with generated names and addresses. Listing 9.3 shows the 16.172.in-addr.arpa zone file and the undelegated subdomain that it includes.

Listing 9.3   Generating Reverse Mappings for Dynamic Addresses

```
[/var/named]# cat 172.16.reverse
```

Advanced Configurations

PART 3

```
;        Address to host name mappings.
;
$ TTL 1d
@    SOA     wren.foobirds.org. admin.wren.foobirds.org. (
             2000021602   ;   Serial
             21600        ;   Refresh
             1800         ;   Retry
             604800       ;   Expire
             900 )        ;   Negative cache TTL
             NS      wren.foobirds.org.
             NS      parrot.foobirds.org.
             NS      bear.mammals.org.
1.5          PTR     wren.foobirds.org.
2.5          PTR     robin.foobirds.org.
3.5          PTR     parrot.foobirds.org.
4.5          PTR     hawk.foobirds.org.
5.5          PTR     crow.foobirds.org.
17.5         PTR     puffin.foobirds.org.
20.5         PTR     kestrel.foobirds.org.
1.12         PTR     trumpeter.swans.foobirds.org.
1.6          PTR     arctic.terns.foobirds.org.
$INCLUDE 172.16.70.reverse 70
[/var/named]# cat 172.16.70.reverse
$GENERATE 100-250 $ PTR host$net70.foobirds.org.
```

The $INCLUDE directive in the zone file creates the undelegated subdomain. This directive temporarily shifts the origin to 70.16.172.in-addr.arpa and loads the file that contains the data for the new subdomain, which I arbitrarily named 172.16.70.reverse.

The 172.16.70.reverse file contains a single $GENERATE directive that creates all of the address-to-name mappings required to support our DHCP server. The $GENERATE directive in Listing 9.3 iterates from 100 to 250, producing a unique PTR record for each number by replacing the dollar signs ($) in the resource record template. The records produced would look like this:

```
100 PTR host100net70.foobirds.org.
101 PTR host101net70.foobirds.org.
102 PTR host102net70.foobirds.org.
...
248 PTR host248net70.foobirds.org.
```

```
249 PTR host249net70.foobirds.org.
250 PTR host250net70.foobirds.org.
```

The format of the generated host names is arbitrary. You can choose any format you like as long as the name includes the number generated by the $GENERATE directive to ensure that each name is unique. The $GENERATE zone directive makes pre-populating the reverse domain simple and straightforward.

Pre-Populating the Zone

Pre-populating the regular zone file might not be as easy as the reverse zone because you have some choices to make. Can you settle for a PTR to PTR match such as the one used in Chapter 8, "Special BIND Configurations," to map the network address to a name? Or do you require real address records in the zone file for your generated host names? Deciding what is right for you may be more difficult than you think.

PTR records, which are easier to create, may be sufficient for you. PTR records in the zone file are sufficient to make the host names in the reverse zone file valid. Additionally, you may not want remote users entering one of these generated host names to get an address because you don't want them to attempt connecting to the systems that are assigned dynamic addresses. If you can live with PTR records, use a $GENERATE directive to create them. The following directive, placed in the foobirds.org zone, creates PTR records for the generated host names:

```
$GENERATE 100-250 host$net70 PTR $.70.16.172.in-addr.arpa.
```

The problem with this simple solution is that it might be too simple. The PTR record might not be sufficient for every situation. It is possible that an address record might be needed for a generated host name. For example, assume one of your PCs connects to a paranoid remote server that maps the IP address of the PC back to a host name. If it then takes the host name and attempts to map it back to the original address, it might not be satisfied with a PTR record from the forward zone. It might demand an A record. If you need to create A records, you can't do it with the $GENERATE directive. $GENERATE only creates NS, CNAME, or PTR records.

Despite the added difficulty, I create A records for generated host names. The records only need to be created once, and even creating them manually with an editor doesn't take that long. On the other hand, if you wind up troubleshooting a user problem caused by the lack of an A record, you might waste days on a problem that could easily be avoided.

Of course, none of this work is necessary if you decide to use dynamic updates. The remainder of the chapter covers how dynamic updates are enabled and how they are used.

Enabling Dynamic Updates

Dynamic updates are not permitted unless you explicitly permit them with the **allow-update** option. This option is used inside a **zone** statement and can be used on any zone for which your system is authoritative. That means that dynamic updates can be allowed on the slave servers as well as on the master server for a specific zone.

> **WARNING**   Don't permit dynamic updates to the slave server's zone file. DNS already has excellent mechanisms for keeping the domain databases of the master and its slaves well synchronized. Adding unneeded dynamic updates to this mix can only hurt synchronization.

Listing 9.4 shows a **named.conf** file with dynamic updates enabled for both the **foobirds.org** zone and the **16.172.in-addr.arpa** domain.

Listing 9.4   The **allow-update** Option

```
options {
        directory "/var/named";
};

// a master nameserver configuration
//
zone "." {
        type hint;
        file "named.ca";
};

zone "0.0.127.in-addr.arpa" {
        type master;
        file "named.local";
};

zone "foobirds.org" {
        type master;
        file "foobirds.hosts";
        allow-update { 172.16.70.1; };
};

zone "16.172.in-addr.arpa" {
        type master;
```

```
            file "172.16.reverse";
            allow-update { 172.16.70.1; };
    };
```

The `allow-update` option defines the hosts that are permitted to dynamically update the zone. In Listing 9.4, only one host, presumably the DHCP server, is allowed to dynamically update the two zone files. Only the host whose address exactly matches 172.16.70.1 is allowed to update the zones.

The hosts in the `allow-update` option are defined by their IP addresses using an address match list. Addresses in an address match list define individual hosts or entire networks of hosts by combining addresses and address prefix masks. Be careful not to give every system on the network permission to perform dynamic updates. This potentially dangerous power must be as tightly limited as possible. If you need to grant dynamic update privileges to multiple hosts, explicitly define each individual host. In the following `allow-update` option, three hosts are granted dynamic update privileges:

```
    allow-update { 172.16.70.1; 172.16.73.1; 172.17.81.1; };
```

The biggest problem with the `allow-update` option is that it grants a powerful and dangerous privilege on the basis of nothing more than an IP address. As everyone knows who has ever changed the address of a network interface with the `ifconfig` command, it is very easy to make your Linux system appear to be any address you wish. Trusting an IP address doesn't really provide any security. DNS has other types of security, such as DNSSEC, but they can't be used in this case because the DHCP server that runs on Linux does not support DNSSEC. Given this limitation, the only acceptable way to allow a Linux DHCP server to dynamically update a Linux DNS server is to run them on a same host, as in the following example:

```
    allow-update { localhost; };
```

Using Dynamic Updates

Linux provides two tools that use DDNS. One is the `nsupdate` program used earlier in this chapter, and the other is the DHCP server software from the Internet Software Consortium (ISC). The DHCP server that currently ships with Linux is DHCP version 2. It is the current production version of DHCP, which was released in June 1999.

This production version of DHCP does not offer dynamic updates. To get those, you must run version 3 of DHCP, which is currently a beta release. Version 3 of DHCP provides an interim implementation of dynamic updates, but they are not supported. The supported version of dynamic updates has not yet reached the beta stage, and the dynamic updates in DHCP do not support DNS security.

Advanced Configurations

PART 3

DHCP configuration is beyond the scope of this book. See *Linux Network Servers*, Craig Hunt, Sybex, 1999, for information on downloading, installing, and configuring DHCP on a Linux server. If you're really interested in linking DNS to DHCP, you can track the development of the DHCP code at www.isc.org, and you can watch that site for information and documentation on dynamic updates.

The *nsupdate* Program

While linking DHCP to DDNS is the Holy Grail of dynamic zone update technology, DHCP is not the only tool that can be used to dynamically update a zone. BIND provides a program called nsupdate that updates a zone with information typed at the console or read from a file. The nsupdate command accepts two commands: prereq and update.

The *prereq* Command

The prereq command defines the prerequisite conditions that must be met before the server should carry out the update. In effect, this is the prerequisite that goes in the prerequisite section of the DDNS update message. The prereq command can define all of the possible prerequisite conditions defined by the DDNS protocol. There are four separate formats for the prereq command:

prereq yxdomain *name*   The update should only be done if the name exists in the zone.

prereq nxdomain *name*   The update should only be done if the specified name does not exist in the zone.

prereq yxrrset *name* [*class*] *type* [*data*]   The update should be done only if the specified resource records exists. At a minimum, the name and type of the records must be specified. Optionally, the data field of a record can also be defined. This command can check for an RRset by name and type or by name, type, and data.

prereq nxrrset *name* [*class*] *type*   The update should be done only if the specified resource records do not exist in the zone. *class* is optional. It defaults to ANY.

The *update* Command

The update command defines the update action that should be taken once the prerequisites are met. As defined in the DDNS protocol, there are only two possible actions: adding records and deleting records. The update command takes two forms to cover these two possible actions:

update add *name* *ttl* [*class*] *type* *data*   This tells the server to add the specified record. The record must be complete with a valid name, TTL, type, and the appropriate data for the record type.

update delete *name* [*class*] [*type* [*data*]]   This tells the DNS server to delete the specified record. The name field of the targeted record must be provided. Optionally, type and data fields of the record can be provided to provide a more specific match. When deleting records, it is best to be as specific as possible.

Using *nsupdate*

Listing 9.1 illustrated how simply nsupdate can change an address. Listing 9.5 shows a more complex example that checks prerequisites before performing an update.

Listing 9.5   Defining nsupdate Prerequisites

```
[root]# host -t MX robin.foobirds.org.
robin.foobirds.org mail is handled (pri=5) by wren.foobirds.org
[root]# host -t MX hawk.foobirds.org.
[root]# nsupdate
> prereq nxrrset robin.foobirds.org. MX
> update add robin.foobirds.org. 1d MX 5 parrot.foobirds.org.
>
> prereq nxrrset hawk.foobirds.org. MX
> update add hawk.foobirds.org. 1d MX 5 parrot.foobirds.org.
>
> ^D
[root]# host -t MX robin.foobirds.org.
robin.foobirds.org mail is handled (pri=5) by wren.foobirds.org
[root]# host -t MX hawk.foobirds.org.
hawk.foobirds.org mail is handled (pri=5) by parrot.foobirds.org
```

The nsupdate session in Listing 9.5 is surrounded by host commands to illustrate that prerequisites do make a difference. The first two host commands show that an MX record already exists for robin and that no MX record exists for hawk. nsupdate is invoked and the first command defines a condition for the update.

The prerequisite command says that the update should only be done if an MX record does not exist for robin.foobirds.org.. The prerequisite command is then followed by an update command that tells the server to add an MX record for robin that defines parrot as the mail exchange server with a preference of 5.

The next line is a blank line. nsupdate requires that every update end with a blank line. Also, a blank line is used as a separator when more than one update is included in an nsupdate session. The session in Listing 9.5 has two updates.

Advanced Configurations

PART 3

The second update includes a prerequisite that says the update should only be done if no MX record exists for hawk. The update command tells the server to add an MX for hawk that defines parrot as the mail exchange server with a preference of 5—if the prerequisite is met. A blank line ends the update and a Ctrl-D ends the interactive nsupdate session.

Based on what you know about the foobirds.org domain, you know that robin had an MX record before the nsupdate session and that hawk did not. Given the prerequisites defined in the session, the MX record for robin should be unchanged, and hawk should have a new MX record.

The final two host commands show us that this is exactly what happens. The MX record for robin still points to wren, and hawk has a new MX record that points to parrot.

Dynamic updates should use prerequisites to prevent improper updates. I don't use nsupdate in a production environment and I don't recommend that you use it. However, if you absolutely must use it, remember to use prerequisites to help you avoid mistakes.

Clearly, using nsupdate to interactively update a zone is more difficult than directly editing the zone file. And manually typing in dynamic updates doesn't really make sense. nsupdate is more useful for developers who want to analyze its source code or to incorporate it with other tools to build a more complete dynamic update system.

Logging Dynamic Updates

The name server keeps track of dynamic changes to make those changes permanent and to ensure that the changes are propagated to the zone's other authoritative servers. BIND does this by logging the changes that were made and creating an incremental zone transfer (IXFR) file for the changes. The IXFR file contains changes that when applied to the original zone file produces the new zone. The log file contains a record of the changes.

A simple example will make the function of these files understandable. In Listing 9.1, the zone was changed with the following nsupdate session:

```
[root]# nsupdate
> update delete parrot.foobirds.org. A
> update add parrot.foobirds.org. 86400 A 172.16.5.83
>
```

These update commands told the master server to delete the old address of parrot and add a new one. The master server logs these changes in a file and generates a name for that file based on the name of the zone file plus the extension .log. Listing 9.6 shows the foobirds.hosts.log file that the master server created in response to the nsupdate command.

Listing 9.6   A Dynamic Update Log File

```
[root]# cat foobirds.hosts.log
;BIND LOG V8
[DYNAMIC_UPDATE] id 16351 from [172.16.70.1].1025 at 954952067
(named pid 947):
zone:   origin foobirds.org class IN serial 2000020501
update: {delete} parrot.foobirds.org. IN A
update: {add} parrot.foobirds.org. 86400 IN A 172.16.5.83


[INCR_SERIAL] from 2000020501 to 2000020502 Wed Apr  5 12:32:47 2000
```

This file identifies that a dynamic update was received from 172.16.70.1, that the update applied to the zone foobirds.org, and that the update directed the server to delete one record and add another. Furthermore, the file records that the server incremented the zone serial number.

A log file like this would be useful for tracking dynamic changes to the zone, particularly if you fear security problems. But that is not what this log file is for. This is a temporary file used in conjunction with the IXFR file to convert the dynamic changes to permanent changes in the zone file. Once the zone is permanently updated, this log file is deleted. To keep a record of server activity, you need to use the correct logging features. Logging is covered in Chapter 12, "The BIND Log Files." This file is a temporary log of incremental changes, not a permanent log file.

The detailed changes that the master server makes as the result of a dynamic update are stored in the IXFR file in the proper format for an incremental zone transfer file. Listing 9.7 lists the IXFR file created as a result of the nsupdate command.

Listing 9.7   An IXFR File

```
[root]# cat foobirds.hosts.ixfr
;BIND LOG V8
[DYNAMIC_UPDATE] id 16351 from [172.16.70.1].1025 at 954952067
(named pid 947):
zone:   origin foobirds.org class IN serial 2000020501
update: {delete} parrot.foobirds.org. 86400 IN A 172.16.5.3
update: {add} parrot.foobirds.org. 86400 IN A 172.16.5.83
update: {delete} foobirds.org. 86400 IN SOA wren.foobirds.org.
admin.wren.foobirds.org. ( 2000020501 21600 1800 604800 900 )
update: {add} foobirds.org. 86400 IN SOA wren.foobirds.org.
admin.wren.foobirds.org. ( 2000020502 21600 1800 604800 900 )
[END_DELTA]
```

Advanced
Configurations

PART 3

The master server generates a name for the IXFR file by adding the extension `ixfr` to the name of the zone file. In this example, the zone file is `foobirds.hosts`, so the IXFR file is `foobirds.hosts.ixfr`.

Everything between the `[DYNAMIC UPDATE]` label and the `[END_DELTA]` label is one update. The first two records in the update tell the server to delete the old address record for `parrot` and then to add a new address record for `parrot`, which are the `nsupdate` changes received from the remote client. The last two records tell the server to delete the old SOA record and add a new one. The only difference between the two SOA records is that the serial number has been incremented from 2000020501 to 2000020502. This change didn't come from the client, but it is important. Incrementing the serial number is an essential part of making sure that every slave knows about this change. Slaves that support incremental zone file transfers can apply the incremental changes exactly as described in this file. Other slave servers can only use a complete zone file.

During the master server's next maintenance cycle, the server removes the log file and the IXFR file, and overwrites the original zone file with an updated zone file. The new zone file looks substantially different from the one originally created for `foobirds.org` because the server writes out the file as it is stored in memory. Listing 9.8 shows the updated file.

Listing 9.8   A Zone File after a Dynamic Update

```
;BIND DUMP V8
$ORIGIN org.
foobirds    86400    IN    MX      10 wren.foobirds.org.              ;Cl=2
            86400    IN    MX      20 parrot.foobirds.org.            ;Cl=2
            86400    IN    NS      wren.foobirds.org.                 ;Cl=2
            86400    IN    NS      parrot.foobirds.org.               ;Cl=2
            86400    IN    NS      bear.mammals.org.                  ;Cl=2
            86400    IN    SOA     wren.foobirds.org.admin.wren.foobirds.org.
                                   (2000020502 21600 1800 604800 900 ) ;Cl=2
$ORIGIN foobirds.org.
news        86400    IN    CNAME   parrot.foobirds.org.               ;Cl=2
robin       86400    IN    MX      5 wren.foobirds.org.               ;Cl=2
            86400    IN    A       172.16.5.2                         ;Cl=2
puffin      86400    IN    MX      5 wren.foobirds.org.               ;Cl=2
            86400    IN    A       172.16.5.17                        ;Cl=2
wren        86400    IN    A       172.16.5.1                         ;Cl=2
parrot      86400    IN    A       172.16.5.83                        ;Cl=2
crow        86400    IN    A       172.16.5.5                         ;Cl=2
```

```
localhost   86400   IN   A       127.0.0.1                  ;Cl=2
www         86400   IN   CNAME   wren.foobirds.org.         ;Cl=2
bob         86400   IN   CNAME   robin.foobirds.org.        ;Cl=2
redbreast   86400   IN   CNAME   robin.foobirds.org.        ;Cl=2
kestrel     86400   IN   A       172.16.5.20                ;Cl=2
kestral     86400   IN   CNAME   kestrel.foobirds.org.      ;Cl=2
hawk        86400   IN   A       172.16.5.4                 ;Cl=2
```

The file looks very different, but in reality it is only slightly different from the file in Listing 6.3. Only the address of parrot and the serial number of the SOA record are changed. The difference in appearance is merely a matter of formatting.

Notice, however, that the updated zone file contains no evidence of which record changed or of which client ordered the dynamic update. Without logging, it would be very hard to track this change if it was a mistake. Read Chapter 12 for a detailed explanation of logging procedures, and make sure you carefully account for dynamic updates if you decide to use DDNS.

In Sum

This chapter examines the benefits and risks of DDNS. The conclusion that most readers should reach is that DDNS is not stable enough for commercial networks. Currently, the risk outweighs the benefit.

The dynamic update features of the BIND and DHCP software are not yet ready for a production Linux environment. DHCP version 3 is still in beta testing and the DDNS code is not a fully supported part of the Beta. Improvements to DDNS support in BIND are planned for BIND 9. Most sites should limit the use of dynamic updates to test and development networks until BIND 9 and a production release of DHCP version 3 are released.

Security is the primary reason for caution when deploying DDNS. This chapter concludes Part 3, "Advanced Configurations," with a look at an advanced option that has profound security implications. The next part of the book, Part 4, "Maintaining a Healthy Server," begins with a chapter on security. Part 4 covers topics relating to the on-going maintenance of a healthy DNS server. Security is undoubtedly one of the most important of these topics.

Part 4

Maintaining a Healthy System

Featuring:

- Controlling server access with wrapper and `ipchains`
- Securing the hardware and selecting the software of a DNS server
- Limiting access to zone transfers, queries, and recursion
- Understanding and deploying DNSSEC protocols
- Testing DNS with the `host` command
- Using `dig` to evaluate and capture DNS response messages
- Using batch mode `dig` commands
- Using `nslookup` for interactive, real-time testing
- Configuring logging with the `logging` statement
- Using the `named.run` log file
- Using the `named_dump.db` file
- Understanding the `named.stat` file

10

DNS Security

Domain administrators cannot afford to overlook security. The Internet is a dangerous place, full of people who will harm your server for no reason. A DNS server is a critical component of any operational network. To provide continued service to your clients, the DNS server needs to be protected from security threats. There are two basic types of threats:

Unauthorized access This is any time that someone who should not be allowed to access your system gains access. Unauthorized access threatens the secrecy and integrity of data. An intruder can examine files that you don't want disclosed to the general public and can modify the files on your system. Imagine the problems you would have if an intruder controlled your DNS database!

Denial of service This is any security problem that prevents you from using your server to its full capacity. Denial of service is a threat to the availability of data. For a DNS server, this means that the server is unable to respond to queries.

These security problems are the same ones that threaten all computer systems. To counter these threats, you need to follow the same basic security procedures for your DNS server that you would follow for any computer system. These basic security procedures, customized for the special needs of a Linux DNS server, are the first topic of this chapter.

In addition to the basic security problems that all systems face, a DNS server has a unique set of challenges that spring from the fact that the server is part of a globally distributed database system. The integrity and availability of the domain database data are of paramount importance to a DNS server. Integrity and availability are issues for both the data sent in response to a query and the information transferred during a zone update. These special DNS security issues are also discussed in this chapter.

The final topic of this chapter is the DNS Security (DNSSEC) protocol. This topic is of less practical interest than the other topics because DNSSEC is not yet widely deployed and is still under development. But it should be interesting to those readers who want to know where DNS security is heading and to those readers who have very high security needs. DNSSEC is the solution for guaranteed DNS data integrity. Before getting into such an advanced topic, let's begin by looking at the basic steps for securing your server.

Basic Security

A DNS server runs on computer hardware and the Linux operating system just like any other server. A DNS server has the same basic security requirements as an e-mail server or a news server. Don't let the hype over sophisticated network attacks obscure the importance of basic security.

Good fundamental system administration is still the best defense against security problems. Don't assume that a firewall or fancy security tool will really make your site secure. Your system will always be vulnerable to security problems. You should assume you will have problems and that you will need to quickly recover from those problems. Begin your security preparations by securing your hardware.

Securing the Hardware

The best security firewall in the world won't protect your server from a real fire. Floods, fires, earthquakes, storms, and other natural disasters are a real threat to your server. More server time is lost to power outages, disasters, and disgruntled employees than has ever been lost because of a network-based security attack.

Don't overlook obvious physical security issues. Your server can't run without hardware, so you need to protect it. Here are some basic steps for securing your hardware:

Provide an uninterruptible power supply (UPS).   Given the fact that Linux runs on standard PC hardware, it is very simple to provide UPS backup for your DNS server. A small UPS that provides an hour of runtime for a PC may be adequate for your site, depending on the frequency and duration of power outages in your area. If critical systems in your organization have diesel generator backup power, you may be able to tie into that system. For example, one place that I worked had a diesel generator to back up the central telephone switch that was also available for a few critical computer systems. Evaluate your needs and your options, and then make sure you have an adequate level of backup power.

Provide a redundant server in hot standby mode.   All master DNS servers are backed up by their slave servers. The low cost of a Linux DNS server lets you take that a step further. It is easy to configure a second Linux system as a backup master server. Simply configure the hot standby as an unadvertised slave server to keep the domain database synchronized between the master server and the hot backup. If the hardware of the master server fails, shut off the master and reconfigure the hot backup to use the host name and IP address of the master. It will immediately take over service as the master. When the hardware of the old master is repaired, use it as the hot backup for the new master.

Use an off-site backup.   At least one of the slave servers that backs up your domain must be physically separate from your master server and your local network. A single power outage in a headquarters building could knock out all of the servers located there. A single cable cut could isolate all servers connected to a single network. Use a remote backup that is independent from the power, network, and location used by the master server.

Put the DNS server in a locked room.   The server hardware must be in a locked and secured location. If you have a computer room with controlled access that is staffed 24x7, that's ideal. At the very least, the server must be in a locked room. You don't want a disgruntled employee taking an ax to the server. (Think that's farfetched? At the very first place I worked, a berserk contractor used metal cutters on the back plane of an IBM mainframe!) A more common threat is that a disgruntled employee will gain access to the console and use that access to corrupt the data in the DNS server.

Securing the Console

Even placing the DNS server in a locked room may not be enough. Many computer rooms run unattended, and many of those allow access to several different employees. A substantial group of people may have access to the console of the DNS server at odd hours. There are some things you can do to increase the physical security of the server and the console in an unattended computer room.

To prevent unwanted reboots, the server box must be secured. If people have access to the power buttons or power cords of the server, they can force the server to reboot. The only way to completely prevent this is to lock the server and its UPS in a cabinet that itself has a secured power connection. Make sure the cabinet has adequate ventilation to support both the server and the UPS and to prevent overheating.

The keyboard must also be secured to prevent keyboard reboots with the "three-finger salute" (Ctrl+Alt+Del). This can be done by placing the keyboard in a locked cabinet, if one is used, or by disabling the function of the Ctrl+Alt+Del keyboard interrupt in the

/etc/inittab file. Listing 10.1 contains the entry for the keyboard interrupt on a Caldera 2.3 system.

Listing 10.1   Controlling Ctrl+Alt+Del

```
# Trap CTRL-ALT-DELETE
ca:12345:ctrlaltdel:/sbin/shutdown -t3 -r now
```

The first line in Listing 10.1 is a comment that describes the purpose of the second line. Any line in the inittab file that begins with a # is a comment.

The second line is the one that actually processes the keyboard interrupt. The line is composed of four fields separated by colons (:). The definitions for the four fields are as follows:

The label   An arbitrary label is assigned to each line in the inittab file. In the Listing 10.1 example, the label is ca, which is the most common label used for the line that implements the keyboard interrupt.

The runlevels   The runlevels affected by the entry are listed in this field. In this example, all runlevels from 1 to 5 are listed. This is not really necessary. The keyboard interrupt is not part of a system initialization process. For this line, the runlevels field could just as easily be empty.

The action   The action field defines the conditions under which the process runs. In this example, the action field is ctrlaltdel, which is a special action that means the process is to be run when the Ctrl+Alt+Del keyboard interrupt occurs.

The process   The last field is the process that is run when the action occurs. In this example, the process is the shutdown command. The three shutdown arguments used in the Listing 10.1 example tell init to take these steps:

- Wait three seconds between warning the processes of the shutdown and killing the processes.
- Reboot the system after the shutdown.
- Begin the shutdown process right now.

There are two ways to disable the three-finger salute. One is to put a # in front of the ca entry. This effectively removes it from the inittab file by turning it into a comment. Pressing Ctrl+Alt+Del has no effect if no ctrlaltdel action is listed in the inittab file.

Another way to disable the reboot is to replace the shutdown command with another process that doesn't reboot the system. For example, it could be replaced with a process that sends a message to the domain administrator saying that someone is trying to reboot the system. Either method eliminates the threat of keyboard reboots.

Securing Single-User Mode

The danger of having unauthorized people reboot the system goes beyond the inconvenience of having the DNS server offline for a few minutes while it reboots. A person who is knowledgeable of Linux can reboot the server into single-user mode and subtly corrupt the system. To boot the system in single-user mode, the person sitting at the console passes the kernel the `single` argument at the boot prompt.

TIP See the "BootPrompt-HOWTO" document by Paul Grotmaker for more information about the boot prompt. You'll probably find it among the HOWTO documents in the /usr/doc directory of your Linux server.

To prevent an unauthorized person from rebooting to single-user mode, require a password to reboot the system. Do this by placing the `password` and `restricted` commands in the `lilo.conf` file. Listing 10.2 shows a `lilo.conf` file with password protection.

Listing 10.2 Requiring a Password to Reboot the Server

```
# global section
boot = /dev/hda3
prompt
timeout = 50
# default boot image
image = /boot/vmlinuz-2.2.5-15
    label = linux
    root = /dev/hda3
    read-only
    password = Wats?Watt?
    restricted
```

The last two lines in the `lilo.conf` file are the ones that secure the system against an unauthorized reboot. First is the `password` command. This command defines a password that must be entered whenever the system reboots.

The second line, `restricted`, changes the function of the `password` command so that the password is required only when someone attempts to pass instructions to the kernel at the boot prompt. With both `password` and `restricted` set, a person attempting to boot the system into single-user mode would be asked to provide the password, but if the system crashed and rebooted because of a power outage, it would not hang waiting for someone to enter the password. The combination of these two commands gives us just what we want.

Maintaining a
Healthy System

PART 4

There is one problem, however, and that is the fact that the password is stored in the `lilo.conf` file as clear text. By default, the `lilo.conf` file is world-readable. Change the file permissions so that it can only be read by the root user, as in the following example:

```
[root]# ls -l /etc/lilo.conf
-rw-r--r--   1 root  root  315 Jan  6 14:11 /etc/lilo.conf
[root]# chmod 600 /etc/lilo.conf
[root]# ls -l /etc/lilo.conf
-rw-------   1 root  root  315 Jan  6 14:11 /etc/lilo.conf
```

Securing the hardware is only the first step in securing your DNS server. Power outages may be a big source of downtime and insiders may pose a big security threat, but they are only part of the story. Software holes can be as easily exploited as unattended hardware.

Securing the Software

Failure to keep software updated and to fix well-known bugs is the leading cause of network-based break-ins. Most break-ins are not the work of sophisticated security crackers. Experts may be the first to discover a vulnerability, but they rarely waste their time exploiting the vulnerability to break into every small business connected to the Internet. Most break-ins are the work of unsophisticated computer users called "script kiddies."

Script kiddies run attack scripts available from places like `rootshell.com` and `insecure.org`, and let the scripts do the work. The scripts look for and exploit well-known vulnerabilities to give the script kiddie unauthorized access to the target systems. The scripts can be configured to scan thousands of systems for vulnerabilities. Tracking the vulnerabilities exploited by the scripts and closing those holes as they appear are important components of improving the security of your server.

Tracking Vulnerabilities

To secure a system, you need to know its vulnerabilities. Your goal should be to stay as well informed about Linux and DNS vulnerabilities as the vandals are. Frankly, you won't be able to. *You* have a life and responsibilities, so the vandals who have nothing better to do will get ahead of you and may compromise your system. Despite the difficulty, you should do your best to keep up-to-date about security problems.

There are several good sources of information about known security vulnerabilities:

- General information about security vulnerabilities is available at `http://geek-girl.com/bugtraq`.
- Good sites for security advisories are `www.10pht.com` and `www.cert.org`.
- A good site for Linux software updates and security hole announcements is `www.freshmeat.com`.

- The best site for information on DNS vulnerabilities and fixes is www.isc.org.

Track all of the problems that pertain to Linux and DNS. All of these could affect your Linux DNS server. Figure 10.1 shows the DNS security advisories at www.isc.org.

Figure 10.1   DNS security advisories at www.isc.org

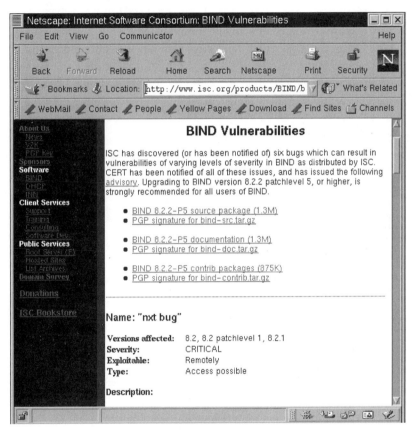

In addition to visiting the sites that report bug and security problems, visit the Web sites that provide attack scripts. Here are two such sites:

- www.rootshell.com
- www.insecure.org.

Make sure that your system is not vulnerable to the old attacks and evaluate the new scripts as they are released to understand the vulnerabilities that they exploit. In addition to providing scripts, these sites provide information about what is currently going on in the network security world.

Closing the Holes

The most important thing you can do to improve the security of your system against network-based attacks is to install security updates as soon as they become available. To update the software, you need to need to know what software needs to be updated and where to find it. Security advisories and vulnerability reports sometimes include fixes.

Unfortunately, the fix is not always included in a vulnerability report, and you may need to look for DNS and Linux fixes yourself. www.isc.org is the best place to look for DNS fixes. Many Linux vendors provide security fixes for their distributions online. For example, on a Red Hat 6 system, all you need to do is click the Red Hat Errata icon on the desktop to go to the location at the Red Hat Web site, shown in Figure 10.2, where security problems and fixes are listed.

Figure 10.2   A Red Hat security advisory

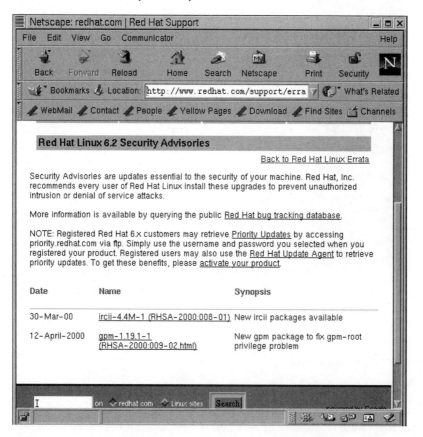

Figure 10.2 shows a security report on the Red Hat Web site. This report describes the problem and provides a link to the software update. Clicking a link leads to a fix that can then be downloaded and installed using the `rpm` command.

If you're looking for a specific fix, you can search through the security advisories on the vendor's Web page. The big advantage of this is that you will often find fixes for bugs that you have never heard of. On the downside, sometimes you find out that a bug you have heard of has not yet been fixed. Nevertheless, you should take all of the bug fixes that are offered and periodically check back to see if the bug you're concerned about does get fixed.

TIP Frequently, administrators complain that the authors of software don't fix bugs, but I find a much more common problem is that system administrators don't use the bug fixes that are out there. Set aside a time each month to download and install the fixes provided by your software vendor. Make it part of your routine.

Vulnerabilities are not limited to Linux and DNS. Most of the network software that runs on your Linux system has vulnerabilities that have been exploited at one time or another. It is not enough to keep the Linux operating system and the BIND software up to date. You must keep all software packages updated to keep your DNS server secure.

Removing Unneeded Software

Reduce the burden of keeping software updated by removing all of the software you don't really need. Unneeded software on a server can open a hole for an intruder. If you have a dedicated DNS server, it needs to run `named` but it doesn't require the `sendmail` daemon, `imapd`, `ftpd`, or a host of other network daemons. Everything you have on your server is a potential tool for an intruder. Think hard about what software is really needed for the server to do its job.

Security is one of the reasons I'm a big fan of dedicated DNS servers built on Linux. Some people recommend putting the master DNS server on a large system that supports several other services. They are even willing to put the DNS master on a server that permits general user accounts.

I think that is a security problem waiting to happen. The only server I would ever co-locate with a DNS master is a DHCP server—and then only to permit more secure dynamic updates. DNS is a critical service that deserves its own dedicated server. At the same time, DNS usually places a minimal load on the computer that can easily be handled by a small Linux system. Using dedicated DNS servers makes it much easier to limit the software installed on the server.

NOTE   I'm arguing for dedicated machines for the master and slave servers. All large, general-purpose network servers run a caching DNS server. The servers that I recommend securing through dedicated systems are the authoritative servers.

There are two ways to limit the software installed on a server. First, don't install what you don't need when you do the initial Linux installation. During the initial installation, you select the software packages that are installed and the daemons that are loaded. Choose carefully based on your plan for the system that you're installing.

NOTE   TurboLinux has a nice feature in their installation that makes it easier to install only those software packages required for a DNS server. TurboLinux displays a list of different servers. Selecting the DNS server installs just the software they think you need for a dedicated DNS server.

The other way to limit the software on a system is to remove it after it is installed. For example, to remove IMAP from a system with `rpm`, you could enter the following command:

```
[root]# rpm -e imap-4.5-3
```

Disabling Unneeded Software

It is not necessary to remove software to prevent it from running. Sometimes you want to keep software so that it can be enabled for special occasions. Other times you want to evaluate the impact before removing software. If you're not sure you want to remove a network daemon, start by not running it until you are sure that doing so has no negative impact on your users or on your server. Once you're sure it is unneeded, the daemon can be permanently removed. There are two simple ways to prevent daemons from running while you evaluate their importance:

Comment unneeded daemons out of the /etc/inetd.conf file.   Most network services are started by `inetd`. The services it starts are listed in the `inetd.conf` file. Removing a service from this file prevents outsiders from using the specified network service, but it does not block you from using the service on outbound connections. Thus, if `ftp` is deleted from `inetd.conf`, you can still use `ftp` to log into remote sites but no one from a remote site can use `ftp` to log into your server.

Remove scripts that launch unneeded daemons during the startup procedure.   Some network service daemons, `named` is a good example, are started at boot time. See Chapter 3, "The BIND Software," for examples of how tools like tksysv, ntsysv, and linuxconf are used to enable and disable startup scripts. Use one of these tools to remove unneeded daemons from the startup. For example, your DNS server does not need to run the httpd startup script because it is not a Web server. You're still able to use a Web browser even if the httpd script is not run at startup.

In addition to installing the latest software and removing unneeded software, limit access to the software and services running on your server to just those systems that you actually want to serve. Linux makes this simple by providing two powerful access control mechanisms: wrapper and ipchain. Both of these access control mechanisms are described in the following sections.

Limiting Login Access

Domain administrators need access to the DNS server to effectively manage the system. On master servers, domain administrators need to edit and maintain the zone files. On all servers, the administrator needs access to the named.conf file and the ndc command. Yet for security reasons, you want to limit remote login access to the server.

Deleting telnet and rlogin from the inetd.conf file, as described in the previous section, eliminates the possibility of remote login access. That provides an ideal level of security but it is usually impractical. Unless all of the domain administrators are physically located close to the console of the server and can use that console for all of their system administration duties, you need to provide secure remote login for the domain administrators.

The secure shell (ssh2) program is probably the most secure remote login software available. It supports secure logins and even supports secure X Windows access. Secure shell is not provided with most Linux distributions but it is available on the Internet. Go to www.cs.hut.fi/ssh for more information about secure shell and to download the latest source code.

Of course, telnet and rlogin may not be the only network daemons that you want to keep on your DNS server. To control access to all services started by inetd, use the wrapper, described in the next section.

Controlling Network Access with Wrapper

The wrapper daemon, named tcpd, is executed by inetd. It is an integral part of most Linux distributions. Using the wrapper on a Linux system is easier than it is on many other systems because the entries in the inetd.conf file already point to the tcpd program. Listing 10.3 contains a few lines from the inetd.conf file on a Red Hat Linux system.

Listing 10.3   Linux is Preconfigured for Wrapper

```
ftp    stream tcp  nowait root /usr/sbin/tcpd in.ftpd -l -a
telnet stream tcp  nowait root /usr/sbin/tcpd in.telnetd
shell  stream tcp  nowait root /usr/sbin/tcpd in.rshd
login  stream tcp  nowait root /usr/sbin/tcpd in.rlogind
talk   dgram  udp  wait   root /usr/sbin/tcpd in.talkd
ntalk  dgram  udp  wait   root /usr/sbin/tcpd in.ntalkd
imap   stream tcp  nowait root /usr/sbin/tcpd imapd
finger stream tcp  nowait root /usr/sbin/tcpd in.fingerd
```

In Listing 10.3, bold text is used to highlight the references to tcpd in each line of the inetd.conf file. The path to tcpd is used in place of the path of each network service daemon. Therefore, when inetd receives a request for a service, it starts tcpd. tcpd then logs the service request, checks the access control information, and, if permitted, starts the real daemon to handle the request.

The wrapper package performs two basic functions: It logs requests for Internet services and it provides an access control mechanism for those services. If the tcpd access control files are not found, tcpd allows every host to have access and simply logs the access request. The wrapper uses the authpriv facility of syslogd to log its messages. Look in the /etc/syslog.conf file to find out where your system logs authpriv messages. (On a Red Hat 6 system, authpriv messages are logged to /var/log/secure.)

Logging requests for specific network services is a useful monitoring function, especially if you are looking for possible intruders. If logging were all it did, wrapper would be a useful package. But the real power of wrapper is its ability to control access to network services.

***tcpd* Access Control Files**   Two files define access controls for tcpd. The hosts.allow file lists the hosts that are allowed to access the system's services, and the hosts.deny file lists the hosts that are denied service. The format of entries in both files is the same:

```
services : clients [: shell-command]
```

The elements in the entry are as follows:

services is a comma-separated list of network services or the keyword ALL. ALL is used to indicate all network services. Otherwise, each individual service is identified by its process name, which is the name that immediately follows the path to tcpd in the inetd.conf file. For example, the process name in the following inetd.conf entry is imapd:

```
imap stream tcp  nowait root /usr/sbin/tcpd imapd
```

clients   is a comma-separated list of host names, domain names, Internet addresses, network numbers, and the keyword LOCAL. Alternately, it can be the keyword ALL. ALL matches all host names and addresses. LOCAL matches all host names that do not include a domain name part. A host name matches an individual host. An IP address can be defined by itself to match a specific host or with an address mask to match a range of addresses. A domain name starts with a dot (.) and matches every host within that domain. A network number ends with a dot (.) and matches every IP address within the network address space.

shell-command   is an optional shell command that tcpd executes when a match occurs. If a match occurs, tcpd logs the access, grants or denies access to the service, and then passes the shell command to the shell for execution. The shell command allows you to define additional processing that is triggered by a match in the access control list. In all practical examples, this feature is used in the hosts.deny file to gather more information about the intruder or to provide immediate notification to the system administrator about a potential security attack.

tcpd reads the hosts.allow file first and then reads the hosts.deny file. It stops as soon as it finds a match for the host and the service in question. Therefore, access granted by hosts.allow cannot be overridden by hosts.deny. For this reason, I usually start by inserting an entry in hosts.deny that denies all access to all systems. The rule in the hosts.deny file that blocks access from all other computers is

```
ALL : ALL
```

Next, I put entries in the hosts.allow file that permit access to just those systems that I really want to provide services to. Here is an example from an imaginary hosts.allow file:

```
ALL : LOCAL, .foobirds.org
in.ftpd,in.telnetd : sr1.sybex.com
```

The keyword ALL in the *services* field indicates that the first rule applies to all network services. In the *clients* field, the keyword LOCAL indicates that all host names without a domain part are acceptable, and the .foobirds.org matches all host names in that domain. By itself, LOCAL would match wren but not wren.foobirds.org. Combining these two tests in a single rule allows every system in our local domain to use all of the network services. The second rule grants ftp and telnet access to users on the remote system sr1.sybex.com.

For a secure DNS server, you want to limit login access to those few computers used by domain administrators. Use hosts.deny to block login access from all remote systems, and then use `hosts.allow` to identify only those few computers that you truly want to grant login access through the blockade.

Wrapper can only protect services started by `inetd` or services, like NIS, that read the `hosts.allow` and `hosts.deny` file on their own. This does not provide security for any other service, such as `named`, that is started at boot time. To control access to services started by boot scripts, use the Linux IP firewall.

Controlling Access with *ipchains*   In its simplest incarnation, a *firewall* is a filtering router that screens out unwanted traffic. Linux includes traffic-filtering features in the kernel, so a DNS server built on Linux can filter its own traffic. The Linux kernel categorizes traffic into three groups and applies different filter rules to each category of traffic. The categories are

Input   Incoming traffic is tested against the input firewall rules before it is accepted.

Output   Outbound traffic is tested against the output firewall rules before it is sent.

Forwarding   Traffic that is being forwarded through a Linux router is tested against the rules for the forwarding firewall.

The Linux kernel maintains a list of rules for each of these categories. These lists of rules are called *chains* and are maintained by the `ipchains` command. Use the `ipchains` command to add rules to a chain with the –A argument or delete rules from a chain with the –D argument. The rules defined in an `ipchains` command specify the source of the traffic with the –s option or the destination of the traffic with the –d option, and they specify the action taken, which is either to accept or reject the traffic, with the –j option. Here are two examples:

```
ipchains -A input -d 172.16.5.1 53 -j accept
ipchains -A input -d 172.16.5.1 -j reject
```

These two commands both add rules to the end of the input rule chain. The first rule checks to see if the traffic is bound for port 52, the DNS port, on the host with the IP address 172.16.5.1. If it is, the traffic is accepted.

The second command has no specific port number so it applies to all ports. That rule says that all traffic bound for any port on host 172.16.5.1 is rejected. `ipchains` rules are applied in order. The first rule accepts DNS traffic and the second rule rejects all other traffic. With the two rules in this example, the server would accept only DNS server-to-server traffic between systems configured to use only port 53.

This section introduced the role that wrapper and `ipchains` can play in limiting network access to your server. Neither of these tools is specific to DNS, so the complete details of the complex syntax of both wrapper and `ipchains` are beyond the scope of this book. If you want to learn more about them, see *Linux Network Servers 24seven*, Craig Hunt, Sybex, 1999.

The next section leaves the topic of general system security and focuses directly on DNS server security.

Securing the DNS Server

Securing hardware, selecting the correct software, and limiting access to network daemons are things done to secure every Linux server. In addition to these basic tasks, BIND has features specifically designed for securing DNS. BIND configuration options can be used to limit queries for DNS information and to limit access to zone transfers. Options are available to limit the impact of DNS spoofing on your server. It is even possible to limit the damage that an intruder who seizes control of named can do to your system. How and why you use all of these features are covered in this section.

Restricting Zone Transfers

Most security experts recommend that you limit the amount of domain information available to outsiders, because there are plenty of miscreants out there trying to exploit every piece of information. Without security, anyone can look at all of the information in your zone through a zone file transfer. Listing 10.4 illustrates this using `nslookup` and the `ls` command.

Listing 10.4   Listing an Entire Zone

```
[craig]$ nslookup
Default Server: wren.foobirds.org
Address: 172.16.5.1

> ls foobirds.org
[wren.foobirds.org]
$ORIGIN foobirds.org.
robin                1D IN A        172.16.5.2
puffin               1D IN A        172.16.5.17
wren                 1D IN A        172.16.5.1
parrot               1D IN A        172.16.5.83
```

```
crow                1D IN A        172.16.5.5
localhost           1D IN A        127.0.0.1
sooty.terns         1D IN A        172.16.30.250
arctic.terns        1D IN A        172.16.30.251
kestrel             1D IN A        172.16.5.20
hawk                1D IN A        172.16.5.4
> exit
```

The ls command of nslookup can be very helpful if you're looking for a system but you don't quite remember how it is spelled or you haven't got the name exactly right. The danger, of course, is that miscreants will use this information to target individual hosts on your network. You need to decide if the risk outweighs the benefit. Security-conscious sites usually prevent unrestricted zone transfers. I'm not sure how much benefit there is in "security through obscurity," but it can't hurt, and BIND makes it easy to restrict zone transfers. Use the allow-transfer option to do this.

Listing 10.5 shows the named.conf file on wren.foobirds.org. An allow-transfer option has been added to the zone statements for the foobirds.org domain and the 16.172.in-addr.arpa domain.

Listing 10.5   The Basic allow-transfer Option

```
options {
        directory "/var/named";
};

zone "." {
        type hint;
        file "named.ca";
};

zone "0.0.127.in-addr.arpa" {
        type master;
        file "named.local";
};

zone "foobirds.org" {
        type master;
        file "foobirds.hosts";
        allow-transfer { 172.16.5.3; 192.168.24.1; };
```

```
        };

        zone "16.172.in-addr.arpa" {
                type master;
                file "172.16.reverse";
                allow-transfer { 172.16.5.3; 192.168.24.1; };
        };
```

The `allow-transfer` option defines the access control list for zone transfers. The `allow-transfer` option can be placed in the `options` statement to control zone transfers for the entire server, or within individual `zone` statements, as it is in Listing 10.5, to control zone transfers for specific zones. The computers listed in the `allow-transfer` option are allowed to transfer the zone, and computers that are not listed in the option are not allowed to transfer the zone. In Listing 10.5, two hosts are identified in each `allow-transfer` option with individual host addresses. Only those two hosts are permitted to transfer the zone. All other hosts are blocked.

Re-running the test from Listing 10.4 on a host not defined in the `allow-transfer` option produces the following result:

```
[craig]$ nslookup
Default Server: wren.foobirds.org
Address: 172.16.12.3

> ls foobirds.org
[wren.foobirds.org]
*** Can't list domain foobirds.org: Unspecified error
> exit
```

A more complex `allow-transfer` option is shown in Listing 10.6. That option says that all of the computers in a large network are permitted zone transfers except for the hosts on a single subnet of the large network.

Listing 10.6   Using ! in an Address Match List

```
        options {
                allow-transfer { !172.16.84/24; 172.16/16; };
        };
```

The `allow-transfer` option in Listing 10.6 defines two addresses. The first is !172.16 .84/24. The dotted decimal address combined with the prefix mask means that this is the network address 172.16.84.0. Normally, an address defined in an `allow-transfer` option is permitted to transfer the zone. The ! that precedes the address changes this. When a ! is used, it means that the address is not allowed to retrieve the zone.

The second address, 172.16/16, defines every computer on the network 172.16.0.0. Because it is not preceded by a !, these computers are allowed zone transfers. Of course, the 172.16.84.0 address that is rejected is part of the 172.16.0.0 address that is accepted. So what happens? Is an address from 172.16.84.0 accepted or rejected? It is rejected because the address matches in the access control list are applied in the order in which they occur in the list. An address from 172.16.84.0 matches the first test !172.16.84/24 and is rejected. It is never compared to the second address match. See the sidebar "Naming Access Control Lists" for more information about the syntax of access control lists.

Naming Access Control Lists

Several BIND configuration options use access control lists to determine to which remote systems the option applies. At the heart of an access control list is an address match list, which is a list of addresses against which the address of the remote system is matched. The address match list can contain several items:

- A host's IP address written in dotted decimal notation, e.g., 172.16.5.3

- A network's IP address written in dotted decimal notation with an address prefix mask defining the network portion of the address, e.g., 198.54.26/24

- The name of a previous defined key identifier (See Appendix B, "named.conf Command Reference," for the syntax of the key statement that is used to define key identifiers.)

- The name of a previously defined access control list

Names are assigned to access control lists so that they can be referred to by name later in the named.conf file. BIND predefines four access control lists and assign them these names:

```
any     matches every possible address.
none    matches no addresses.
localhost  matches all addresses assigned to the local host.
localnet  matches any addresses from any network to which the local
host is directly connected.
```

Naming Access Control Lists *(continued)*

You can create your own access control list and assign it a name using the acl statement. The following example creates a list that matches three different network
addresses and assigns the list the name mammal-net:

```
acl mammal-net {
192.168.24/24;
192.168.32/24;
192.168.84/24;
};
```

Once a list is defined, it can be used in subsequent configuration commands. An
allow-transfer option that referenced the newly created list might look something
like the following:

```
allow-transfer { localnets; mammal-net; };
```

Note that the acl command must occur in the named.conf file before any other command that references the list name. Forward references are not allowed in the
named.conf file.

Limiting Queries

A DNS server normally accepts all of the queries it receives, regardless of the source of
those queries. The reason that the domain name system exists is to disseminate information about hosts and addresses. Yet it is possible that a security-conscious organization
won't want to disseminate information about all of its hosts to everyone. Use the allow-
query option to restrict the sources from which queries will be accepted.

The allow-query option can be defined in the options statement to affect all queries or
in the zone statement to affect only those queries that request information from a specific
zone. Listing 10.7 shows an interesting named.conf file that uses allow-query options
in both the options statement and the zone statement.

Listing 10.7   The allow-query Option

```
acl mammal-net {
        192.168.24/24;
        192.168.32/24;
        192.168.84/24;
};
```

Maintaining a
Healthy System

PART 4

```
options {
        directory "/var/named";
        allow-query { 172.16/16; mammal-net; }
};

zone "." {
        type hint;
        file "named.ca";
};

zone "0.0.127.in-addr.arpa" {
        type master;
        file "named.local";
};

zone "foobirds.org" {
        type master;
        file "foobirds.hosts";
        allow-transfer { 172.16.5.3; 192.168.24.1; };
        allow-query { any; };
};

zone "16.172.in-addr.arpa" {
        type master;
        file "172.16.reverse";
        allow-transfer { 172.16.5.3; 192.168.24.1; };
        allow-query { any; };
};
```

The first allow-query option is found in the options statement. It specifies that queries for any information will be accepted from any client whose address is found on the network 172.16.0.0 or whose address is found on one of the networks lumped together under the name mammal-net. Network 172.16.0.0 is the foobird.org network and the networks labeled mammal-net belong to our good friends at mammals.org.

In effect, this option tells the server to accept any and all queries from foobirds.org and mammals.org, and to reject queries from all other sources. On the surface, that seems a little harsh. After all, this is the master server for the foobirds.org and 16.172.in-addr-arpa domains and as such, is expected to answer all queries it receives for those domains.

The `allow-query` options found in the `zone` statements soften this harsh restriction and ensure that the server meets its obligations to the `foobirds.org` and `16.172.in-addr.arpa` domains. An `allow-query` option in a `zone` statement overrides the global `allow-query` option for the specific zone. The `allow-query` options in the `zone` statements in Listing 10.7 permit the server to answer queries from any source for information about the `foobirds.org` domain and the `16.172.in-addr.arpa` domain. These `allow-query` options permit full access to the information within this server's zone of authority while the `allow-query` option in the `options` statement limits queries for information outside of the server's zone of authority to only those hosts in `foobirds.org` and `mammals.org`.

The reason why you might want to restrict queries for information outside of your zone of authority while permitting all queries for information within your zone of authority is subtle and related to recursion. To fully understand this, you need to understand the material covered in Chapter 2, "DNS Protocols." Clients that identify the server in their `resolv.conf` files or that configure the server as a forwarder send recursive queries to the server. Other DNS clients send queries to your server through their local servers. When a query comes from another server, it should be a non-recursive query. If it isn't, security-conscious organizations become suspicious because it is possible for a miscreant to send a recursive query to your server asking for information that that person knows is corrupted in order to get your server to cache data that the miscreant knows is bad data. This is one way for bad guys to spoof DNS. *DNS spoofing* simply means getting DNS to provide false or erroneous information

The configuration shown in Listing 10.7 solves this problem. Even recursive queries for information within a server's zone of authority do not have to be forwarded to any other server that might return corrupted data. All of the information necessary to answer any query about a zone for which the server is authoritative can be found right on the server. Therefore, queries about these zones can safely be accepted from any source. Other queries that might require the server to get answers from the remote server are only accepted if the query originates from a trusted source. In Listing 10.7, the trusted sources are the hosts in `foobirds.org` and `mammals.org`.

BIND provides other techniques for controlling recursion and limiting the records cached from other server. These techniques are described in the next section.

Controlling Recursion

Another way to prevent miscreants from using recursive queries to spoof DNS is to disable recursion completely. Paranoid domain administrators like this approach because they fear that a trusted query source might be compromised and become the source of cache corruption. Turning off recursion means that no query source is trusted, and therefore no

Maintaining a
Healthy System

PART 4

query source is a threat. Advocates of disabling recursion also claim that it reduces the load on the server. If you decide to completely eliminate recursion, BIND makes it easy to do. Just use the `recursion` option. The command in Listing 10.8 disables recursion.

Listing 10.8   Disabling Recursion

```
options {
        recursion no;
};
```

Personally I disagree with this approach. There is no way to completely eliminate recursion from your DNS architecture. Your users want information about the outside world. Your servers use recursion to find that information. At least some of the servers on your network *must* be recursive servers. It is possible to make some servers recursive and some non-recursive.

The most common approach is to make the master and its slaves non-recursive while leaving all non-authoritative servers recursive. The problem with this approach is that none of the clients on your network would be able to list the master or its slaves in their `resolv.conf` file or as a forwarder. If they did, they would have DNS lookup failures. Tracking down configuration problems for your clients is a much bigger threat to your time and productivity than DNS spoofing is.

A better and more flexible approach that generally requires less maintenance and is more robust combines the `allow-query` option described in the previous section with the `allow-recursion` option. First, you configure the authoritative servers with the `allow-query` option, as shown in Listing 10.7. Then you add an `allow-recursion` option to all servers on the network, authoritative and non-authoritative. The `allow-recursion` option defines an access control list for recursion. Recursive queries are accepted from only those computers identified in the `allow-recursion` option. Listing 10.9 is an example of how the `allow-recursion` option is used.

Listing 10.9   Using the `allow-recursion` Option

```
options {
        allow-recursion { 172.16/16; };
};
```

With the `allow-recursion` option in Listing 10.9, the server will accept recursive queries from any host on network 172.16.0.0. Recursive queries from any other source will be rejected.

Running *named* without Root Privilege

In addition to corrupting DNS data, miscreants try to exploit the named process to gain unauthorized access to the server. The security advisory shown in Figure 10.2 describes one way that intruders use DNS to break into the system. There are some steps that you can take to limit the damage caused by an intruder who takes over DNS.

One way to limit damage is to run named with fewer privileges. Normally, named is run as a process owned by the root user. Any intruder gaining control of named might also be able to assume the privileges of the root user. It is not, however, necessary to run named under the root user id.

First, create a new user id and a new group id for the named process. I don't use a user id or group id used by any other process or user so that I ensure that only named has access to the files and directories. Normally I call the new user id and the group id "named." This might seem confusing but I think it clearly identifies these as the user id and group id of the named process.

Next, make sure that all of the files required by named can be read and written by the new user id. named.conf is read by named before it gives up the root privilege, so the file permissions for named.conf do not need to be changed. Every other file must be changed to grant read and write permission to the new user. Do this by changing the ownership for the /var/named directory and all of the files it contains to the new user id and group id. The chown commands that accomplish this change are shown in Listing 10.10.

Listing 10.10 Changing the Ownership of /var/named

```
[root]# chown -R named:named /var/named
[root]# ls -l /var/named
total 21
-rw-r--r-- 1 named named    698 Apr  5 12:24 172.16.reverse
-r--r--r-- 1 named named   1891 Apr  5 16:39 foobirds.hosts
-rw-r--r-- 1 named named   2769 Mar 21  1999 named.ca
-rw-r--r-- 1 named named    187 Dec 10 15:24 named.local
-rw-r--r-- 1 named named   2860 Jan  3 13:49 named.memstats
-rw-r--r-- 1 named named   4000 Jan  3 13:49 named.stats
-rw-r--r-- 1 named named   6094 Feb  7 15:20 named_dump.db
```

Next, make sure that all of the files needed by named are now available. We know we don't have to worry about named.conf because named is still running as root when it reads that file. Setting the directory option in the named.conf file takes care of all of the zone files by placing them in the directory that is now owned by the new user id. Other options in the named.conf file define paths for five other files:

- named-xfer, which defines the path to the named-xfer program
- dump-file, which defines the path to the named_dump.db file
- memstatistic-file, which defines the path to the named.memstats file
- pid-file, which defines the path to the named.pid file
- statistics-file, which defines the path to the named.stats file

The last three lines in Listing 10.10 show that the memstatistic-file, statistics-file, and dump-file options are already configured to write their respective files into the /var/named directory.

The named-xfer file is not a file that is written by named. It is a program used to handle zone file transfers. Check that it can be executed by the new user id. The following example from a Red Hat system uses whereis to find named-xfer and ls to check the permission.

```
[root]# whereis named-xfer
named-xfer: /usr/sbin/named-xfer /usr/man/man8/named-xfer.8
[root]# ls -l /usr/sbin/named-xfer
-rwxr-xr-x 1 root root 285076 Nov 11 00:04 /usr/sbin/named-xfer
```

With world-execute permission, named-xfer will still be available to named. That leaves only the PID file unaccounted for. Clearly it is not being written to the /var/named directory or it would have appeared in Listing 10.10. That's to be expected. On most Linux systems, the PID file is written to the /var/run directory. Change the pid-file option in the named.conf file to write the file to the /var/named directory, as in the following example:

```
options {
    directory /var/named;
    pid-file /var/named/named.pid;
};
```

Now that the file permissions are all set, use the –u and –g arguments to start named with the new user id and group id, as in the following example:

```
[root]# named -u named -g named
```

Of course, named is not usually started from the command line. See the discussion of the named and ndc commands in Chapter 3 for information about how arguments can be passed to named through ndc and for information about the scripts that start named at boot time. To ensure that named starts with the correct user id and group id after every reboot, you must make sure that the scripts that start named provide the correct arguments.

When named is run under a different user id, the process does not have the privileges of the root account, but it does still have the privileges of a normal user. An intruder gaining access to the system through DNS would have the same potential to do damage as any user logged into the system. Running named in a chroot jail is one way to place additional limitations on the potential damage an intruder can do.

Running *named* in a *chroot* Jail

Readers who come to Linux without a Unix background may not understand what a chroot jail is. Remember that the Linux file system is a rooted hierarchy much like DNS. In the same way that we created a private root for DNS in Chapter 8, "Special BIND Configurations," we can create a private root in the Linux file system that is completely separate from the true root of the file system. Just as the private DNS root cuts the system off from information known to the true DNS root, a private file system root cuts a program off from all of the information known to the true file system root. Why would you want to run a program that was cut off from all of the data and software stored on your system? Security!

To run named in a chroot jail, create a minimal copy of the root file system. This copy should include /dev, /etc, /usr, and /var directories. Those directories should include just the files named needs to run properly:

/dev   must define the null device, /dev/null. Build a null device in this directory with the mknod command. You can find the exact syntax of the correct mknod command by looking in the /dev/MAKEDEV file on your system.

/etc   needs to contain the named.conf file and the resolv.conf file. It also needs a minimal /etc/group file and a minimal /etc/passwd file that contain only the group and user entries for named. Finally, the directory should contain a copy of /etc/localtime, which is used by named for the timestamp of the log entries.

/var   must contain the working directories and files needed by named. Create two subdirectories: /var/named and /var/run. named will write the PID file in /var/run and it will write log files and working files in /var/named. Copy all of the zone files need by named to the newly created /var/named directory.

/usr   must contain the DNS programs. Create a /usr/sbin directory and copy the named-xfer program and a statically linked copy of the named program to that new directory.

WARNING If you don't use a statically linked version of named for the chroot jail, you must create copies of the necessary dynamic link libraries in the chroot directory.

To find out more about running named in a chroot jail, see the paper "Securing DNS" by Craig Rowland, located at www.psionic.com/papers/dns.

Once the private root is created, run named with the −t option to point named to the chroot jail. Assume for example, that you create the minimal copy of the root in /home/ named. You would then run named with the following command:

```
[root]# named −t /home/named
```

Why You Shouldn't *chroot*

I have a big problem with running named in a chroot jail. To me, this is a technique more directed to the Unix past than to the Linux present. Ten years ago, Unix boxes were big and expensive. All functionality was consolidated on one large system and it was necessary in a high-security environment to separate the different servers from each other using chroot. Today, functions are separated by using separate dedicated systems. There is no need to use chroot on a dedicated server because named is already isolated from all other servers and users on its own machine. The entire system is, in effect, a much improved chroot jail. If you find yourself using chroot to secure DNS, I suggest that you take a good hard look at the design of your DNS architecture. You would be better off placing DNS on a dedicated Linux server.

Coexisting with a Firewall

DNS is a vector of attack on your network. Therefore, access to DNS is generally limited by a firewall. Your DNS architecture must be adjusted to work within the limits set by your firewall.

One of the functions of a firewall is to direct the flow of traffic between the outside world and internal servers. It is common for a firewall to place a limit on the number of DNS servers allowed to send queries to the outside world and an even tighter limit on the number of servers allowed to accept queries from the outside world. The firewall blocks DNS traffic unless it comes from or is bound to one of the selected servers. Inside the secured network, all of the other DNS servers are configured to use the selected servers as forwarders.

The first adjustment to your architecture is to limit the number of systems running as DNS servers. Caching-only servers are not used, and authoritative servers pick up the workload. On a firewalled network, the resolv.conf file of every client is configured to use only the authoritative servers of the zone to which the client belongs. For example, every client in the terns.foobirds.org zone would have the following resolv.conf file:

```
nameserver 172.16.30.250
nameserver 172.16.30.251
search terns.foobirds.org
```

In turn, the authoritative servers for the subdomains must adjust to the fact that they are no longer permitted to directly query servers outside of the secured network. They handle this restriction in two ways:

1. The forwarders option is used to send all queries about the outside world to the selected servers. These are often the authoritative servers for the domain. In our sample domain, this would be the servers for foobirds.org.

2. The subdomain servers are configured as unadvertised slaves for all of the other subdomains within the internal network. This is used to limit the number of unnecessary queries sent to the forwarders. Without this, all queries for other subdomains within the enterprise domain would be sent to the forwarders, even if the local server knows the authoritative server for the other subdomain.

In the foobirds.org domain, the named.conf files for the authoritative servers of the terns.foobirds.org subdomain would add the following lines:

```
options {
    directory "/var/named";
    forwarders { 172.16.5.1; 172.16.5.3; };
    forward only;
};
zone "ducks.foobirds.org" {
    type slave;
    master { 172.16.55.1; };
    file "ducks.foobirds.hosts";
};
```

The foobirds.org servers are defined as the forwarders. Additionally, this server makes itself secondary for the other subdomain.

Finally, the servers for foobirds.org that are acting as the forwarders are configured to accept recursive queries only from the internal network. External queries are accepted only for information about the `foobirds.org` domain. This type of configuration was shown in Listing 10.7.

Using a Split Namespace

Some highly secure organizations do not like to have outsiders query all of the information about the domain. These organizations create a split namespace with a public and a private version of the domain. The private version contains all of the domain information, but the public version contains only the names and addresses of the few servers available for outside access. The server for the public version of the domain is placed outside of the firewall or is accessible to the outside world by a tunnel through the firewall. A public version of `foobirds.org` might contain the following lines:

```
$TTL 86400
;
;       The public domain database
;
@       SOA     dove.foobirds.org. admin.dove.foobirds.org. (
                2000020501 ; Serial
                21600      ; Refresh
                1800       ; Retry
                604800     ; Expire
                900 )      ; Negative Cache TTL
;Define the nameservers
                NS      dove.foobirds.org.
                NS      bear.mammals.org.
;   Define the mail servers
                MX      10 wren.foobirds.org.
                MX      20 parrot.foobirds.org.
;   Define the hosts in this zone
wren            A       172.16.5.1
parrot          A       172.16.5.3
dove            A       172.16.62.1
*               MX      10 wren.foobirds.org.
                MX      20 parrot.foobirds.org.
www             CNAME   wren.foobirds.org.
```

Notice that the remote server and a specially created server, `dove.foobirds.org`, are the servers for the public version of the domain. These must be the servers registered through the `.org` domain. The private servers are defined in the configuration of internal servers as forwarders and are reached in that manner. The public domain only lists the advertised servers and a wildcard for delivering mail. This is probably all that the outside world needs.

Port Number Filtering

A final topic before leaving the subject of firewalls is the use of port numbers. Most firewalls filter on port numbers. They expect the well-known DNS port number, which is port number 53, to be used. Port 53 is the server port. Resolvers connecting to a DNS server use a dynamically generated port as the source port and port 53 as the destination port. By default, a Linux server also uses a randomly generated port number when sending a query to a remote server, because the local server is acting as a client to the remote server. Thus, from the point of view of port numbers, server-to-server queries and resolver-to-server queries look the same.

Some firewall designers prefer to have the local server send queries on port 53 so that all server traffic can be clearly distinguished from resolver traffic. The `ipchain` example earlier in this chapter depends on this. Setting the following option in the `named.conf` file forces the server to send all traffic, even queries, via port 53:

```
options {
    query-source * port 53;
};
```

When this option is used, the firewall can tell that a packet originated from a server because both the source and destination ports are 53. Traffic originating from a client has a source port greater than 1024 and a destination port of 53. Some firewall designers find this desirable. If this setting is needed for your enterprise firewall, it is the responsibility of the security officer to tell you.

DNS Security Protocols

The DNS Security (DNSSEC) protocol is defined in RFC 2535, "Domain Name System Security Extensions." At this writing, RFC 2535 is about a year old. Complex protocols that affect critical systems such as DNS do not get widely implemented in one year. This section describes DNSSEC to help you understand the shape of things to come. If you run a DNS server for a commercial enterprise, don't plan on implementing DNSSEC any time soon. Right now, DNSSEC is being tested by universities, government agencies, and network research organizations. Let them work out the kinks before you consider deploying it in your enterprise.

DNSSEC ensures the integrity and authenticity of DNS information. It also makes it possible to distribute cryptographic keys from secured domain name servers. To accomplish these tasks, DNSSEC uses cryptography to authenticate DNS communications. This isn't a book about cryptography; however, some cryptographic concepts are essential for understanding DNSSEC.

Encryption and Cryptography

There are two basic types of cryptography: *secret key,* which is also called *symmetric cryptography,* and *public key.* Symmetric cryptography is easy to understand. Cooperating systems use the same key and the same algorithm to encrypt and decrypt data. The problem with symmetric cryptography is that a prior agreement must be reached among all participating systems about the key and the algorithm to be used. The secret key in a secret key system is far from being a secret because every system must have a copy of the key. As everyone knows, a shared secret is no secret at all. And the more systems sharing the secret, the greater the possibility that the secret will be compromised.

Public key cryptography is a much more interesting system. It uses two keys: a public key that can be openly available to everyone and a private key that does not need to be shared with anyone. When the public key is used to encrypt a message, the message can only be decrypted with the private key. As a result, anyone can encrypt a message bound for the target system by using the public key, but only the target system can decrypt and read the message using its private key. Equally important, only messages encrypted with the private key can be decrypted with the public key. Thus anyone who can decrypt a message with the public key knows that the message comes from the owner of the private key.

This elegant system is not without complexity. Two elements are required to make it work:

authentication   In a secret key cryptography system, the mere fact that a message is properly encrypted means that it must have come from a trusted system that has the secret key. A public key system is different. Because the public key is available to everyone, a method for authenticating the source of an encrypted message is needed. Messages are authenticated by a digital signature. A *digital signature* is produced by running a cryptographic checksum using the content of the message as the data for the checksum and the private key of the source of the message for the encryption. Since the digital signature was produced with the source's private key, it can only be decrypted with the source's public key, proving the message came from the source. Additionally, the fact that the checksum was produced using the original content of the message means that the recipient can detect corrupted data by re-running the checksum. Authentication of both the source and the content! Cool!

secure key distribution   A weakness of public key cryptography is that you must trust the source of the public key. Everything—authentication, encryption, and decryption—depends on the public key. A key obtained from a corrupted server undermines the security of everything. A trusted public key infrastructure is not yet a reality, although there are some commercial outfits offering this service. Many organizations create bilateral agreements establishing trust between the organizations for the purpose of distributing keys. In effect, an organization tells its partners to trust a specific server as the source of its public keys.

The DNSSEC protocol provides both of these essential ingredients so that public key cryptography can be used for DNS.

Authentication and Integrity

The first thing that pops into my head when I hear the word "cryptography" is secret communications intended to provide confidentiality. DNSSEC, as defined in RFC 2535, is not designed to encrypt communications between DNS clients and servers. The RFC assumes that those communications are open and should be open. DNSSEC focuses on guaranteeing the authenticity and integrity of DNS data through the use of digital signatures.

From the discussion in the previous section, you know that authenticated data requires public keys, private keys, and digital signatures. RFC 2535 defines a new resource record to hold the public key, a new record to hold digital signatures, and a new record to authenticate negative domain information. Notice that there is no record to hold the private key. The RFC assumes that private keys are safely stored offline.

The KEY Resource Record

RFC 2535 defines the syntax of the KEY resource record as follows:

```
name ttl class KEY flags protocol algorithm public_key
```

The KEY record holds the public key for the domain object identified by the *name* field. The named object can be a zone, a host or a subdomain, or a user. A key that is defined for a zone can be used for anything within that zone. A key for a specific host can be used for any RR associated with that host. Finally, a key for a user is intended for use with a user account. A future mail service might use the user's key to authenticate that mail is from the user. Because DNSSEC is not yet widely used, speculation about how the keys will be used in the future is just that—speculation.

NOTE   If you're a security expert, you may wonder if the KEY record is a *certif-icate*—a record that binds a public key to support information, such as the key's validity interval, with a cryptographic signature. The KEY record is not a certificate and RFC 2535 does not define a certificate record. Certificates are proposed by another RFC. If you're interested in certificates, see RFC 2538, "Storing Certificates in the DNS."

The data field of a KEY record contains four components:

flags   The *flags* component of the data field defines how the key is used and clarifies whether the name in the *name* field is a zone, host, or user. *flags* contains four active subfields:

A/C   These two bits define whether the key is used for authentication or for confidentiality. If the first bit is 1 (10), the key cannot be used for authentication. If the second bit is 1 (01), the key cannot be used confidentially. Thus, 00 means the key can be used for either task, and 11 means that the zone is not secured. Despite the fact that 00 covers both authentication and confidentiality, DNSSEC only supports authentication. Some other protocol would be needed to make use of the key for confidentiality.

XT   This bit is reserved for the future when more than one *flags* field may be required. If set to 1, it means that the flags are extended to a second 16-bit word. Currently, the value must be 0 because there are no valid extensions.

NAMTYP   These two bits identify what type of domain name is found in the name field. 00 means that the name is a username such as would be found on an RP or SOA record. 01 means that the name is the domain name of the zone. 10 means that the name is the name of an object, such as a host or subdomain, contained within the zone. 11 is reserved for future use.

SIG   These four bits indicate whether or not the key can be used to sign updates for dynamic DNS. If the field is non-zero, the key can be used to sign dynamic DNS updates. If the field is 0, the key can only be used to sign a DNS update if the NAMTYP field contains 01, i.e., if the name type is zone and the update is for the specified zone.

protocol   The *protocol* component defines the protocol that will use the public key. The currently valid values for *protocol* are: 1 for TLS, 2 for e-mail, 3 for DNSSEC, and 4 for IPSEC.

algorithm   The *algorithm* component defines the algorithm used to generate the public key. The valid values for *algorithm* are: 1 for RSA/MD5, 2 for Diffie-Hellman, or 3 for DSA.

public_key The *public_key* is just that—the encryption key used for public key cryptography when communicating with the object identified by *name*.

Listing 10.11 shows these components in an actual KEY record.

Listing 10.11 A DNSSEC KEY Record

```
foobirds.org. IN KEY 16641 3 3
    ANAzGsrwr9oMDkt8g0P6cUK+iOV1py25SWHa/pYDUVmmzXyxuGDwDkk
    4xrD3MeV3omHs4+fjEFhp9nOo4qDepHiQZof8PF3uSiFSuj+yDhOo5I
    iZSbGHarEEU7W+8g2OooG7N1MbOgOKXMmhayDT/hw7U01t66T67WZ5H
    1MdNmPLp+3jWv+De2rtDjsa42Is6dPr7VgZtqe1zQgxQjr/uR+gjIYf
    2hVBuOsD73YAJVkwjsznX9FS5h1Fpi/zgEtOfJuab5SSYZKLsTDTRm5
    ufj6VN96
```

The name field contains the name of our domain foobirds.org.. The first component of the data field is the flags field. Its value is 16641, which is the default for a zone key. The flags mean that the name is a zone name and that the key is used for authentication, not confidentiality.

Next comes a 3 in the protocol field, which means that the protocol that will use the key is DNSSEC. This is followed by a second 3 in the algorithm field, which means that DSA was the algorithm used to generate the key. Finally, comes the public key itself.

Even if you understand all of the fields in a KEY record, generating a KEY record by hand would be nearly impossible. See the sidebar, "Using dnskeygen," for information on a tool that can generate the KEY record for you.

Using *dnskeygen*

dnskeygen is a program provided with BIND that generates public and private key pairs. Arguments provided to dnskeygen tell it everything it needs to know to generate a valid KEY record. The basic syntax of the dnskeygen command follows:

dnskeygen [-[DHR] *size*] **-[zhu] [-a] [-c] [-p** *num*] **-n** *name*

The elements of this command include

    -n *name* is the name of the domain object for which the key is to be generated.

    -[zhu] defines the name type: –z for a zone, –h for a host or subdomain, and –u for a user account.

Using *dnskeygen* (continued)

[-a][-c]   sets the A/C values in the flags field. Use –a to set the value to 10. Use –c to set the value to 01. Use both to set the value to 11. If neither –a nor –c is defined, the correct value for DNSSEC is set as a default.

[-p *num*]   defines the protocol the key will be used for. It can be any of the protocol numbers that are valid in a KEY record. The default is 3, DNSSEC.

-[DHR] *size*   defines the algorithm used: –D is DSA, –H is HMAC-MD5, and –R is RSA. *size* is the length of the key to be generated.

To generate a DSA key for the foobirds.org zone, enter the following command:

```
[root]# dnskeygen -D 512 -z -n foobirds.org.
Generating 512 bit DSS Key for foobirds.org.

Generated 512 bit Key for foobirds.org. id=57430 alg=3
flags=16641
```

The dnskeygen command produces two files. One file holds the private key that can be used to sign records in the zone. The other file holds the KEY record for the zone. Files created by dnskeygen start with an uppercase K and the name of the object for which the key was generated. Here are the two files created by the preceding dnskeygen command:

```
[root]# ls Kfoobirds.org.*
Kfoobirds.org.+003+57430.key
Kfoobirds.org.+003+57430.private
```

The file with the extension .key contains the exact KEY record shown in Listing 10.11. The file with the extension .private contains the private key which must be safeguarded to maintain security.

The SIG Resource Record

The SIG resource record digitally signs an RRset to guarantee the authenticity and integrity of the RRset. The format of the SIG records is

```
name ttl class SIG type_list (
    algorithm
    labels
    original_ttl
```

```
signature_expiration

signature_ inception

key_tag

signer_name

signature )
```

The fields for the SIG record are as follows:

type_list   is a list of the resource record types for the specified domain name that are digitally signed by this SIG record.

algorithm   is the encryption algorithm used to produce the digital signature. There are three *algorithm* values currently available:

1   for the RSA/MD5 algorithm defined in RFC 2537, "RSA/MD5 KEYs and SIGs in the Domain Name System (DNS)."

2   for the Diffie-Hellman algorithm defined in RFC 2539, "Storage of Diffie-Hellman Keys in the Domain Name System (DNS)."

3   for the DSA algorithm defined in RFC 2536, "DSA KEYs and SIGs in the Domain Name System (DNS)."

labels   specifies the number of parts in the domain name. For example, foobirds.org has two parts, foobirds, and org, so it has a *labels* value of 2. terns.foobirds.org has three parts and thus, a *labels* value of 3.

orginal_ttl   is the TTL value from the original resource record that was used when the digital signature was calculated. Because the TTL is decremented by servers that hold records in their caches, the *orginal_ttl* is needed to recalculate the signature when verifying the record.

signature_expiration   defines the date that the signature becomes invalid.

signature_inception   defines the date on which the signature was created.

key_tag   is a 16-bit identifier that is used to select the correct key. The *key_tag* field must match the id value that was displayed by **dnskeygen** when the key was created.

signer_name   is the domain name of the entity that created the digital signature. It is usually the domain name of the zone that contains the signed records.

signature   is the digital signature that authenticates the resource records.

The data field of a SIG record contains nine different pieces of data, which can make things complicated. The example in Listing 10.12 should help to clarify the structure and meaning of the SIG record.

Maintaining a Healthy System

PART 4

Listing 10.12 DNSSEC SIG Record

```
foobirds.org. 86400 IN SOA wren.foobirds.org.
   admin.wren.foobirds.org. (
               2000020501 ; serial
                       6H ; refresh
                      30M ; retry
                       1W ; expiry
                     15M ) ; minimum
        86400 IN SIG SOA 3 2 86400 (
                         20000521211449 20000420211449
                         57430 foobirds.org.
                         AAKB63gqDeRoB/ryQm6Nc7aOocr6LC
                         aYzzjOa3YJgnl3Whx6h4RzGL4= )
```

Listing 10.12 contains the SOA record and its associated SIG record from a secured version of the foobirds.org zone. Look at the components of the data field of the SIG record. In order, each component has the following meaning:

SOA   This is the digital signature for the SOA record.

3   The Digital Signature Algorithm (DSA) was used to generate the digital signature.

2   The number of labels in the name is 2.

86400   The original TTL used to calculate the digital signature was 86400 seconds (one day).

20000521211449   The digital signature will expire sometime during the day on May 21, 2000.

20000420211449   The digital signature became valid sometime during the day of April 20, 2000.

57430   The *key_tag* is 57430.

foobirds.org.   The signer's name for this record is foobirds.org..

AAKB63...RzGL4=   The SIG record concludes with the digital signature.

WARNING   As the *signature_expiration* and *signature_inception* fields show, digital signatures are time dependent. This goes not only for the SIG records but also for the transaction signatures described later in this chapter. For this reason, secure servers and clients need to be time synchronized. To do this, these systems need to run the Network Time Protocol (NTP). Describing NTP is beyond the scope of this book. See RFC 1305, "Network Time Protocol," for a description of NTP.

Again, understanding these fields does not mean you will be able to create a SIG record manually. SIG records are created by software. For example, a DHCP server that dynamically updates a secure zone should create the appropriate KEY records and SIG records for the update. To secure an existing zone, you must use a tool such as dnssigner. See the sidebar, "Using dnssigner," for more information about signing your own zone file.

Using *dnssigner*

dnssigner is a tool that can be used to process a zone file and sign the records it contains. It is not included with the basic BIND software but it is available from ISC in the bind-contrib.tar.gz file.

Use tar to extract and uncompress this file into the directory you're using for BIND software. In Chapter 3, we used /usr/local/src/bind8.2.2 as the directory for the BIND software. After the installation described in Chapter 3, that directory contains two subdirectories, doc and src. After extracting the bind-contrib.tar.gz file, a third subdirectory named contrib is added.

Change to the newly created contrib/dns_signer directory and type **make**. On a Linux system, dnssigner should compile without error because the compilation of BIND done in Chapter 3 produced the correct Makefile.set and make is smart enough to use it for the dnssigner compile. The full path of the dnssigner program is now /usr/local/src/bind8.2.2/dns_digner/signer/dnssigner. Move dnssigner to a more convenient directory. It is now be ready to run.

To sign a zone, tell dnssigner the name of the zone, the path to the file containing the zone, where it should put the signed zone file, and where it can find the key. The following command signs the foobirds.org zone:

```
[root]# ./dnssigner -or foobirds.org. -zi foobirds.hosts \
-zo foobirds.signed -k1 foobirds.org. dsa 57430
```

The original zone file is foobirds.hosts. We chose to call the output file foobirds.signed. The key we are using is the DSA zone key for foobirds.org, identified by key tag 57430.

The newly created foobirds.signed file contains more than twice as many records as the original file and is about five times larger in total bytes. The added records are the NXT records and the SIG records. If the file is correct, the signed file should be made the new zone file.

The NXT Resource Record

The final resource record defined by RFC 2535 does not deal directly with cryptographic signatures, but it does fill an important role in providing complete information about a secured domain. You learned earlier in this book from the discussions of negative caching that negative information about a zone is almost as important as the data that the zone contains. That is true whether the zone is unsecured or secured. However, in a secured zone, all information needs to be digitally signed, and a record must exist before a cryptographic signature can be generated. The NXT record is the record for non-existent information.

When a zone file is signed, a NXT record is added to the RRset for each host name. The NXT record creates an ordered sequence in the zone by sorting each part of the domain name. The NXT record contains the next host name in sequence that is currently in use. Thus, by knowing the name in the name field of the NXT record and the name in the data field of the record, you know that all other names that would appear in sequence between these names do not exist.

Negative wording always makes things hard to explain. An example should help. In the foobirds.org zone, puffin follows parrot in name sequence. The response to a query for partridge.foobirds.org has an RCODE of NXDOMAIN and an authority section containing the NXT records for parrot and puffin. The parrot NXT record says that puffin is the next name. partridge, which would fall between parrot and puffin if it existed, clearly does not exist. Because the NXT records for parrot and puffin can be digitally signed, the information that partridge does not exist can be authenticated.

The format of the NXT record is

```
name ttl class NXT next_name type_list
```

The *next_name* field contains the name of the next object in name sequence. The *type_list* is a list of the types of resource records in the RRset of the current object, which is identified by *name*. Because A, RP, and now NXT records exist for the domain name parrot.foobirds.org and puffin.foobirds.org is the next name in sequence, parrot might have the following NXT record:

```
parrot.foobirds.org. IN NXT puffin.foobirds.org. A RP NXT
```

You don't really need to worry about creating NXT records. They are created by the program that signs the zone when you create a secure zone. In the previous example, dnssigner created the NXT record.

Statically Configured Public Keys

On the surface, it looks as if KEY records and SIG records solve the problem of defining and distributing public keys. But there is a problem. Unless the parent zones above your zone are also secured, the security of your zone is in doubt. The KEY record for your zone should be signed by a secured parent to maintain traceability through a secured DNS hierarchy. In a perfect world, a client or server should be able to get a copy of the public key of your zone from your parent, signed by your parent, along with the pointers to your zone. The chain of signed keys in the perfect world would be unbroken all the way to the root. Of course, the world is not perfect so it doesn't work this way.

The best you can really do is to secure your enterprise domain and all of its children. You cannot reasonably expect the people who run the root servers to digitally sign the KEY record for your domain. You must rely on the physical security of the root to keep the top-level domains secure and create your own security in your domain and its children. Beyond the domains you control, you cannot rely on DNS to distribute the keys. An alternative to distributing keys through DNS is to distribute keys through a side channel, such as UPS or Federal Express, and then to manually add those keys to the configuration. BIND provides ways to manually define keys in the named.conf file.

The *pubkey* Option

Use the pubkey option in the zone statement to define the public key for a zone when no parent of the zone will be secured. To create a properly formatted pubkey option, copy the flags, protocol, algorithm, and public key from your zone's KEY record and paste them onto the keyword pubkey. Listing 10.13 shows an example for the foobirds.org domain.

Listing 10.13 Using the pubkey Option

```
zone "foobirds.org" {
        type slave;
        file "foobirds.hosts";
        pubkey 16641 3 3
        "ANAzGsrwr9oMDkt8gOP6cUK+iOV1py25SWHa/pYDUVmmzXyxuG
        DwDkkT4xrD3MeV3omHs4+fjEFhp9nOo4qDepHiQZof8PF3uSiFS
        uj+yDhOo5IiZSbGHarEEU7W+8g2OooG7NlMbOgOKXMmhayDT/hw
        7UO1t66T67WZ5HlMdNmPLp+3jWv+De2rtDjsa42Is6dPr7VgZtq
        e1zQgxQjr/uR+gjIYf2hVBuOsD73YAJVkwjsznX9FS5h1Fpi/zg
        EtOfJuab5SSYZKLsTDTRm5ufj6VN96";
};
```

Listing 10.13 is a very realistic example. If you secure the `foobirds.org` zone on the master server, you must use the `pubkey` option to provide the public key to all of the slave servers for that zone. The slaves cannot ask the parent zone, `.org`, for the key because root servers do not store or sign KEY records. And without the key, the slaves would not be able to verify the zone when it was loaded. At the very least, the slave servers of your enterprise domain must be statically configured with the public key using the `pubkey` option.

The *trusted-keys* Statement

Slave servers, of course, are not the only servers loading information from your domain. Non-authoritative servers that insist on maintaining a chain of trust for secure domain information statically define the public key with the `trusted-keys` statement. Listing 10.14 shows a full `named.conf` file with a `trusted-keys` statement for the `foobirds.org` key.

Listing 10.14 Using the `trusted-keys` Statement

```
options {
        directory "/var/named";
};


trusted-keys {
    foobirds.org. 16641 3 3
            "ANAzGsrwr9oMDkt8gOP6cUK+iOV1py25SWHa/pYDUVmmzXyxuG
            DwDkkT4xrD3MeV3omHs4+fjEFhp9nOo4qDepHiQZof8PF3uSiFS
            uj+yDhOo5IiZSbGHarEEU7W+8g2OooG7N1MbOgOKXMmhayDT/hw
            7U01t66T67WZ5H1MdNmPLp+3jWv+De2rtDjsa42Is6dPr7VgZtq
            e1zQgxQjr/uR+gjIYf2hVBuOsD73YAJVkwjsznX9FS5h1Fpi/zg
            EtOfJuab5SSYZKLsTDTRm5ufj6VN96";
};


zone "." {
        type hint;
        file "named.ca";
};


zone "0.0.127.in-addr.arpa" {
        type master;
        file "named.local";
};
```

Each entry in the `trusted-keys` statement defines the key for one domain. Each entry starts with a domain name followed by the flags, protocol, algorithm, and public key values from that domain's KEY record. The entire `named.conf` file is shown in Listing 10.14 to illustrate that `trusted-keys` is a stand-alone statement and not part of a `zone` statement, and to illustrate that the `trusted-keys` statement is not used by servers that are authoritative for the domain defined in the `trusted-keys` statement.

Transaction Security

The various keys, records, and commands discussed thus far are used to guarantee the authenticity and integrity of the domain database. Another level of security is needed to guarantee the authenticity and integrity of the DNS requests and responses that move over the network. A request and the response to that request is a *transaction*. Like the DNS database itself, the authenticity and integrity of DNS transactions is guaranteed by digital signatures, which in the case of transactions are called *transaction signatures (TSIGs)*. A TSIG is *not* a resource record; it is a technique for digitally signing DNS messages. Furthermore, transaction signatures are not yet standardized; the TSIG RFC is still only a draft. Yet BIND provides transaction security that can be used on your Linux DNS server.

Use the `key` statement to assign a key identifier to the algorithm and secret key pairing that will be used for transaction security. The syntax of the `key` statement follows:

```
key key_id {
  algorithm hmac-md5;
  secret secret_string;
};
```

The *key_id* is any descriptive name that you want to assign to the algorithm and secret key pairing—it is this name that is used as the key identifier. BIND 8.2.2 only supports the `hmac-md5` algorithm, so the algorithm is always that value. (This could change in the future.) The *secret_string* is a base-64 encoded key used by the algorithm. Use the `dnskeygen` utility to generate the *secret_string* value or manually create your own value.

Once a key identifier is defined, it can be used in an access control list or in the `keys` option of a `server` statement. Listing 10.15 contains a few statements from a `named.conf` file to illustrate how to define and use a key identifier.

Listing 10.15 The key Statement

```
key bear-wren-key {
    algorithm hmac-md5;
    secret "SqkS32+izd9aaKClmzPhrQ==";
};
server 192.168.32.4 {
    keys { bear-wren-key; };
};
```

The first statement in Listing 10.15 is a key statement. It defines a pairing identified as bear-wren-key. This key is then referenced in the keys option of a server statement, which means that this key will be used to secure transactions with the server at IP address 192.168.32.4. For the communications to be secured in both directions, the server at 192.168.32.4 must also secure the transactions with a matching key statement, as follows:

```
key bear-wren-key {
    algorithm hmac-md5;
    secret "SqkS32+izd9aaKClmzPhrQ==";
};
server 172.16.5.1 {
    keys { bear-wren-key; };
};
```

Notice that the configuration on the remote system is identical to that on the local system, except for the address in the server statement. The key identifier as well as the secret key value must be the same on both systems for transaction security to function properly.

In both examples, the key statement precedes any reference to the key identifier. This is necessary. named.conf does not allow forward references. Place the key statement before any other configuration command that references it.

A Final Word on DNSSEC

DNSSEC is a cool security tool. Network research organizations, high security sites, and sites that allow dynamic updates should be working with it now. But DNSSEC is not yet ready for prime time. Some features, such as TSIG, are only in draft form. Most commercial sites should avoid anything that is not yet even a proposed standard, unless it fills a clear and pressing need.

For many of us, the risk of DNSSEC is greater than the reward. DNSSEC is not a security cure-all. DNSSEC does not secure the hardware. It does not protect the server from break-ins. It cannot prevent all denial of service attacks. All of the security techniques needed to deal with these threats are still needed even after you deploy DNSSEC.

What DNSSEC does is protect the integrity of the DNS database. Clearly, running DNSSEC is less work than tracking down and fixing corruption after the database has been maliciously corrupted. But has your zone file ever been maliciously corrupted? Probably not. If you choose to run a secure zone, you will need to manually distribute keys to your partners and you will need to manually run `dnssigner` every time you update the zone. Ask yourself if you'll spend more time than you'll save. Time is always the critical factor for a system administrator at a commercial site, so make this determination before jumping into DNSSEC. Some will benefit from DNSSEC in its current form. Many will not.

Currently, I'm recommending that average commercial sites wait. Future versions of BIND 9 will simplify DNSSEC configuration and management. Researchers and sites with advanced security requirements will clean up the bugs. After DNSSEC is stable and debugged, re-evaluate it for your site's security needs.

In Sum

The only people who like security are security experts and bad guys. For the rest of us, security is a necessary evil that steals time away from making things better. It's like putting iron bars on your windows; they don't make your house better, they just make it safer. Securing your DNS server won't improve performance or make life better for your users; it will just help you limit the amount of damage done to your system by intruders.

The glamour of automated solutions and advanced cryptography often put the focus of security on those things. But there are many other simple things that can be done to improve the security of the hardware and software of your system. This chapter has covered the full range of security options, from basic to advanced. For most organizations, the best security is good system administration. Making security a fundamental part of your on-going system maintenance is an essential part of maintaining a healthy server.

The next chapter covers the test tools that can be used to examine the content of the DNS database. Use these tools to test local and remote servers when problems arise.

Maintaining a
Healthy System

PART 4

11

Testing DNS

DNS is a complex system with many different configuration options and a substantial number of different database records. Beyond the challenge of creating your own server, there is a world of equally complex DNS servers upon which your server depends. The global, distributed DNS database system creates complex interdependencies. You need test tools that allow you to test and validate remote servers as easily as you can test your own.

BIND provides powerful tools for testing DNS. You have seen examples of the use of the three test tools, `host`, `dig`, and `nslookup`, throughout this book. In this chapter, these tools are described in detail. You'll see why the tools are used, how each tool is used, and when a specific tool is the best choice. Each tool has advantages and disadvantages. Understanding them will help you select the best tool for the job. We begin by looking at the `host` command, which is the simplest of the three commands.

The *host* Command

The `host` command is a simple, straightforward command. It is most often used to obtain the IP address of a host name with the minimum muss and fuss. Listing 11.1 contains a simple example of the `host` command.

Listing 11.1 The Basic host Command

```
[craig]$ host redbreast.foobirds.org.
redbreast.foobirds.org is a nickname for robin.foobirds.org
robin.foobirds.org has address 172.16.5.2
robin.foobirds.org mail is handled (pri=5) by wren.foobirds.org
```

There are two advantages to such a simple command:

- It is easy to script. A complete host command can be built on a single line and stored in a script. Not only is the command simple, the response to the command is also simple, which makes it easy to extract the critical information from the response. The ability to extract information from a response and process it is an important part of scripting.

- It is useful for quick tests. A classic example of this is shown in Listing 4.8, where a change is made to the system, and a host command is used to make sure that the change has taken effect. Simple, quick tests are the host command's forte.

The *host* Command Syntax

Of course, the host command is not always as simple as the example shown in Listing 11.1. In Listing 7.7, the host command is used to test advertised name servers before delegating a new zone. For that test, a few command-line arguments were necessary. The full syntax of the host command is

```
host [-w] [-v] [-r] [-d] [-l] [-t type] [-a] name [server]
```

The options for the host command are as follows:

−w   causes the host command to wait forever for a response from the server. Without it, host times out using the normal resolver timeout. I believe that a test should simulate reality, so I want host to use the normal timeout. Therefore, I don't use this argument.

−v   tells the host command to produce verbose output. Normally, host displays a short response.

−r   causes host to send a non-recursive query to the server. Normally, the host command sends out recursive queries.

−d   turns on debugging, which traces the DNS transactions.

−l   lists the complete domain by performing a zone file transfer.

−t *type*   requests a specific type of resource record. The type field can contain any of the valid record types found in Table 6.1 or the keyword ANY for the entire RRset associated with the domain name.

−a   requests all of the records for the domain name in verbose format. The −a argument produces the same output as combining the −t any and the −v argument.

name   defines the name of the domain object for which information is sought. If the name does not contain at least one dot, the default domain from the resolver configuration is used to complete the name.

server   defines the name of the server to which the query should be sent. If the name of a server is not provided, the resolver configuration is used and the query is sent to the server normally used by the system. The server name is position-dependent. The second name on the command line is always assumed to be the server name.

Combining the various host command arguments allows you to extend the usefulness of the host command well beyond the basic example used in Listing 11.1. The following sections describe different ways that these arguments can be used.

Testing a Remote Server

All the BIND test tools, host, dig, and nslookup, make it just as easy to test a remote DNS server as it is to test your own server. The power of these tools is that they can be configured to bypass your local server and go directly to the remote server. Thus, problems with your local server do not affect the outcome of the test.

Any tool that allows you to segment a problem is worth its weight in gold. These tools allow you to segment a problem by focusing the test on an individual server, which makes it possible to locate the server that has the problem. Listing 7.7 uses this feature of the host command to check the advertised servers for a domain. Listing 11.2 contains an expanded version of that test and explains the individual host commands.

Listing 11.2   Testing Different DNS Servers with the host Command

```
[craig]$ host -r -t NS ducks.foobirds.org ruddy.ducks.foobirds.org
Using domain server:
Name: ruddy.ducks.foobirds.org
Address: 172.16.50.1
Aliases:

ducks.foobirds.org name server ruddy.ducks.foobirds.org
ducks.foobirds.org name server wren.foobirds.org
ducks.foobirds.org name server bear.mammals.org
[craig]$ host -r -t soa ducks.foobirds.org wren.foobirds.org
```

```
Using domain server:
Name: wren.foobirds.org
Address: 172.16.5.1
Aliases:

ducks.foobirds.org SOA ruddy.ducks.foobirds.org dan.ruddy.ducks.foobirds.org(
                    2000032201   ;serial (version)
                         10800   ;refresh period
                          1800   ;retry refresh this often
                        604800   ;expiration period
                           900   ;negative TTL
                             )
```

[craig]$ **host -r -t soa ducks.foobirds.org ruddy.ducks.foobirds.org**
```
Using domain server:
Name: ruddy.ducks.foobirds.org
Address: 172.16.50.1
Aliases:

ducks.foobirds.org SOA ruddy.ducks.foobirds.org dan.ruddy.ducks.foobirds.org(
                    2000032201   ;serial (version)
                         10800   ;refresh period
                          1800   ;retry refresh this often
                        604800   ;expiration period
                           900   ;negative TTL
                             )
```
[craig]$ **host -r -t soa ducks.foobirds.org bear.mammals.org**
```
Using domain server:
Name: ns1.foobirds.org
Address: 172.22.13.2
Aliases:

Host not found.
```

Listing 11.2 shows the four host commands in bold text. (All of the other text is output that appears in response to the host commands.) In Chapter 7, "Creating Subdomains," this test was used to prevent a lame delegation by checking that each authoritative server for the ducks.foobirds.org domain had a zone file for that domain before the ducks zone was delegated.

The test in Listing 11.2 begins by asking for the list of authoritative servers from the master server of the `ducks` domain. The master server is `ruddy.ducks.foobirds.org`. The authoritative servers are the servers identified in the NS records for the zone `ducks.foobirds.org`. The command that asks for this information is as follows:

```
host -t ns ducks.foobirds.org ruddy.ducks.foobirds.org
```

The command begins with the keyword `host`, which is followed by the `-t ns` argument that requests NS type records. The records are requested for the object identified by the name `duck.foobirds.org`, which is the name of a subdomain. The query for the NS records is sent directly to the master server `ruddy.ducks.foobirds.org`. `ruddy` returns a list of servers that it advertises as authoritative for the zone.

Using the list of name servers, each server is queried in turn for the SOA record of the `ducks.foobirds.org` zone. It is essential that each server be queried directly. If the local server answered these queries, it would answer from its cache. Once it obtained an answer from the first server, it would not query the other servers. The only way to be sure that each server can answer the query is to ask each server directly.

> **NOTE**   Notice that when a remote server is used on the host command line, the output of the command begins by listing the name and address of the server that is being used.

A different but somewhat related issue is recursion. By default, the `host` command sends recursive queries to the server. Most of the time this is just what you want. You want the `host` command to act like a normal application interacting with the resolver. But on occasion, you want to check what the server knows, not what it can learn from other servers.

To ensure that the server answers from its own database of knowledge, use the –r argument to turn off recursion. The server will answer a non-recursive query if it can, but it will not recursively pursue an answer for the query by checking other servers.

Getting More Information Out of the *host* Command

The `host` command often provides a one- or two-line answer to a query. Listing 11.1 is a good example of this. Even when longer answers are provided, as in Listing 11.2, `host` tries to keep the output to a minimum and to make the output as readable as possible. By default, `host` prints out a short sentence identifying the address of a host instead of displaying the raw address record. An entire zone file can be printed out in this text format using the –l argument. Listing 11.3 shows such a listing of the `foobirds.org` domain.

Listing 11.3   Listing an Entire Domain with the host Command

```
[craig]$ host -l foobirds.org. 172.16.5.1
Using domain server 172.16.5.1:
foobirds.org name server wren.foobirds.org
foobirds.org name server parrot.foobirds.org
foobirds.org name server bear.mammals.org
ducks.foobirds.org name server ruddy.ducks.foobirds.org
ducks.foobirds.org name server wren.foobirds.org
ducks.foobirds.org name server bear.mammals.org
robin.foobirds.org has address 172.16.5.2
puffin.foobirds.org has address 172.16.5.17
wren.foobirds.org has address 172.16.5.1
parrot.foobirds.org has address 172.16.5.3
crow.foobirds.org has address 172.16.5.5
localhost.foobirds.org has address 127.0.0.1
terns.foobirds.org name server sooty.terns.foobirds.org
sooty.terns.foobirds.org has address 172.16.30.250
terns.foobirds.org name server arctic.terns.foobirds.org
arctic.terns.foobirds.org has address 172.16.30.251
kestrel.foobirds.org has address 172.16.5.20
hawk.foobirds.org has address 172.16.5.4
foobirds-net.foobirds.org domain name pointer 0.0.16.172.in-addr.arpa
```

The –l argument shows the limitation of the text output used by the host command. For simple queries, the sentence structure that the host command uses for answers is very readable. For complex queries, it is less useful. There are several command-line arguments available to change the default output format.

Requesting Verbose Output

An obvious choice for changing the amount of information displayed by the host command is the verbose (–v) argument. Listing 11.4 shows two queries for puffin.foobirds .org, one with and one without the –v argument.

Listing 11.4   The host Command –v Argument

```
[craig]$ host puffin.foobirds.org.
puffin.foobirds.org has address 172.16.5.17
puffin.foobirds.org mail is handled (pri=5) by wren.foobirds.org
```

```
[craig]$ host -v puffin.foobirds.org.
rcode = 0 (Success), ancount=1
puffin.foobirds.org       86400 IN         A         172.16.5.17
For authoritative answers, see:
foobirds.org     86400 IN        NS        wren.foobirds.org
foobirds.org     86400 IN        NS        parrot.foobirds.org
foobirds.org     86400 IN        NS        bear.mammals.org
Additional information:
wren.foobirds.org         86400 IN         A         172.16.5.1
parrot.foobirds.org       86400 IN         A         172.16.5.3
foobirds.org              86400 IN         KEY       ???
```

The –v argument displays the RCODE and answer count from the DNS message header. The content of the answer section, the authority section, and the additional section of the DNS message are also displayed.

Notice that the two host queries in Listing 11.4 are not exactly the same. The second host command produces both more and less information than the first. It puts out more details about the address query, but it doesn't display any information at all about the MX record for puffin. The default for the host command is to query for both address and MX records, except when the –v argument is used. Then the host command only queries for address records.

Requesting All Records

To cover the same ground as the first query, another host command would need to be issued that had both a –t mx argument and a –v argument. If you really want verbose output for multiple record types, an easier way to do it is with the –a argument.

The –a argument provides verbose output for all of the resource records associated with a host name. Listing 11.5 shows the output produced when the –a argument is used in a query for information about puffin.foobirds.org.

Listing 11.5   The host Command –a Argument

```
[craig]$ host -a puffin.foobirds.org.
rcode = 0 (Success), ancount=3
puffin.foobirds.org       86400 IN         RP        admin@foobirds.org
    hotline.foobirds.org
puffin.foobirds.org       86400 IN         MX        5 wren.foobirds.org
puffin.foobirds.org       86400 IN         A         172.16.5.17
```

Maintaining a
Healthy System

PART 4

```
For authoritative answers, see:
foobirds.org      86400 IN          NS       wren.foobirds.org
foobirds.org      86400 IN          NS       parrot.foobirds.org
foobirds.org      86400 IN          NS       bear.mammals.org
Additional information:
wren.foobirds.org         86400 IN       A        172.16.5.1
parrot.foobirds.org       86400 IN       A        172.16.5.3
foobirds.org              86400 IN       KEY      ???
```

The host name `puffin.foobirds.org` has three resource records assigned: an RP record, an MX record, and an A record. To get this same output using the –v argument, you would need to issue three separate `host` commands, one for each record type. Clearly, the –a argument gives you more information, but it is still not the option that provides the most detailed output.

Running *host* in Debug Mode

The –d argument turns on debugging, which displays the query as well as the response in more detail than any other `host` command argument. If the –t argument is not used with the –d argument, the `host` command first queries for the host's A record and then for the host's MX record. Listing 11.6 shows the result of using the –d argument with the –t argument to query for the address record of `puffin.foobirds.org`.

Listing 11.6   The host Command –d Argument

```
[craig]$ host -d -t A puffin.foobirds.org.
;; res_nmkquery(QUERY, puffin.foobirds.org, IN, A)
;; res_send()
;; ->>HEADER<<- opcode: QUERY, status: NOERROR, id: 64070
;; flags: rd; QUERY: 1, ANSWER: 0, AUTHORITY: 0, ADDITIONAL: 0
;;      puffin.foobirds.org, type = A, class = IN
;; Querying server (# 1) address = 0.0.0.0
;; got answer:
;; ->>HEADER<<- opcode: QUERY, status: NOERROR, id: 64070
;; flags: qr aa rd ra; QUERY: 1, ANSWER: 1, AUTHORITY: 3, ADDITIONAL: 3
;;      puffin.foobirds.org, type = A, class = IN
puffin.foobirds.org.    1D IN A      172.16.5.17
foobirds.org.           1D IN NS     wren.foobirds.org.
foobirds.org.           1D IN NS     parrot.foobirds.org.
foobirds.org.           1D IN NS     bear.mammals.org.
```

```
wren.foobirds.org.      1D IN A      172.16.5.1
parrot.foobirds.org.    1D IN A      172.16.5.3
foobirds.org.           1D IN KEY    0x4101 3 3 (
         ANAzGsrwr9oMDkt8gOP6cUK+iOV1py25SWHa/pYDUVmmzXyx
         uGDwDkkT4xrD3MeV3omHs4+fjEFhp9nOo4qDepHiQZof8PF3
         uSiFSuj+yDhOo5IiZSbGHarEEU7W+8g2OooG7NlMbOgOKXMm
         hayDT/hw7U01t66T67WZ5HlMdNmPLp+3jWv+De2rtDjsa42I
         s6dPr7VgZtqe1zQgxQjr/uR+gjIYf2hVBuOsD73YAJVkwjsz
         nX9FS5h1Fpi/zgEtOfJuab5SSYZKLsTDTRm5ufj6VN96 )
rcode = 0 (Success), ancount=1
puffin.foobirds.org has address 172.16.5.17
```

More than anything else, the output in Listing 11.6 will remind you of the dig output you first saw in Listing 2.1. The host command with the –d argument provides details of the DNS message header just like dig does, and just like dig, these details are set off by semi-colons. The advantage of this is that the semi-colons make these informational lines comments.

The problem that I have with the output from the host command when compared to dig is that it does not make all of the informational messages into comments. The last two lines in Listing 11.6 are informational messages from the host command, but they are not set off by semi-colons.

To me, the host command is at its best when it is used for basic queries and it is allowed to format the responses to those queries into simple sentences fit for human consumption. Look at the reverse query shown in Listing 11.7.

Listing 11.7 Doing a Reverse Lookup with the host Command

```
[craig]$ host 172.16.5.17
17.5.16.172.IN-ADDR.ARPA domain name pointer puffin.foobirds.org
```

Nothing could be easier or more understandable than the reverse query in Listing 11.7. There is no need to reverse the address into the proper form or to request the PTR record type. The host command does all of the work for you and then displays the answer in an easy-to-read sentence. This is the host command at its best. Other BIND test tools are better suited for more complex queries.

The *dig* Command

The power of the dig test tool comes from the amount of detail it provides about a DNS query, and the fact that it formats that information in a way that can be directly used by named. There are three significant advantages to the dig command:

- It is easy to script. A complete dig command can be built on a single line and stored in a script file. dig goes beyond simple shell scripting by offering a special "batch mode" execution. dig commands stored in a file can be executed by dig in batch mode to add features that are not available when executing dig commands through the shell.

- It is useful for viewing and controlling the structure of DNS messages. The dig command was used in Listing 2.1 to illustrate the structure of DNS messages because it does an excellent job of following the format of a DNS query response. dig provides access to query options to let you control the DNS message header settings.

- It produces output that is properly formatted for a DNS zone file. Output from a dig command can, and often is, loaded directly into named as part of a zone file.

Let's begin our discussion of the dig command by taking a detailed look at its syntax.

The Syntax of the *dig* Command

Because of added features such as batch mode and the ability to control the query header, the syntax of the dig command is more complex than that of the host command. A simplified version of the dig command syntax is

```
dig name [type] [class] [@server] [-option] [+query-option] [%comment]
```

The dig syntax is a curious mixture of positional and position-independent command-line arguments. The position-independent arguments are tagged by special characters, as follows:

- The string that begins with an @ must be the host name or the IP address of the server to which the query will be sent.

- Any string that begins with a – must be a dig command-line option.

- Any string that begins with a + must be an option for the DNS query.

- Any string that begins with a % is treated as a comment.

The relative positions of the three remaining arguments determine the function of each argument. The arguments that begin with special characters can occur anywhere on the command line—before the positional arguments, after them, or between them. But the positional arguments must occur in the following order:

- The first argument that does not begin with a special character must be the name of the domain object for which information is sought. The *name* field is required.

- The second argument that does not start with a special character is interpreted as the resource record type. If supplied, it must be a valid resource record type. (Table 6.1 lists the most commonly used record types.) The *type* field is optional. If it is not supplied, dig asks for address records.

- The third argument that does not start with a special character is interpreted as the database class. It defaults to IN for Internet class records. I never use the *class* field because all of the records in all of the DNS zones I work with are Internet records.

Try this out yourself. Do a simple dig query for the address record of a host. Start with the server first, followed by the host name and the type argument. Then, run dig with the server at the end of the command. Finally, run dig with the server name between the host name and the type argument. The results are the same in all cases. The three dig commands in Listing 11.8 all produce the same output.

Listing 11.8   The Placement of dig Command Arguments

```
dig @172.16.5.3 puffin.foobirds.org. a
dig puffin.foobirds.org. @172.16.5.3 a
dig puffin.foobirds.org. a @172.16.5.3
```

The mixture of positional and position-independent arguments on the dig command line can make it hard to read dig commands written by other people. Some administrators like to put the server first; others like to put it at the end of the command. Just remember these rules, and you should be able to read anyone's dig command.

Mixing positional and position-independent arguments on the same command line is not the only thing that makes dig syntax complex. The volume of command arguments and query options can also be overwhelming.

dig Command Options

The dig command accepts 10 different command options. Two of these provide an alternate way to define the optional positional arguments:

-t *type*   defines the type of resource records sought by this query. *type* must be a valid DNS query type, specified by either the numeric value of the query type or the mnemonic. Appendix C, "Resource Record Reference," lists the resource records in numeric sequence from query type 1 to 41. I prefer to use mnemonics, such as those listed in Table 6.1.

−c *class*   defines the class of records sought by the query. This option defaults to IN, which is correct for DNS Internet information.

Some people find the −t option preferable to the positional *type* argument because they feel that the clear −t marking is more understandable and thus more readable. dig commands that are easier to read and understand are beneficial when the commands are stored in batch files, particularly when the administrator reading the file may not be the one who wrote it. The following dig commands produce the same results. The one you use is primarily a matter of personal preference:

```
dig puffin.foobirds.org. @172.16.5.3 mx
dig puffin.foobirds.org. @172.16.5.3 -t mx
```

Like the positional class argument, there is rarely any reason to use the −c option because the default value is correct for almost every system. The −c option is not the only command option that is rarely used. Two other dig command-line options that don't see much use are

−p *port*   defines an alternate port for DNS traffic. If your server uses a port number other than the standard DNS port number of 53, use the −p option to define that port. People use non-standard ports for testing or security. I have never worked with a server that used a non-standard port. Therefore, I have never needed to use this option. But it is there if you need it.

−P *ping*   tells dig to launch a ping command after the query. dig displays statistics after the query. The idea behind this option is to compare the response time of a ping command to the response time of a DNS query. This is supposed to tell you if the DNS server application is running particularly slow, but the value of such a comparison is marginal at best. Additionally, this option does not work properly on Linux systems. See the sidebar, "Fixing the −P Option," for more information about this problem.

Fixing the –P Option

The basic –P option does not work on Linux systems. Here is a dig command with the –P option and the last few lines of output from the command. (I deleted lots of unneeded lines.)

```
  [craig]$ dig @172.16.5.1 puffin.foobirds.org -P
...Many lines deleted...
  ;; Total query time: 3 msec
  ;; FROM: 24seven.wrotethebook.com to SERVER: 172.16.5.1
```

Fixing the −P Option *(continued)*

```
;; WHEN: Tue Apr 25 15:50:47 2000
;; MSG SIZE  sent: 37  rcvd: 393
usage: ping [-LRdfnqrv] [-c count] [-i wait] [-l preload]
[-p pattern] [-s packetsize] [-t ttl] [-I interface address] host
```

The last two lines of output are ping trying to explain the proper ping command format. This problem is caused by the fact that dig sends a ping command to the shell that is incompatible with Linux. dig uses an old BSD ping syntax that is rejected by Linux and most current Unix systems.

The −P option accepts a ping command as an optional argument. Using the optional argument is the first step in attacking the problem. But even the optional ping command argument does not completely solve the problem. dig sends a ping query in the following format:

ping −s *server size count*

The optional ping command argument that can be provided with −P only replaces the ping −s value at the beginning of the command issued by dig. The *server*, *size*, and *count* fields are still provided as positional arguments to the ping command, which is not the format needed by Linux. What Linux wants is a command in the following format:

ping −c *count* **−s** *size server*

To handle this, create a tiny shell script that takes the values provided by dig and properly formats them for Linux. I call the following two-line shell script mungeping:

```
[craig]$ cat mungeping
#!/bin/sh
ping -c $3 -s $2 $1
```

The mungeping shell script is called from dig by using it as the argument with −P. (Notice that in the example that follows, there is no space between −P and its argument.) The shell script is called as follows:

```
[craig]$ dig @172.16.5.1 puffin.foobirds.org -Pmungeping
   ...Many lines deleted...
;; Total query time: 3 msec
;; FROM: 24seven.wrotethebook.com to SERVER: 172.16.5.1
;; WHEN: Tue Apr 25 16:29:53 2000
;; MSG SIZE  sent: 37  rcvd: 393
--- 172.16.5.1 ping statistics ---
3 packets transmitted, 3 packets received, 0% packet loss
round-trip min/avg/max = 0.1/0.1/0.1 ms
```

Fixing the –P Option *(continued)*

Now the ping command is properly formatted to run on Linux. dig prints its statistics, runs ping, and displays the ping summary statistics after its own. Again, I'm not sure what this comparison shows you, but at least it works.

I know I have been pointing out options that I don't find useful, but there are some useful dig options. One option that I find very useful is the –x argument. –x properly formats reverse domain queries. Listing 11.9 shows a reverse domain query using the –x argument.

Listing 11.9 Using dig for a Reverse Domain Query

```
[craig]$ dig -x 172.16.5.17

; <<>> DiG 8.2 <<>> -x
;; res options: init recurs defnam dnsrch
;; got answer:
;; ->>HEADER<<- opcode: QUERY, status: NOERROR, id: 6
;; flags: qr aa rd ra; QUERY: 1, ANSWER: 1, AUTHORITY: 1, ADDITIONAL: 1
;; QUERY SECTION:
;;      17.5.16.172.in-addr.arpa, type = ANY, class = IN

;; ANSWER SECTION:
17.5.16.172.in-addr.arpa.  1D IN PTR  puffin.foobirds.org.

;; AUTHORITY SECTION:
16.172.in-addr.arpa.       1D IN NS   wren.foobirds.org.

;; ADDITIONAL SECTION:
wren.foobirds.org.         1D IN A    172.16.5.1

;; Total query time: 1 msec
;; FROM: 24seven.wrotethebook.com to SERVER: default -- 0.0.0.0
;; WHEN: Tue Apr 25 13:57:29 2000
;; MSG SIZE  sent: 42  rcvd: 129
```

*dig B*atch Mode Options

Two of the dig command options are used only for batch mode:

–T *seconds*   defines the delay between the start of each successive dig command when dig is run in batch mode. This option is used to keep multiple batch runs roughly synchronized.

–f *path*   provides the path to the file that contains the dig commands for a batch run. This option causes dig to run in batch mode.

Comments are most often used on the dig command line during batch mode execution. In batch mode, dig commands are stored in a file—sometimes for a long period of time. Comments are useful reminders about the meaning and purpose of a command. Listing 11.10 shows a dig batch file that includes comments.

Listing 11.10 Using the dig Command in Batch Mode

```
[craig]$ cat dig-soa
dig @129.6.13.2 -t soa nist.gov. %Check_the_master_SOA
dig @132.163.4.9 -t soa nist.gov. %Check_1st_slave_SOA
dig @172.16.5.1 -t soa nist.gov. %Check_2nd_slave_SOA
[craig]$ dig -f dig-soa
```

Listing 11.10 starts with a cat command that displays the contents of the batch file. Notice that this file contains full dig command lines. These lines contain comments to illustrate how they are used to clarify the purpose of each line.

Listing 11.10 concludes with the dig command that executes the batch file. The –f option is the key to running in batch mode. For the sake of brevity, the output of this command is not shown in Listing 11.10. The output is the sum of all of the output of the three dig commands from the batch file, so it is extensive.

Of the seven options described so far, only three are really useful in a production environment:

- The –t option is used to improve the readability of dig commands when they are stored in batch files.
- The –x option is needed for reverse queries.
- The –f option is absolutely essential for running dig in batch mode.

While you probably want to know that they exist and what they do, the four options –c, –p, –P, and –T can safely be ignored. The remaining three command options relate to defining the dig environment.

Maintaining a
Healthy System

PART 4

The *dig* Environment

The dig command lets you control how the execution environment is passed between different instantiations of the dig process. Because the dig command can run both as a command-line process and as a batch process, it is important to be able to manage and maintain the execution environment. The large number of arguments, command options, and query options make this particularly important.

If a large number of configuration parameters need to be set the same way every time you run dig, it might be useful to save those parameters for successive runs. dig allows you to do this with the –envsav option. When –envsav is specified on the command line, the current dig execution environment is written to a file named DiG.env in the current directory. Subsequent dig runs read the DiG.env file and use the configuration parameters it contains.

You can select a different name for the environment file using the LOCALDEF environment variable. LOCALDEF is specific to dig and does not affect any other applications. Using LOCALDEF makes it possible to create and save several different execution environments. Listing 11.11 shows a simple example of how it is used.

Listing 11.11 Listing 11.11: The LOCALDEF Environment Variable

```
[craig]$ LOCALDEF=./mydig.env
[craig]$ echo $LOCALDEF
./mydig.env
[craig]$ export LOCALDEF
[craig]$ dig puffin.foobirds.org –envsav
[craig]$ ls -l mydig.env
-rw-------   1 craig    craig    512 Apr 26 08:49 mydig.env
```

Maintaining the environment between different instantiations of dig is particularly important when dig is run in batch mode. dig provides two command options for this purpose:

–envset sets the execution environment for a batch file. Adding –envset to a dig command in a batch file causes the current execution environment used by that command to become the default execution environment for subsequent dig commands in the batch file. The –envset option can be used on more than one dig command. Each time it is used, the current environment becomes the default environment.

–[no]stick controls whether or not the default environment is restored before each dig command is executed in a batch file. Normally, the environment in a batch file is cumulative. As each `dig` command changes the environment, the changed environment is passed on to subsequent `dig` commands. This is the –nostick default. The –stick option tells the batch file to stick to the default environment as inherited by the batch run or as defined by a –envset option, and not to change the environment with each `dig` command.

One reason that maintaining the `dig` environment is an issue is that the environment can be complex. One cause for this complexity is the large number of query options available to `dig`.

dig Query Options

The `dig` command accepts 30 different query options. These options control the format of the query sent to the server, and they control the output displayed by `dig`. Table 11.1, which is derived directly from the `dig` manual page, lists all of the available options.

Table 11.1   The `dig` Query Options

Option	Abbreviation	Purpose
[no]debug	[no]deb	Enable or disable debugging
[no]d2		Enable or disable additional debugging
[no]recurse	[no]rec	Enable or disable recursion
[no]defname	[no]def	Use the default domain name
[no]search	[no]sea	Use the search list
[no]ignore	[no]i	Ignore truncation errors
[no]primary	[no]pr	Send the query to the zone's master server
[no]aaonly	[no]aa	Set the authoritative answer bit in the query
[no]ko		Keep the connection open when TCP is used
[no]vc		Use TCP for the query
domain=*name*	do=*name*	Define the default domain
retry=*num*	ret=*num*	Set the number of retries
time=*num*	ti=*num*	Set the number of seconds for a query to time out

Maintaining a
Healthy System

PART 4

Table 11.1   The dig Query Options *(continued)*

Option	Abbreviation	Purpose
[no]cmd		Display the dig command
[no]stats	[no]st	Display the query statistics
[no]Header	[no]H	Display the header
[no]header	[no]he	Display the header flags
[no] ttlid	[no]tt	Display the TTL values
[no]cl		Display the class value
[no]qr		Display the query
[no]reply	[no]rep	Display the response
[no]ques	[no]qu	Display the question section
[no]answer	[no]an	Display the answer section
[no]author	[no]au	Display the authority section
[no]addit	[no]ad	Display the additional section
pfdef		Use the default print flags
pfmin		Use the minimal default print flags
pfset=*num*		Set the print flags to a numeric value
pfand=*num*		Bitwise AND the number to the print flags
pfor=*num*		Bitwise OR the number to the print flags

Many of the query options are Boolean. To enable a Boolean option, specify it by name. To disable a Boolean option, use the name of the option with the no prefix. For example, +debug enables debugging and +nodebug disables it.

Table 11.1 also shows that several of the commands can be abbreviated. For example, +recurse and +rec are equivalent; both request recursion.

Listing 11.12 shows how query options are used. In this listing, `dig` is run with the following three query options:

+noqu   tells `dig` not to display the question section of the DNS message.

+noau   tells `dig` not to display the authority section of the DNS message.

+noad   tells `dig` not to display the additional section of the DNS message.

The result of these options is that the only resource records displayed by `dig` are those found in the answer section of the DNS message.

Listing 11.12 Using Query Options to Control `dig` Output

```
[craig]$ dig puffin.foobirds.org +noqu +noau +noad

; <<>> DiG 8.2 <<>> puffin.foobirds.org +noqu +noau +noad
;; res options: init recurs defnam dnsrch
;; got answer:
;; ->>HEADER<<- opcode: QUERY, status: NOERROR, id: 19942
;; flags: qr aa rd ra; QUERY: 1, ANSWER: 1, AUTHORITY: 2, ADDITIONAL: 3
;; ANSWER SECTION:
puffin.foobirds.org.    1D IN A       172.16.5.17

;; Total query time: 1 msec
;; FROM: 24seven.wrotethebook.com to SERVER: default -- 172.16.5.1
;; WHEN: Wed Apr 26 08:42:26 2000
;; MSG SIZE  sent: 37  rcvd: 366
```

I never use most of the query options available for `dig`. The query options that control the amount of output can be useful for batch files, but the other options are simply too complex for the way that I use `dig`. I find it clumsy to enter complex queries at the command line, and I don't submit complex queries frequently enough to script them or to save them in batch files. I use `nslookup` for complex or iterative testing. For me, the power of `dig` is best utilized when I want to examine the detailed output from a query, or when I want to capture information that can be read back into `named`, as in the next section of this chapter.

Using *dig to* Create a Hint File

Putting all of these pieces together, a simple `dig` command can demonstrate the power of the `dig` test tool. Chapter 5, "Caching and Slave Server Configuration," introduced a file called the *hint file* that contains a list of root servers. That chapter also explained the importance of keeping that file up to date. Using dig is one way to keep the hint file updated. dig can go directly to the source, the master root server, and ask that server for the list of root name servers. Listing 11.13 shows the dig command that is used to query the master root server for the root server list.

Listing 11.13 Building named.ca with dig

```
[craig]$ dig @a.root-servers.net . -t ns +norec >named.ca
[craig]$ cat named.ca
; <<>> DiG 8.2 <<>> @a.root-servers.net . -t +norec
; (1 server found)
;; res options: init defnam dnsrch
;; got answer:
;; ->>HEADER<<- opcode: QUERY, status: NOERROR, id: 33910
;; flags: qr aa; QUERY: 1, ANSWER: 13, AUTHORITY: 0, ADDITIONAL: 13
;; QUERY SECTION:
;;., type = NS, class = IN

;; ANSWER SECTION:
.           6D IN NS     A.ROOT-SERVERS.NET.
.           6D IN NSH.ROOT-SERVERS.NET.
.           6D IN NS     C.ROOT-SERVERS.NET.
.           6D IN NS     G.ROOT-SERVERS.NET.
.           6D IN NS     F.ROOT-SERVERS.NET.
.           6D IN NS     B.ROOT-SERVERS.NET.
.           6D IN NS     J.ROOT-SERVERS.NET.
.           6D IN NS     K.ROOT-SERVERS.NET.
.           6D IN NS     L.ROOT-SERVERS.NET.
.           6D IN NS     M.ROOT-SERVERS.NET.
.           6D IN NS     I.ROOT-SERVERS.NET.
.           6D IN NS     E.ROOT-SERVERS.NET.
.           6D IN NS.ROOT-SERVERS.NET.

;; ADDITIONAL SECTION:
A.ROOT-SERVERS.NET.   6D IN A       198.41.0.4
H.ROOT-SERVERS.NET.   6D IN A       128.63.2.53
C.ROOT-SERVERS.NET.   6D IN A       192.33.4.12
G.ROOT-SERVERS.NET.   6D IN A       192.112.36.4
F.ROOT-SERVERS.NET.   6D IN A       192.5.5.241
```

```
B.ROOT-SERVERS.NET.     6D IN A        128.9.0.107
J.ROOT-SERVERS.NET.     5w6d16h IN A   198.41.0.10
K.ROOT-SERVERS.NET.     5w6d16h IN A   193.0.14.129
L.ROOT-SERVERS.NET.     5w6d16h IN A   198.32.64.12
M.ROOT-SERVERS.NET.     5w6d16h IN A   202.12.27.33
I.ROOT-SERVERS.NET.     6D IN A        192.36.148.17
E.ROOT-SERVERS.NET.     6D IN A        192.203.230.10
D.ROOT-SERVERS.NET.     6D IN A        128.8.10.90

;; Total query time: 475 msec
;; FROM: 24seven.wrotethebook.com to SERVER: a.root-servers.net  198.41.0.4
;; WHEN: Tue Apr 25 15:04:50 2000
;; MSG SIZE  sent: 17  rcvd: 436
```

The output of the `dig` command in Listing 11.13 is redirected into the `named.ca` file. The interesting thing is that the `named.ca` file created in this manner is ready to use. It does not require any editing. The `cat` command shows that the `named.ca` file produced by `dig` contains many `dig` status messages. But all of the status messages and statistics written by `dig` begin with a semi-colon. This means that `named` treats those lines as comments when it loads this `named.ca` file. Information retrieved by `dig` is directly useable by `named`.

nslookup

The power of the `nslookup` command can best be seen when it is used as an interactive test tool. `nslookup` can be used as a single-line command, just like `host` or `dig`. But when used in that manner, it doesn't add anything that can't be done just as well, or better, with one of the other tools. It is when `nslookup` is used interactively to track down a problem in real time that the true potential of this tool shines through. The advantage of `nslookup` is real-time problem solving.

Running *nslookup* Interactively

To run `nslookup` in interactive mode, simply type **nslookup** at the shell prompt. Listing 11.14 shows a basic interactive session with `nslookup`. The session starts when `nslookup` is invoked. The user enters the domain name **puffin.foobirds.org** at the `nslookup` prompt, and receives the address of `puffin` as the response. The first two lines displayed after starting `nslookup`, and the first two lines displayed after every query identify the name and address of the server being used. The user ends the session with the `exit` command.

Maintaining a Healthy System

PART 4

Listing 11.14 Running nslookup Interactively

```
[craig]$ nslookup
Default Server:  wren.foobirds.org
Address:  172.16.5.1

> puffin.foobirds.org
Server:  wren.foobirds.org
Address:  172.16.5.1

Name:     puffin.foobirds.org
Address:  172.16.5.17
> exit
[craig@24seven craig]$
```

A basic address query, such as the one shown in Listing 11.14, is not very impressive. The same result could have been obtained much more simply with the host command. To really utilize nslookup, you need to make multiple interrelated queries, and to do that, you need to understand the set command.

The *set* Command

The set command defines the optional values used to build the query that nslookup sends to the server. By default, when a domain name is entered at the nslookup prompt, nslookup queries for address records for that domain name. Listing 11.15 shows how the set command is used to change this default to look for MX records.

Listing 11.15 Using the nslookup set Command

```
[craig]$ nslookup
Default Server:  wren.foobirds.org
Address:  172.16.5.1

> set type=MX
> puffin.foobirds.org
Server:  wren.foobirds.org
Address:  172.16.5.1

puffin.foobirds.org    preference = 5, mail exchanger = wren.foobirds.org
foobirds.org    nameserver = wren.foobirds.org
```

```
foobirds.org     nameserver = parrot.foobirds.org
wren.foobirds.org       internet address = 172.16.5.1
parrot.foobirds.org     internet address = 172.16.5.3
> robin.foobirds.org
Server:  wren.foobirds.org
Address:  172.16.5.1

robin.foobirds.org       preference = 5, mail exchanger = wren.foobirds.org
foobirds.org     nameserver = wren.foobirds.org
foobirds.org     nameserver = parrot.foobirds.org
wren.foobirds.org       internet address = 172.16.5.1
parrot.foobirds.org     internet address = 172.16.5.3
> hawk.foobirds.org
Server:  wren.foobirds.org
Address:  172.16.5.1

foobirds.org
        origin = wren.foobirds.org
        mail addr = admin.wren.foobirds.org
        serial = 2000020501
        refresh = 21600 (6H)
        retry  = 1800 (30M)
        expire = 604800 (1W)
        minimum ttl = 900 (15M)
> exit
```

Listing 11.15 shows that once a query type is set, that type stays in force until it is explicitly reset to a different query type by another **set** command. In the example in Listing 11.15, the query type is set to MX, and queries are made for MX records for puffin, robin, and hawk.

The queries for puffin and robin return the MX record from the answer section of the response, along with the names of the authoritative servers for the zones from the authority section, and their addresses from the additional section. Notice that hawk does not have an MX record. Instead of getting an MX record in response to the query, we get an SOA record from the authority section. As you'll recall from Chapter 2, "The DNS Protocols," this means the MX record does not exist, and it tells the local system how long to cache this negative information.

Listing 11.15 shows the basic format of the `set` command. It begins with the command `set`, which is followed by a keyword that is either a Boolean or an argument that is set equal to a value. The `set` command is not limited to setting the query type. It can set a very large number of query options, including the following:

`all`   displays all of the values that are currently set. This option was used in Chapter 4, "Configuring the Resolver," to test the effects of placement in the `resolv.conf` file on the `domain` and `search` commands by displaying the values inherited by `nslookup` from the resolver configuration. Use `set all` any time you need to examine the `nslookup` settings.

`class=value`   defines the class used for the query. This defaults to IN, which is correct for almost every system.

`[no]debug`   enables or disables debugging. For `nslookup`, debugging just means that more information about the response packet is printed.

`[no]d2`   enables or disables increased debugging. When enabled, `nslookup` displays information about the query as well as the response.

`domain=name`   defines the default domain name.

`[no]defname`   specifies whether or not `nslookup` should append the default domain name to host names when constructing queries. If this value is set, which is the default, the default domain name is appended to any host name that does not contain a dot.

`srchlist=name/name/...`   defines the domain search list. The search list is defined as a series of up to six domain names separated by slash characters (/).

`[no]search`   specifies whether or not the search list should be used to extend the host name used in the query before it is sent to the server. If this value is set, which is the default, the search list is used to extend any name that does not contain a dot. A query is sent to the server for each domain in the search list until the server answers the query.

`type=type`   defines the type of resource records requested by the query. `type` can be any valid resource record type defined in Appendix C. The most common resource record types are those listed in Table 6.1. Both the keyword `querytype` and `query` are valid alternative spellings for the keyword `type`.

`[no]recurse`   specifies whether or not recursion is requested for the query. By default, recursion is requested. This option can be abbreviated `[no]rec`.

`retry=num`   defines the number of retries `nslookup` will issue when the server does not respond to queries.

timeout=*seconds*   defines the number of seconds that nslookup will wait for a response from the server. This value defines the initial timeout interval. As explained in Chapter 4, "Configuring the Resolver," the timeout is doubled for each successive retry. The default is 5 seconds.

port=*num*   defines an alternate port for the query. By default, the port number is 53, which is the standard port used for DNS on all servers. If the server uses a non-standard port, define that port with the port option.

root=*server*   defines the root server used by nslookup.

[no]ignoretc   specifies whether or not nslookup should ignore truncation error. By default, errors are not ignored.

[no]vc   specifies whether or not nslookup should send all queries over a TCP connection. Most DNS traffic runs over UDP, so the default is novc, which should be correct for most systems.

The 16 different options that work with set can cover most conceivable situations. These options do not have to be defined with the set command; they also can be set from the nslookup command line. Listing 11.16 illustrates this.

Listing 11.16 Setting Options on the nslookup Command Line

```
[craig]$ nslookup
Default Server:  wren.foobirds.org
Address:  172.16.5.1

> set all
Default Server:  wren.foobirds.org
Address:  172.16.5.1

Set options:
  nodebug        defname        search         recurse
  nod2           novc           noignoretc     port=53
  querytype=A    class=IN       timeout=5      retry=4
  root=a.root-servers.net.
  domain=foobirds.org
  srchlist=foobirds.org

> exit
[craig]$ nslookup -type=MX -norec -retry=3
Default Server:  wren.foobirds.org
```

Maintaining a Healthy System

PART 4

```
Address:  172.16.5.1

> set all
Default Server:  wren.foobirds.org
Address:  172.16.5.1

Set options:
    nodebug          defname          search           norecurse
    nod2             novc             noignoretc       port=53
    querytype=MX     class=IN         timeout=5        retry=3
    root=a.root-servers.net.
    domain=foobirds.org
    srchlist=foobirds.org

> exit
```

In Listing 11.16, nslookup is run twice, and both times it is run, set all is used to display the option settings. However, the second time that nslookup is run, three of the options are set to non-default values on the command line. Examining the results of the set all command shows that the options are indeed modified.

I don't do this. I find that setting configuration options on the nslookup command line is just as clumsy as setting them on the dig command line. I define these values interactively as I need them, using the set command inside the nslookup session. On the rare occasions that I find it necessary to set the same options every time I run nslookup, I store the options in the .nslookuprc file in my home directory. Listing 11.17 illustrates this.

Listing 11.17 Using the .nslookuprc File

```
[craig]$ cat .nslookuprc
root=d.root-servers.net
domain=mammals.org
norec
[craig]$ nslookup
Default Server:  wren.foobirds.org
Address:  172.16.5.1

> set all
Default Server:  wren.foobirds.org
Address:  172.16.5.1
```

```
Set options:
  nodebug         defname         search          norecurse
  nod2            novc            noignoretc      port=53
  querytype=A     class=IN        timeout=5       retry=4
  root=d.root-servers.net
  domain=mammals.org
  srchlist=mammals.org
```

> **exit**

Listing 11.17 shows an .nslookuprc file that contains three options: root, domain, and norecurse. The set all command in the nslookup session shows that these options affected the configuration without requiring any options on the nslookup command line.

Setting configuration options is not the only thing you need to do to get the most out of nslookup. There are several more nslookup commands in addition to set.

Requesting a Server

The set command is probably the most versatile nslookup command, but the server command is easily just as important. The server command lets you bypass your local server and go directly to the remote server for information. This is an essential component of any real test system.

NOTE An alternate spelling for the server command is lserver.

In Listing 11.18, the server command is used to go directly to the authoritative server for a domain to ask for information. When nslookup is invoked, it starts by using the local domain server as the default. The server command attaches the session directly to the remote server.

Listing 11.18 The nslookup server Command

```
[craig]$ nslookup
Default Server:  wren.foobirds.org
Address:  172.16.5.1

> server 10.252.116.61
Default Server:  legacy-ns3.dns.fakeisp.net
Address:  10.252.116.61
```

```
> set query=any
> smtp.fakeisp.com
Server:  legacy-ns3.dns.fakeisp.net
Address:  10.252.116.61

smtp.fakeisp.com   canonical name = smtp.mail.fakeisp.net
fakeisp.com        nameserver = auth2.dns.fakeisp.net
fakeisp.com        nameserver = auth3.dns.fakeisp.net
fakeisp.com        nameserver = auth4.dns.fakeisp.net
fakeisp.com        nameserver = auth1.dns.fakeisp.net
auth2.dns.fakeisp.net      internet address = 10.13.11.20
auth3.dns.fakeisp.net      internet address = 10.172.3.21
auth4.dns.fakeisp.net      internet address = 10.172.3.22
auth1.dns.fakeisp.net      internet address = 10.172.3.20
> exit
```

Specifying the server with the query is an alternative to changing the default server when you know you won't be send multiple queries to the server. In Listing 11.18, only one query is sent to the remote server. The same thing could have been done in the following manner:

```
[craig]$ nslookup
Default Server:  wren.foobirds.org
Address:  172.16.5.1

> auth1.dns.fakeisp.net 10.252.116.61
Server:  legacy-ns3.dns.fakeisp..net
Address:  10.252.116.61

Name:    auth1.dns.fakeisp.net
Address:  209.1.78.11

> exit
```

In this case, the address of the remote server immediately follows the domain name for which information is sought. This technique for specifying a server is preferable when only one query is being sent, and the **server** command is preferable when multiple queries are to be sent.

TIP The root command sets the default server to the root server. I never use it. The root servers are busy enough without being bothered by my test queries.

Listing a Complete Domain

nslookup includes the ls command to simplify listing an entire domain. nslookup uses a zone transfer to gather the information for the ls command, which makes it a good tool for testing zone transfers and the security you use to limit zone transfers, as you saw in Chapter 10, "DNS Security." The basic ls command used in Listing 10.4 only listed host names and addresses for an entire zone. That is enough to test security, but ls can gather much more information.

The full syntax of the ls command is

```
ls [option] domain [>|>> file]
```

These fields are used as follows:

domain the name of the domain to be transferred and listed.

file an optional file that the domain listing is copied to, if the > character is used, or appended to if the >> characters are used.

option the type of information that ls should gather about the domain. It can be any of the following values:

–a all of the aliases, i.e., CNAME records, in the domain.

–d all records in the domain.

–h any HINFO records in the domain. (HINFO is a rarely used record type.)

–s any WKS records in the domain. (WKS is a rarely used record type.)

–t *type* a specific record type.

In Listing 11.19, all of the records in the foobirds.org zone are captured to a file named foobirds.txt using the ls command. The user then exits nslookup and uses a shell command to examine the foobirds.txt file that nslookup just created.

Notice that the first two lines of the foobirds.txt file display the ls command used to create the file and the name of the server from which the data in the file was obtained. In addition to these status lines at the beginning of the file, for some obscure reason nslookup repeats the SOA record at the end of the file. The repeated SOA record is not shown in Listing 11.19 because a head command is used to list only the first 20 lines of the foobirds .txt file in order to keep the listing to a reasonable length. But trust me. The repeated record is there at the end of the file.

Maintaining a Healthy System

PART 4

Listing 11.19 The nslookup ls Command

```
[craig]$ nslookup
Default Server:  wren.foobirds.org
Address:  172.16.5.1

> ls -d foobirds.org > foobirds.txt
[wren.foobirds.org]
Received 41 answers (41 records).
> exit
[craig]$ head -20 foobirds.txt
> ls -d foobirds.org
[wren.foobirds.org]
$ORIGIN foobirds.org.
@                         1D IN SOA        wren admin.wren (
                          2000020501       ; serial
                          6H               ; refresh
                          30M              ; retry
                          1W               ; expiry
                          15M )            ; minimum

                          1D IN NS         wren
                          1D IN NS         parrot
                          1D IN RP         admin hotline
                          1D IN MX         10 wren
                          1D IN MX         20 parrot
ducks                     1D IN NS         ruddy.ducks
                          1D IN NS         wren
                          1D IN NS         bear.mammals.org.
news                      1D IN CNAME      parrot
robin                     1D IN RP         admin hotline
```

WARNING   The nslookup program provides a built-in view command for examining a file captured by ls. The view command doesn't work properly under Linux. To look at the file, exit nslookup and use shell commands.

Putting It All Together

The interactive nature of nslookup allows you to adjust your test plan as the results from individual tests lead you in a different direction. The large number of options and the amount of control you have over those options let you fine-tune each test. Using nslookup, it is possible to directly connect to various remote servers to compare how the different servers respond in order to isolate the source of a reported problem. An example using some of the previously discussed features of nslookup will illustrate the usefulness of this program.

Assume that an intermittent DNS problem has been detected. Users are attempting to connect to a popular remote site on the host dolphin.mammals.org. The problem is affecting some of the systems on your network, but not all of them. Even some of the users who have the problem have it only occasionally.

Nonetheless, they have reported to management that *your* server is broken. A quick test with the host command shows that your server currently knows the address of dolphin.mammals.org. Use nslookup as follows to see what the remote servers know about dolphin.mammals.org:

```
[craig]$ nslookup
Default Server: wren.foobirds.org
Address:  172.16.5.1

> set type=NS
> mammals.org.
Server:  wren.foobirds.org
Address:  172.16.5.1

mammals.org        nameserver = goat.mammals.org
mammals.org        nameserver = shark.fish.org
mammals.org        nameserver = whale.mammals.org
goat.mammals.org   inet address = 172.32.3.2
shark.fish.org     inet address = 172.30.8.2
whale.mammals.org  inet address = 172.32.3.1
```

Start nslookup in interactive mode. When it starts, nslookup indicates that it is using your local server as the default server. You need the NS records to locate the name servers for the remote domain you wish to test. Set the query type to NS, and then enter the domain name you want to query. In this example, the domain name is mammals.org. The local name server returns three NS records, identifying goat.mammals.org, whale .mammals.org, and shark.fish.org as the servers for that domain. Now that you know the authoritative servers, connect to one of them to run the next phase of the test using the following commands:

```
> server goat.mammals.org
Default Server:  goat.mammals.org
Address:  172.32.3.2

> set type=ANY
> dolphin.mammals.org
Server:  goat.mammals.org
Address:  172.32.3.2

dolphin.mammals.org   inet address = 172.32.3.8
```

To connect directly to the remote server, use the `server` command. In this example, I choose to connect to `goat`. Then set the query to the type of resource records you're interested in. This can be the keyword ANY for all available resource records or any of the standard resource record types. The ANY query is particularly useful because it provides all of the information available from the name server.

A successful test tells you that the remote server is responding and can resolve the desired host name. If the test fails completely, the user may have the wrong host name. If the test works but your local server is having trouble with the host name, the problem could be in your local server or in one of the other remote servers. We know it is not either of these problems because the local system can resolve the name and the remote master server provides information about the name.

Sometimes remote servers get out of synchronization, so querying all of the authoritative remote servers is worthwhile when you have intermittent problems resolving a host name. Because we're having intermittent problems resolving the host name `dolphin.mammals`
`.org`, we run identical tests with the other two authoritative servers, as follows:

```
> server whale.mammals.org
Default Server:  whale.mammals.org
Address: 172.32.3.1

> dolphin.mammals.org
Server:  whale.mammals.org
Address:  172.32.3.1

dolphin.mammals.org   inet address = 172.32.3.8
> server shark.fish.org
```

```
Default Server:  shark.fish.org
Address:  172.30.8.2

> dolphin.mammals.org
Server:  shark.fish.org
Address:  172.30.8.2

*** shark.fish.org can't find dolphin.mammals.org:
    Non-existent domain
```

In this case, the third authoritative server disagrees with the first two. goat and whale resolve the query for dolphin.mammals.org to an address, but shark can't. The most likely cause for this problem is that the servers have two different copies of the zone file. Check the SOA records on each system to see if the serial numbers are different as in the following example:

```
> set type=SOA
> mammals.org.
Server:  shark.fish.org
Address:  172.30.8.2

mammals.org        origin = goat.mammals.org
   mail addr = amanda.goat.mammals.org
     serial=10164, refresh=43200, retry=3600, expire=3600000,
   min=2592000
> server goat.mammals.org
Default Server:  goat.mammals.org
Address:  172.32.3.2

> mammals.org.
Server:  goat.mammals.org
Address:  172.32.3.2

mammals.org        origin = goat.mammals.org
   mail addr = amanda.goat.mammals.org
     serial=10164, refresh=43200, retry=3600, expire=3600000,
   min=2592000

> exit
```

In this example, the serial numbers are the same. This is bad news. If the serial numbers were different, the problem might be a temporary one that would be resolved as soon as the slave server updated the zone from the master server. The fact that the serial numbers are the same but the contents of the zone files are different is a major problem that must be addressed by the remote domain administrator. Luckily, the SOA record tells you who that is. Send mail to amanda@goat.mammals.org and report the problem. She needs to get this fixed!

In Sum

BIND provides three powerful test tools that can be used in a variety of situations:

- host is the simplest tool, and is well suited for basic DNS queries and for use in shell scripts.

- dig is a more complicated tool that is very useful for examining the complete contents of the DNS message sent in response to a query. dig commands can be grouped together in a file and executed in batch mode. The output from the dig command is properly formatted so that it can be used directly by named.

- nslookup is well suited for real-time, iterative testing. With nslookup you can interactively run a series of evolving tests in a simple, natural manner.

All of these tools allow you to test remote servers as well as your local server. This important feature helps you determine which problems can be addressed locally and which problems need to be referred to a remote domain administrator.

When test tools point to problems on the local DNS server, you need to know how that system is running. The log files created by BIND are an important part of monitoring the health of your server. The next chapter concludes the book with a look at the logging services available with BIND.

12

The BIND Log Files

BIND creates various log files to record the status of the server and the amount and nature of the DNS traffic that the server has handled. These log files provide the domain administrator with a useful window into the state of the server. Use the log files as a way to monitor the system.

Monitoring your system does not mean studying the log files in detail. Much of the information in the log files is intended for BIND software designers and others who are trying to debug source code. That level of detail is not of interest to a DNS administrator, and even if it is, I have never known an administrator who had enough free time to undertake a detailed analysis of any log file.

This chapter does not recommend that you drop everything and start studying log files. What it does recommend is that you periodically scan these files to get a sense of how your server is normally used and how it is currently operating. Monitoring the server log files helps with the following:

Capacity planning The statistics recorded in the log files can give you a sense of the workload that your server is handling and can help you properly size any future server upgrades. I keep telling you that a small system can handle most domains. But I don't know the workload of your domain. Only you can know that, and the log files are one source of information about your system's workload.

Problem detection Error messages in the log files can help you anticipate developing problems before they become real problems.

Security   Sudden changes from normal activity can indicate an intruder or a denial-of-service attack.

This chapter provides an overview of each of the log files produced by BIND. The chapter also describes the logging configuration commands that you can use to control what information is logged and where the information is written. Let's begin by looking at the basic log files.

The Dump File

The dump file is a dump of the contents of the DNS cache. You produce the dump file by sending named the INT signal or, more simply, by issuing the following ndc command:

```
[root]# ndc dumpdb
Database dump initiated.
```

By default, the dump file is written to the file named_dump.db in the /var/named directory. Use the dump_file option in the named.conf file to change the path of the dump file.

TIP   Don't change the default path of any of the log files. It makes it harder for the other administrators that work with you to monitor the files.

The longer the server has been running, the larger the dump file becomes. The reason, of course, is that the longer the server has been running, the more information it has added to its cache. Even the very small dump file used in this chapter is a pretty long listing. For this reason, I have divided the file into three distinct parts. The divisions used in this chapter are natural divisions that named places in the dump file. The following list identifies the labels that named uses to segment the dump file:

zone table   lists all of the zones for which the server is authoritative.

Cache & Data   contains all of the DNS data known to the server. This is all of the data that the server loaded from its own zone files and all of the information that the server cached from queries.

Hints   contains all of the information loaded from the hint file.

NOTE   The dump file is one contiguous file. This chapter uses three separate listings to improve readability. Your file will print as one long listing.

The Zone Table Section

The first section of the dump file is the zone table. Listing 12.1 shows the zone table section of a dump file from wren.foobirds.org taken a few minutes after the server started.

Listing 12.1   The Zone Table in a named_dump.db File

```
; Dumped at Tue May  2 10:49:12 2000
;; ++zone table++
; . (type 6, class 0, source Nil)
;       time=0, lastupdate=0, serial=0,
;       refresh=0, retry=0, expire=0, minimum=0
;       ftime=0, xaddrcnt=0, state=0000, pid=0
; . (type 3, class 1, source named.ca)
;       time=0, lastupdate=922045767, serial=0,
;       refresh=0, retry=0, expire=0, minimum=0
;       ftime=922045767, xaddrcnt=0, state=0040, pid=0
; 0.0.127.in-addr.arpa (type 1, class 1, source named.local)
;       time=0, lastupdate=0, serial=1997022700,
;       refresh=0, retry=14400, expire=3600000, minimum=86400
;       ftime=944857474, xaddrcnt=0, state=0041, pid=0
; foobirds.org (type 1, class 1, source foobirds.hosts)
;       time=0, lastupdate=0, serial=2000020501,
;       refresh=0, retry=1800, expire=604800, minimum=900
;       ftime=956773960, xaddrcnt=0, state=0041, pid=0
; 16.172.in-addr.arpa (type 1, class 1, source 172.16.reverse)
;       time=0, lastupdate=0, serial=2000021602,
;       refresh=0, retry=1800, expire=604800, minimum=900
;       ftime=954951897, xaddrcnt=0, state=0041, pid=0
;; --zone table--
```

The dump file begins by displaying the date and time that the dump was taken. Labels at the start and end of this section delimit the zone table. From Listing 12.1, you can tell that this server has a zone statement in its named.conf file for the following domains:

.   the root domain, which was loaded from a source file called named.ca. This is the hint file described in Chapter 5, "Caching and Slave Server Configuration."

0.0.127.in-addr.arpa   the loopback domain, which, in Listing 12.1, is loaded from the source file named.local.

foobirds.org   the foobirds.org domain, which is loaded from the
foobirds.hosts source file.

16.172.in-addr.arpa   the reverse domain 16.172.in-addr.arpa, which is
loaded from the 172.16.reverse file.

The values from the SOA record of each zone are also printed. In Listing 12.1, every zone
except the root (.) has an SOA record.

The zone table section identifies every zone for which the server has authority. It tells you
where the server obtained the information about the zone, and it tells you which defaults
are set for the zone by the SOA record.

The Cache & Data Section

The second section of the dump file is by far the longest. This is the section that contains
all of the DNS information known to the server. Listing 12.2 contains the Cache & Data
information from a sample dump taken on wren.foobirds.org.

Listing 12.2   The Cache & Data Section in a named_dump.db File

```
; Note: Cr=(auth,answer,addtnl,cache) tag only shown for non-auth RR's
; Note: NT=milliseconds for any A RR which we've used as a nameserver
; --- Cache & Data ---
$ORIGIN .
.       513482    IN      NS      H.ROOT-SERVERS.NET.    ;Cr=auth
        513482    IN      NS      C.ROOT-SERVERS.NET.    ;Cr=auth
        513482    IN      NS      G.ROOT-SERVERS.NET.    ;Cr=auth
        513482    IN      NS      F.ROOT-SERVERS.NET.    ;Cr=auth
        513482    IN      NS      B.ROOT-SERVERS.NET.    ;Cr=auth
        513482    IN      NS      J.ROOT-SERVERS.NET.    ;Cr=auth
        513482    IN      NS      K.ROOT-SERVERS.NET.    ;Cr=auth
        513482    IN      NS      L.ROOT-SERVERS.NET.    ;Cr=auth
        513482    IN      NS      M.ROOT-SERVERS.NET.    ;Cr=auth
        513482    IN      NS      I.ROOT-SERVERS.NET.    ;Cr=auth
        513482    IN      NS      E.ROOT-SERVERS.NET.    ;Cr=auth
        513482    IN      NS      D.ROOT-SERVERS.NET.    ;Cr=auth
        513482    IN      NS      A.ROOT-SERVERS.NET.    ;Cr=auth
COM     515224    IN      NS      A.ROOT-SERVERS.NET.    ;Cr=addtnl
        515224    IN      NS      G.ROOT-SERVERS.NET.    ;Cr=addtnl
        515224    IN      NS      F.GTLD-SERVERS.NET.    ;Cr=addtnl
        515224    IN      NS      F.ROOT-SERVERS.NET.    ;Cr=addtnl
```

```
            515224    IN    NS      I.ROOT-SERVERS.NET.     ;Cr=addtnl
            515224    IN    NS      E.ROOT-SERVERS.NET.     ;Cr=addtnl
            515224    IN    NS      J.GTLD-SERVERS.NET.     ;Cr=addtnl
            515224    IN    NS      K.GTLD-SERVERS.NET.     ;Cr=addtnl
            515224    IN    NS      A.GTLD-SERVERS.NET.     ;Cr=addtnl
            515224    IN    NS      M.GTLD-SERVERS.NET.     ;Cr=addtnl
            515224    IN    NS      H.GTLD-SERVERS.NET.     ;Cr=addtnl
            515224    IN    NS      C.GTLD-SERVERS.NET.     ;Cr=addtnl
$ORIGIN GTLD-SERVERS.NET.
K           515224    IN    A       195.8.99.11            ;NT=12 Cr=addtnl
A           515224    IN    A       198.41.3.38            ;NT=8 Cr=addtnl
M           515224    IN    A       210.176.152.18         ;NT=21 Cr=addtnl
C           515224    IN    A       205.188.185.18         ;NT=75 Cr=addtnl
F           515224    IN    A       198.17.208.67          ;NT=6 Cr=addtnl
H           515224    IN    A       216.33.75.82           ;NT=23 Cr=addtnl
J           515224    IN    A       198.41.0.21            ;NT=15 Cr=addtnl
$ORIGIN ROOT-SERVERS.NET.
K           599882    IN    A       193.0.14.129           ;NT=9 Cr=answer
A           599882    IN    A       198.41.0.4             ;NT=10 Cr=answer
L           599882    IN    A       198.32.64.12           ;NT=5 Cr=answer
M           599882    IN    A       202.12.27.33           ;NT=15 Cr=answer
B           599882    IN    A       128.9.0.107            ;NT=5 Cr=answer
C           599882    IN    A       192.33.4.12            ;NT=165 Cr=answer
D           599882    IN    A       128.8.10.90            ;NT=12 Cr=answer
E           599882    IN    A       192.203.230.10         ;NT=6 Cr=answer
F           599882    IN    A       192.5.5.241            ;NT=1021 Cr=answer
G           599882    IN    A       192.112.36.4           ;NT=1023 Cr=answer
H           599882    IN    A       128.63.2.53            ;NT=6 Cr=answer
I           599882    IN    A       192.36.148.17          ;NT=7 Cr=answer
J           599882    IN    A       198.41.0.10            ;NT=6 Cr=answer
$ORIGIN org.
foobirds    86400    IN    MX       10 wren.foobirds.org.       ;Cl=2
            86400    IN    MX       20 parrot.foobirds.org.     ;Cl=2
            86400    IN    NS       wren.foobirds.org.          ;Cl=2
            86400    IN    NS       parrot.foobirds.org.        ;Cl=2
      86400 IN SOA wren.foobirds.org. admin.wren.foobirds.org.(
             . 2000020501 21600 1800 604800 900 )     ;Cl=2
```

```
$ORIGIN foobirds.org.
ducks          86400    IN    NS       ruddy.ducks.foobirds.org.      ;Cl=2
               86400    IN    NS       wren.foobirds.org.             ;Cl=2
               86400    IN    NS       bear.mammals.org.              ;Cl=2
news           86400    IN    CNAME    parrot.foobirds.org.           ;Cl=2
robin          86400    IN    MX       5 wren.foobirds.org.           ;Cl=2
               86400    IN    A        172.16.5.2                     ;Cl=2
puffin         86400    IN    MX       5 wren.foobirds.org.           ;Cl=2
               86400    IN    A        172.16.5.17                    ;Cl=2
wren           86400    IN    A        172.16.5.1                     ;Cl=2
parrot         86400    IN    A        172.16.5.3                     ;Cl=2
crow           86400    IN    A        172.16.5.5                     ;Cl=2
localhost      86400    IN    A        127.0.0.1                      ;Cl=2
terns          86400    IN    NS       sooty.terns.foobirds.org.      ;Cl=2
               86400    IN    NS       arctic.terns.foobirds.org.     ;Cl=2
www            86400    IN    CNAME    wren.foobirds.org.             ;Cl=2
bob            86400    IN    CNAME    robin.foobirds.org.            ;Cl=2
redbreast      86400    IN    CNAME    robin.foobirds.org.            ;Cl=2
kestrel        86400    IN    A        172.16.5.20                    ;Cl=2
kestral        86400    IN    CNAME    kestrel.foobirds.org.          ;Cl=2
hawk           86400    IN    A        172.16.5.4                     ;Cl=2
foobirds-net   86400    IN    PTR      0.0.16.172.in-addr.arpa.       ;Cl=2
$ORIGIN terns.foobirds.org.
arctic         86400    IN    A        172.16.30.251                  ;Cl=2
sooty          86400    IN    A        172.16.30.250                  ;Cl=2
$ORIGIN 172.in-addr.arpa.
16             86400    IN    NS       wren.foobirds.org.             ;Cl=4
      86400 IN SOA wren.foobirds.org. admin.wren.foobirds.org. (
               2000021602 21600 1800 604800 900 )        ;Cl=4
$ORIGIN 6.16.172.in-addr.arpa.
1              86400    IN    PTR      arctic.terns.foobirds.org.   ;Cl=4
$ORIGIN 12.16.172.in-addr.arpa.
3              86400    IN    PTR      wren.foobirds.org.             ;Cl=4
$ORIGIN 5.16.172.in-addr.arpa.
20             86400    IN    PTR      kestrel.foobirds.org.        ;Cl=4
4              86400    IN    PTR      hawk.foobirds.org.           ;Cl=4
2              86400    IN    PTR      robin.foobirds.org.          ;Cl=4
17             86400    IN    PTR      puffin.foobirds.org.         ;Cl=4
```

```
5               86400    IN   PTR    crow.foobirds.org.      ;Cl=4
3               86400    IN   PTR    parrot.foobirds.org.    ;Cl=4
$ORIGIN 0.127.in-addr.arpa.
0               86400    IN   NS     localhost.              ;Cl=5
        86400   IN   SOA  localhost. root.localhost. (
                1997022700 28800 14400 3600000 86400 )  ;Cl=5
$ORIGIN 0.0.127.in-addr.arpa.
1               86400    IN   PTR    localhost.              ;Cl=5
```

Listing 12.2 is extremely long, even though the dump was taken shortly after the server started and only a few queries had been processed. The bulk of this listing is information loaded from the local zone files, but there is also a good deal of cached information. Large chunks of the cache are the result of information provided in the authority and additional sections of the query responses. At least as much data enters the cache in this manner as enters as a result of the specific answers to queries. Just looking at the large number of NS entries and the A records for those NS entries makes this clear.

The Cache & Data section is segmented by $ORIGIN directives. All of the other lines in this section are clearly identifiable DNS resource records. But some additional information is appended to the end of each record as a comment. Three comments that the server commonly adds to a record are the following:

Cl   identifies the number of fields in the current origin. Therefore, when the origin is 0.0.127.in-addr.arpa, the Cl value is 5, and when the origin is foobirds.org, the Cl value is 2. The root (.) is assigned a Cl value of 0.

Nt   is the round-trip time for queries to the specified name server. This comment is only added to the address records of name servers. The round-trip time helps named select the best server for a given query.

Cr   is the credibility tag, which defines the authority level of the source of cached information. BIND has three authority levels:

auth   is an authoritative answer.

answer   is an answer from a non-authoritative source.

addtnl   is a record learned from the authority or additional section of a query response.

The Cr value is used by named when a record is received that already exists in the name server's cache. If the record received has a higher credibility rating than the record in the cache, the new record replaces the cached record. If the new record has a lower credibility rating than the record in the cache, the cached record is retained. Of the Cr values, auth is the most credible and addtnl is the least credible.

The comments at the end of a record are not the only comments that you might see in the Cache & Data section of a dump file. Negative cached information also appears in the dump as a comment. There are no examples of this in Listing 12.2, but if there were, you would see a normal resource record that starts with a semi-colon. In other words, the negative cached information appears as a resource record that has been commented out of the file. Additionally, the record has the tag NXDOMAIN written near the end of the record.

The Hints Section

The last section in the dump file is the Hints section. This section contains the list of root name servers loaded from the hint file. This list is only used when the name server starts. Once the server starts, one of the root servers is queried for an authoritative list of root servers. Defining and using the hint file is discussed in Chapter 5.

Listing 12.3 contains the Hints section of the named_dump.db file from wren.foobirds .org. Notice that all of the name servers in the Hints section have an Nt number assigned. named queries each server to establish a round-trip time to select the best root server to use.

Listing 12.3   The Hints in the named_dump.db File

```
; --- Hints ---
$ORIGIN .
.           3600000         IN      NS      A.ROOT-SERVERS.NET.     ;Cl=0
            3600000         IN      NS      B.ROOT-SERVERS.NET.     ;Cl=0
            3600000         IN      NS      C.ROOT-SERVERS.NET.     ;Cl=0
            3600000         IN      NS      D.ROOT-SERVERS.NET.     ;Cl=0
            3600000         IN      NS      E.ROOT-SERVERS.NET.     ;Cl=0
            3600000         IN      NS      F.ROOT-SERVERS.NET.     ;Cl=0
            3600000         IN      NS      G.ROOT-SERVERS.NET.     ;Cl=0
            3600000         IN      NS      H.ROOT-SERVERS.NET.     ;Cl=0
            3600000         IN      NS      I.ROOT-SERVERS.NET.     ;Cl=0
            3600000         IN      NS      J.ROOT-SERVERS.NET.     ;Cl=0
            3600000         IN      NS      K.ROOT-SERVERS.NET.     ;Cl=0
            3600000         IN      NS      L.ROOT-SERVERS.NET.     ;Cl=0
            3600000         IN      NS      M.ROOT-SERVERS.NET.     ;Cl=0
$ORIGIN ROOT-SERVERS.NET.
K           3600000         IN      A       193.0.14.129            ;NT=2 Cl=0
L           3600000         IN      A       198.32.64.12            ;NT=5 Cl=0
```

A	3600000	IN	A	198.41.0.4	;NT=6 Cl=0
M	3600000	IN	A	202.12.27.33	;NT=10 Cl=0
B	3600000	IN	A	128.9.0.107	;NT=134 Cl=0
C	3600000	IN	A	192.33.4.12	;NT=8 Cl=0
D	3600000	IN	A	128.8.10.90	;NT=24 Cl=0
E	3600000	IN	A	192.203.230.10	;NT=2 Cl=0
F	3600000	IN	A	192.5.5.241	;NT=22 Cl=0
G	3600000	IN	A	192.112.36.4	;NT=2 Cl=0
H	3600000	IN	A	128.63.2.53	;NT=22 Cl=0
I	3600000	IN	A	192.36.148.17	;NT=2 Cl=0
J	3600000	IN	A	198.41.0.10	;Cl=0

The purpose of dumping the DNS cache is to examine how data is stored internally by DNS and what data is stored. Examining the authoritative information that you provide to the server in the zone files will give you insight into how that data is being stored. Examining the other data in the cache shows you how your users use DNS. Learning how DNS is normally used can help identify when usage patterns change. A sudden change can indicate that an intruder is misusing your system.

BIND also offers a log file that provides summary statistics about your name server. That file is described in the next section of this chapter.

The Statistics Files

The named.stats log file captures name server usage statistics. The file is written to the /var/named directory when the following ndc command is issued:

```
[root]# ndc stats
Statistics dump initiated.
```

You can change the path name of the named.stats file with the statistics-file option in the named.conf file. However, there is no real advantage in changing the name, and the potential disadvantage is that changing the name could make it harder for other people to troubleshoot your system if they can't locate the file.

Listing 12.4 contains the statistics file from wren.foobirds.org. The file was written shortly after the system booted, so there is very little activity recorded by the file. Nevertheless, the meaning and purpose of each line is independent of how much traffic has been recorded. This file lists statistics for every possible query number, even though many query types are not yet implemented. (To save space and make the listing more readable, I deleted 200 lines of unused query counters from the listing.)

Listing 12.4   The `named.stats` File

```
+++ Statistics Dump +++ (957297236) Tue May  2 15:53:56 2000
23202    time since boot (secs)
23202    time since reset (secs)
0        Unknown query types
13       A queries
1        NS queries
0        MD queries
0        MF queries
0        CNAME queries
0        SOA queries
0        MB queries
0        MG queries
0        MR queries
0        NULL queries
0        WKS queries
6        PTR queries
0        HINFO queries
0        MINFO queries
0        MX queries
0        TXT queries
0        RP queries
0        AFSDB queries
0        X25 queries
0        ISDN queries
0        RT queries
0        NSAP queries
0        NSAP_PTR queries
0        SIG queries
0        KEY queries
0        PX queries
0        GPOS queries
0        AAAA queries
0        LOC queries
0        NXT queries
0        EID queries
0        NIMLOC queries
```

```
0          SRV queries
0          ATMA queries
0          NAPTR queries
0          KX queries
0          CERT queries
0          38 queries
... Many lines deleted ...
0          249 queries
0          TSIG queries
0          IXFR queries
3          AXFR queries
0          MAILB queries
0          MAILA queries
1          ANY queries
++ Name Server Statistics ++
(Legend)
RR      RNXD     RFwdR    RDupR     RFail
RFErr   RErr     RAXFR    RLame     ROpts
SSysQ   SAns     SFwdQ    SDupQ     SErr
RQ      RIQ      RFwdQ    RDupQ     RTCP
SFwdR   SFail    SFErr    SNaAns    SNXD
(Global)
5 0 4 0 0  0 0 3 0 0  2 18 3 3 1  24 0 0 0 3  4 0 0 0 3
[172.16.12.1]
0 0 0 0 0  0 0 3 0 0  0 18 0 0 0  24 0 0 0 3  4 0 0 0 0
-- Name Server Statistics --
--- Statistics Dump --- (957297236) Tue May  2 15:53:56 2000
```

The first two lines of the statistics file indicate how long the server has been running. The remainder of the named.stats file contains two basic types of information: counters for each type of query received and statistics for each host that the server has interacted with.

Query Counters

The named.stats file contains a list of every possible query type and a count of how many of each query type the server has received. Appendix C, "Resource Record Reference," explains each query type that maps to a resource record. The query types with values greater than 249 are special queries for multiple records; these queries are explained in Chapter 2, "The DNS Protocols."

The main thing you will learn from the query counters on your server is that most query types are never used. All queries are concentrated on approximately 10 query types. The remaining query types have become obsolete or are not yet used in production environments.

Name Server Statistics

The second part of the file starts with the label Name Server Statistics. This part of the file lists statistics for each system with which your server has interacted. The first part of this file is a section identified as Legend, which lists five groups of five mnemonics. These groups exactly map to the five groups of five numbers listed after each host. Each host that the server interacted with is listed by IP address and is followed by 25 numbers that are the statistics for that host. The mnemonics are supposed to help you interpret the number, but the mnemonics themselves need some explanation.

The first group of five numbers for each host map to these five mnemonics:

RR   This is the number of responses received from the host.

RNXD   This is the number of NXDOMAIN answers received from the host.

RFwdR   This is the number of answers received from the host that were forwarded on to the application that started the query.

RDupR   This is the number of duplicate responses received from the host.

RFail   This is the number of times that RCODE 2, the name server failure RCODE, was received from the host.

The second group of five numbers for each host map to the following five mnemonics:

RFErr   This is the number of times that RCODE 1, the format error RCODE, was received from the host.

RErr   This is the number of errors received from the host that were not either RCODE 1 or 2.

RAXFR   This is the number of zone transfers initiated by the host.

RLame   This is the number of lame delegations made to this host. The host must be a name server that is delegated a zone for which the host is not authoritative.

ROpts   This is the number of packets received from this host that contained IP options.

The third group of five numbers for each host map to these five mnemonics:

SSysQ   This is the number of system queries sent by the local server to the host. *System queries* are queries generated by **named** itself for such tasks as fetching glue records.

SAns   This is the number of answers sent to the host.

SFwdQ   This is the number of queries sent to this host as part of a recursive search.

SDupQ   This is the number of duplicate queries sent to the host. If a query was previously sent to any other server, it counts as a duplicate.

SErr   This is the number of times that a message sent to the host produced a transmission error.

The fourth group of five numbers for each host map to the following five mnemonics:

RQ   This is the number of queries received from the host.

RIQ   This is the number of inverse queries received from the host.

RFwdQ   This is the number of queries received from the host that required a recursive search before they could be answered.

RDupQ   This is the number of duplicate queries received from the host.

RTCP   This is the number of queries received from the host that arrived via TCP instead of via UDP.

The fifth group of five numbers for each host map to these five mnemonics:

SFwdR   This is the number of responses from remote name servers that the local server forwarded to the host.

SFail   This is the number of times that the local server sent a DNS message with the RCODE set to 2 to the host. RCODE 2 indicates server failure.

SFErr   This is the number of responses sent to the host with the RCODE set to 1, i.e., the RCODE value indicates a format error.

SNaAns   This is the number of non-authoritative answers sent to the host.

SNXD   This is the number of times that NXDOMAIN was sent to the host.

The first group of statistics is labeled Global. These are the summary statistics for the local server. In Listing 12.4, these statistics are as follows:

```
(Global)
5 0 4 0 0   0 0 3 0 0   2 18 3 3 1   24 0 0 0 3   4 0 0 0 3
```

Using the mnemonics from the Legend in Listing 12.4 as a guide, these statistics are interpreted as follows:

- 5 responses were received (5 RR).
- 4 responses were returned to applications to answer specific queries (4 RFwdR).

- 3 requests for zone file transfers were received (3 RAXFR).
- 2 system queries were sent (2 SSysQ).
- 18 answers were sent (18 SAns).
- 3 queries required a recursive search (3 SFwdQ).
- 3 duplicate queries were sent (3 SDupQ).
- 1 send failed on a transmission error (1 SErr).
- 24 queries were received (24 RQ).
- 3 requests arrived via TCP (3 RTCP). This maps to the three zone file transfer requests.
- 4 responses were forwarded from remote name servers (4 SFwdR).
- 3 NXDOMAIN responses were sent (3 SNXD).

This snapshot was taken so soon after the reboot that it doesn't contain much significant information, although I was surprised to see one transmission failure. Use these statistics to get a feel for how your server is used. The list of hosts in the Name Server Statistics section on your server will be very large. That list will help you understand how many and which servers your server works with.

The *named.memstats* File

There is one other statistics file—it records statistics about the server's memory usage. This file is `named.memstats`. It might be useful if you have memory problems on your server, or you suspect a memory leak. I have never had these problems, and I have never had occasion to use this file. The content is more useful for a code developer than for a domain administrator.

The `named.memstats` file is produced by the same `ndc stats` command that produces the `named.stat` file, so if you're curious about memory usage, this file is available in the `/var/named` directory for your perusal.

In addition to examining long-term usage statistics, BIND makes it possible for you to monitor specific name server events through its debugging facility. The final log file that we'll examine in this chapter is `named.run`, which is the file that holds debugging and trace information.

The Trace File

The default trace file used by BIND is called `named.run` and it is found in the `/var/named` directory. Unlike the log files covered in the previous sections, the standard path name of the trace file cannot be changed with a simple option in the named.conf file. The contents of the named.run file can be controlled with the logging statement, which is described later in this chapter. But whenever tracing is turned on, the named.run file is created.

Turning Tracing On and Off

The trace file captures an enormous amount of information. In most cases, tracing is turned on to capture an event and then turned off soon after the event. If this isn't done, the file can become so large and so full of different types of information that it is almost as difficult to locate the information in the file as it is to diagnose the problem without the information. There are three ways to enable tracing:

- Use the ndc trace command to turn on tracing. After the event is captured, turn tracing off with the ndc notrace command.

- Send the USR1 signal to named to turn on tracing, and send the USR2 signal to turn tracing off.

- Use the –d option on the named command line to enable tracing. If tracing is enabled in this manner, it must be disabled using either the USR2 signal or the ndc notrace command.

NOTE The named command-line options, the named signals, and the ndc commands are all explained in Chapter 3, "The BIND Software."

Setting the Debug Level

The debug level controls the amount of detail captured in a trace. The debug level is an optional numeric argument that can be provided with the –d command-line option or with the ndc trace command. If you use signals, you need to send one USR1 signal for each debug level, so debug level 4 requires four separate kill commands. (Why bother with USR1? Use ndc. It is better and easier.)

There are 11 different debug levels. The levels are cumulative, so level 4 includes all of the trace detail covered by levels 1 through 4. Not all 11 debug levels are useful. The debug levels that produce useful results are as follows:

1   provides basic status messages and transaction traces. This is the default and it provides the most concise output.

2   adds details about SOA values for zone transfers and information about the remote servers used for queries.

3   adds details about the name server updating its database, about system queries, and about the remote servers involved in resolving queries.

4 adds full packet traces of the query and response messages that the server receives.

10 adds full packet traces of the query and response messages that the server sends.

The sample named.run file described in this chapter captures the trace of a zone file transfer at debug level 1. The commands shown in Listing 12.5 were used to start and stop the trace to capture the specific event.

Listing 12.5 Using ndc to Control Tracing

```
[root]# ndc trace
Debug level: 1
... Waited for the remote server to run the test...
[root]# ndc notrace
Debugging turned off.
```

The *named.run* File

The trace file produced by the pair of ndc commands shown in Listing 12.5 captured a zone file transfer. Listing 12.6 contains the actual trace captured in the named.run file by those commands.

Listing 12.6 An Event Trace in the named.run File

```
Debug level 1
Version = named 8.2.2-P3 Thu Nov 11 00:04:50 EST 1999
        /usr/src/bs/BUILD/bind-8.2.2_P3/src/bin/name
conffile = /etc/named.conf
datagram from [172.16.12.1].1025, fd 22, len 42
req: nlookup(1.5.16.172.in-addr.arpa) id 6455 type=12 class=1
req: found '1.5.16.172.in-addr.arpa' as '1.5.16.172.in-addr.arpa' (cname=0)
ns_req: answer -> [172.16.12.1].1025 fd=22 id=6455 size=122 rc=0
IP/TCP connection from [172.16.12.1].1026 (fd 6)
req: nlookup(foobirds.org) id 6456 type=252 class=1
req: found 'foobirds.org' as 'foobirds.org' (cname=0)
approved AXFR from [172.16.12.1].1026 for "foobirds.org"
finddata(): buflen=65493
zone transfer (AXFR) of "foobirds.org" (IN) to [172.16.12.1].1026
datagram from [172.16.12.1].1025, fd 22, len 35
```

```
req: nlookup(hawk.foobirds.org) id 48166 type=17 class=1
req: found 'hawk.foobirds.org' as 'hawk.foobirds.org' (cname=0)
ns_req: answer -> [172.16.12.1].1025 fd=22 id=48166 size=161 rc=0
datagram from [172.16.12.1].1025, fd 22, len 37
req: nlookup(hawkrp.foobirds.org) id 46401 type=16 class=1
req: found 'hawkrp.foobirds.org' as 'hawkrp.foobirds.org' (cname=0)
ns_req: answer -> [172.16.12.1].1025 fd=22 id=46401 size=159 rc=0
```

The first three lines in the named.conf file in Listing 12.6 provide background information. These lines state that the trace is running at debug level 1, that the version of named running on the server is BIND 8.2.2-P3, and that the configuration file used by named is /etc/named.conf.

The next four lines trace a reverse domain lookup. Each line has the following meaning:

datagram from   A DNS message was received from the specified address. In Listing 12.6, the requestor's address is 172.16.12.1.

req: nlookup   A request to look up DNS information was received. In this line of Listing 12.6, the specific information requested was the PTR record, which is a type 12 record, for 1.5.16.172.in-addr.arpa.

req: found   The requested information was found. Not only that, the information was found to be a canonical name and not a nickname, which is what (cname=0) means.

ns_req: answer   The answer was sent to the requestor.

We wanted to capture a zone transfer but some other stuff is also in the trace file. This reverse lookup was caused by the way that the administrator at the remote system ran the test. The administrator used nslookup. When the administrator typed **server 172.16.5.1** at the nslookup command prompt, nslookup issued a reverse lookup for 172.16.5.1 in order to display the server name as well as the server address. Look at the nslookup examples in Chapter 11, "DNS Test Tools," and you'll see that nslookup displays the server name and address with every test.

The next six lines are the heart of the trace. It is these six lines that trace the file transfer. Two of the lines, req: nlookup and req: found, were described previously. The meaning of these lines is the same; only the type of information requested is different. In this case, the query type is 252 (AXFR), which is a zone file transfer.

These two lines, however, are the only similarities. From the start, the zone transfer doesn't look like the other query. First off, it does not start with the receipt of a datagram.

Instead, it starts with a TCP connection, as indicated by the IP/TCP connection entry in the trace file. Zone transfers run over TCP; all other DNS queries normally use UDP.

This server also checks to see if zone transfers are limited by an allow-transfer option. The approved AXFR entry shows that, even if they are, this requestor is allowed to receive zone transfers.

Finally, the trace reports the buffer size being used for TCP traffic, and the successful transfer of the foobirds.org zone to the requestor at 172.16.12.1. The administrator running the test at the remote location should successfully receive the zone file.

That's the test we wanted, but there are eight more lines in the trace file. Four of those lines are from a query for the RP record of hawk, and four are from a query for the supporting TXT record hawkRP. These extra lines are just part of the reality of trace files. If the server is being used at all, there will always be some additional stuff in the trace that you're not interested in. Before I could type **ndc notrace**, these extra queries were received. They can just be ignored. When working with a trace, you must learn to focus on just those lines relating to your test.

This chapter describes the named_dump.db file, the named.stats file, and the named.run file. Among them, named logs a tremendous amount of information. But named is not finished. It also logs information through the system log service.

System Log Messages

All Linux systems use syslogd to log system messages. The log files created by syslogd and the information written to those files are defined in the /etc/syslog.conf file. Listing 12.7 shows the syslog.conf file from a Red Hat 6 system.

Listing 12.7   The syslog.conf File

```
# Log all kernel messages to the console.
#kern.*                                 /dev/console

# Log anything of level info or higher except mail and
# private authentication messages to /var/log/messages
*.info;mail.none;authpriv.none          /var/log/messages

# Log authpriv messages to /var/secure.
authpriv.*                              /var/log/secure
```

```
# Log all mail messages to /var/maillog.
mail.*                                /var/log/maillog

# Log emergency messages in all log files.
*.emerg                               *

# Log critical uucp and news message to /var/log/spooler.
uucp,news.crit                        /var/log/spooler

# Log all boot messages to /var/log/boot.log
local7.*                              /var/log/boot.log
```

Comments in the `syslog.conf` file start with a # and are ignored by `syslogd`. Active entries in the file start with a semi-colon–separated list of the messages being logged and end with the path name of the file where the messages are logged.

`syslogd` categorizes log entries by *facility* and *severity*. A facility identifies the source of the message, and `syslogd` recognizes several sources. The `syslog.conf` file in Listing 12.7 identifies some of these, such as `mail`, `news`, and `kern` (for the kernel). One of the most common facility values is `daemon` because it is the default used by most daemon processes. Listing 12.7 does not contain an explicit entry for the `daemon` facility, but the * in the facility field of two of the entries in the sample `syslog.conf` file covers all facilities, including `daemon`.

A severity is assocsiated with each facility. The severity of a message is identified by a keyword that is separated from the facility keyword by a period. A few severity values are shown in Listing 12.7, such as `info` and `crit` for informational and critical messages, respectively. The * in the severity field means that messages of all severity levels are logged for the identified facility. A severity of `none` means that no messages are logged for the facility.

This information about the `syslogd` facility and severity values will come in handy if you decide to create a custom logging configuration with the `logging` statement. BIND uses the same facility and severity values in its configuration.

DNS Messages in */var/log/messages*

By default, `named` logs messages with `syslogd` using the `daemon` facility. Given the Red Hat configuration in Listing 12.7, all of the messages that `named` logs through `syslogd` are stored in the `/var/log/messages` file. The messages from `named` are stored there, along with most of the other information logged by `syslogd`, which is usually a very large amount of information.

Maintaining a
Healthy System

PART 4

Use a tool like grep to pick out just the named messages from the mass of data in the messages file. In Listing 12.8, grep is used to select only named messages and only those named messages written on May 3.

Listing 12.8 Using grep to Find Messages in the System Log

```
[root]# grep '^May  3' /var/log/messages | grep named
May  3 09:17:21 wren named[831]: starting.  named 8.2.2-P3 Thu Nov 11 00:04:50
EST 1999 /usr/src/bs/BUILD/bind-8.2.2_P3/src/bin/named
May  3 09:17:21 wren named[831]: hint zone "" (IN) loaded (serial 0)
May  3 09:17:21 wren named[831]: Zone "0.0.127.in-addr.arpa" (file
named.local): No default TTL set using SOA minimum instead
May  3 09:17:21 wren named[831]: master zone "0.0.127.in-addr.arpa" (IN)
loaded (serial 1997022700)
May  3 09:17:21 wren named[831]: master zone "foobirds.org" (IN) loaded
(serial 2000020501)
May  3 09:17:21 wren named[831]: master zone "16.172.in-addr.arpa" (IN) loaded
(serial 2000021602)
May  3 09:17:21 wren named[831]: listening on [127.0.0.1].53 (lo)
May  3 09:17:21 wren named[831]: listening on [172.16.5.1].53 (eth0)
May  3 09:17:21 wren named[831]: listening on [208.58.211.84].53 (ppp0)
May  3 09:17:21 wren named[831]: Forwarding source address is [0.0.0.0].1027
May  3 09:17:21 wren named[832]: Ready to answer queries.
May  3 09:17:40 wren named[832]: Sent NOTIFY for "foobirds.org IN SOA"
(foobirds.org); 1 NS, 1 A
May  3 09:19:35 wren named[832]: IP/TCP connection from [172.16.12.1].1026 (fd
6)
May  3 09:19:35 wren named[832]: approved AXFR from [172.16.12.1].1026 for
"foobirds.org"
May  3 09:19:35 wren named[832]: zone transfer (AXFR) of "foobirds.org" (IN)
to [172.16.12.1].1026
May  3 10:17:21 wren named[832]: Cleaned cache of 0 RRsets
May  3 10:17:21 wren named[832]: deleting interface [208.58.211.84].53
May  3 10:17:21 wren named[832]: USAGE 957363441 957359841 CPU=0u/0.01s
CHILDCPU=0u/0s
May  3 10:17:21 wren named[832]: NSTATS 957363441 957359841 PTR=1 TXT=1 RP=1
AXFR=1
May  3 10:17:21 wren named[832]: XSTATS 957363441 957359841 RR=1 RNXD=0
RFwdR=0 RDupR=0 RFail=0 RFErr=0 RErr=0 RAXFR=1 RLame=0 ROpts=0 SSysQ=2 SAns=3
SFwdQ=0 SDupQ=2 SErr=0 RQ=4 RIQ=0 RFwdQ=0 RDupQ=0 RTCP=1 SFwdR=0 SFail=0
SFErr=0 SNaAns=0 SNXD=0
May  3 11:17:21 wren named[832]: Cleaned cache of 0 RRsets
May  3 11:17:21 wren named[832]: USAGE 957367041 957359841 CPU=0u/0.01s
CHILDCPU=0u/0s
```

```
May  3 11:17:21 wren named[832]: NSTATS 957367041 957359841 PTR=1 TXT=1 RP=1
AXFR=1

May  3 11:17:21 wren named[832]: XSTATS 957367041 957359841 RR=1 RNXD=0
RFwdR=0 RDupR=0 RFail=0 RFErr=0 RErr=0 RAXFR=1 RLame=0 ROpts=0 SSysQ=2 SAns=3
SFwdQ=0 SDupQ=2 SErr=0 RQ=4 RIQ=0 RFwdQ=0 RDupQ=0 RTCP=1 SFwdR=0 SFail=0
SFErr=0 SNaAns=0 SNXD=0
```

The messages log file provides an interesting glimpse into the activities of this server. The first few messages show that the name server was started and that it loaded the hint file, the localhost file, and the zone files for the foobirds.org domain and for the 16.172.in-addr.arpa domain. The server is listening for DNS queries on all of its network interfaces, which is the default. (Use the listen-on option in the named.conf file to change this behavior.) No forwarders have been configured, and the server is ready for queries.

The server in Listing 12.8 is a master server. It sends out a NOTIFY message to its slaves. The slave then initiates a zone file transfer. That is the only client activity recorded for this server because it is a demonstration system set up on a private network. Your operational server will record much more activity.

The last two entries are interesting because they show the periodic cache maintenance that occurs at fixed intervals when a server is running. From the timestamp, you can tell that the periodic cache maintenance occurs every 60 minutes. (Use the cleaning-interval option to change this maintenance interval.)

All of the files examined thus far are the default logging services provided by BIND. For most sites, these services are far more than adequate. They provide more information than most domain administrators ever need. Most administrators don't need to change the logging configuration. But if you do, BIND gives you extensive control over the logging configuration.

Configuring Logging

The logging statement in the named.conf file defines the logging configuration for your server. The syntax of the logging statement is as follows:

```
logging {
  [ channel channel_name {
  ( file pathname
      [ versions number|unlimited ]
      [ size size ]
  |syslog kern|user|mail|daemon|auth|syslog|lpr
          |news|uucp|cron|authpriv|ftp
```

Maintaining a
Healthy System

PART 4

```
                    |local0|local1|local2|local3
                    |local4|local5|local6|local7
        |null;

        [ severity critical|error|warning|notice
                        |info|debug [level]|dynamic; ]
        [ print-category yes|no; ]
        [ print-severity yes|no; ]
        [ print-time yes|no; ]
      }; ]


      [ category category_name {
        channel_name; [ channel_name; ... ]
      }; ]
      ...
    };
```

The syntax of the logging statement looks worse than it is because it contains a whole list of syslogd facility values and severity values. In reality, the logging statement comes down to two basic clauses:

- The channel clause, which defines where messages are logged and how they are handled
- The category clause, which defines what messages are sent to a channel

The *channel* Clause

The channel clause defines a target where messages are logged and assigns that target an arbitrary name. In the syntax, the name is identified as *channel_name*, and it can be anything you want that does not conflict with an existing name.

The target for the messages can be a file, the system log service, or the null device. If the null device is used, the messages are discarded. If the system log is used, a valid syslogd facility value must be specified.

If a file is the target for the messages, you can optionally define how many versions of the file should be kept and how large the file should be allowed to grow. Assume that you defined the channel clause in Listing 12.9.

Listing 12.9   Defining a Logging Channel

```
logging {
    channel maintenance_log {
        file "maintenance.log";
            versions 2;
    };
};
```

This `logging` statement defines a channel arbitrarily named `maintenance_log`. The messages sent to this channel will be written to a file named `maintenance.log`. Two prior versions of the file will be kept. The current version of the file is `maintenance.log`, the previous version is `maintenance.log.0`, and the oldest version is `maintenance.log.1`. `named` creates a new log and rotates the old logs every time `named` starts or is forced to reload.

Versions have nothing to do with file size. If the file-size option is used, `named` stops writing to the log file when it reaches the maximum size, but it does not open a new file or rotate the logs if multiple versions are allowed.

Defining How Messages are Handled

The `severity` option in the `channel` clause filters the messages that are logged via the channel. The `severity` option is just like the severity value in a `syslog.conf` file, and it serves the same purpose. Only messages that carry a severity that is equal to or higher than the value defined in the `severity` option are written to the log. The syntax of the `severity` option is

```
[ severity critical|error|warning|notice
            |info|debug [level]|dynamic; ]
```

The severity values are listed in the syntax in descending order. `critical` is the highest severity and **debug** is the lowest, which means that a severity setting of **debug** will log all messages and a setting of `critical` will log only critical messages.

I didn't mention `dynamic` in this hierarchy because it is a special form of **debug**. The **debug** setting captures debug messages at a specific level along with all other messages. The `dynamic` setting captures debug messages at the current debug level along with all other messages. `dynamic` is more flexible than **debug** because it uses the current debug level, regardless of what that level is.

Maintaining a
Healthy System

PART 4

When used in a `channel` clause, the severity setting is not specific to the `syslog` option. All messages, whether the channel directs them to the system log, to a file, or to the null device, can be filtered on their severity value.

The three remaining options in the `channel` clause define how messages are formatted:

`print-time`   specifies whether or not a timestamp should be added to the message when it is written to the log file.

`print-severity`   specifies whether or not the severity of the message should be printed in the log file.

`print-category`   specifies whether or not the category of the message is written to the log file.

Message categories and how they are mapped to channels is the topic of the next section.

The *category* Clause

The `category` clause maps a category of messages to the channel that will log those messages. There are currently 22 different categories of messages. See Table B.2 in Appendix B, "`named.conf` Command Reference," for a full listing of all of these categories. An example will make the purpose of the `category` clause clear.

In Listing 12.9, a channel was defined to write messages to a file named `maintenance.log`. The channel was assigned the name `maintenance_log`. To send maintenance messages, which are one of the categories of messages, to the new channel, add a `category` clause to the `logging` statement. Listing 12.10 shows the completed `logging` statement with a `channel` clause and a `category` clause.

Listing 12.10 Mapping a Category to a Channel

```
logging {
    channel maintenance_log {
        file "maintenance.log";
            versions 2;
    };
    category maintenance {
        maintenance_log;
    };
};
```

Now, messages that have a category value of `maintenance` are sent to the `maintenance.log` file. All other messages are handled just as before, according to the rules of the predefined channels and categories built in to BIND.

The Predefined Channels and Categories

The BIND documentation identifies four predefined channels and defines them as shown in Listing 12.11.

Listing 12.11 The Predefined Logging Channels

```
logging {
  channel default_syslog {
    syslog daemon;
    severity info;
  };
  channel default_debug {
    file "named.run";
    severity dynamic;
  };
  channel default_stderr {
    file "<stderr>";
    severity info;
  };
  channel null {
    null;
  };
  category default { default_syslog; default_debug; };
  category panic { default_syslog; default_stderr; };
  category packet { default_debug; };
  category eventlib { default_debug; };
};
```

These predefined channels are not really defined in the standard syntax of a `logging` statement. In reality, these values are defined inside the `named` source code. This means that you cannot redefine these channels yourself. For example, you could not create your own channel and name it `default_syslog`. Nor could you create a channel using `<stderr>` as the name of a file. Internal file descriptors cannot be used as filenames in a `channel` clause.

What you can do is use these predefined channels in your own configuration. For example, if you want to send security messages to the console, you could add the following `category` clause to your own configuration:

```
logging {
  category security { default_stderr; };
};
```

WARNING I don't recommend putting messages out on the console. This is just an illustration.

The `logging` statement provides lots of flexibility in configuring your system. Play with it to find the configuration that works best for you.

In Sum

Periodic review of the `named` log files is essential to monitoring the health of your server. A Linux DNS server offers exhaustive logging services. By default, a wide array of server status messages are logged via `syslogd` using the `daemon` facility. In addition to logging via `syslogd`, `named` creates four other log files:

`named_dump.db` is created by the `ndc dumpdb` command and contains a dump of the information in the server's cache.

`named.stats` is created by the `ndc stats` command and contains server usage statistics.

`named.memstats` is created whenever the `named.stats` file is created and contains memory usage statistics.

`named.run` is created by the `ndc trace` command and contains a trace of name server events.

Despite the fact that the default logging facilities are adequate for almost every situation, BIND provides the `logging` statement in the `named.conf` file for you to customize logging to meet your own personal needs. Extensive services that are also highly configurable are a hallmark of the BIND software.

This chapter completes a book in which you and I have shared the full story of DNS and BIND, and of how a Linux system can be configured as a DNS server. We started with the architecture and protocols of DNS, and the BIND software that implements it. We examined how most Linux systems are configured to run DNS, and discussed the wide range of configuration options available to meet special needs. We covered the ongoing tasks that are necessary to maintain a healthy server.

I believe that the time we have shared discussing these topics will give you the insight you need to tackle the tough tasks of DNS server administration. I enjoyed writing this book for you. I hope you enjoyed reading it and can benefit from it.

Appendixes

BIND 9

A major change is coming to BIND, and it should be arriving soon. The change is from BIND 8 to BIND 9. BIND 9 is currently in its second beta release, so it is not quite ready for production use. But when it is, you can bet that Linux will be among the first systems to offer it.

You may not welcome the news of a major change coming in the software on which your DNS server depends. You have put lots of time and effort into mastering BIND 8 and configuring your server. At this point, fears that BIND 9 will somehow make all of that effort for naught could be plaguing you.

Have no fear; the work that you invest in BIND 8 and the BIND 8 advice provided in this book apply to the upcoming BIND 9 release as well. BIND 9 keeps the features of BIND 8 and adds some new ones. The configuration files you create for BIND 8 should work just fine with BIND 9.

New Features

BIND 9 is a redesign and rewrite of the underlying BIND code. BIND is being rewritten to take advantage of changes in computer architectures, including multithreaded systems, multiprocessor hardware, and high-performance backend database systems. This rewrite will provide the performance enhancements needed to support very large domains, and the rewritten code will be easier for developers to maintain and to port to different operating systems.

In addition to improved performance, several features are being added or improved in BIND 9. Expect the following functionality to be enhanced:

- support for DNSSEC
- support for TSIG
- support for DDNS
- support for IXFR
- support for NOTIFY
- support for EDNS0
- support for IPv6

For many domain administrators, the benefits of BIND 9 are indirect. Most of us do not run very large domains, and we don't really need a multithreaded multiprocessor to run BIND. But all of us depend on the root servers and indirectly benefit from performance enhancements that help the root servers. Additionally, code improvements that help the developers maintain BIND mean quicker and better bug fixes for all of us.

BIND 9 also means that DNSSEC and DDNS will be usable at more sites. Most domain administrators don't have a pressing need for DDNS and DNSSEC, but if you do, you might want to start experimenting with the BIND 9 beta.

Installing the BIND 9 Beta

The second beta of BIND 9 is available now from `www.isc.org`. Follow the links from the ISC home page and download the `bind-9.0.0b2.tar.gz` file. Use `tar` to uncompress and restore the files.

When the files are in place, change to the `bind-9.0.0b2` subdirectory created by `tar`. Run the `./configure` command to create the correct `Makefile` files for your Linux system. Then run `make`. BIND 9 should compile without errors. The BIND 9 documentation only lists Red Hat Linux under the systems that are known to have successful builds, but I have also compiled it under Caldera 2.3 without problems. Finally, run the `make install` command to move the executables to the `/usr/local/sbin` directory.

TIP If you want to place the executables in a directory other than /usr/local/ sbin, define that directory on the ./configure command line with the --prefix argument.

Once it is installed, the BIND 9 beta can be configured and used like any other Linux DNS server. But this is a beta. Not everything you expect in BIND is implemented.

The Limitations of Beta 2

Don't try to use an early beta release as a production server. Use the beta release to learn about BIND 9 and to evaluate which features in BIND 9 may be important for your environment. Production environments need to wait for the formal release of BIND 9 before moving any operational servers.

The `bind-9.0.0b2/doc/misc/options` file that comes with the BIND 9 beta release is a summary of the configuration language changes from BIND 8 to BIND 9. This is a very useful list, and it is the basis for the information in the next few sections of this appendix. This information is current for BIND 9 beta release 2, but it will undoubtedly change as new betas and then a production version of BIND 9 are released. Check the documentation that comes with your version of BIND 9 to make sure there are no new surprises.

One of the most important things in the `doc/misc/options` file is the list of configuration options that are not yet implemented in the beta. Listing A.1 shows these options. Use this list to decide whether or not the current beta is ready for the testing you want to do.

Listing A.1   Options That Are Unavailable in BIND 9 Beta 2

```
allow-update-forwarding      also-notify
blackhole                    bogus
check-names                  coresize
datasize                     dialup
dump-file                    fetch-glue
files                        forward
forwarders                   heartbeat-interval
host-statistics              lame-ttl
max-ixfr-log-size            max-ncache-ttl
memstatistics-file           min-roots
notify                       pubkey
rfc2308-type1                rrset-order
serial-queries               sortlist
stacksize                    statistics-file
statistics-interval          topology
type forward                 type stub
controls                     trusted-keys
```

Many of these options have not yet been implemented because they are low priority. Examples of these are maintenance intervals, file sizes, and file path names, none of which are essential for testing. Others, such as `notify` and `allow-update-forwarding`, require new or rewritten code that isn't ready yet. Evaluate the importance of these features before testing BIND 9 at your site.

Most commercial sites won't run the BIND 9 beta. But I believe at some point in the future, you will run BIND 9.

Appendixes

Configuration Changes

You may not think you'll use BIND 9, but you probably will. If you don't have an enormous domain, or any need for DNSSEC, DDNS, or IPv6, then you don't have an immediate need for BIND 9. But you'll use it anyway. The reason is simple—future releases of Linux will include BIND 9 once it becomes the production release of BIND. You need to know how it will affect you.

The good news is that the named.conf file you created for BIND 8 will probably work without modification. The bad news is that I said "probably." Simple configurations, such as those covered in Part 2, "Essential Configuration," will work without a problem. Advanced configurations options, such as the options that support IXFR, will change. You should check the named.conf file carefully when moving from BIND 8 to BIND 9. Some BIND 8 configuration options are obsolete in BIND 9, and some new configuration options have been added.

Obsolete Configuration Options

One of the most important items in the doc/misc/options file is the list of obsolete configuration options. These are BIND 8 configuration options that are considered outdated by BIND 9. Many of these options are simply ignored by BIND 9 and therefore can be in a named.conf file without causing BIND 9 any problems. But I don't believe in leaving unused junk in a configuration file. Use the list of obsolete options in Table A.1 to clean up your named.conf file before running BIND 9.

Table A.1   Obsolete Configuration Options

Option	Usage in BIND 9
allow-update	Supported. The new update-policy option is preferred.
deallocate-on-exit	Ignored. Always enabled.
fake-iquery	Ignored. Always disabled.
has-old-clients	Ignored and unused.
ixfr-base	Supported. ixfr-tmp-file is an alternative.
maintain-ixfr-base	Obsolete. Use the provide-ixfr option instead.
multiple-cnames	Ignored. Always disabled.

Table A.1   Obsolete Configuration Options *(continued)*

Option	Usage in BIND 9
named-xfer	Ignored. Zone transfer is integrated in BIND. named-xfer is not used.
support-ixfr	Deprecated. Instead, use provide-ixfr or request-ixfr.
treat-cr-as-space	Ignored. BIND 9 reads files in both formats.
use-id-pool	Ignored. Always enabled.

New Configuration Options

The doc/misc/options file also lists the new configuration options that have been added to BIND 9. The following new options are those that are identified in beta 2, as listed here:

allow-update-forwarding   identifies the hosts from which a slave server will accept dynamic updates. The slave server then forwards the updates on to the master server. This new feature is not implemented in beta 2.

max-transfer-idle-in   defines the amount of time an inbound zone transfer can sit idle. By default, if no packets have been received in the last 60 minutes, the transfer is terminated.

max-transfer-idle-out   defines the amount of time that an outbound zone transfer can sit idle. By default, if no packets can be sent for 60 minutes, the transfer is terminated.

max-transfer-time-out   defines the maximum amount of time an outbound zone transfer can take. By default, if the transfer cannot be completed in 120 minutes, it is terminated.

provide-ixfr   specifies whether or not the master will provide incremental zone file transfers to its slaves.

query-source-v6   defines a specific interface and port for sending out IPv6 queries. By default, any available interface is used. This option performs the same function as the BIND 8 query-source option, except it does it for IPv6.

recursive-clients   defines the maximum number of concurrent recursive lookups that the server will perform for its clients. The default is 100.

Appendixes

`request-ixfr` specifies whether or not a slave server will request incremental zone file transfers from its master.

`tcp-clients` defines the maximum number of concurrent TCP connections that the server will accept from its clients. The default is 100.

`transfer-source-v6` identifies a specific interface that will be used for inbound IPv6 zone file transfers. By default, the best available interface is used. This option performs the same function as the BIND 8 `transfer-source` option, except that it does it for IPv6.

NOTE All of these options are available for test and evaluation in beta 2 except for the `allow-update-forwarding` option.

Another configuration command that is described in the draft BIND 9 documentation but that is not listed in the `doc/misc/options` file is the `view` command. The `view` command simplifies the implementation of a split DNS namespace by offering different views of the DNS data to different clients. If you use a split namespace to support a private network number or to coexist with a firewall, the `view` command might be useful to you. The `view` command is not implemented in BIND 9 beta 2 and its syntax is not finalized. Monitor the BIND 9 releases for information about the developing `view` command.

Final Words

BIND 9 will have little direct impact on most domain administrators. The configuration language that you mastered for BIND 8 will still work as advertised. While all of us will benefit from improved performance and better code maintenance, the real demand for BIND 9 is among those sites that need advanced features. Most of us can wait for our Linux vendors to adopted BIND 9 as a part of the basic Linux distribution before tackling this new system. When it becomes a stable part of Linux, the DNSSEC, DDNS, and IXFR protocols will become much more widely used.

named.conf
Command Reference

This appendix provides a reference to the syntax and structure of BIND 8.2.2 configuration commands. It is a reference; it is not a tutorial. Tutorial material is provided in the main body of the book. Use this appendix to read unfamiliar commands and to verify the syntax of commands in your own configuration file.

The following conventions describe the syntax of the commands:

- **Bold** means that something must be typed as shown.
- *Italic* means that you must provide your own value for the specified field.
- Square brackets [ ] mean that the item is optional.
- Vertical bar | means choose one keyword or the other.

NOTE My source for much of this information is the online documentation at the www.isc.org Web site. Check that Web site for the latest information.

The named.conf file is used to configure BIND 8. This file defines the BIND operational environment and points to the sources of DNS database information. The file is composed of eight basic configuration statements: key, acl, options, logging, zone, server, controls, and trusted-keys.

In addition to these configuration commands, an include statement can be used. It loads an external file, which can contain any or all of the eight basic configuration statements, into the named.conf file. For example,

    include /var/named/keys

copies the file /var/named/keys, which might be a file containing key and trusted-key commands, into the named.conf file at the current location. The include statement must be the only command on the line; it cannot be embedded inside another command.

The eight other commands are used to create the actual configuration. These commands are described in the remainder of this appendix.

The *key* Statement

The key statement assigns a name to an authentication method used for transaction security. Assigning a name to an authentication method makes it easier to reference that method later in the configuration. key statements usually occur near the start of the configuration because forward references are not allowed. The syntax of the key statement is shown in Listing B.1.

Listing B.1 key Statement Syntax

```
key key_id {
  algorithm algorithm_id;
  secret secret_string;
};
```

The *key_id* is the name assigned to the authentication method. Use any descriptive name you like. Avoid using names that can be confused with configuration commands or options.

The *algorithm_id* identifies which authentication algorithm is used. BIND 8.2.2 only supports the hmac-md5 algorithm. Thus, with BIND 8.2.2, hmac-md5 is the only value that is valid for *algorithm_id.*

The *secret_string* is a base-64 encoded key used by the algorithm. Use the dnskeygen utility to generate the *secret_string* value. Chapter 10, "DNS Security," provides examples of the key statement and describes how to use dnskeygen.

The *acl* Statement

The access control list (acl) command assigns a name to an address match list so that it can be referenced later in the configuration. Forward references are not allowed. Therefore, any acl commands usually occur near the start of the named.conf file. The syntax of the acl command is shown in Listing B.2.

Listing B.2   acl Statement Syntax

```
acl name {
    address_match_list
};
```

name is any descriptive name you wish. Avoid using names that can be confused with configuration commands or options. For example, don't assign names such as trusted-keys or allow-query. Additionally, there are four names already assigned to predefined access control lists. The predefined names are

any   match every possible address.

none   match no address.

localhost   match every address assigned to the local host.

localnet   match every address where the network portion of the address is the same as the network portion of any address assigned to the local hosts.

An *address_match_list* is a list of addresses that can include an IP address written in standard dotted decimal notation with an optional address mask prefix. For example, 172.16.0.0/16 matches every address where the first 16 bits are 172.16. An exclamation point (!) before an address means "don't match" the value. Therefore, placing an exclamation in front of our sample address would match everything *except* addresses where the first 16 bits are 172.16.

An *address_match_list* can also contain a previously defined access control list name, including the four predefined names described earlier in this section, or a previously defined *key_id*. The keyword key must precede a *key_id* when used in an *address_match_list*. See Chapter 10 for access control list and *address_match_list* examples.

Appendixes

The *options* Statement

The options statement defines global options that affect the operation of BIND and the DNS protocol. The syntax of the options command is shown in Listing B.3.

Listing B.3 options Statement Syntax

```
options {
    [ version string; ]
    [ directory pathname; ]
    [ named-xfer pathname; ]
    [ dump-file pathname; ]
    [ memstatistics-file pathname; ]
    [ pid-file pathname; ]
    [ statistics-file pathname; ]
    [ auth-nxdomain yes|no; ]
    [ deallocate-on-exit yes|no; ]
    [ dialup yes|no; ]
    [ fake-iquery yes|no; ]
    [ fetch-glue yes|no; ]
    [ has-old-clients yes|no; ]
    [ host-statistics yes|no; ]
    [ multiple-cnames yes|no; ]
    [ notify yes|no; ]
    [ recursion yes|no; ]
    [ rfc2308-type1 yes|no; ]
    [ use-id-pool yes|no; ]
    [ treat-cr-as-space yes|no; ]
    [ also-notify { address-list; };
    [ forward only|first; ]
    [ forwarders { address-list; }; ]
    [ check-names master|slave|response warn|fail|ignore; ]
```

```
[ allow-query { address_match_list }; ]
[ allow-transfer { address_match_list }; ]
[ allow-recursion { address_match_list }; ]
[ blackhole { address_match_list }; ]
[ listen-on [ port ip_port ] { address_match_list }; ]
[ query-source [address ip_addr|*] [port ip_port|*] ; ]
[ lame-ttl number; ]
[ max-transfer-time-in number; ]
[ max-ncache-ttl number; ]
[ min-roots number; ]
[ serial-queries number; ]
[ transfer-format one-answer|many-answers; ]
[ transfers-in number; ]
[ transfers-out number; ]
[ transfers-per-ns number; ]
[ transfer-source ip_addr; ]
[ maintain-ixfr-base yes|no; ]
[ max-ixfr-log-size number; ]
[ coresize size; ]
[ datasize size; ]
[ files size; ]
[ stacksize size; ]
[ cleaning-interval number; ]
[ heartbeat-interval number; ]
[ interface-interval number; ]
[ statistics-interval number; ]
[ topology { address_match_list }; ]
[ sortlist { address_match_list }; ]
[ rrset-order { order_spec ; [ order_spec ; ... ] ] };
};
```

There are many different options and almost a dozen different types of values for those options. Two options, check-names and transfer-format, accept keyword values. The Boolean options accept either yes or no. All other options expect an appropriate value that you must provide. The italic labels in the syntax identify the format of the value you must provide for each option. The meaning of each label is described in the following list.

string   is a text string.

ip_port   is an IP port number.

number   is just that, a number.

size   is the size of a file in bytes, which can be abbreviated with K for kilobyte or M for megabytes; e.g., 5M is 5 million bytes.

pathname   is a path name. The path name provided to the directory option must be an absolute path from the root. All other path values can be relative to the value provided for the directory option or absolute paths from the root.

ip_addr   is a single IP address.

address-list   is a list of IP addresses separated by semi-colons.

address_match_list   is a list of addresses, ACL names, and key_ids. See the description of the *address_match_list* in "The acl Statement" section earlier in this appendix.

order_spec   is a multi-part rule that defines how resource records are ordered when multiple records are sent in response to a single query. The structure of an *order_spec* is

    [**class** *class*][**type** *type*][**name** "*domain*"] **order** *order*

class   can be ANY, IN, HS, or CH. The default is ANY, which means that all classes are processed by this rule.

type   is the keyword ANY, or one of the valid resource record types listed in Appendix C, "Resource Record Reference." The default is ANY, which means that all resource record types are processed by this *order_spec*.

domain   is a fully qualified domain name. If no *domain* is provided, the ordering rule applies to resource records from all domains handled by this server. *order* defines the ordering rule. There are three possible values:

   fixed   The order in which records are defined in the zone file is maintained.

   random   Resource records are shuffled into a random order.

   cyclic   The resource records are rotated in a round-robin manner. The default order is cyclic.

The options statement supports a large number of options. Each option is described in Table B.1.

Table B.1   BIND 8 Configuration Options

Option	Meaning
version	The string returned when the server is queried for its version.
directory	The path of the working directory from which the server reads and writes files.
named-xfer	The path to the named-xfer program.
dump-file	The file where the database is dumped if named receives a SIGINT signal. The default filename is named_dump.db.
memstatistics-file	The file where memory usage statistics are written if deallocate-on-exit is set. The default filename is named.memstats.
pid-file	The file where the process ID is stored.
statistics-file	The file where statistics are written when named receives a SIGILL signal. The default filename is named.stats.
auth-nxdomain	yes causes the server to respond as an authoritative server. The default is yes.
deallocate-on-exit	yes is used to detect memory leaks. The default is no.
dialup	yes causes the server to optimize operation for a dial-up network connection. The default is no.
fake-iquery	yes causes the server to respond to inverse queries with a fake reply instead of an error. The default is no.

Table B.1   BIND 8 Configuration Options *(continued)*

Option	Meaning
fetch-glue	yes causes the server to fetch all of the glue records for a response. The default is yes.
has-old-clients	yes sets auth-nxdomain and maintain-ixfr-base to yes and rfc2308-type1 to no.
host-statistics	yes causes the server to keep statistics on every host. The default is no.
multiple-cnames	yes allows multiple CNAME records for a domain name. The default is no.
notify	yes causes the server to send DNS NOTIFY messages when a zone is updated. The default is yes.
recursion	yes causes the server to recursively seek answers to queries. The default is yes.
rfc2308-type1	yes returns NS records with the SOA record for negative caching. no returns only the SOA record to be compatible with old servers. no is the default.
use-id-pool	yes causes the server to track outstanding query IDs to increase randomness. no is the default.
treat-cr-as-space	yes causes named to treat carriage returns as if they were spaces when loading a zone file. no is the default.
also-notify	Lists unofficial name servers to which the server should send DNS NOTIFY messages.
forward	first causes the server to first query the servers listed in the forwarders option and then look for the answer itself. only causes the server to query only the servers listed in the forwarders option.
forwarders	Lists the IP addresses of the server to which queries are forwarded. The default is not to use forwarding.

Table B.1   BIND 8 Configuration Options *(continued)*

Option	Meaning
check-names	Checks host names for compliance with RFC 952.
allow-query	Queries will only be accepted from hosts in the address list. The default is to accept queries from all hosts.
allow-transfer	Only hosts in the address list are allowed to receive zone transfers. The default is to allow transfers to all hosts.
allow-recursion	Lists hosts that are allowed to make recursive queries through this server. The default is to do recursive queries for all hosts.
blackhole	Lists hosts from which this server will not accept any queries or responses.
listen-on	Defines the interfaces and ports on which the server provides name service. By default, the server listens to the standard port (53) on all installed interfaces.
query-source	Defines the address and port used to query other servers.
lame-ttl	The amount of time a lame server indication will be cached. The default is 10 minutes.
max-transfer-time-in	Sets the maximum amount of time the server waits for an inbound transfer to complete. The default is 120 minutes (2 hours).
max-ncache-ttl	The amount of time this server will cache negative answers. The default is 3 hours and the maximum acceptable value is 7 days.
min-roots	The minimum number of root servers that must be reachable for queries involving the root servers to be accepted. The default is 2.

Appendixes

Table B.1 BIND 8 Configuration Options *(continued)*

Option	Meaning
serial-queries	The number of outstanding SOA queries a slave server can have at one time. The default is 4.
transfer-format	one-answer transfers one resource record per message. many-answers transfers as many resource records as possible in each message. For compatibility with older systems, the default is one-answer.
transfers-in	Sets the maximum number of concurrent inbound zone transfers. The default value is 10.
transfers-out	Limits the number of concurrent outbound zone transfers.
transfers-per-ns	Limits the number of concurrent inbound zone transfers from any one name server. The default value is 2.
transfer-source	The IP address of the network interface this server uses to transfer zones from remote masters.
maintain-ixfr-base	yes causes the server to keep a log of incremental zone transfers. no is the default.
max-ixfr-log-size	Sets the maximum size of the incremental zone transfer log file.
coresize	Sets the maximum size of a core dump file.
datasize	Limits the amount of data memory the server may use.
files	Limits the number of files the server may have open concurrently. The default is unlimited.
stacksize	Limits the amount of stack memory the server may use.

Table B.1   BIND 8 Configuration Options *(continued)*

Option	Meaning
cleaning-interval	Sets the time interval for the server to periodically remove expired resource records from the cache. The default is 60 minutes.
heartbeat-interval	Sets the time interval used for periodic zone maintenance when the dialup option is set to yes. 60 minutes is the default.
interface-interval	Sets the time interval for the server to scan the network interface list looking for new interfaces or interfaces that have been removed. The default is 60 minutes.
statistics-interval	Sets the time interval for the server to log statistics. The default is every 60 minutes.
topology	Forces the server to prefer certain remote name servers over others. Normally, the server prefers the remote name server that is topologically closest to itself.
sortlist	Defines a sort algorithm applied to resource records before sending them to the client.
rrset-order	Specifies the ordering used when multiple records are return for a single query.

The *logging* Statement

The logging statement defines the logging options for the server. The logging statement can include two different types of subordinate clauses: the channel clause and the category clause. The syntax of the logging statement is shown in Listing B.4.

Listing B.4   logging Statement Syntax

```
logging {
  [ channel channel_name {
```

```
( file pathname
    [ versions number|unlimited ]
    [ size size ]
  |syslog kern|user|mail|daemon|auth|syslog|lpr
              |news|uucp|cron|authpriv|ftp
              |local0|local1|local2|local3
              |local4|local5|local6|local7
  |null;

    [ severity critical|error|warning|notice
                |info|debug [level]|dynamic; ]
    [ print-category yes|no; ]
    [ print-severity yes|no; ]
    [ print-time yes|no; ]
  }; ]

  [ category category_name {
    channel_name; [ channel_name; ... ]
  }; ]
  ...
};
```

The channel clause defines how logging messages are handled. Messages are written to a file (file), sent to syslogd (syslog), or discarded (null). If a file is used, you can specify how many old versions are retained (version), how large the log file is allowed to grow (size), and the severity of the messages written to the log file (severity). You can specify that the time (print-time), category (print-category), and severity (print-severity) of the message be included in the log.

The category clause defines the category of messages sent to the channel. Thus the category clause defines what is logged and the channel clause defines where it is logged. The logging categories are listed in Table B.2.

Table B.2   BIND 8 Logging Categories

Category	The Type of Messages Logged
cname	Messages recording CNAME references.
config	Messages about configuration file processing.
db	Messages that log database operations.
default	Various types of messages. This is the default if nothing is specified.
eventlib	Messages containing debugging data from the event system.
insist	Messages that report internal consistency check failures.
lame-servers	Messages about lame server delegations.
load	Messages about loading the zone.
maintenance	Messages reporting maintenance events.
ncache	Messages about negative caching.
notify	Messages tracing the NOTIFY protocol.
os	Messages reporting operating system problems.
packet	Messages containing dumps of all of the packets sent and received.
panic	Messages generated by a fault that causes the server to shut down.
parser	Messages about configuration command processing.
queries	Messages about every DNS query received.
response-checks	Messages reporting the results of response checking.
security	Messages concerning the application of security criteria. These are most meaningful if the allow-update, allow-query, and allow-transfer options are in use.

Appendixes

Table B.2   BIND 8 Logging Categories *(continued)*

Category	The Type of Messages Logged
statistics	Messages containing server statistics.
update	Messages concerning dynamic updates.
xfer-in	Messages recording inbound zone transfers.
xfer-out	Messages recording outbound zone transfers.

The *zone* Statement

The zone statement identifies the zone being served and defines the source of domain database information. There are four variants of the zone statement: one for the master server, one for the slave servers, one for the root cache zone, and a special one for forwarding. The syntax of each variant is shown in Listing B.5.

Listing B.5   zone Statement Syntax

```
zone domain_name [ in|hs|hesiod|chaos ] {
    type master;
    file pathname;
    [ forward only|first; ]
    [ forwarders { address-list; }; ]
    [ check-names warn|fail|ignore; ]
    [ allow-update { address_match_list }; ]
    [ allow-query { address_match_list }; ]
    [ allow-transfer { address_match_list }; ]
    [ dialup yes|no; ]
    [ notify yes|no; ]
    [ also-notify { address-list }; ]
    [ ixfr-base pathname; ]
    [ pubkey flags protocol algorithm key; ]
};
```

```
zone domain_name [ in|hs|hesiod|chaos ] {
  type slave|stub;
  [ file pathname; ]
  [ ixfr-base pathname; ]
  masters [port ip_port] { address-list };
  [ forward only|first; ]
  [ forwarders { address-list; }; ]
  [ check-names warn|fail|ignore; ]
  [ allow-update { address_match_list }; ]
  [ allow-query { address_match_list }; ]
  [ allow-transfer { address_match_list }; ]
  [ transfer-source ip_addr; ]
  [ dialup yes|no; ]
  [ max-transfer-time-in number; ]
  [ notify yes|no; ]
  [ also-notify { address-list };
  [ pubkey flags protocol algorithm key; ]
};

zone "." [ in|hs|hesiod|chaos ] {
  type hint;
  file pathname;
  [ check-names warn|fail|ignore; ]
};

zone domain_name [in|hs|hesiod|chaos] {
  type forward;
  [ forward only|first; ]
  [ forwarders { address-list; }; ]
  [ check-names warn|fail|ignore; ]
};
```

The zone statement starts with the keyword zone, followed by the name of the domain. For the root cache, the domain name is always " . ". This is then followed by the data class. This is always IN for Internet DNS service, which is the default if no value is supplied.

The type option defines whether this is a master server, a slave server, a forwarded zone or the hint file for the root cache. A stub server is a slave server that loads only the NS records instead of the entire domain.

The file option for a master server points to the source file from which the zone is loaded. For the slave server, it points to the file to which the zone is written and the master clause points to the source of the data written to the file. In the root cache statement, the file option points to the source file for the hints used to initialize the cache. A forwarded domain does not have a file option because no data for the forwarded domain is stored on the local server.

With the exception of the pubkey option, all of the options available for the zone statement are covered in Table B.1. Other than their scope, they function the same in a zone statement as they do in an options statement.

The pubkey option defines the DNSSEC public encryption key for the zone when there is no trusted mechanism for distributing public keys over the network. pubkey defines the DNSSEC flags, protocol, and algorithm, as well as a base-64 encoded version of the key. The remote server that will be accessing this domain through DNSSEC defines the same settings using the trusted-key command described later in this appendix. See Chapter 10 for details about DNSSEC.

The *server* Statement

The server statement defines the characteristics of a remote server. Its syntax is shown in Listing B.6.

Listing B.6   server Statement Syntax

```
server address {
    [ bogus yes|no; ]
    [ support-ixfr yes|no; ]
    [ transfers number; ]
    [ transfer-format one-answer|many-answers; ]
    [ keys { key_id [key_id ... ] }; ]
};
```

The options in the server statement only apply to the remote server identified by *address*. This is particularly useful for the transfers-format command. Use the more efficient many-answers format in the options statement and then use individual server statements to fall back to the more compatible one-answer setting for servers that cannot handle the newer format.

Except for the transfer-format option, the server statement contains options not seen before in this appendix. The other options included in the server statement are

bogus yes   prevents the local server from sending queries to this server. The default is no, which permits queries to the remote server.

support-ixfr yes   indicates that the remote server can support incremental transfers. no, which is the default, says that the remote server cannot perform incremental transfers.

transfers   defines the maximum number of concurrent inbound transfers permitted from this server. In BIND 8.2.2, this feature is not yet implemented.

keys   specifies the key required by the remote host for transaction security. The *key_id* must be previously defined in the named.conf file by a key statement. The key is used to sign requests sent to the remote server.

The *controls* Statement

The controls statement defines the control channels used by ndc. Chapter 3, "The BIND Software," describes the ndc program and the "ndc Control Modes" section of that chapter describes what control channels are and how they are used. Recall from that discussion that ndc can use a Unix socket or a network socket as a control channel. The controls statement defines those sockets. The syntax of the controls statement is shown in Listing B.7.

Listing B.7   controls Statement Syntax

```
controls {
  [ inet ip_addr
    port ip_port
    allow { address_match_list; }; ]
  [ unix pathname
    perm file_permissions
    owner uid
    group gid; ]
};
```

Appendixes

The first three options, inet, port, and allow, are used to define a network socket as a control channel. The IP address that follows the inet keyword is the address on which named listens for control commands. The port number that follows the port keyword is the port named listens on. It is the pairing of the IP address and the port number that creates the socket. The allow option is used to limit access to the control channel.

WARNING   Creating a control channel that is accessible from the network is a risky thing to do. Whoever gains access to that channel has control over the name server process.

The last four options, unix, perm, owner, and group, define the Unix control socket. The Unix socket appears as a file in the file system. It is identified by a normal file *pathname*, e.g., /var/run/ndc. Like any file, the Unix socket is assigned the user id (*uid*) of its owner and a valid group id (*gid*). It is protected by standard file permissions. Only numeric *uid*, *gid*, and *file_permissions* values are acceptable. The *file_permissions* value must start with a 0. For example, to set owner read and write, group read, and world no permission, the numeric value would normally be 640. For *file_permissions*, it would be 0640.

The *trusted-keys* Statement

DNSSEC, which is described in Chapter 10, is a public key security system. An underlying premise of such a system is that a secure key distribution system exists from which trusted public keys can be obtained. This is not always the case. The trusted-keys statement makes it possible to define manually the public key for a remote domain when that key cannot be securely obtained from the network. The syntax for the trusted-keys statement is shown in Listing B.8.

Listing B.8   trusted-keys Statement Syntax

```
trusted-keys {

[ domain_name flags protocol algorithm key; ]

};
```

The arguments for the trusted-keys statement are as follows:

domain_name   is the name of the remote domain.

flags, *protocol*, and *algorithm*   are attributes of the authentication method used by the remote domain.

key   is a base-64 encoded string representing the remote domain's public key.

These values must be securely obtained from the administrator of the remote domain, because, by definition, they cannot be securely obtained from the network. If you can securely obtain the public key of the remote domain from the network, don't use the `trusted-keys` statement.

Resource Record Reference

BIND supports a full array of zone resource records. 41 different record types are defined in the `include/arpa/nameser.h` header file. This appendix provides a full list of those records with a description of each. The records are listed here in the same order that they are listed in the header file, which is in numeric order from query type 1 to query type 41.

Most of the resource records supported by BIND are never used to configure an operational domain database. BIND software is at the forefront of DNS development. When a new resource record is proposed, it is often implemented in BIND for testing and evaluation. After testing, many of these records are found to be of limited value for operational networks. They never advance beyond the experimental stage and never win any widespread support.

Some BIND record types are so new that they have not yet been defined in an RFC. Some are only used for server-to-server messages and are not manually created by the domain administrator. This appendix lists all kinds of records, even those that you will never use. The essential resource records are covered earlier in this book, and it is those records you will actually use to build your DNS database.

This appendix is a reference. It is here to provide some insight into what all of the resource records were designed to do. This can be particularly helpful when you see documentation about unfamiliar resource records and you want to know if they are useful to you.

To be frank, most of them are not. However, you need sufficient data to make your own informed decision.

Every resource record has the same basic components:

- A *name* field that defines the domain object to which the record pertains—for example, the name of an individual host or an entire domain.
- A *ttl* field that defines the amount of time that servers are allowed to cache the record.
- A *class* field that always has the value IN for Internet database records.
- A *type* field that contains a short acronym, such as A for address or PTR for pointer, to identify the type of the resource record.
- A *data* field that varies from record to record, depending on the purpose of the record. For example, address records have an address in this field.

Chapter 6, "Creating a Master Server," provides a tutorial that includes detailed examples of these fields, as well as examples of how the records are used to define domain information. In this appendix, the records supported by BIND are simply listed in numeric order.

When the syntax of a record is described, the following conventions are used:

- **Bold** means that something must be typed as shown.
- *Italic* means that you provide your own value for the specified field.
- Square brackets [ ] mean that the item is optional.
- Vertical bar | means choose one keyword or the other.

Address Record (A)   The Address records map domain names to IP addresses. The format of the A record is

> *host ttl class* **A** *ip_address*

You will use the A record to build your domain database. The A record is used extensively in this text, and it is defined in RFC 1035, "Domain Names – Implementation and Specification."

Name Server Record (NS)   Name Server records define the advertised name servers for a domain. The format of the NS record is

> *domain ttl class* **NS** *server_name*

Your domain database will include NS records as described in the tutorial section of the text. RFC 1035 defines the NS record.

Mail Destination Record (MD)   The Mail Destination record, which defined the final delivery point of mail, has been obsolete for more than a decade. It was replaced by the MX record and is no longer used.

Mail Forwarder Record (MF)   The Mail Forwarder record, which defined intermediate mail relays, has been obsolete for more than a decade. It was replaced by the MX record and is no longer used.

Canonical Name Record (CNAME)   The CNAME record maps a host alias to the canonical name of the host. The format of the CNAME record is

```
alias ttl class CNAME canonical_name
```

CNAME records are used in most domain databases and are explained in the text. The CNAME record is defined in RFC 1035.

Start of Authority Record (SOA)   The Start of Authority record marks the beginning of the zone and defines administrative information for the zone. The format of the SOA record is

```
zone ttl class SOA master contact (
serial_number
refresh_cycle
retry_cycle
expiration
negative_cache_ttl )
```

The data field of the SOA record contains seven items:

- The host name of the master server (*master*)
- The e-mail address of the domain administrator (*contact*)
- The revision number of the zone file (*serial_number*)
- The maximum amount of time that slave servers should wait before checking for a new version of the zone file (*refresh_cycle*)
- The maximum amount of time that a slave server should keep zone information that cannot be updated (*expiration*)
- The maximum amount of time that a remote server can cache negative information about the zone (*negative_cache_ttl*)

Every zone that you create will begin with one SOA record. See Chapter 6 for examples of this essential record. RFC 1035 defines the SOA record.

Appendixes

Mailbox Record (MB)   The obsolete Mailbox record defined mail delivery information for an individual user. Every user in the domain needed a unique MB record. This record has been obsolete for many years. The mail server, not DNS, handles forwarding mail to individuals. The MX record provides the DNS mail delivery function.

Mail Group Record (MG)   The obsolete Mail Group record defined mail delivery instructions for mailing lists. Mailing lists are processed by mail servers, not by DNS. This record is no longer used.

Mail Rename Record (MR)   The obsolete Mail Rename record defined mail aliases. A mail alias is a nickname for a user that permits mail addressed to the nickname to be delivered to the real user. For example, `postmaster@foobirds.org` might be an alias for `david@foobirds.org`. The `sendmail` program handles aliases. This function is not handled by DNS.

Null Record (NULL)   While this is called the Null record, there is no null record that can be defined for a DNS zone file. The Null record is actually a block of undefined data. It is supposed to be used by DNS developers when testing out new code. It has nothing to do with DNS configuration or administration.

Well Known Services Record (WKS)   The Well Known Services record advertises the network services offered by a host. The format of the WKS record is

```
host ttl class WKS address protocol services
```

The data field of the WKS record contains three fields:

address   is the IP address of the host advertising the services. This address must be one of the addresses that are valid for the computer identified by the host field.

protocol   is either UDP or TCP. To advertise services for both transport protocols, use one WKS record for UDP and one for TCP for each host.

services   is the list of advertised services. The services should be identified using the names found in the `/etc/services` file.

These two WKS records are an example of advertising UDP and TCP services for the host `crow`:

```
crow IN WKS 172.20.5.5 TCP ftp telnet
crow IN WKS 172.20.5.5 UDP domain tftp
```

The WKS record is rarely used. There are no widely distributed programs that take advantage of WKS record and there is the threat that network intruders will use the information in the WKS record to exploit your system.

Pointer Record (PTR)   The Pointer record maps one host name to another. It is primarily used to map an IP address back to a host name. PTR records make up the bulk of every reverse domain. The format of the PTR record is

```
name ttl class PTR hostname
```

In a reverse domain, the *name* field contains a numeric IP address reversed and transformed into a DNS name. The data field contains the actual domain name that the IP number maps to. See Chapter 6 for examples of PTR records and reverse zone files. The PTR record is defined in RFC 1035.

Host Information Record (HINFO)   The Host Information record provides a short description of the hardware and operating system used by a host. The format of the HINFO record is:

```
host ttl class HINFO hardware software
```

Originally, the hardware and software items in the data field were supposed to come from an official list of hardware and software registered in RFC 1700, "Assigned Numbers." That might have worked in the days of mainframes when computer models changed slowly but it wouldn't work today. Administrators who use this record simply make up descriptive entries for the hardware and software. Consider the following example:

```
crow IN HINFO "IBM Aptiva 590" Linux
```

The quotation marks are required for the hardware field in the sample because the description contains blanks.

I don't use this record. It can provide information to network intruders and it doesn't provide information to any programs that I use. RFC 1035 defines the HINFO record.

Mailbox Information Record (MINFO)   The obsolete Mailbox Information record defined control information for mailing lists. This record was directly related to the obsolete Mail Group record. Mailing lists and the administrative information about mailing lists are defined in the sendmail configuration. This record is not used.

Mail Exchange Record (MX)   Mail Exchange records define the mail servers for a domain or a host. The MX record supercedes all of the other (MD, MF, MB, MG, MR, and MINFO) records that were defined to handle mail. The MX record simply points the remote mail server to the local mail server. The sendmail program on the local mail server is responsible for handling all of the e-mail–specific information, such as mail aliases and mailing lists. The format of the MX record is

```
name ttl class MX preference server
```

Appendixes

The *name* field contains the name of the domain or host to which the mail is addressed. The *server* field contains the name of the server to which the mail is delivered. *preference* is a number used to select the most preferred server when a domain or host has multiple MX records, with low numbers preferred over high numbers. See Chapter 6 for more information about using the MX record, which is defined in RFC 1035.

Text Record (TXT)   The Text record is used to define free-form information about the named object. Its format is simple

```
name ttl class TXT string
```

On Linux systems, the TXT record is generally used to provide information about a host to the technical support group. The following example illustrates this use:

```
buzzard IN TXT "Accounting Department server in room B152"
```

Because of its free-form nature, the TXT record has been used over time for special purposes, such as providing input to locally developed scripts that collect domain information. An earlier version of BIND that runs on some Unix systems even uses these records to define security information. Linux, of course, uses the latest version of BIND so it does not need to use TXT records for security. RFC 1035 defines the TXT record.

Responsible Person Record (RP)   The Responsible Person record identifies the point of contact for a host or domain. The format of the RP record is

```
name ttl class RP mail_address text_pointer
```

The *mail_address* is the e-mail address of the responsible person. The @ usually included in an e-mail address is replaced with a dot. Thus, craig@foobirds.org becomes craig.foobirds.org. The *text_pointer* is the domain name of a TXT record that contains additional information about the responsible person. Here's an example of how an RP record is used with a TXT record:

```
ibis.foobirds.org.    IN RP craig.foobirds.org. ibisRP
ibisRP.foobirds.org. IN TXT "Craig Hunt (301)555-1234 X237"
```

The RP record states that the person responsible for ibis.foobirds.org can be reached via e-mail at craig@foobirds.org and that additional information about the person can be obtained in the TXT records for ibisRP.foobirds.org. The TXT record provides the contact person's name and phone number.

Use RP records to make it easier for system administrators to contact each other when things go wrong. Unfortunately, most domains don't use RP records. Maybe the system administrators don't want people to know how to get in touch with them. But if you don't use RP records, remote administrators will contact the domain administrator when the problem is really a problem related to a single host. The RP record is defined in RFC 1183, "New DNS RR Definitions."

Andrew File System Database Record (AFSDB)   The experimental AFSDB record points to the server for an AFS or DCE cell. AFS, originally called the Andrew File System, is a distributed file system that is optimized for use over wide area networks (WANs). DCE, the Distributed Computing Environment, is just that, a distributed computing environment. AFS and DCE systems use DNS to point to their servers. They do this by using cell names that are compatible with DNS domain names. The AFSDB record maps the cell name to the correct server. The format of an AFSDB record is

        `cell_name ttl class` **AFSDB** `type server`

The `cell_name` looks just like a domain name. In fact, if `terns.foobirds.org` installed an AFS or a DCE server, the name of the cell would probably be `terns.foobirds.org`. The `type` field contains a 1 if the server is an AFS server or a 2 if it is a DCE server. The `server` field contains the DNS domain name of the AFS or DCE server. The AFSDB record is defined in RFC 1183.

X.25 Address Record (X25)   The experimental X25 record maps a domain name to an X.25 address, called an X.121 address. X.25 is an international standard for public packet-switched networks. X.25 networks have not been widely used in the United States for many years. The advent of personal computers and the Internet made them largely obsolete, though some countries still use X.25. The format of the X25 records is

        `name ttl class` **X25** `X.121_address`

The X25 record is rarely used because most X.25 networks provide their own facilities for mapping X.121 addresses to IP addresses. The scale of the Internet makes it impossible for X.25 networks, or any other network for that matter, to ignore IP. In fact, implementations of IP that run directly over X.25 have long been available. The X25 record is defined in RFC 1183.

ISDN Address Record (ISDN)   The experimental ISDN record maps a domain name to an ISDN address. Integrated Services Digital Network (ISDN) is a digital telephone service that can carry voice and data. Poor price/performance has limited the number of ISDN users in the United States, but it is popular in many other countries. The format of the ISDN record is

        `name ttl class` **ISDN** `ISDN_address subaddress`

The ISDN record is rarely used because most IP-to-ISDN bridges have internal mechanisms to map IP addresses to ISDN addresses. The ISDN record is defined in RFC 1183.

Route Through Record (RT)   The experimental RT record points to a gateway that can be used to route packets to networks that are not part of the Internet. The X.25 and ISDN networks mentioned earlier are good examples. The format of the RT record is

    name ttl class **RT** *preference gateway*

The *preference* value in the RT record is similar to the preference value of an MX record. It is a numeric value and the lower the number, the more preferred the gateway. *preference* permits DNS to define multiple gateways to the remote host, allowing applications that use the RT records to select the best route. When a server returns an RT record as the response to a query, it also includes all A, X25, and ISDN records that define addresses for the gateway. This allows applications on various types of networks to find addressing and routing information from DNS.

The RT record is rarely used. There are no widely available applications designed to use it. Routing protocols handle the distribution of routing information. RT was primarily of interest as a possible technique for integrating dissimilar networks. The RT record is defined in RFC 1183.

ISO NSAP Address Record (NSAP)   The outdated NSAP record assigns an International Standards Organization (ISO) Network Service Access Point (NSAP) address to a domain name. About ten years ago, everyone was looking for a way to increase the address range of the Internet. There was a competition to create a next generation Internet Protocol. One group proposed *TCP and UDP with Big Addresses (TUBA),* which used the ISO NSAP address. TUBA was not chosen as the next generation IP so the need for NSAP records faded away. RFC 1637, "DNS NSAP Resource Records," defines the NSAP record.

ISO NSAP Pointer Record (NSAP_PTR)   The NSAP_PTR record is the reverse of the NSAP record. It maps NSAP addresses back to domain names. This record is no longer used. It is defined in RFC 1637.

Security Signature Record (SIG)   The Security Signature record provides a digital signature to authenticate a set of resource records. The format of the SIG records is

    name ttl class **SIG** *type_list* (
            algorithm
            labels
            original_ttl
            signature_expiration
            signature_ inception

```
key_tag

signer_name

signature )
```

The fields for the SIG record are as follows:

type_list   is a list of the resource record types for the specified domain name that are digitally signed by this SIG record.

algorithm   is the encryption algorithm used to produce the digital signature. There are three *algorithm* values currently available:

1   for the RSA/MD5 algorithm defined in RFC 2537, "RSA/MD5 KEYs and SIGs in the Domain Name System (DNS)."

2   for the Diffie-Hellman algorithm defined in RFC 2539, "Storage of Diffie-Hellman Keys in the Domain Name System (DNS)."

3   for the DSA algorithm defined in RFC 2536, "DSA KEYs and SIGs in the Domain Name System (DNS)."

labels   specifies the number of parts in the domain name. For example, foobirds.org has two parts, foobirds and org, so it has a *labels* value of 2. terns.foobirds.org has three parts and thus, a *labels* value of 3.

orginal_ttl   is the TTL value from the original resource record that was used when the digital signature was calculated. Because the TTL is decremented by servers that hold records in their caches, the *orginal_ttl* is needed to recalculate the signature when verifying the record.

signature_expiration   defines the date that the signature becomes invalid. The date is stored internally as the number of seconds from January 1, 1970.

signature_inception   defines the date on which the signature was created. The date is stored internally as the number of seconds from January 1, 1970.

key_tag   is a 16-bit identifier of the key that is used to select the correct key when multiple possible keys are involved. For all other algorithms, the *key_tag* field holds a checksum of the SIG resource record.

signer_name   is the domain name of the entity that created the digital signature. It is usually the domain name of the zone that contains the signed records.

signature   is the digital signature that authenticates the resource records.

Examples of the SIG record and how it is used in DNSSEC are covered in Chapter 10, "DNS Security." RFC 2535, "Domain Name System Security Extensions," defines the SIG record.

Appendixes

Security Key Record (KEY)   The Security Key record provides the public key for a given domain name. The format of the KEY record is

```
name ttl class KEY flags protocol algorithm public_key
```

The *public_key* is just that—the encryption key used for public key cryptography when communicating with the object identified by *name*. The value of the *algorithm* field can be 1 for RSA/MD5, 2 for Diffie-Hellman, or 3 for DSA. The *protocol* field defines the protocol that will use the public key. The currently valid values for *protocol* are

1   for TLS

2   for e-mail

3   for DNSSEC

4   for IPSEC

The *flags* field is a binary bit mask that contains several different subfields. Figure C.1 shows each bit in the *flags* field.

Figure C.1   The flags bit mask

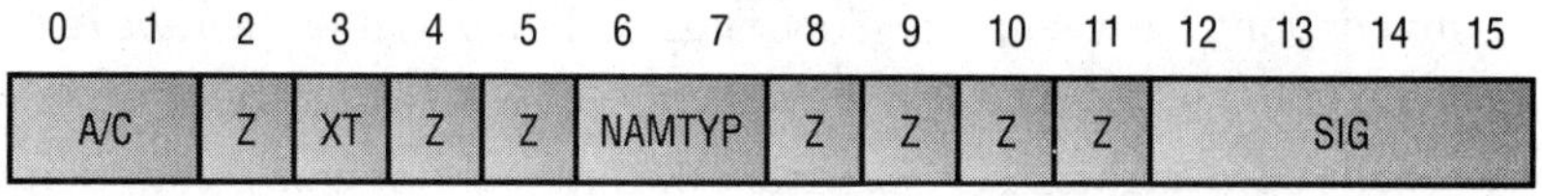

Every bit marked with a Z in Figure C.1 is reserved for future use and must be set to 0. That leaves four active subfields:

A/C   These two bits define whether the key is used for authentication or for confidentiality. If the first bit is 1 (10), the key cannot be used for authentication. If the second bit is 1 (01), the key cannot be used confidentiality. Thus, 00 means the key can be used for either task, and 11 means that the zone is not secured.

XT   This bit is reserved for the future when more than one *flags* field may be required. If set to 1, it means that the flags are extended to a second 16-bit word. Currently, the value must be 0 because there are no valid extensions.

NAMTYP   These two bits identify which type of domain name is found in the name field. 00 means that the name is a username such as would be found on an RP or SOA record. 01 means that the name is the domain name of the zone. 10 means that the name is the name of an object, such as a host or subdomain, contained within the zone. 11 is reserved for future use.

SIG   These four bits indicate whether or not the key can be used to sign updates for Dynamic DNS. If the field is non-zero, the key can be used to sign Dynamic

DNS updates. If the field is 0, the key can only be used to sign a Dynamic DNS update if the NAMTYP field contains 01, i.e., if the name type is zone and the update is for the specified zone.

Chapter 10 contains examples of using the KEY record for DNS security. The KEY record is defined in RFC 2535.

X400 Mail Record (PX)   The PX record defines a mapping between an Internet e-mail address and an X.400 e-mail address. The format of the PX record is

```
name ttl class PX preference RFC822_address X400_address
```

The *preference* number is used just like it is on an MX record, to sort the PX records into preference order when more than one address mapping is provided. The *RFC822_address* and the *X400_address* are e-mail addresses formatted in the manner defined by RFC 1327, "Mapping between X.400(1988) / ISO 10021 and RFC 822."

This record is rarely used. All existing X.400 e-mail gateways already have a technique for converting Internet e-mail addresses to X.400 e-mail addresses and for converting X.400 addresses to Internet addresses. The purpose of this record is to create an improved conversion process, but it has not been widely adopted and is still considered experimental. RFC 1664, "Using the Internet DNS to Distribute RFC 1327 Mail Address Mapping Tables," defines the PX record.

Geographical Positioning Record (GPOS)   The GPOS record was supposed to map domain names to physical locations, but the record was withdrawn and is not supported.

IPV6 Address Record (AAAA)   The AAAA record maps a domain name to an Internet Protocol version 6 (IPv6) address. The format of the AAAA record is

```
name ttl class AAAA ipv6_address
```

The format is the same as an A record, except that the address provided in the data field is a 128-bit IPv6 address instead of a 32-bit IP address. Instead of the dotted decimal notation used to write an IP address, an IPv6 address is written as eight, 16-bit hexadecimal numbers separated by colons, as in the following example:

```
big6 IN AAAA 1234:a:b:c:d:e:f:9876
```

The traditional PTR record is used to map IPv6 addresses back to domain names. A new top-level reverse-mapping domain was created called ip6.int. When IPv6 addresses are converted to names in the reverse-mapping domain, they are reversed and written out as 32, four-bit nibbles separated by dots. Thus the IPv6 address 1234:a:b:c:d:e:f:9876 becomes

```
6.7.8.9.f.0.0.0.e.0.0.0.d.0.0.0.c.0.0.0.b.0.0.0.a.0.0.0.4.3.2.1.ip6.int.
```

Appendixes

Only systems that use IPv6 are assigned IPv6 addresses, and only systems that run the IPv6 protocol stack need to look up AAAA records. Unless you run IPv6 on your network, you won't use this record. Currently, IPv6 has a relatively small share of the network market. The AAAA record, which is defined in RFC 1886, "DNS Extensions to Support IP Version 6," is superseded in BIND 9 by the A6 record.

Location Information Record (LOC)   The Location Information record defines physical location information for a domain object. The format of the LOC record is

```
name ttl class LOC (
        latitude
        longitude
        altitude
        [size]
        [horizontal_precision]
        [vertical_precision] )
```

The data field of the LOC record contains up to six items that define the physical location of the named object. The first three items are required. The last three items are optional. The six items in the data field are

latitude and *longitude*   are written in degrees, minutes, seconds, and direction using the following format:

```
    degree [minutes [seconds]] N|S|E|W
```

altitude   is written as meters of elevation.

size   is square meters. It defaults to one square meter, which is the approximate size of a computer system.

horizontal_precision   sets the limit as to how accurate the longitude and latitude figures are. It defaults to 10,000 meters, which is the approximate size of a ZIP code area.

vertical_precision   sets the accuracy limit for the altitude figure. It defaults to 10 meters.

An example of a LOC record should make the structure clear. This is the LOC record for the Ethernet in my home

```
    wrotethebook.com LOC 39 08 8.621 N 77 14 6.986 W 200m
```

NOTE This location information was obtained from www.geocode.com/ eagle.html-ssi.

People have been working to create a database of network locations for years. One example is the abandoned GPOS record described earlier in this appendix. When the DNS system was first created, you were required to provide the longitude and latitude of your master server in order to register a domain. People who study the Internet are interested in this information. Yet most domain administrators have no interest in the LOC record and see very little use for it, and the LOC record is not widely used.

Next Domain Security Record (NXT)   The Next Domain record provides a way to authenticate non-existent domain information. The SIG record described earlier is used to authenticate domain database records. However, a digital signature can only be calculated against an existing record. By its very nature, the information involved in negative caching has no database record to be authenticated. If the information returned by the authoritative name server states that no MX record exists for a given domain name, how is that information authenticated before being added to the cache? The NXT record is the solution. The format of the NXT record is

        `name ttl class` **NXT** `next_name type_list`

The `type_list` is a list of the types of resource records that do not exist for the object identified by name, which by inference indicates the records that do not exist for that object. Thus, if A, RP, and NXT records existed for the domain name `parrot.foobirds.org`, you might have the following NXT record:

        `parrot.foobirds.org. IN NXT puffin.foobirds.org. MX`

The function of the `next_name` field is a little more obscure. This field contains the next domain name in canonical order as defined by RFC 2535. A simple way to think of canonical ordering is as if each label in the names were sorted without regard to case. The `next_name` field is used to provide evidence that a name does not exist.

Examples of the NXT record are provided in Chapter 10. The NXT record is defined in RFC 2535.

Endpoint Identifier Record (EID)   The proposed EID record maps Nimrod endpoint labels to endpoint identifiers. In the Nimrod architecture, the *endpoint identifier* is essentially the address of the endpoint, and the name of the endpoint is called an *endpoint label*. Nimrod is a proposed routing architecture that is still a work in progress. Nimrod records are experimental and are not used in operational DNS servers. The EID record is not yet standardized in an RFC.

Appendixes

Nimrod Locator Record (NIMLOC) The proposed Nimrod Locator record assigns locators to nodes in the Nimrod architecture. Locators are used in the Nimrod routing process. Nimrod is a proposal that is still a work in progress. It is not used in operational environments. The NIMLOC resource record is not yet standardized in an RFC.

Server Selection Record (SRV) The Server Selection record provides a standardized way to locate network servers. Generic names such as `www.foobirds.org` and `ftp.foobirds.org` are widely used to locate network servers, but these names are not really a standard. The SRV record provides a standard convention for creating generic server names, and it adds features for server selection and load-balancing. The format of the SRV record is

> `_service._protocol.name ttl class` **SRV** `preference weight port server`

The name field of the SRV record has a unique `_service._protocol.name` format. Dots are used to separate the components in the name field just as they are in any domain name. The underscore characters (_) are used to prevent the service name and the protocol name from colliding with real domain names. `service` is the name of the offered service as listed in the `/etc/services` file. `protocol` is the protocol name associated with that service in the `/etc/services` file. `name` is a standard host or domain name that would be found in any name field. Using these criteria, the name that could be used to find the FTP servers for the `foobirds.org` domain would be `_ftp._tcp.foobirds.org`.

The data field contains four values:

> `preference` is a number used to select the most preferred server when multiple SRV records exist for the same service. The servers are sorted by preference number, so the server with the lowest number is the most preferred. All traffic is sent to the most preferred servers; servers with a higher preference number are only used if the preferred servers are not available.

> `weight` is used to balance the load among servers with the same preference number. `weight` is a number that defines the share of traffic sent to a server with 1 being the base. If server A has a weight of 1 and server B has a weight of 2, then B gets twice as much traffic as A.

> `port` is the port number used for the service. Normally, this is the port number defined in the `/etc/services` file for the specified service. But it is possible to specify a non-standard port number for services equipped to use non-standard numbers.

> `server` is the canonical host name of the computer running the requested service.

See Chapter 8, "Special BIND Configurations," for more information about the SRV record and when it is used. The SRV record is defined in RFC 2052, "A DNS RR for Specifying the Location of Services (DNS SRV)."

ATM Address Record (ATMA)   The proposed ATMA record maps a name to an Asynchronous Transfer Mode (ATM) address. ATM is a high-speed fiber-optic network technology. It transmits small chunks of information that are only 53 bytes long to make it easier to optimize support for real-time traffic such as voice and video. The ATMA record is not yet standardized in an RFC.

Naming Authority Pointer Record (NAPTR)   The experimental Naming Authority Pointer record maps a domain name to a universal resource identifier (URI). A URI can be a universal resource locator (URL), which everyone is familiar with from the Web, or it can be a universal resource name (URN), which is a modified URL that is supposed to be more robust. The format of the NAPTR record is

```
name ttl class NAPTR (
        order
        preference
        flags
        service
        regular_expression|replacement )
```

The data field of the NAPTR record includes six different components:

order   is a number that defines the order in which the records *must* be processed if multiple records are returned for a single query. A low number is processed before a high number.

preference   defines the order in which records *should* be processed when multiple records are returned for a single query. A low number is preferred over a high number.

flags   indicate special processing. There are currently three flag values defined:

A   means that the next query should be for address records.

S   means the next query should be for SRV records.

P   means that the remaining processing should be carried out in a protocol-specific manner, and that no further DNS queries are required.

service   identifies an available resolution service, and optionally, a protocol used to communicate with the service. The format of the service field is

```
[protocol] + resolution_services
```

The possible protocols are `rcds`, `tthtp`, `hdl`, `rwhois`, and `z3950`. The resolution services are

N2L   Converts a URN to a URL.

N2Ls   Converts a URN to a set of URLs.

N2R   Processes a URN and returns the resource.

N2Rs   Processes a URN and returns a set of the resources.

N2C   Processes a URN returning a collection of information about the resource.

N2Ns   Maps a given a URN to all URNs that also identifies the resource.

L2R   Processes a URL and returns the resource.

L2Ns   Maps a given URL to all the URNs that also identify the resource.

L2Ls   Maps a given URL to all URLs for the same resource.

L2C   Processes a URL returning a description of the resource.

regular_expression   is a template used to construct the next domain name for the server to look up. The original URL is used as input to the template to create the name. If the *regular_expression* is used, the replacement field will be empty.

replacement   is the name value used to locate the next NAPTR record, or if the flag field was S or A, the next SRV or address record. When the *replacement* field is used to specify the next domain name, the *regular_expression* field is empty.

The NAPTR is a complex resource record that requires substantial processing. Currently, there are no widely available applications to make use of this record. However, the idea is that in the future, the NAPTR record will make it possible to relocate named services more easily. NAPTR is not used in operational servers. The NAPTR record is defined in RFC 2168, "Resolution of Uniform Resource Identifiers Using the Domain Name System."

Key Exchange Record (KX)   The Key Exchange record defines a server that is authorized to distribute security keys for a specified domain object. It is used to direct key requests for an individual, a host, or an entire domain to a server in the same way that the MX record is used to direct mail to a server. The format of the KX record is

   name ttl class **KX** *preference server*

preference is a numeric field used to sort servers in order of precedence, with a low preference number preferred over a high preference number.

Because KX records point to trusted key distribution servers, they are only valid if they are retrieved from a secured zone. The KX record has not been proposed for standardization, and it currently is used in only limited situations. The KX record is defined in RFC 2230, "Key Exchange Delegation Record for the DNS."

Certification Record (CERT)   The Certification record provides a certificate of authenticity for public encryption keys. The format of the CERT record is

name ttl class **CERT** *cert_type key_tag algorithm certificate*

The data field of the CERT record contains the following components:

cert_type   is a numeric field that defines the type of certificate provided by the CERT resource record. The currently supported certificate types are

1   an X.509 PKIX certificate

2   a SPKI certificate

3   a PGP certificate

key_tag   is a 16-bit value derived from the encryption key stored in the certificate. The *key_tag* makes it easier to select CERT records for a specific key. The *key_tag* can only be used for encryption keys that are valid for a KEY resource record. If a key is used that is not supported by the KEY record, this field must be 0.

algorithm   defines the encryption algorithm used to authenticate the certificate. There are four possible values:

0   for an algorithm that is not yet standardized for DNS

1   for the RSA/MD5 algorithm defined in RFC 2537

2   for the Diffie-Hellman algorithm defined in RFC 2539

3   for the DSA algorithm defined in RFC 2536

certificate   is a base-64 encoded string representing the digital certificate. The certificate itself is formatted according to the standards defined for the type of certificate used. In other words, a valid PKIX, SPKI, or PGP certificate must be created and then converted to base-64 encoding to provide the value for this field.

See Chapter 10 for more information about certificates. The CERT record is defined in RFC 2538, "Storing Certificates in the Domain Name System (DNS)."

IPV6 Address Record (A6)   The A6 record maps a domain name to an IPv6 address. It will supercede and replace the older AAAA record in BIND 9. The A6 record has not yet been formally defined in an RFC.

DNS Name Redirection Record (DNAME)   The DNAME record maps all names within a domain to another domain. The purpose of this record is to simplify maintenance when a domain is renamed or renumbered. The format of the DNAME record is

name ttl class **DNAME** *new_name*

Appendixes

name is the original name of the domain, and *new_name* is the name that has replaced the original name. If the server gets an address query for a host in the original domain, the server returns the DNAME record, along with the address record of the host using the host's new name.

The DNAME record only works if all of the clients and servers involved in the query understand DNAME records and can handle them properly. It will take awhile before this new record is widely implemented. The DNAME record is defined in RFC 2672, "Non-Terminal DNS Name Redirection."

Kitchen Sink Record (SINK)   Query type 40 is held in reserve for the experimental Kitchen Sink record, which has not yet been defined in an RFC.

Extended DNS Option Record (OPT)   The OPT record is a mechanism for extending DNS. The basic DNS message has a limited number of fields, most of which are already used. The OPT record is loaded in the additional section of the DNS message to provide information about extended features. See the description of the DNS message in Chapter 2, "The DNS Protocols."

The OPT record has the same fields as any resource record but they are used in a different way. The type field, of course, contains OPT and the length field contains the length of the data field. But the name field is always empty. The class field contains the size of the largest UDP packet that the sender can handle. (In traditional DNS, the largest packet is 512 bytes. This feature permits the servers to negotiate a better packet size.) The TTL field contains extended RCODE and flag values. (A TTL is not needed because OPT records are not cached and one of the primary motivations of the record is to extend the number of RCODE and flags available.) The data field contains attribute/value pairs that will be used to describe new features as they emerge.

The OPT record is not created by the domain administrator and is not stored in the zone file. The server generates the OPT record to negotiate new DNS features. The OPT record is described in RFC 2671, "Extension Mechanisms for DNS (EDNS0)."

Configuring Network Information Service

Network Information Service (NIS) is a network server that centralizes control of several system administration databases. NIS simplifies the management of Unix and Linux desktop clients by making it possible for those clients to use administrative files that are maintained on a central server. There is no need for users of desktop systems to create their own `/etc/passwd` or `/etc/aliases` files; they simply use the files that you maintain on the NIS server. Table 4.1 in Chapter 4, "Configuring the Resolver," provides a full list of the administrative databases that are supported by an NIS server.

This is an unusual appendix. Unlike most appendixes, this is a how-to tutorial instead of a reference. And unlike the other appendixes in this book, this appendix has very little to do with DNS. This book includes an appendix about NIS because NIS provides a centralized method for accessing the host table, and some small networks use the host table as an alternative to DNS. This appendix is also included to clarify the relationship between DNS and NIS, and to explain the role of NIS introduced in the discussion of the `/etc/nsswitch.conf` file in Chapter 4.

NIS is a client/server system. `ypbind` is the client process that is used to locate the NIS server. Once a server is located, the client is bound to the server, and all of the client's NIS queries are sent to the server. `ypserv` is the server process that answers client queries. This appendix provides an overview of the installation and configuration of both ypbind and ypserv. Let's start with a look at the ypbind process that runs on all NIS clients and servers.

> **NOTE** NIS was previously known as the Sun Yellow Pages Server. For that reason, most NIS commands start with the letters "yp".

Installing the *ypbind* Client

Linux vendors include NIS client software as part of the basic Linux distribution. On most Linux systems, ypbind can be installed during the initial software installation. If you didn't install it at that time, ypbind can easily be installed from the Linux distribution CD-ROM at a later time using the vendor's software package manager. In Listing D.1, the administrator uses the rpm command to check that the ypbind software is installed and discovers that it is indeed already installed.

Listing D.1   Managing ypbind Software with rpm

```
[root]# rpm -q ypbind
ypbind-3.3-20
```

ypbind runs as a daemon started as part of the boot process. Once installed, ypbind must be enabled using a tool like tksysv or linuxconf. See the discussion of these tools in Chapter 3, "The BIND Software."

> **WARNING** Don't enable NIS client software until the server is up and running. NIS provides critical administrative databases that may be needed for the boot process. Clients can hang during the boot looking for a non-existent server if clients are configured to run NIS before the NIS server is configured.

Configuring a NIS Client

The ypbind process locates the server for the client's NIS domain. An *NIS domain* is a name that identifies a grouping of NIS clients and servers. An NIS domain usually encompasses a single network or a small department. It is not the same as a DNS domain, although system administrators frequently use a DNS domain name as the NIS domain name. The only real requirement for an NIS domain name is that the server and its clients use the same NIS domain name.

The NIS domain name can be configured in two ways:

- The `nisdomainname` command can be used to define or display the NIS domain name.
- The NIS domain name can be configured in the `yp.conf` file.

Setting the NIS domain name with the `nisdomainname` command is very simple. In the following example, the NIS domain name is set to `terns` and then checked with the `nisdomainname` command:

```
[root]# nisdomainname terns
[root]# nisdomainname
terns
```

Linux systems provide three alternate forms of the `nisdomainname` command. The command can be entered as **nisdomainname**, **domainname**, or **ypdomainname**. All three commands work in the same way and do the same thing.

By default, `ypbind` uses the NIS domain name returned by the `nisdomainname` command and broadcasts it to the network in a request for the NIS server for that domain. This default behavior can be modified using the `yp.conf` file.

> **NOTE**   Caldera names the configuration file `nis.conf` instead of `yp.conf`. Also, on a Red Hat 6 system, the ypbind daemon is started by the script `/etc/rc.d/init.d/ypbind`, while on a Caldera 2.3 system, the ypbind daemon is started by the `/etc/rc.d/init.d/nis-client` script. While the script names and configuration file names may vary from system to system, most systems use filenames that match the ones used by Red Hat, which are the filenames used in this appendix. If your system uses different filenames, don't worry, they are easy to guess—just look for files beginning with "yp" or "nis".

The *yp.conf* File

The `/etc/yp.conf` file defines the `ypbind` configuration. If the `yp.conf` file is not found, `ypbind` uses the NIS domain name returned by the `nisdomainname` command and it uses broadcasts to locate a server for that domain. `ypbind` binds the client to the first server that responds to the request for services for the given domain. The `yp.conf` file provides the following two configuration options to change this default behavior:

ypserver *hostname*

domain *nisdomain* **broadcast** | **server** *hostname*

Use the ypserver configuration option to define a specific server for the client. When the yp.conf file contains a ypserver option, the client uses the NIS domain name returned by the nisdomainname command, and sends a request for services for that domain to the server identified by the *hostname* field of the ypserver command. An IP address for *hostname* must be found in the local /etc/hosts file on the client. The ypserver option forces a client to bind to a specific server.

Use the domain configuration option to define the NIS domain name inside the yp.conf file, and to specify whether the client should use broadcasting to locate a server for the domain or should send a request for services directly to an individual server. Again, if the host name of a server is used, the IP address for that server must be defined in the local /etc/hosts file of the client.

Listing D.2 contains a sample yp.conf file.

Listing D.2   Defining an NIS Client Configuration

```
# /etc/yp.conf - ypbind configuration file
#
domain terns server sooty
```

The yp.conf file in Listing D.2 defines terns as the NIS domain name and sooty as the server for that domain. The name sooty must have an IP address in the local /etc/hosts file.

Once the yp.conf file is configured, a SIGHUP signal can be sent to the ypbind process to force it to re-read the configuration file. Listing D.3 is an example of sending SIGHUP to ypbind.

Listing D.3   Sending a Signal to ypbind

```
[root]# cat /var/run/ypbind.pid
  2502
[root]# kill -HUP 2502
```

An NIS client needs ypbind software, a valid NIS domain name, and a server for that domain. The bulk of the NIS configuration takes place on the server.

Creating an NIS Server

Like a client, the server requires the correct software and a valid NIS domain name. In addition to these, a server needs the database files that supply the answers to client queries. Configuring an NIS server requires the installation and configuration of the server software and the creation of the NIS database files.

Installing *ypserv*

The ypserv software is included with the Linux distribution and is often installed during the initial installation. If it isn't, it can be installed from the distribution CD-ROM. Figure D.1 shows the Package Info window of gnorpm on a Red Hat 6 system as the ypserv software is about to be installed.

Figure D.1 Installing ypserv with gnorpm

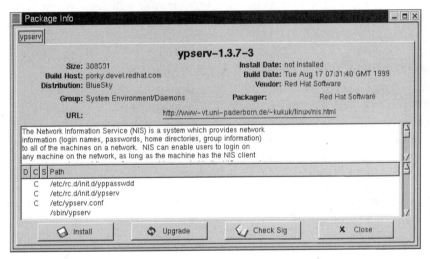

To get to the point shown in Figure D.1, take the following steps:

1. Run gnorpm.
2. Click the Install button in the gnorpm window. A small Install window opens.
3. Click Add and select ypserv from the list of software.
4. Close the Add Packages window.
5. Highlight ypserv in the Install window and click Query.

If the information displayed in the Package Info window shows this is the software you want (as it is in Figure D.1), click Install to install the software on your system. Once the software is installed, the server needs to be configured and the database files need to be prepared.

Appendixes

Building the NIS Databases

The databases provided by the NIS server, called *NIS maps*, are built from the traditional flat files used by Linux system administrators. An example is the /etc/passwd file that lists user account information. Lookups in databases are much faster than they are in flat files. NIS indexes the databases created from a flat file in various ways to take full advantage of the increased speed.

The commands used to build the NIS databases vary depending on the server architecture you plan to use. Every physical network within your enterprise should have its own NIS server. If you have only one server for your NIS domain, you can create a standalone server. If you have more than one server for your NIS domain, one server should be the master server for the domain, and all other servers for that NIS domain should be slave servers.

Creating a Stand-Alone Server

Initialize a stand-alone server and build the NIS maps for that server with the make command. The /var/yp/Makefile contains the instructions necessary to build the databases. Review the Makefile to ensure that the directory names and filenames are correct for your system. make will display error messages if you attempt to build maps for which your system lacks the proper input files. Edit the line labeled all: to select the maps that you want to build.

Listing D.4 shows the initialization process of a stand-alone server for the terns NIS domain.

Listing D.4   Building NIS Maps with make

```
[root]# nisdomainname terns
[root]# cd /var/yp
[root]# make
gmake[1]: Entering directory `/var/yp/terns'
Updating passwd.byname...
Updating passwd.byuid...
Updating hosts.byname...
Updating hosts.byaddr...
Updating rpc.byname...
Updating rpc.bynumber...
Updating services.byname...
Updating netid.byname...
Updating protocols.bynumber...
Updating protocols.byname...
Updating mail.aliases...
gmake[1]: Leaving directory `/var/yp/terns'
```

In Listing D.4, the administrator ensures that nisdomainname is set to the correct value, changes to the /var/yp directory, and then runs make. Notice that the make process creates a subdirectory within the /var/yp directory that has the same name as the NIS domain. This new /var/yp/terns subdirectory contains all of the maps for the terns domain.

Creating Master and Slave Servers

Use the ypinit command to initialize a master server and create the NIS maps. By default, ypinit does exactly what the make command did in Listing D.4—it builds the NIS maps for a stand-alone server. To create a master server that will have slave servers, you need to edit /var/yp/Makefile. Locate the NOPUSH entry in the Makefile and set it to NOPUSH=false. After making the change, run ypinit with the –m argument, as shown in Listing D.5.

Listing D.5   Creating a Master NIS Server with ypinit

```
[root]# nisdomainname terns
[root]# cd /var/yp
[root]# /usr/lib/yp/ypinit -m

At this point, we have to construct a list of the hosts
which will run NIS servers.  sooty.terns.foobirds.org is
in the list of NIS server hosts.  Please continue to add
the names for the other hosts, one per line.  When you are
done with the list, type a <control D>.
          next host to add: sooty.terns.foobirds.org
          next host to add: arctic.terns.foobirds.org
          next host to add: black.terns.foobirds.org
          next host to add:
The current list of NIS servers looks like this:

sooty.terns.foobirds.org
arctic.terns.foobirds.org
black.terns.foobirds.org

Is this correct?  [y/n: y]  y
We need some  minutes to build the databases...
Building /var/yp/terns/ypservers...
Running /var/yp/Makefile...
gmake[1]: Entering directory `/var/yp/terns'
Updating passwd.byname...
Updating passwd.byuid...
Updating hosts.byname...
Updating hosts.byaddr...
Updating rpc.byname...
Updating rpc.bynumber...
Updating services.byname...
```

```
Updating netid.byname...
Updating protocols.bynumber...
Updating protocols.byname...
Updating mail.aliases...
gmake[1]: Leaving directory `/var/yp/terns'
```

Listing D.5 shows that the `ypinit` command asks for a list of NIS servers. Enter the name of each slave server when prompted and finish the list with Ctrl+D. Listing D.5 lists three servers: two slaves and the master. This list starts with the name of the master server, but you don't have to type it in; `ypinit` fills in that entry for you.

The `ypinit` command finishes by running the same `make` process shown earlier in Listing D.4. The only difference between `ypinit` and running `make` yourself is the list of NIS servers that `ypinit` creates and places in the `/var/yp/ypservers` file. The master server uses that list to determine which servers should get NIS updates.

> **TIP**   If `ypinit` complains that ypserv is not registered with RPC, enter **ypserv** at the shell prompt and then run `ypinit`.

The NIS master "pushes" updates to its slaves. On a Linux NIS server, NOPUSH is set to `true` by default, which means that the server will not send updates to its slave. Changing NOPUSH to `false` enables NIS updates, and providing the list of servers to `ypinit` tells the master which server should receive the updates. To support the transfer of maps from the master to the slaves, run the map transfer daemon `rpc.ypxfrd`.

Slaves require much less configuration than the master does. The master has all of the map files. The slaves simply need to know which server is the master. Configure slaves by running `ypinit` with the –s option. For example, the following command would initialize a slave server and tell it that the master server is `sooty`:

```
[root]# /usr/lib/yp/ypinit -s sooty
```

For this to work, the IP address of `sooty` must be in the `/etc/hosts` file of the slave.

Security

Security is a concern for NIS because NIS provides network access to a wide range of system administration database files. Security-conscious system administrators don't want outsiders reading the information in these files. On most Linux systems, NIS uses the same `hosts.allow` and `hosts.deny` files used by the `tcpd` wrapper. The normal security configuration created for your system applies to NIS just like it does to other network servers.

Wrapper security is the most desirable and reliable security available for NIS. To find out if your server uses the wrapper files for security, run ypserv with the --version argument. Listing D.6 shows the results of this command.

Listing D.6   Checking for Wrapper Support

```
[root]# ypserv --version
ypserv - NYS YP Server version 1.3.7 (with tcp wrapper)
```

The configuration and use of the hosts.allow and hosts.deny files are described in Chapter 10, "DNS Security." ypserv uses the same files in the same manner as its preferred security mechanism.

The *securenets* File

In Listing D.6, the response clearly shows that the server supports tcpd wrapper. If your NIS server does not use the wrapper security files, you can define security for the server in the /var/yp/securenets file. This file lists the addresses and address masks that define the systems that are given access to the server.

The securenets file that comes with Red Hat 6 grants the local host and all other systems access to the NIS server. In Listing D.7, that default file has been edited to change the security settings so that the local host and all computers on network 172.16.5.0 are granted NIS server access. All systems that are not explicitly granted access by the securenets file are denied access to the NIS server.

Listing D.7   Using the securenets File

```
#
# securenets
# This file defines the access rights to your NIS server
# for NIS clients. This file contains netmask/network
# pairs. A clients IP address needs to match with at least
# one of those.
#
# One can use the word "host" instead of a netmask of
# 255.255.255.255. Only IP addresses are allowed in this
# file, not hostnames.
#
# Always allow access for localhost
255.0.0.0        127.0.0.0

# This line gives access to everybody. PLEASE ADJUST!
#0.0.0.0         0.0.0.0

# Allow access to every host on subnet 172.16.5.0
255.255.255.0    172.16.5.0
```

Appendixes

Listing D.7 is the `securenets` file that is delivered with Red Hat 6, with one line commented out and one line added. Comments begin with a #. Each active entry in the file contains a network mask followed by the address to which the mask applies. Combining masks and addresses makes it possible to define any address, from an individual host to an entire network. As shipped, the file contains a line with a mask of 0.0.0.0 and an address of 0.0.0.0, which permits all hosts to access the server. To increase security, remove that line and add a line that defines just those hosts that should really use this server. In Listing D.7, the line that started with the 0.0.0.0 mask was commented out by placing a # at the start of the line. The last line in Listing D.7 was added to grant access to all computers on subnet 172.16.5.1.

The *ypserv.conf* File

The last line of defense for `ypserv` is the security that can be defined in the `ypserv.conf` file. This is considered the least desirable and the least secure security mechanism. It is only described here so that you know how to read a `ypserv.conf` file if you come across one.

Define security using the wrapper files, if you can, and using `securenets` if you must. Don't use the `ypserv.conf` file for security. That said, the syntax of a security entry in the `ypserv.conf` file is

    host:*map*:*security*:[*mangle*[:*field*]]

These fields have the following meanings:

host   The computer being granted or denied access is defined by an address/ mask pair. Both the address and the mask are written in dotted decimal notation. For example, 172.16.5.0/255.255.255.0 defines all hosts on subnet 172.16.5.0. Use * in the *host* field to indicate all hosts.

map   This field represents the name of the NIS map for which this entry controls access. Listing D.4 shows the list of maps created on our sample server. An example is `passwd.byuid`. Use * in the *map* field to indicate all available NIS maps.

security   The type of access being granted is defined by one of four keywords. The following security keywords are valid:

   `none`   Allow access. Don't enforce security.

   `port`   Allow access from a privileged port. With this setting, connections are only accepted if the source port number is less than 1024.

   `deny`   Block access.

   `des`   Require Digital Encryption Standard (DES) authentication before granting access. Nice idea, but DES is not implemented by the clients.

[*mangle*[:*field*]]   Identifies a field that should be overwritten with "x" characters before the response is sent to the client. *mangle* is set to yes or no to enable or disable this feature. By default, *mangle* is disabled. *field* is a numeric value that indicates the position of the field that is to be overwritten—1 for the first field, 2 for the second, etc. By default, the second field is overwritten. The idea is that sensitive information like passwords can be masked in a response. But why let someone unreliable query the system at all? Most people don't use *mangle* because they prefer to block access rather than allow unreliable systems to access part of the information they request.

The two entries in the ypserv.conf file that would have the same affect as the securenets file shown in Listing D.7 are contained in Listing D.8.

Listing D.8   ypserv.conf Security Entries

```
# Host                      : Map  : Security  : Mangle
#
172.16.5.0/255.255.255.0  : *    : none      : no
*                          : *    : deny      : no
```

Comments start with #. The first active entry in Listing D.8 grants access to all maps to all hosts on subnet 172.16.5.0. The second entry denies access to all other hosts.

The ypserv.conf file can also be used to set the following NIS server configuration options:

dns   This option causes the NIS server to query DNS when a host name is not found in the NIS map. By default, this option is set to no. See the sidebar, "Don't Worry About NIS Working With DNS," for more information.

xfr_check_port   This option causes the server to refuse map transfer requests unless they come from a privileged port. This is the default. Don't change it. Setting xfr_check_port to no undermines the security of your server.

sunos_kludge   This is an outdated option that is no longer supported, although it is still documented.

These configuration options are rarely used. Add to this the fact that better security is provided by the wrapper files, and it is easy to see why most Linux system administrators ignore the ypserv.conf file that comes with their Linux distribution.

Appendixes

Don't Worry About NIS Working With DNS

There are options in the /var/yp/Makefile and in the ypserv.conf file that can cause confusion for an administrator who runs both NIS and DNS. The Makefile contains the following lines:

```
# Set the following variable to "-b" to have NIS servers use DNS
# for hosts not in the NIS hosts map. This is only needed
# if you have SunOS slave YP server that gets maps from this
# server. The NYS YP server will ignore the YP_INTERDOMAIN key.
#B=-b
B=
```

This comment along with old documentation can make you think you need to set the B variable to –b. You don't. SunOS systems of this type have not been manufactured for several years. Ignore this line and leave it as it is.

The ypserv.conf file adds to the confusion with the dns argument. The sample ypserv.conf file that comes with Red Hat 6 contains the following lines:

```
# Some options for ypserv. This things are all not needed, if
# you have a Linux net.
dns: no
```

The comments in the ypserv.conf file are not very clear, and a nervous system administrator could easily think dns should be set to yes when DNS and NIS run on the same system. Don't be nervous. You can safely ignore this option.

The Makefile B variable and the ypserv.conf dns option can be ignored because the resolver, not NIS, selects the source of host name and address information. The nsswitch.conf file described in Chapter 4 is the file that determines when and in what order NIS and DNS are used. Don't use NIS configuration to do a job that is more properly done by the resolver.

Starting the Server

Once the server is configured, it can be run with the ypserv command. If it is already running, use either the SIGHUP signal to make the server read the new configuration, or run the startup script with the restart option to start a new copy of the server daemon with the new configuration. Listing D.9 shows how the server is restarted on a Red Hat 6 system using the startup script.

Listing D.9   Restarting the NIS Server

```
[root]# /etc/rc.d/init.d/ypserv restart
Stopping YP server services:                    [  OK  ]
Starting YP server services:                    [  OK  ]
```

After starting the NIS server, run ypbind to bind the client side of NIS to the server. ypbind is the only part of NIS that runs on clients, but servers run both the ypserv server and the ypbind client. The client software can be started with the ypbind command, or it can be restarted by passing the restart argument to the ypbind startup script, as shown in Listing D.10.

Listing D.10   Restarting the NIS Client

```
[root]# /etc/rc.d/init.d/ypbind restart
Shutting down NIS services:                     [  OK  ]
Binding to the NIS domain...                    [  OK  ]
Listening for an NIS domain server: sooty
```

Listings D.9 and D.10 are examples of starting the server and the client from the shell prompt. Of course, you also want to make sure that the server and the client start at every boot. Use a tool like linuxconf to enable ypserv and ypbind as part of the boot process.

In addition to starting the server and the client at boot time, make sure that the NIS domain name is properly set every time that the system restarts and that supporting processes are started. The NIS domain name must be set very early in the boot process, in a script such as rc.sysinit or rc.

On some systems, you may need to create your own nisdomainname command and store it in one of these files. On a Red Hat system, the code already exists for setting the NIS domain name. All you need to do is define the NIS domain name in the /etc/sysconfig/networks file in the following manner:

```
NISDOMAIN=terns
```

Other required processes, such as rpc.ypxfrd, can be added to the rc.local script. Remember, rpc.ypxfrd only needs to run on the master NIS server.

Testing NIS

With everything configured, a few quick tests tell you if NIS is running properly. The NIS client should be bound to a server. Use the ypwhich command to check if the client has

Appendixes

bound to a server and to make sure it has bound to the correct server. Listing D.11 is a ypwhich test.

Listing D.11 Testing NIS with ypwhich

```
[root]# ypwhich
sooty.terns.foobirds.org
```

If the client is bound to the correct server, use ypcat to examine the information provided by the server. In Listing D.12, the ypcat command is used to display the contents of the host table stored on a NIS server.

Listing D.12 Testing NIS with ypcat

```
[root]# ypcat hosts
172.16.30.2      black.terns.foobirds.org black
127.0.0.1        localhost localhost.localdomain
172.16.30.250    sooty.terns.foobirds.org sooty
172.16.30.251    arctic.terns.foobirds.org arctic
```

These simple tests prove that both the NIS client and the NIS server are up and running.

A Step-by-Step Summary

These are the steps used to configure a NIS server:

1. Install the ypserv and ypbind software.

2. Define a NIS domain name.

3. Run the ypinit -m command on the master server. Run the ypinit -s command on the slave servers.

4. Start ypserv.

5. Start ypbind.

6. Start rpc.ypxfrd on the master server.

These are the steps used to install and configure a NIS client:

1. Install the ypbind software.

2. Define the NIS domain name.

3. Run ypbind.

That's it. NIS is a useful tool for managing Unix and Linux clients on a local area network. This appendix gives you all the information you need to configure and use NIS.

Index

Note to the Reader: Page numbers in **bold** indicate the principal discussion of a topic or the definition of a term. *Italicized* page numbers indicate illustrations.

Index

Praise for Craig Hunt

Reviewers praise Craig Hunt's *Linux Network Servers 24seven* (Sybex, 1999)!

If I had to pick a reference book for a new Linux administrator or to have as a reference guide to Linux administration in the office this would be it.

Alan Cox, www.linux.org.uk

Linux Network Servers 24seven does an outstanding job of explaining how to turn a machine running Linux 2.2 ...into a reliable, high-performance provider of network services. This book will help you build a fire-and-forget network server on the Linux platform.

David Wall, Amazon.com

To master Linux networking you have to understand how to use and configure a surprisingly large number of applications. Fortunately, Craig Hunt knows his subject. This is a valuable read...

Amazon.co.uk

I loved this book. This book gets into the nitty-gritty with helpful examples and expert-commentary.

Recommendo.com

The Craig Hunt Linux Library

◆ Written under the direction of Craig Hunt, renowned Linux and TCP/IP guru
◆ Developed specifically for networking professionals working in Linux environments
◆ Offers the most advanced and focused coverage of key topics for Linux Administrators

Craig Hunt is a noted TCP/IP and Linux expert who lectures regularly on the topics at the NetWorld+Interop, ComNet, and other networking trade shows. His other books include the best-selling *Linux Network Servers 24seven* from Sybex™ and the classic *TCP/IP Network Administration* from O'Reilly & Associates.

by Craig Hunt
0-7821-2736-3 • $39.99

by Charles Aulds
0-7821-2734-7 • $39.99
3rd Quarter 2000

by Vicki Stanfield
0-7821-2735-5 • $39.99
4th Quarter 2000

by Roderick W. Smith
0-7821-2740-1 • $39.99
4th Quarter 2000

by Craig Hunt
0-7821-2737-1 • $39.99
4th Quarter 2000

by Craig Hunt
0-7821-2741-x • $39.99
4th Quarter 2000

The Linux standard on your bookshelf.

www.sybex.com SYBEX®